MONO™

The Old Curiosity Shop

P A C I F I C

PROSPERO RISING

V O L U M E
O N E

A creature born in storms

arcane, forged in war, and

tempered by servitude.

MONO.

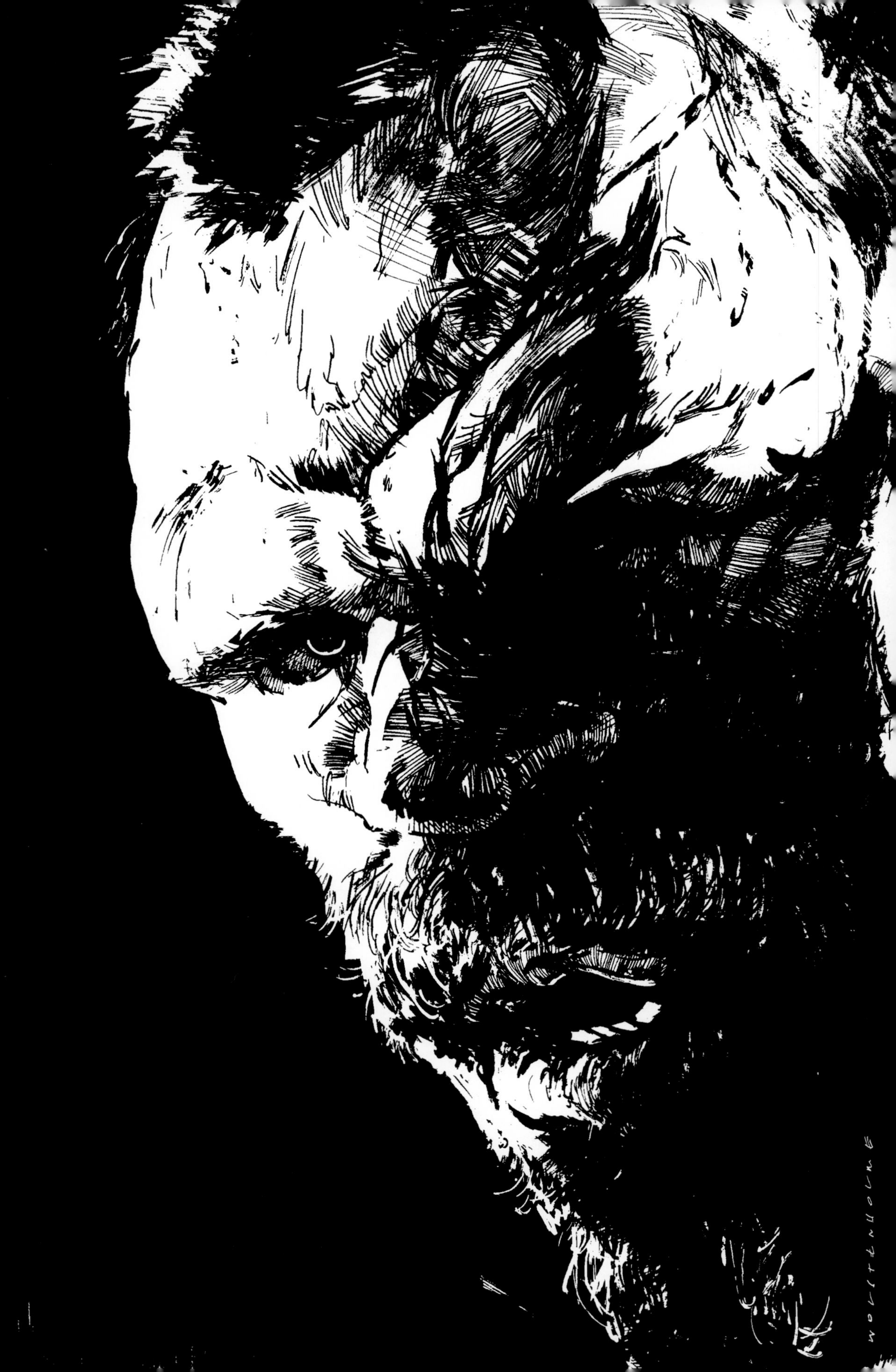

Foreword
By Mr. Dave Gibbons

That Ben Wolstenholme doesn't make his living by drawing comics only adds to my admiration for his talent. In real life, he's a founder of the international Moving Brands agency, moving effortlessly amongst the worlds of Silicon Valley, A-list companies, and corporate advertising; and, although his skills there are a kind of visual storytelling, it is only in his spare time that he wields pen and ink to provide some of the most stirring and engaging hand-drawn narratives you will find anywhere.

Synthesizing aspects of the great illustrators of the past, from Daniel Vierge through to Joseph Clement Coll, and modern masters like Mike Kaluta and Gary Gianni, Ben's line is spontaneous yet precise, effortlessly describing form and atmosphere. Equally stunning is his mastery of movement and physical action, bringing life not only to the printed page but to the digital arena, where this material was first presented, under the banner of Madefire's 'Motion Books'.

The evocative, muscular, pulp-inspired script is provided by co-plotter Liam Sharp; a hugely talented writer-artist in his own right, Ben's long-time friend and a co-founder of Madefire.

> *"Beautifully drawn, MONO is a unique blend of action and emotion unlike anything else out there."*

With colourist Fin Cramb and letterer Jim Campbell adding their peerless talents, *Mono* combines the craft of the past with technology of today, presented here in a volume that will be treasured by readers for a long time to come.

—Dave Gibbons

Co-creator Watchmen.

Co-creator Kingsman: The Secret Service.

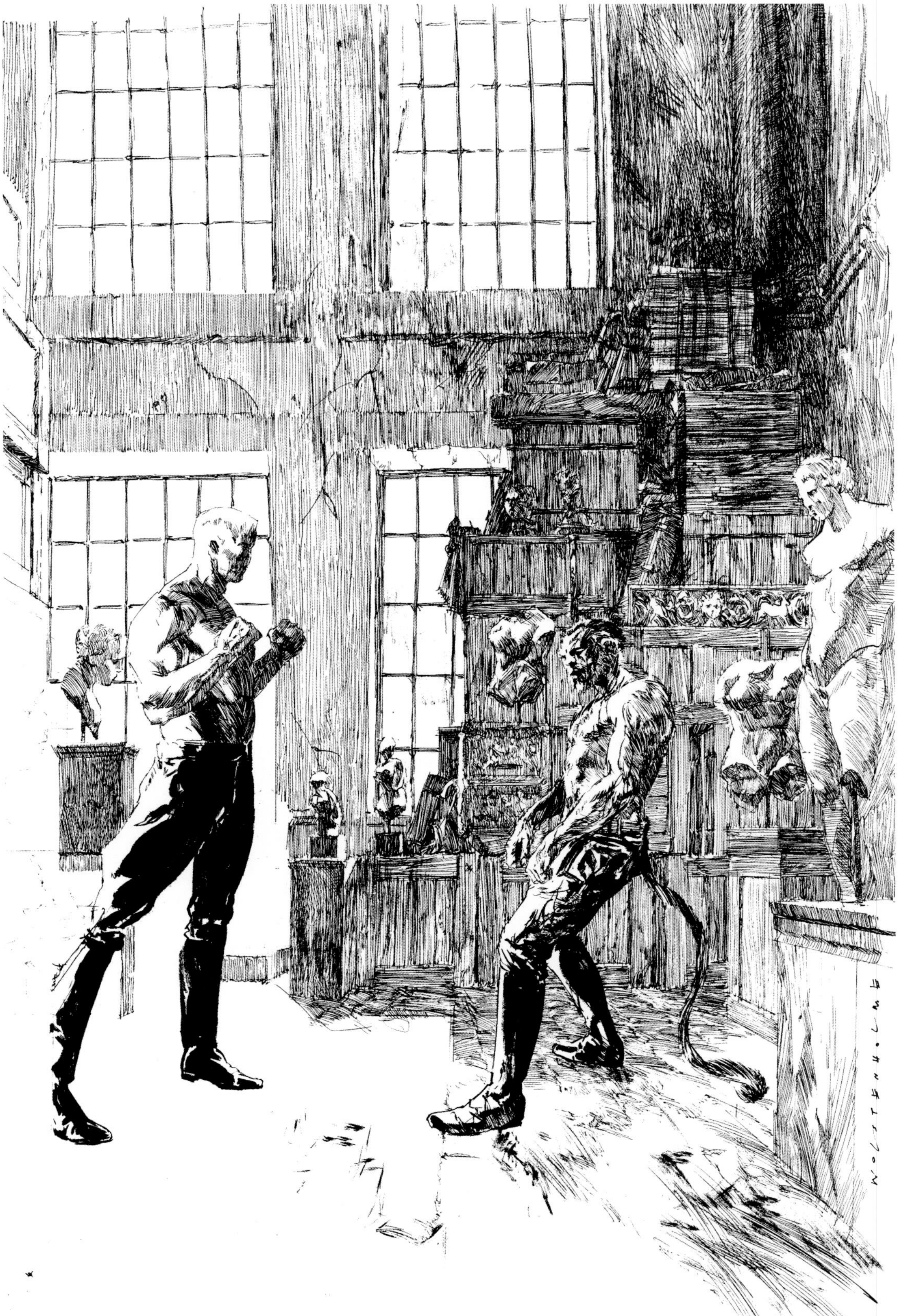
WOLSTENHOLME

MONO
VOLUME ONE

Contents

Published by Titan Comics
A division of Titan Publishing Group Ltd.
144 Southwark St.
London, SE1 0UP
Great Britain

A CIP catalogue record for this title is available from the British Library.

First edition: October 2015.
ISBN: 9781782762850
Printed in China.
Titan Comics. TC0605

MADEFIRE

Collection Editor Kevin Buckley
Collection Designer Ben Wolstenholme
Executive Producers Ben Wolstenholme, Liam Sharp, Eugene Walden
Business Development & Operations Eugene Walden, Graves Englund, Josh Wilkie
Marketing Richard Watson
Engineering Dan Bostonweeks, Joshua Worby, Ben Lee
Special thanks to Ben Abernathy and Joe 'Otis' Costello

Become a fan on Facebook.com/Madefire
Follow us on Twitter @Madefire
Download the Madefire app for iOS, Android & Windows
www.madefire.com

TITAN COMICS

Collection Editor Steve White
Collection Designer Russell Seal
Titan Comics Editorial Andrew James, Lizzie Kaye, Kirsten Murray, Tom Williams
Production Supervisors Jackie Flook, Maria Pearson
Production Assistant Peter James
Production Controller Obi Onuora
Art Director Oz Browne
Studio Manager Selina Juneja
Circulation Manager Steve Tothill
Senior Marketing & Press Office Owen Johnson
Marketing Manager Ricky Claydon
Advertising Manager Michelle Fairlamb
Publishing Manager Darryl Tothill
Publishing Director Chris Teather
Operations Director Leigh Baulch
Executive Director Vivian Cheung
Publisher Nick Landau

Become a fan on Facebook.com/comicstitan
Follow us on Twitter @ComicsTitan
www.titan-comics.com

10 9 8 7 6 5 4 3 2 1

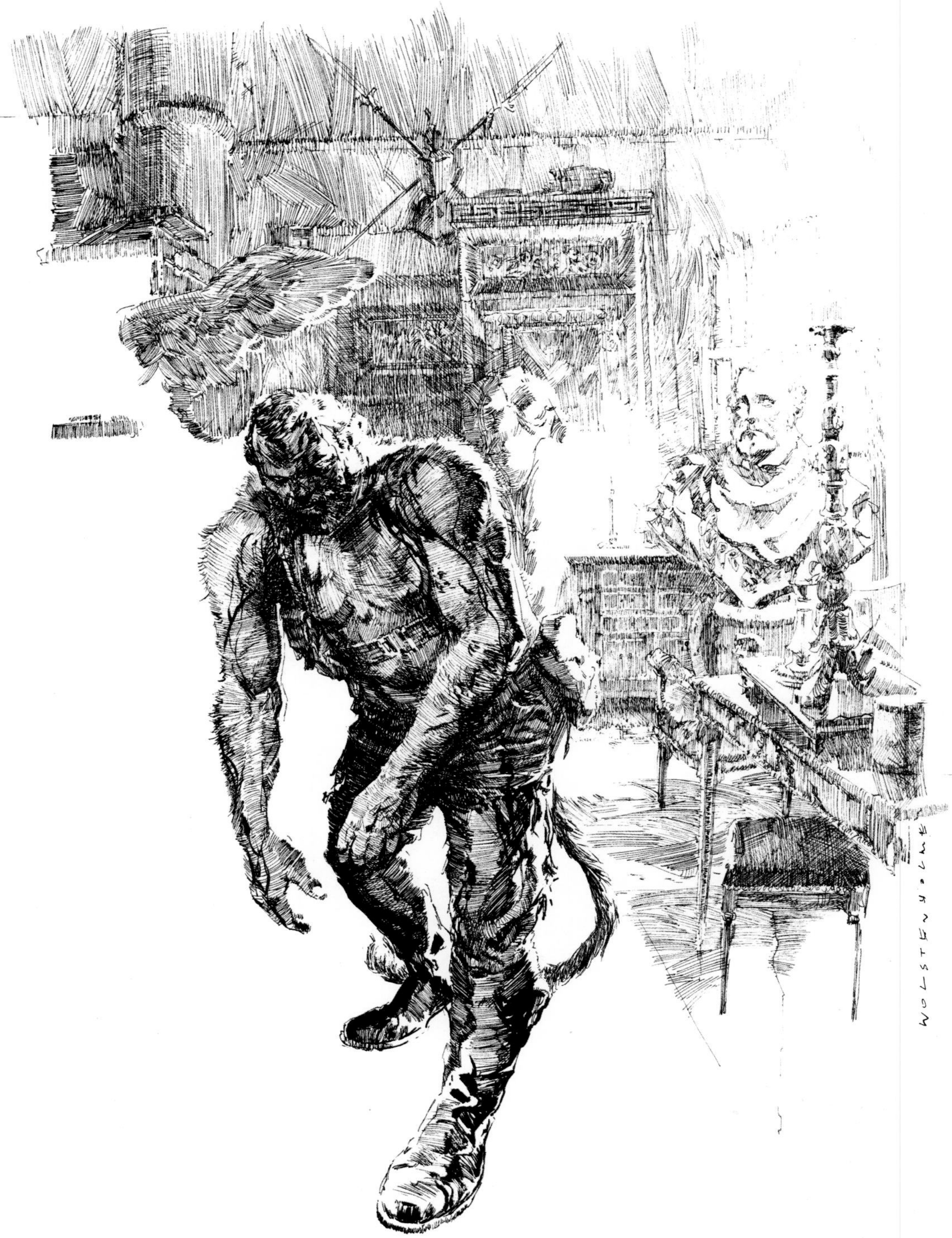
WOLSTENHOLME

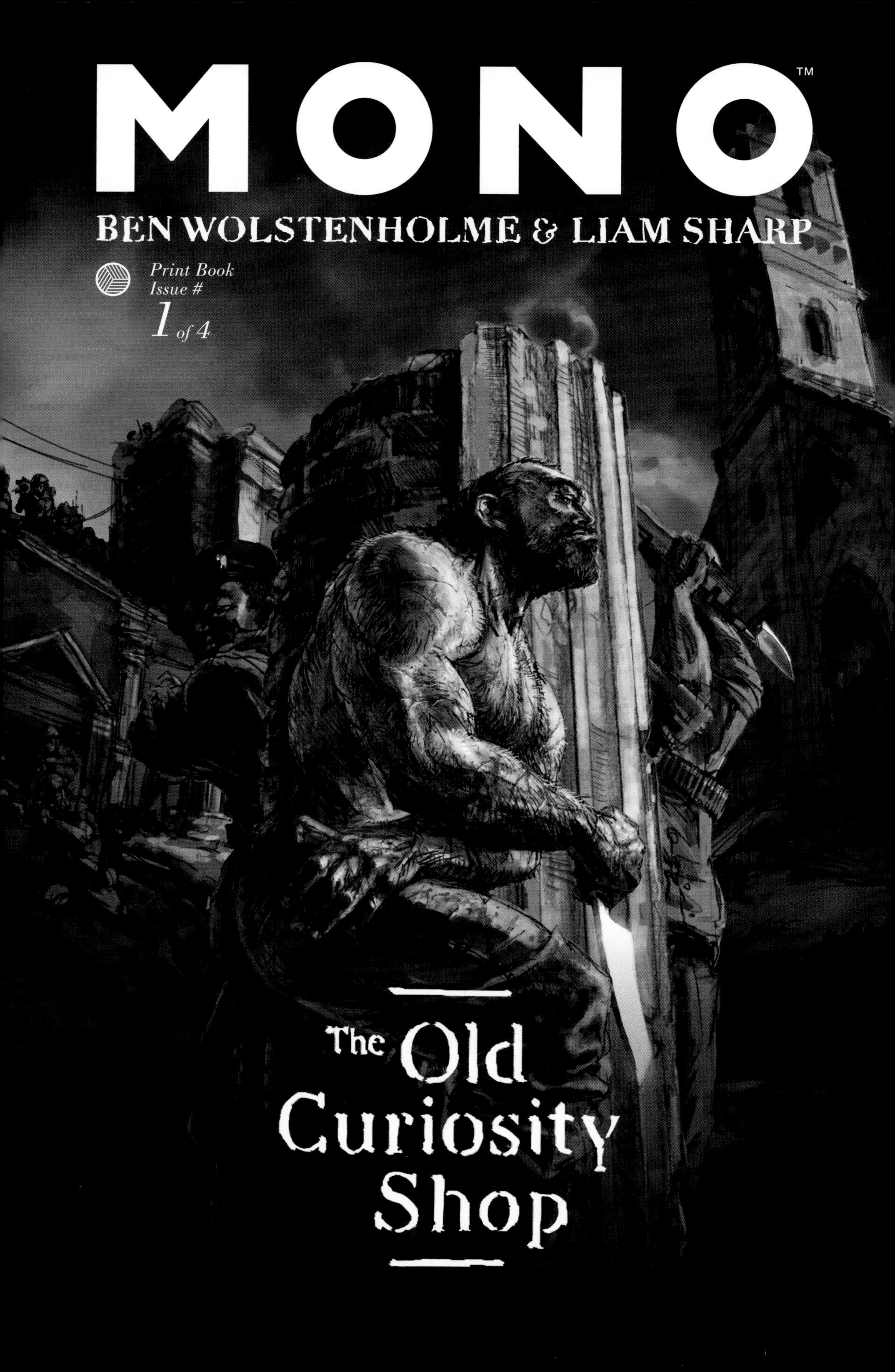
MONO™
BEN WOLSTENHOLME & LIAM SHARP
Print Book
Issue #
1 of 4
The Old Curiosity Shop

THESE... BOOKS.

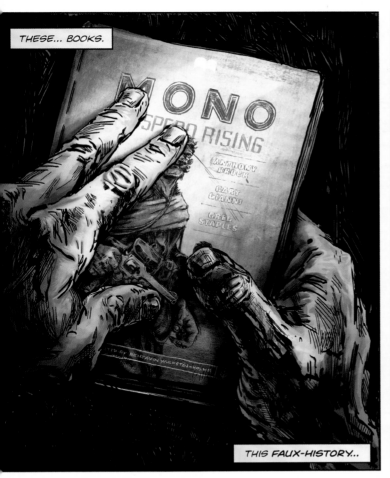

MONO
SPEED RISING

ANTHONY BROCK
GARY GIANNI
GREG STAPLES

THIS FAUX-HISTORY...

I ONCE THOUGHT TO REWRITE IT -- TO TELL THE *TRUTH OF THE MATTER* --

TO MAKE RIGHT WHAT IS *WRONG* IN THESE PULP FICTIONS.

BUT TO WHAT END?

WHAT DO EVEN I, WHO WAS SO CLOSE TO THE MAN, REALLY KNOW OF THE TRUTH AFTER ALL THESE YEARS?

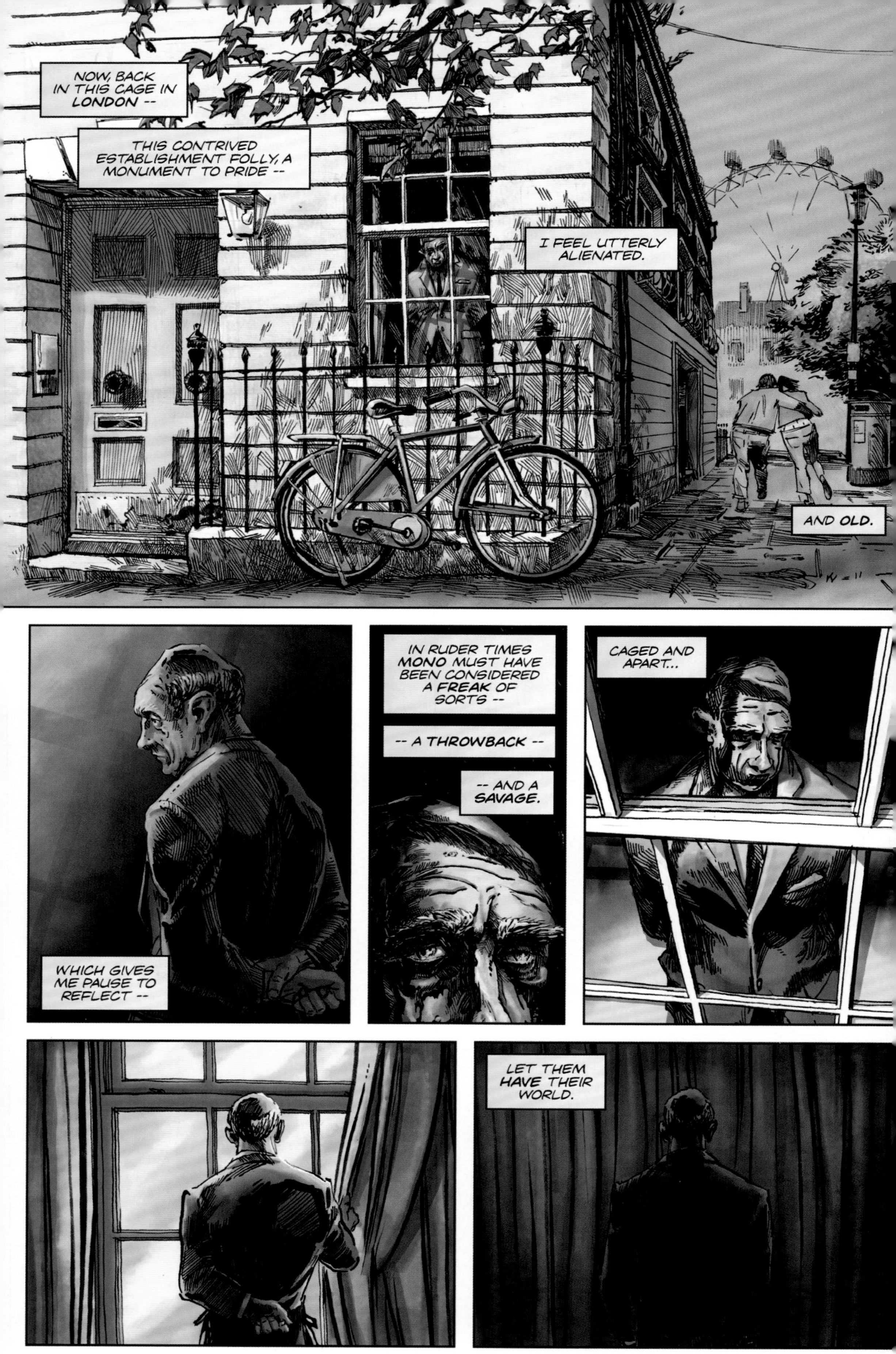
NOW, BACK IN THIS CAGE IN LONDON --
THIS CONTRIVED ESTABLISHMENT FOLLY, A MONUMENT TO PRIDE --
I FEEL UTTERLY ALIENATED.
AND OLD.
WHICH GIVES ME PAUSE TO REFLECT --
IN RUDER TIMES MONO MUST HAVE BEEN CONSIDERED A FREAK OF SORTS --
-- A THROWBACK --
-- AND A SAVAGE.
CAGED AND APART...
LET THEM HAVE THEIR WORLD.

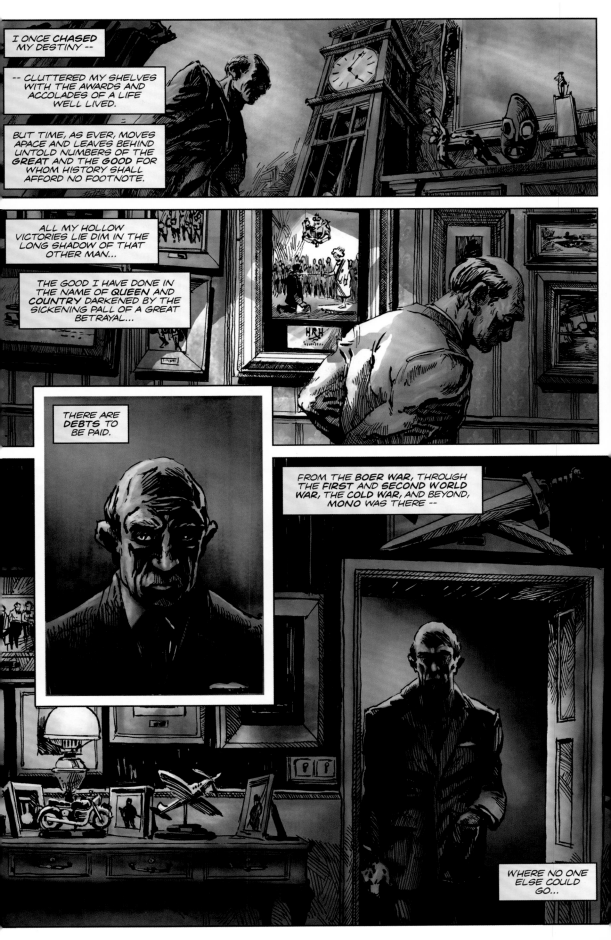

I ONCE CHASED MY DESTINY --

-- CLUTTERED MY SHELVES WITH THE AWARDS AND ACCOLADES OF A LIFE WELL LIVED.

BUT TIME, AS EVER, MOVES APACE AND LEAVES BEHIND UNTOLD NUMBERS OF THE GREAT AND THE GOOD FOR WHOM HISTORY SHALL AFFORD NO FOOTNOTE.

ALL MY HOLLOW VICTORIES LIE DIM IN THE LONG SHADOW OF THAT OTHER MAN...

THE GOOD I HAVE DONE IN THE NAME OF QUEEN AND COUNTRY DARKENED BY THE SICKENING PALL OF A GREAT BETRAYAL...

THERE ARE DEBTS TO BE PAID.

FROM THE BOER WAR, THROUGH THE FIRST AND SECOND WORLD WAR, THE COLD WAR, AND BEYOND, MONO WAS THERE --

WHERE NO ONE ELSE COULD GO...

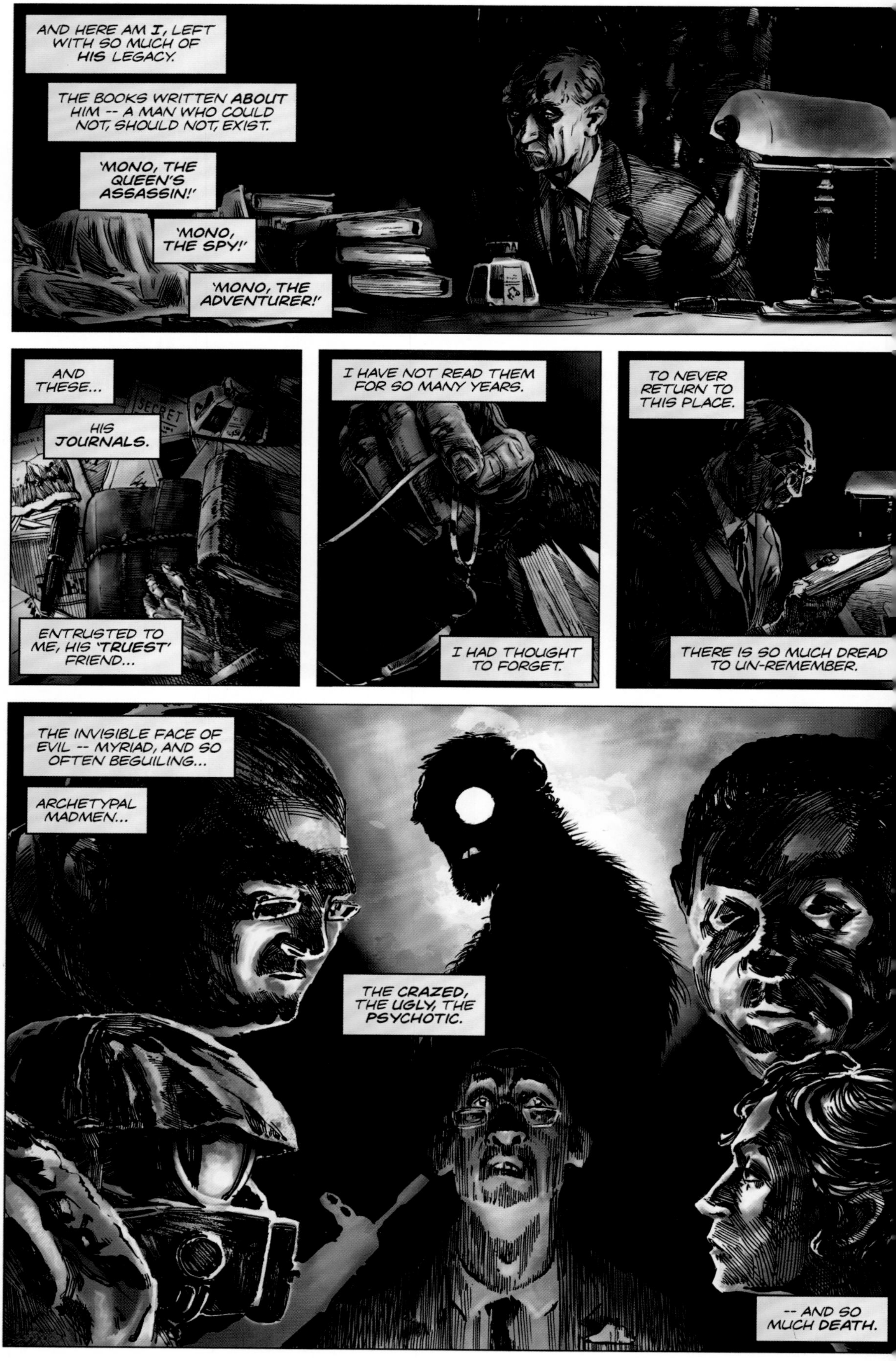
AND HERE AM I, LEFT WITH SO MUCH OF HIS LEGACY.
THE BOOKS WRITTEN ABOUT HIM -- A MAN WHO COULD NOT, SHOULD NOT, EXIST.
'MONO, THE QUEEN'S ASSASSIN!'
'MONO, THE SPY!'
'MONO, THE ADVENTURER!'
AND THESE...
HIS JOURNALS.
ENTRUSTED TO ME, HIS 'TRUEST' FRIEND...
I HAVE NOT READ THEM FOR SO MANY YEARS.
I HAD THOUGHT TO FORGET.
TO NEVER RETURN TO THIS PLACE.
THERE IS SO MUCH DREAD TO UN-REMEMBER.
THE INVISIBLE FACE OF EVIL -- MYRIAD, AND SO OFTEN BEGUILING...
ARCHETYPAL MADMEN...
THE CRAZED, THE UGLY, THE PSYCHOTIC.
-- AND SO MUCH DEATH.

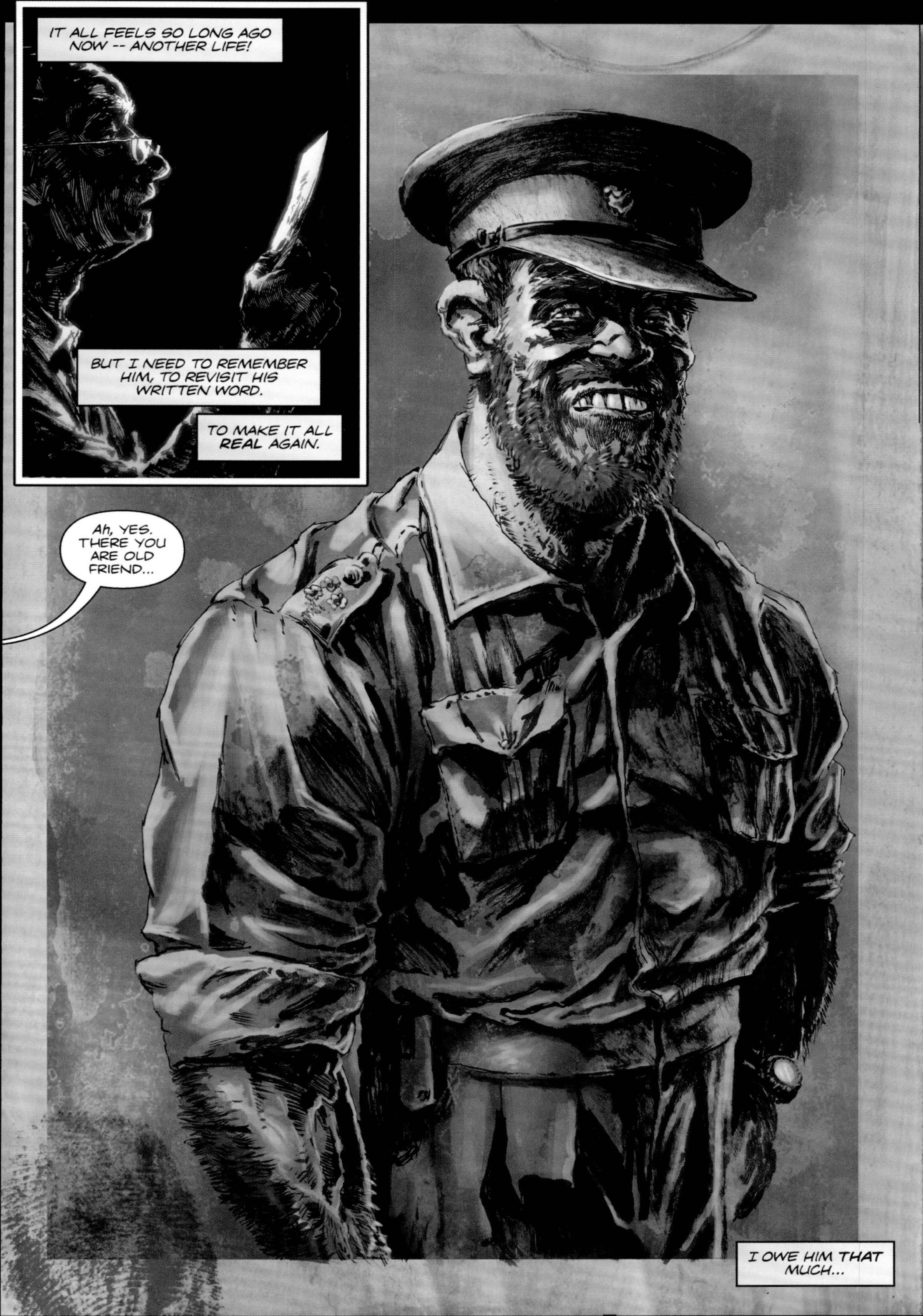

IT ALL FEELS SO LONG AGO NOW -- ANOTHER LIFE!
BUT I NEED TO REMEMBER HIM, TO REVISIT HIS WRITTEN WORD.
TO MAKE IT ALL REAL AGAIN.
Ah, YES. THERE YOU ARE OLD FRIEND...
I OWE HIM THAT MUCH...

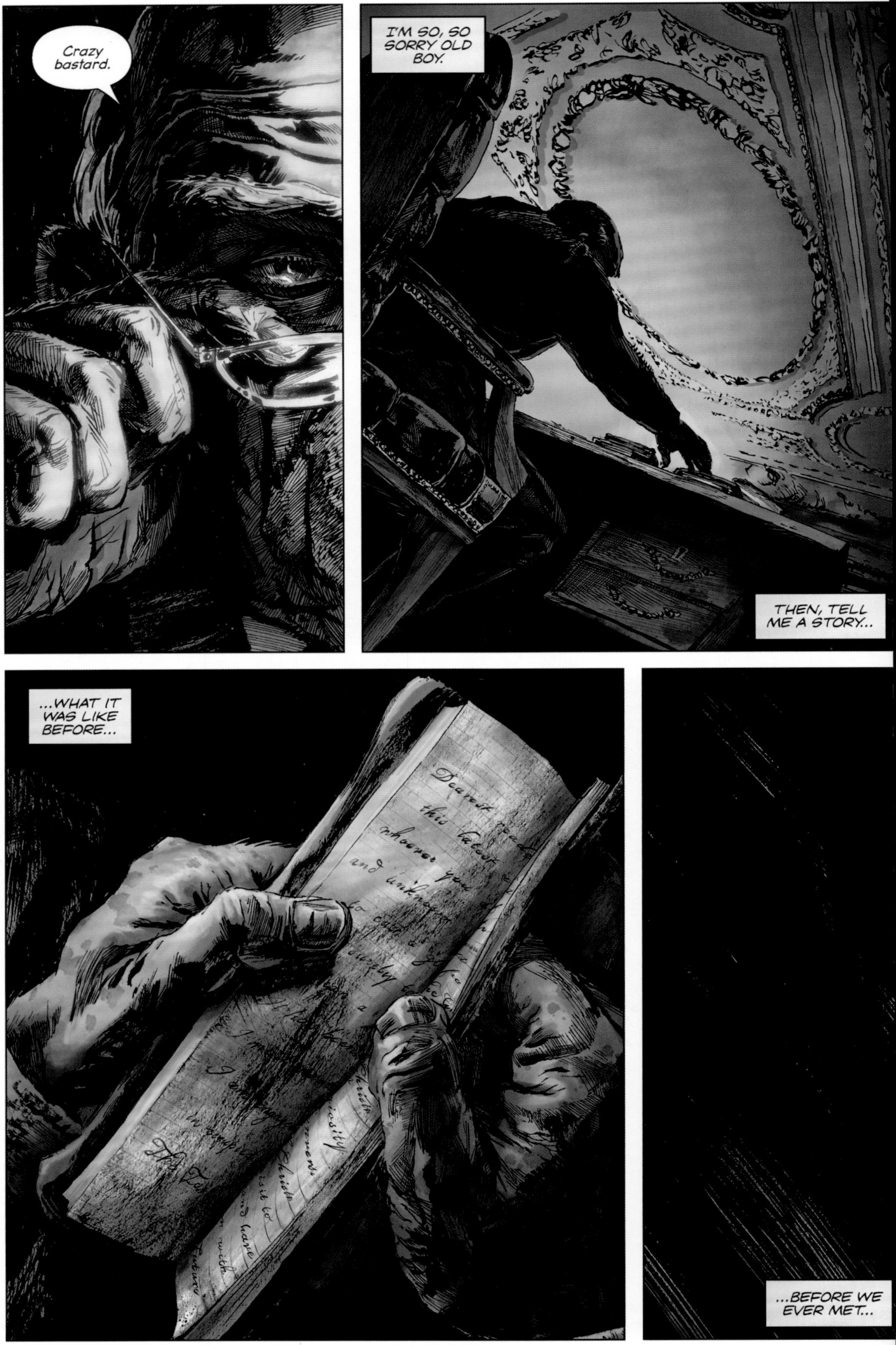
Crazy bastard.
I'M SO, SO SORRY OLD BOY.
THEN, TELL ME A STORY...
...WHAT IT WAS LIKE BEFORE...
...BEFORE WE EVER MET...

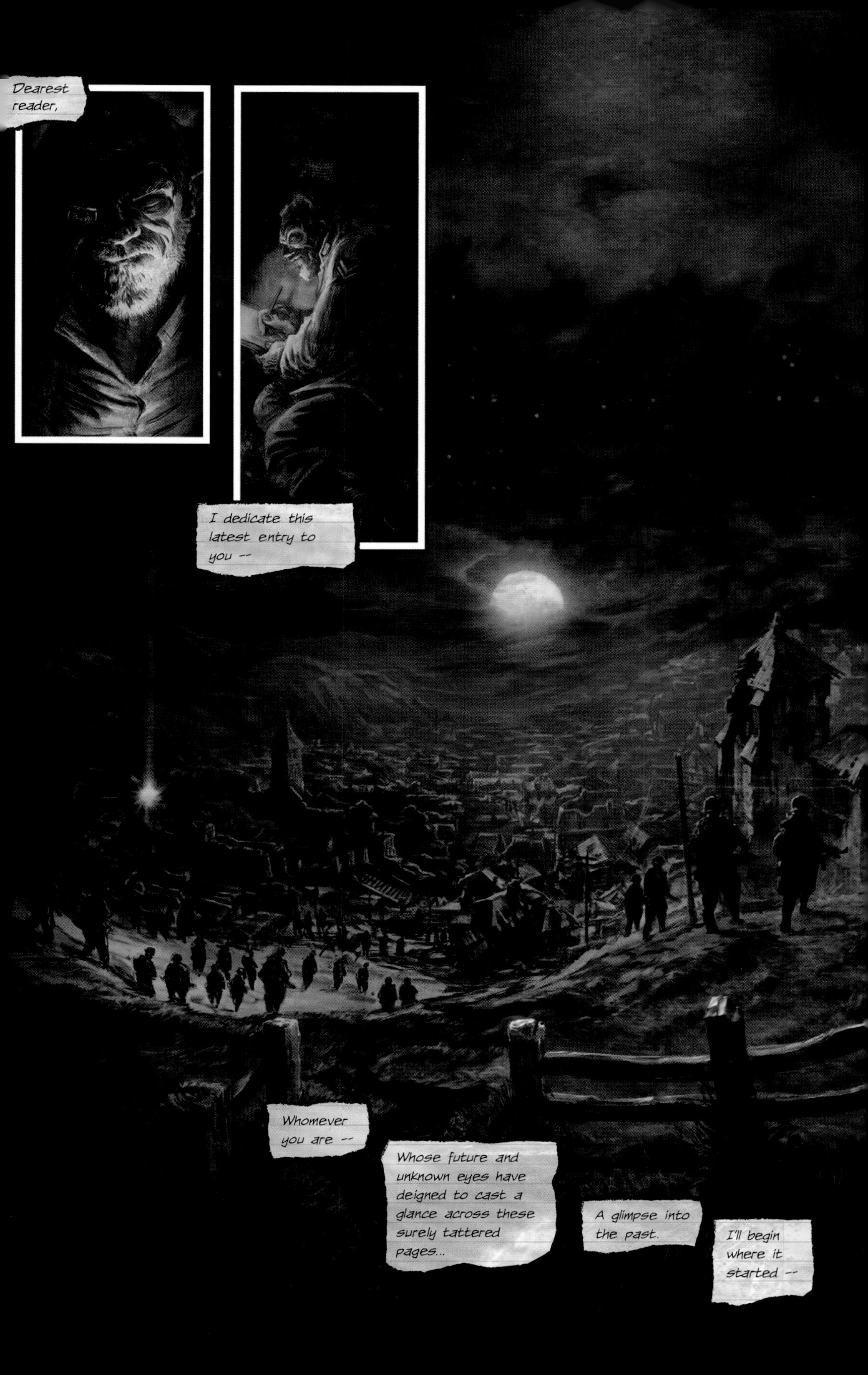

Dearest reader,
I dedicate this latest entry to you --
Whomever you are --
Whose future and unknown eyes have deigned to cast a glance across these surely tattered pages...
A glimpse into the past.
I'll begin where it started --

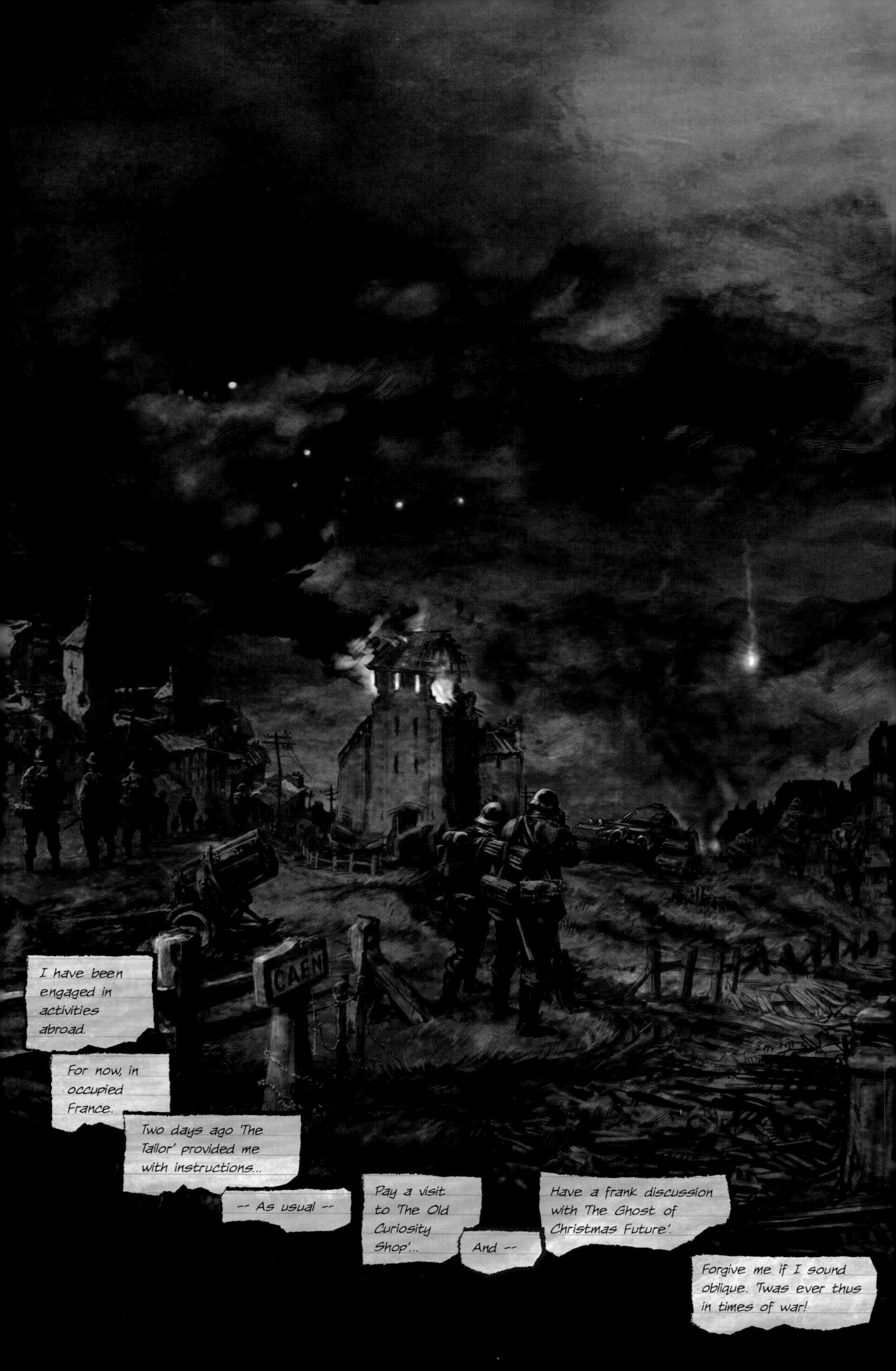
CAEN
I have been engaged in activities abroad.
For now, in occupied France.
Two days ago 'The Tailor' provided me with instructions...
-- As usual --
Pay a visit to 'The Old Curiosity Shop'...
And --
Have a frank discussion with 'The Ghost of Christmas Future'.
Forgive me if I sound oblique. 'Twas ever thus in times of war!

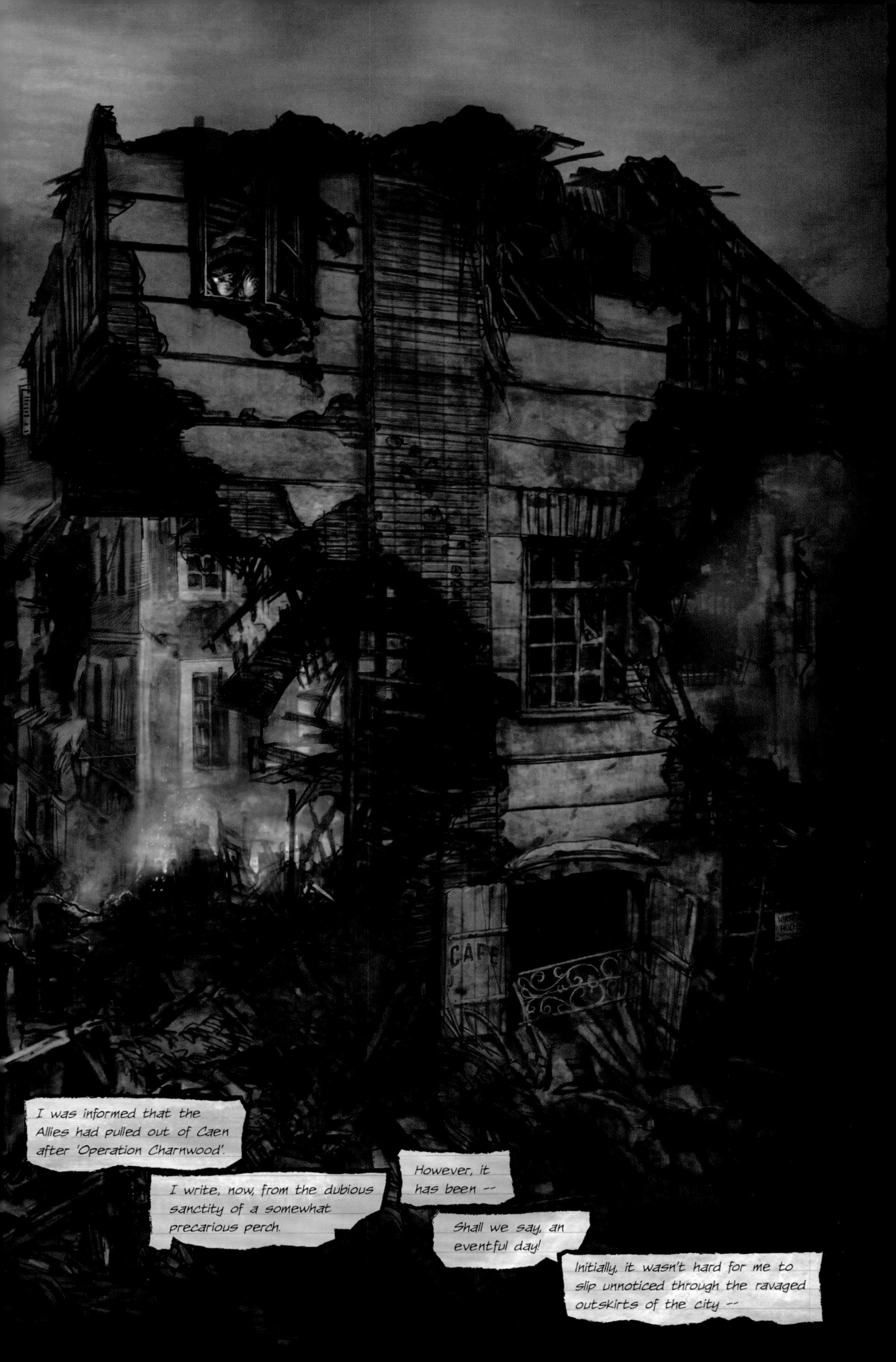
I was informed that the Allies had pulled out of Caen after 'Operation Charnwood'.
I write, now, from the dubious sanctity of a somewhat precarious perch.
However, it has been --
Shall we say, an eventful day!
Initially, it wasn't hard for me to slip unnoticed through the ravaged outskirts of the city --

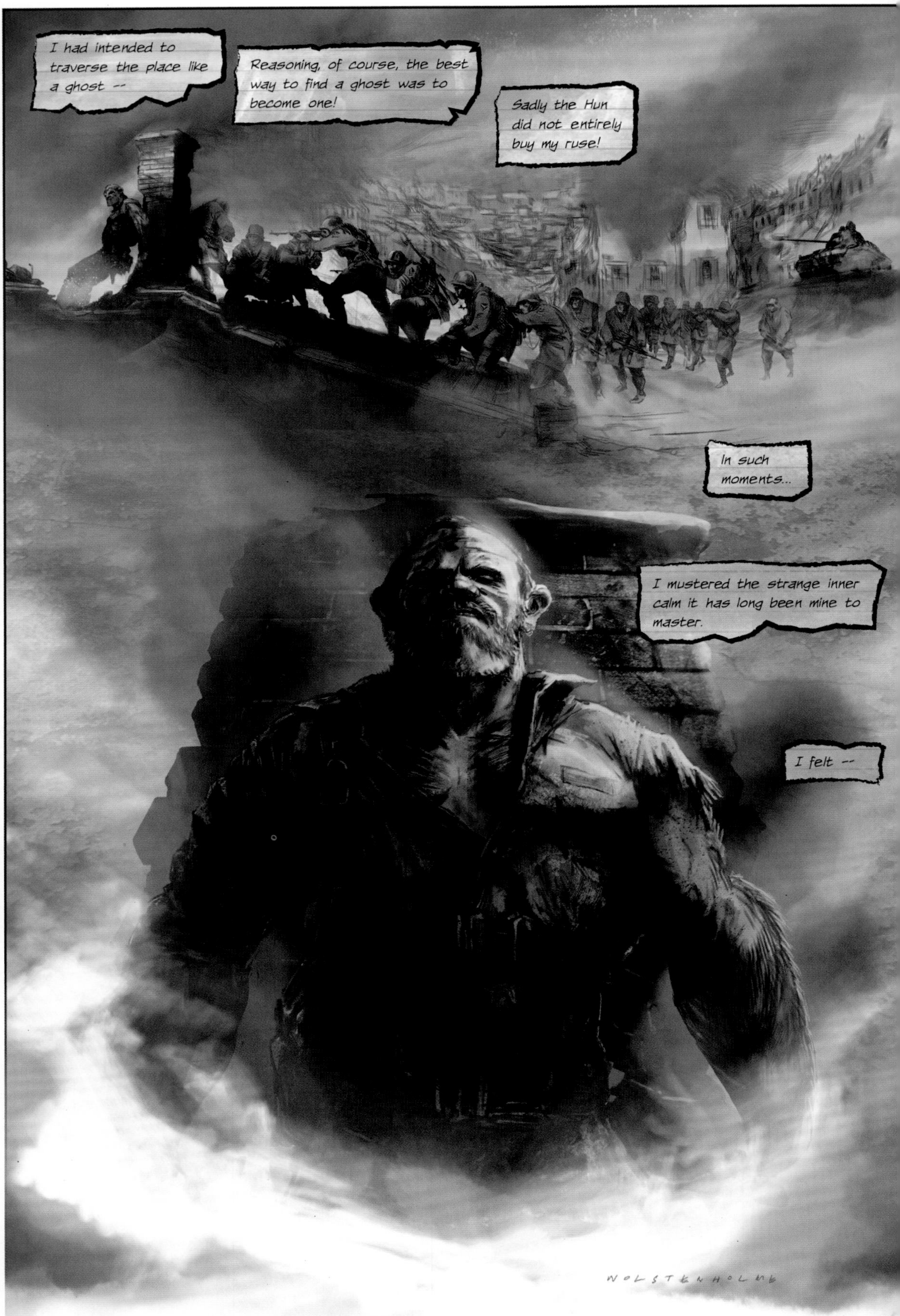
I had intended to traverse the place like a ghost --
Reasoning, of course, the best way to find a ghost was to become one!
Sadly the Hun did not entirely buy my ruse!
In such moments...
I mustered the strange inner calm it has long been mine to master.
I felt --
WOLSTENHOLME

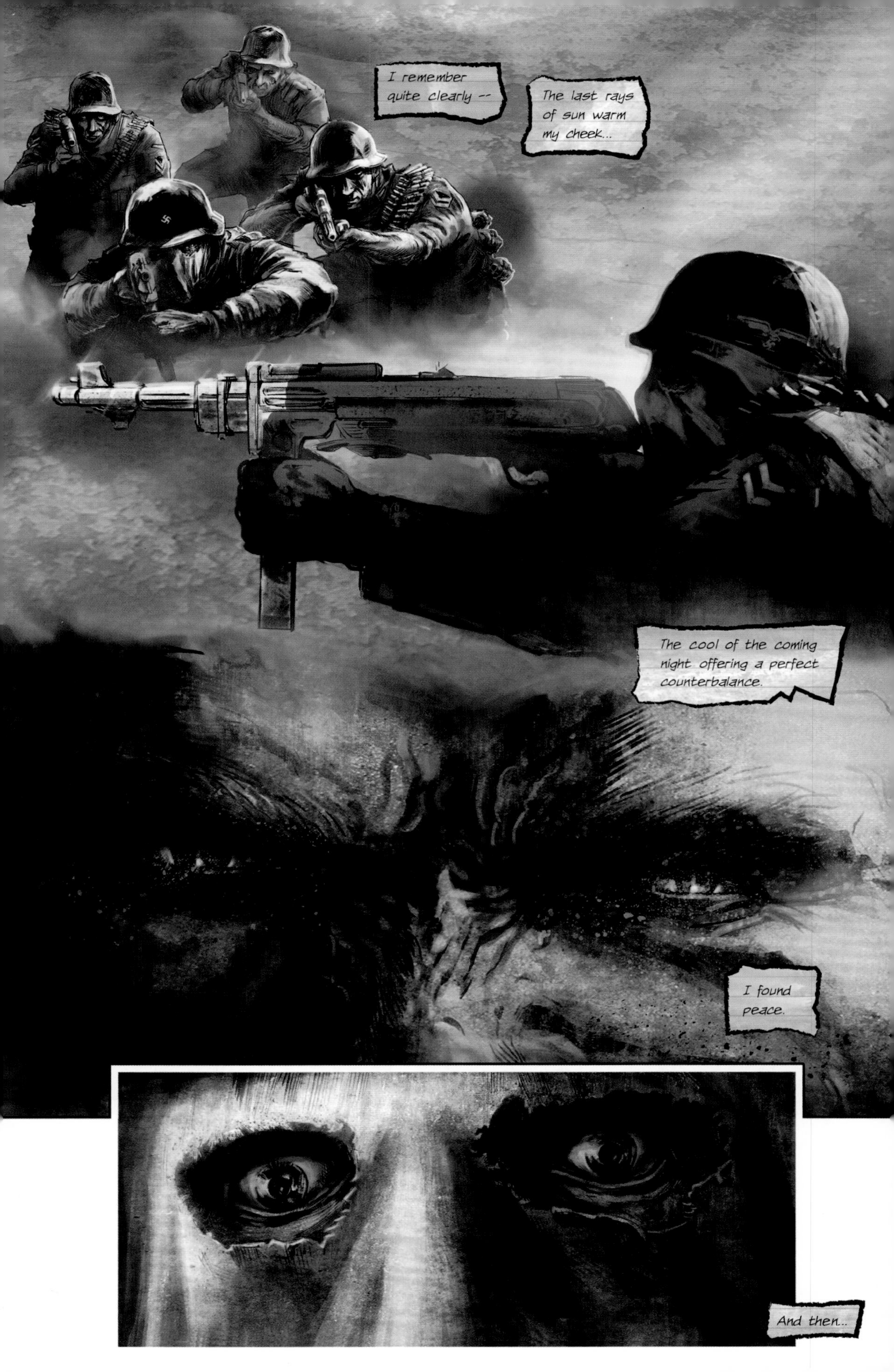
I remember quite clearly --
The last rays of sun warm my cheek...
The cool of the coming night offering a perfect counterbalance.
I found peace.
And then...

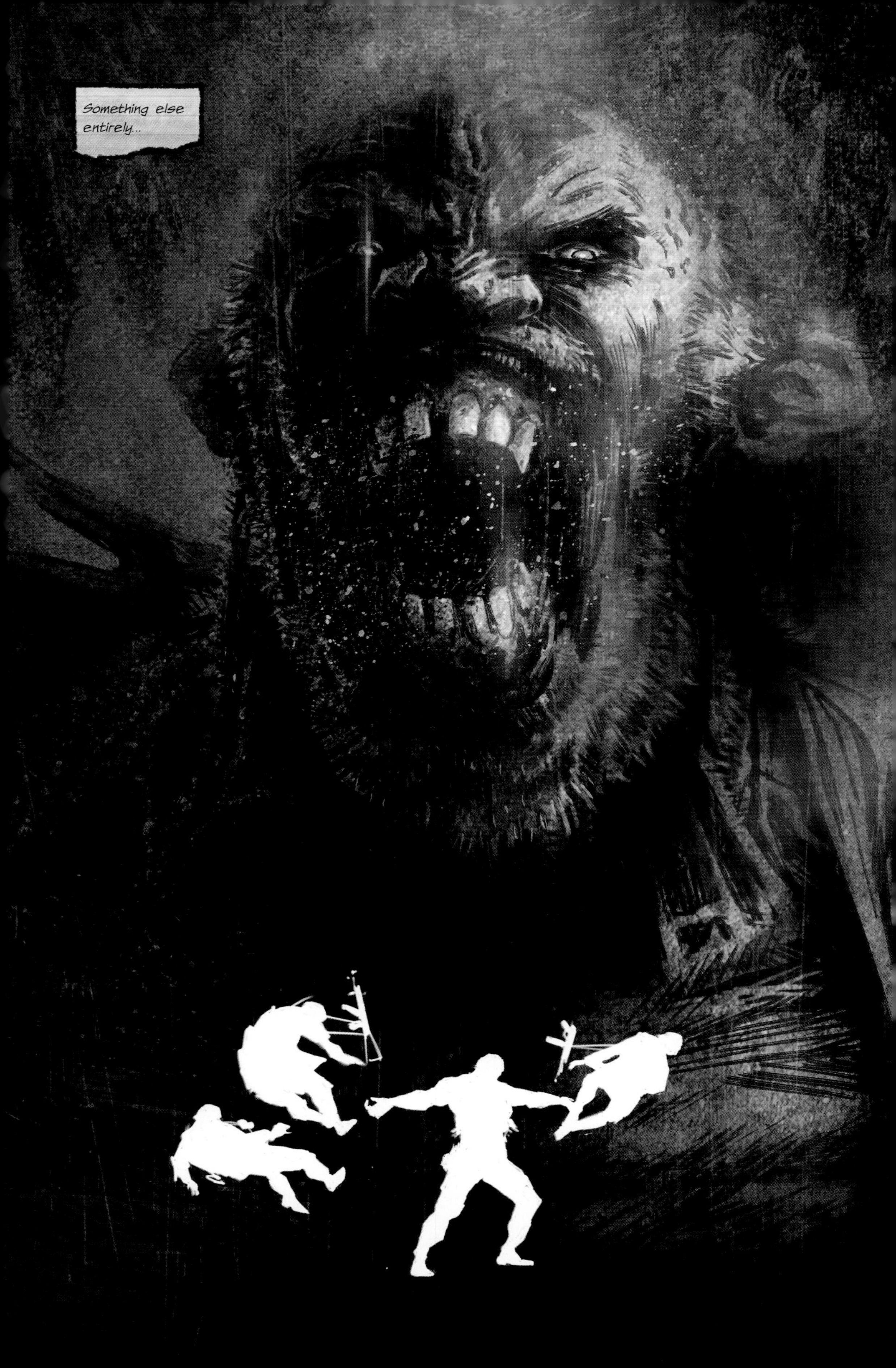
Something else entirely...

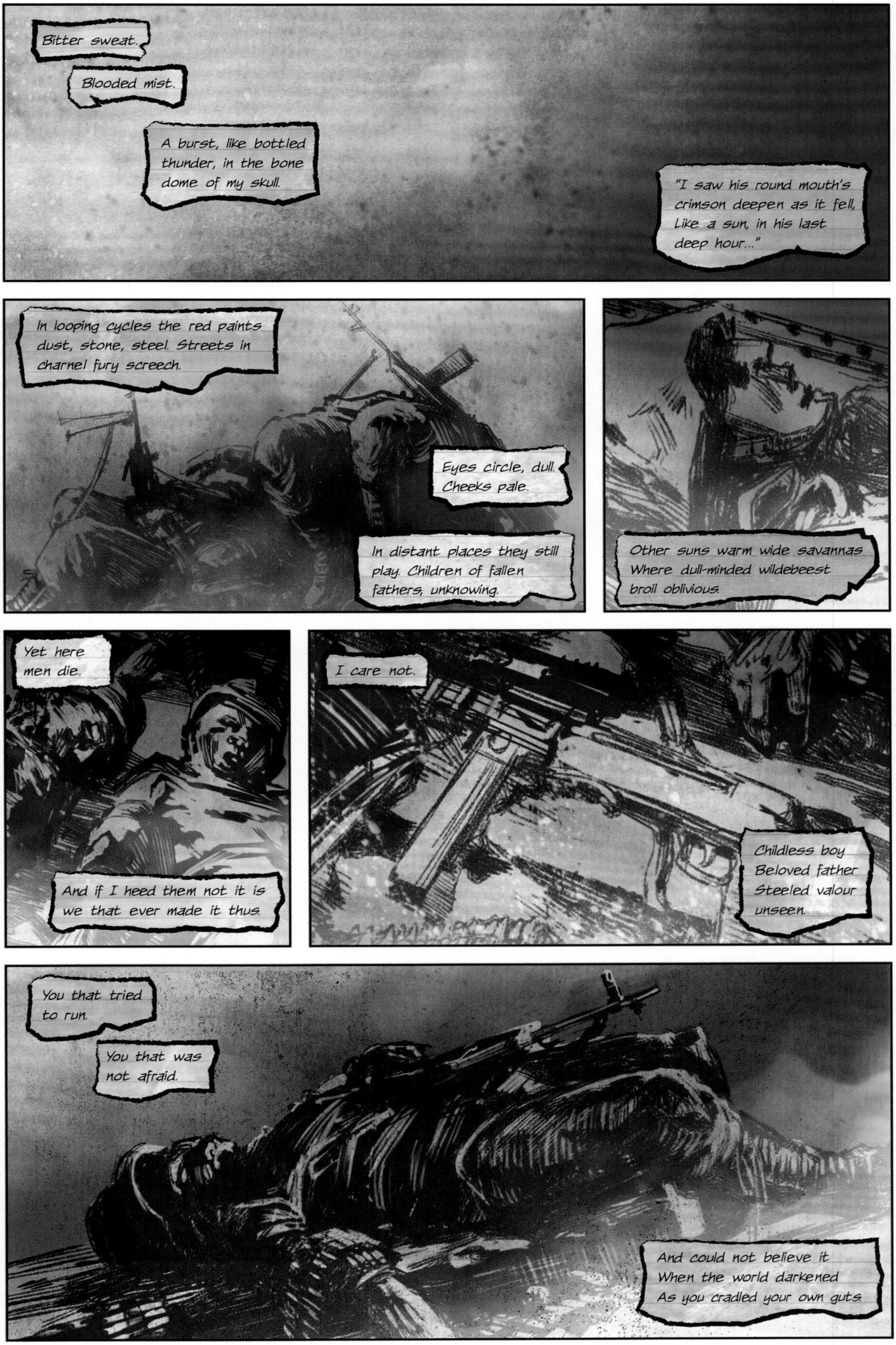
Bitter sweat.
Blooded mist.
A burst, like bottled thunder, in the bone dome of my skull.
"I saw his round mouth's crimson deepen as it fell, Like a sun, in his last deep hour..."
In looping cycles the red paints dust, stone, steel. Streets in charnel fury screech.
Eyes circle, dull. Cheeks pale.
In distant places they still play. Children of fallen fathers, unknowing.
Other suns warm wide savannas Where dull-minded wildebeest broil oblivious.
Yet here men die.
And if I heed them not it is we that ever made it thus.
I care not.
Childless boy Beloved father Steeled valour unseen.
You that tried to run.
You that was not afraid.
And could not believe it When the world darkened As you cradled your own guts.

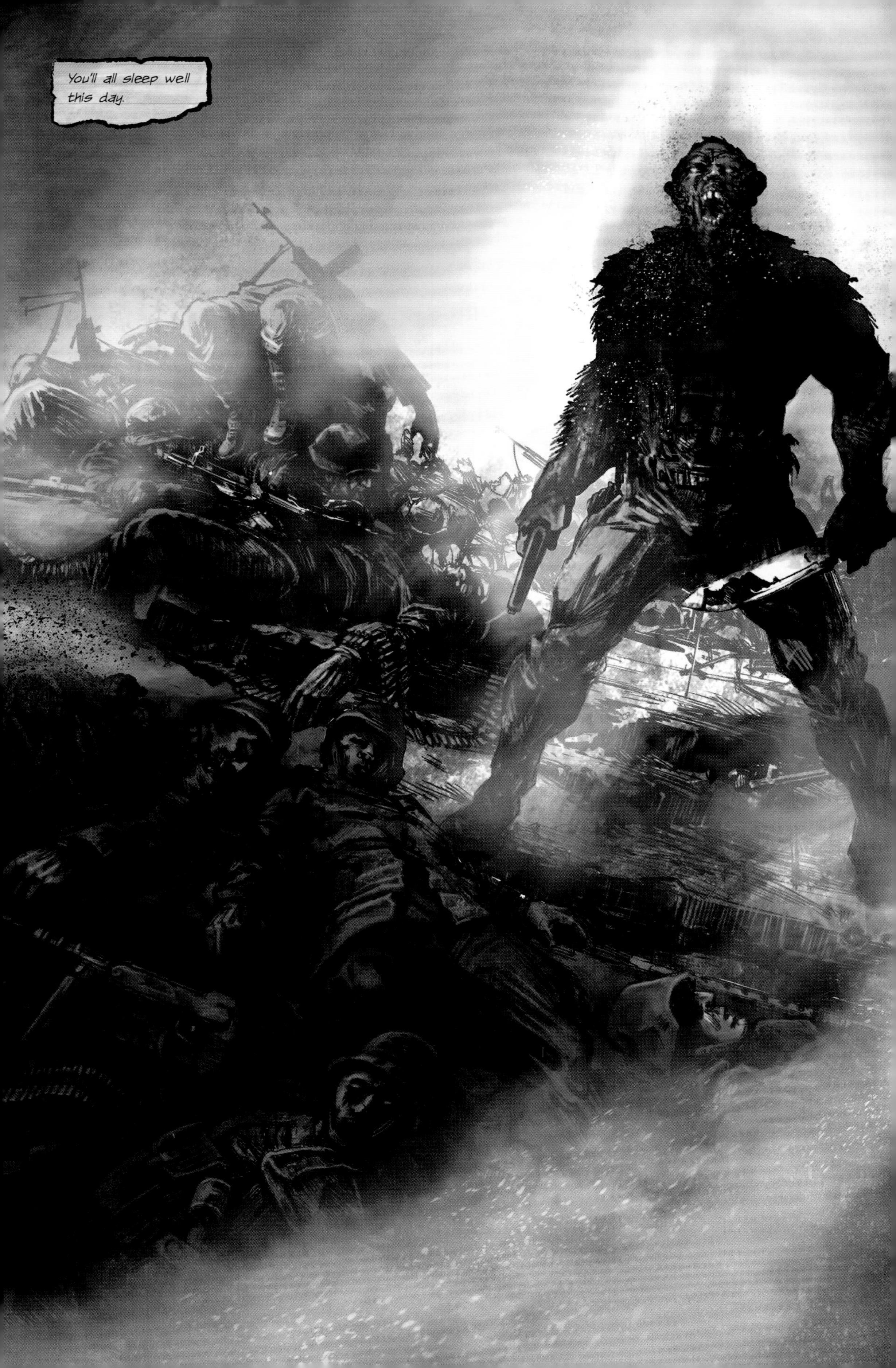
You'll all sleep well this day.

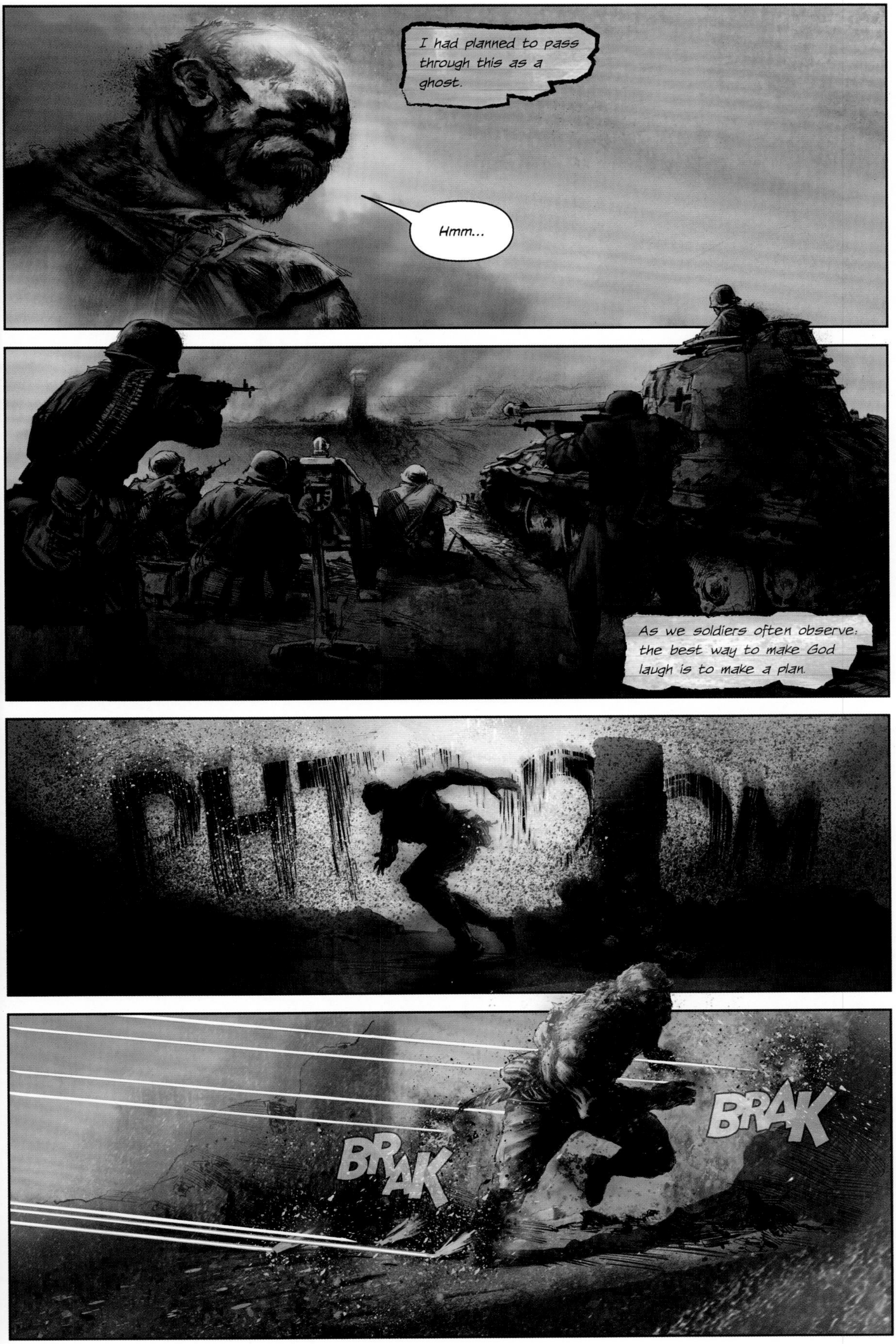

I had planned to pass through this as a ghost.
Hmm...
As we soldiers often observe: the best way to make God laugh is to make a plan.
BRAK
BRAK

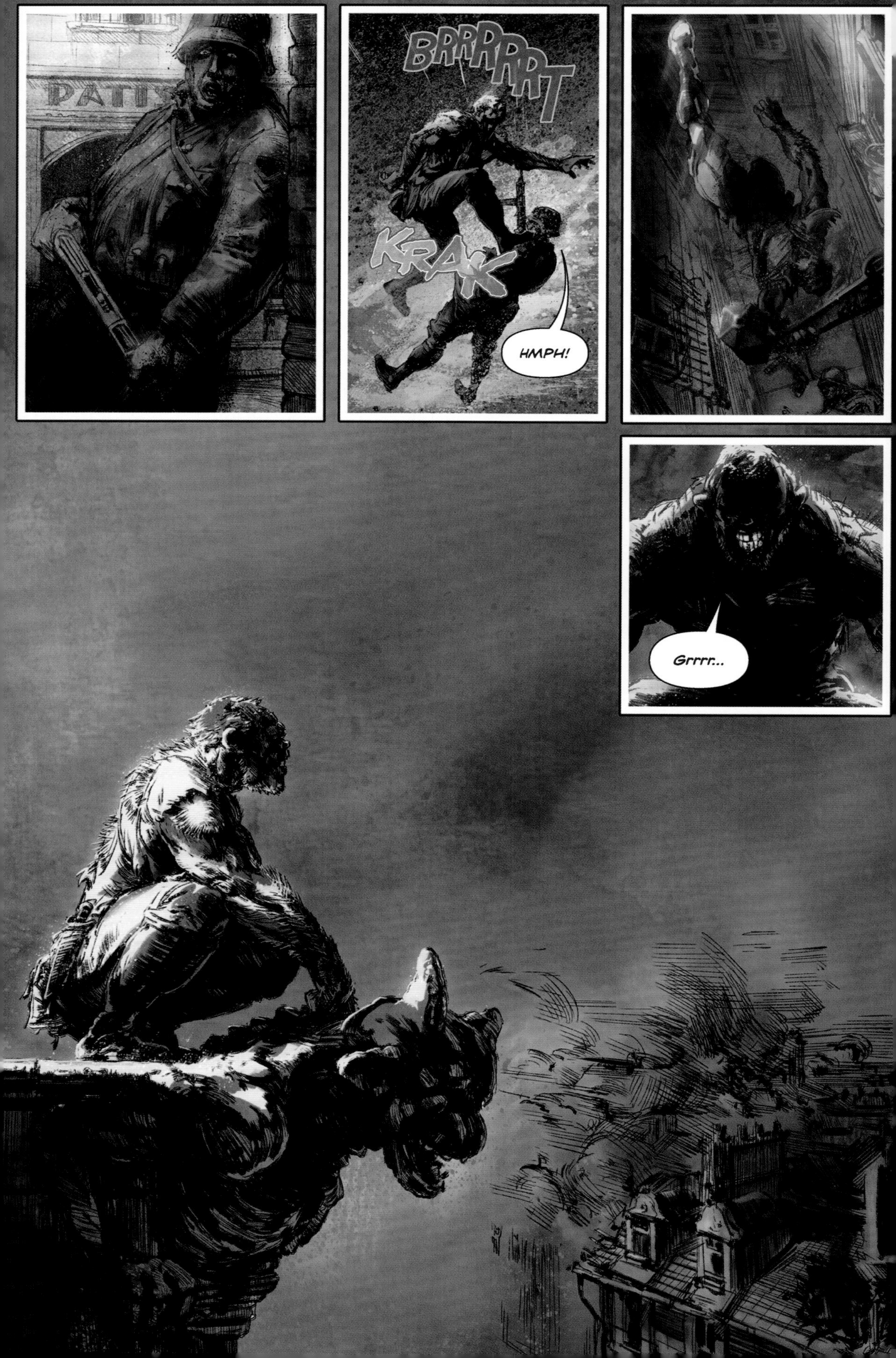
BRRRRRRT
KRAK
HMPH!
Grrrr...

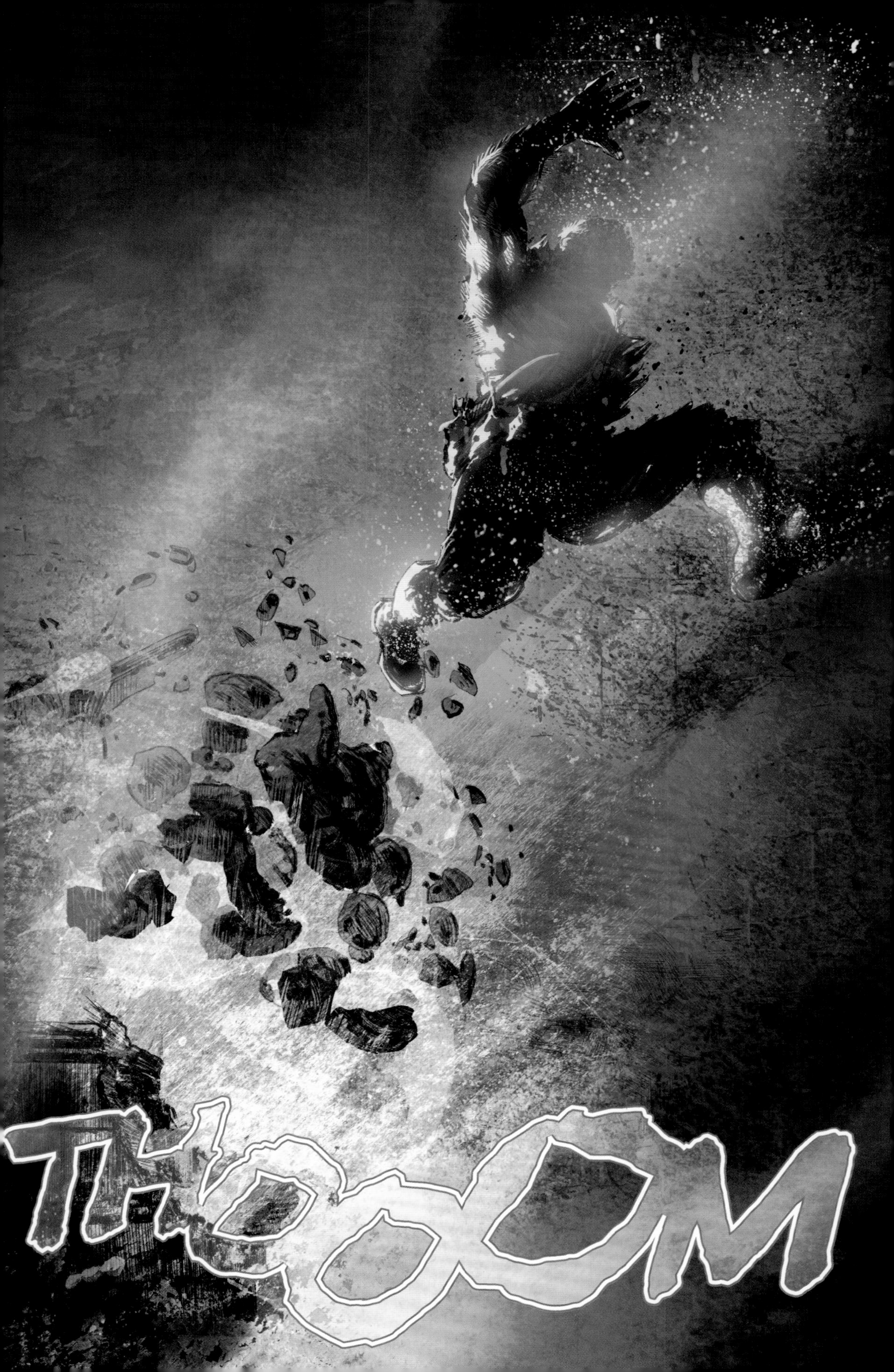
THOOOM

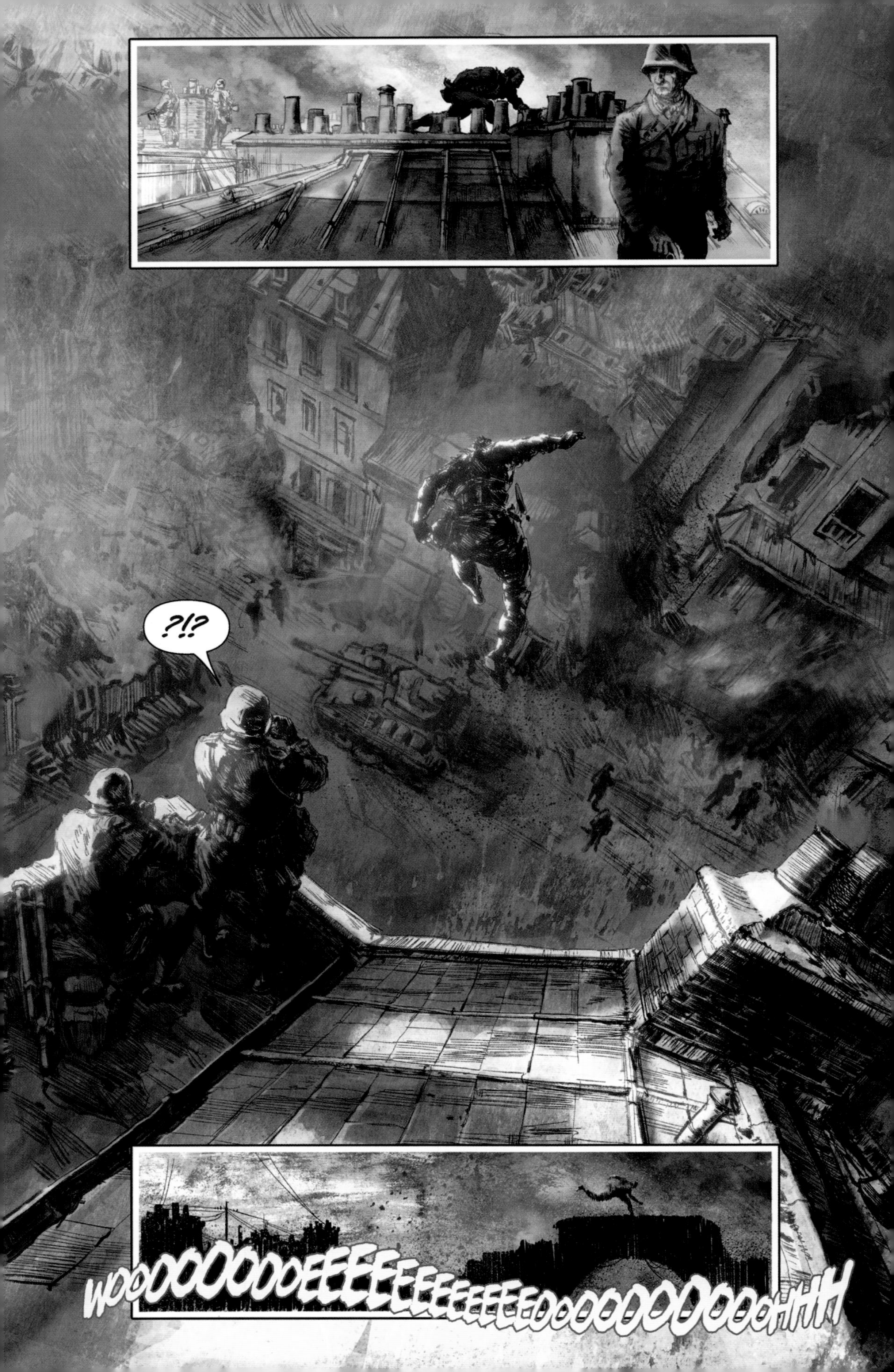
?!?
WOOOOOOOOOEEEEEEEEEEEEEEEEOOOOOOOOOOOOOOHHHH

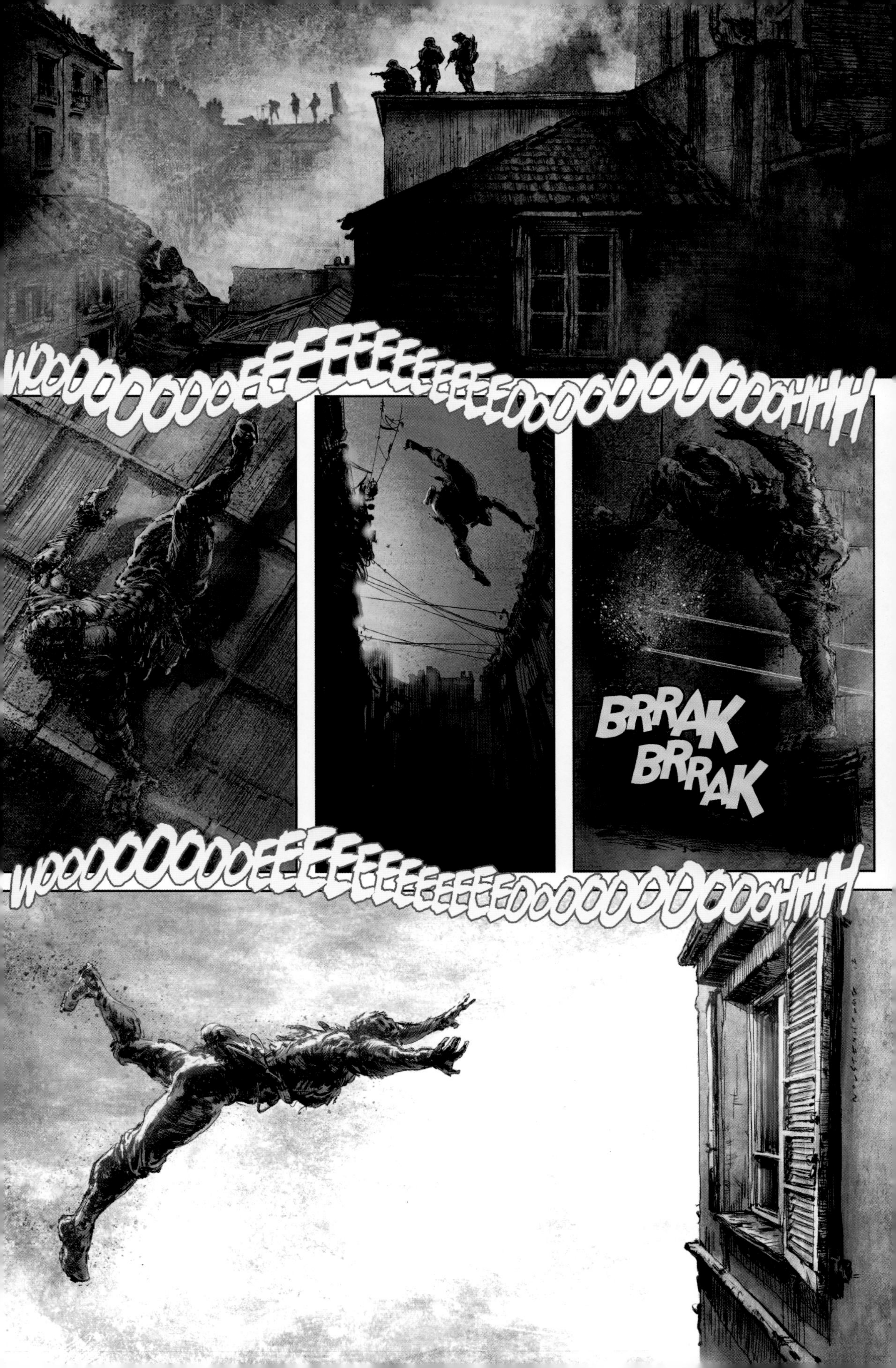

WOOOOOOOOOEEEEEEEEEEEEEEOOOOOOOOOOOOHHH
BRRAK BRRAK
WOOOOOOOOOEEEEEEEEEEEEEEEOOOOOOOOOOOOHHH

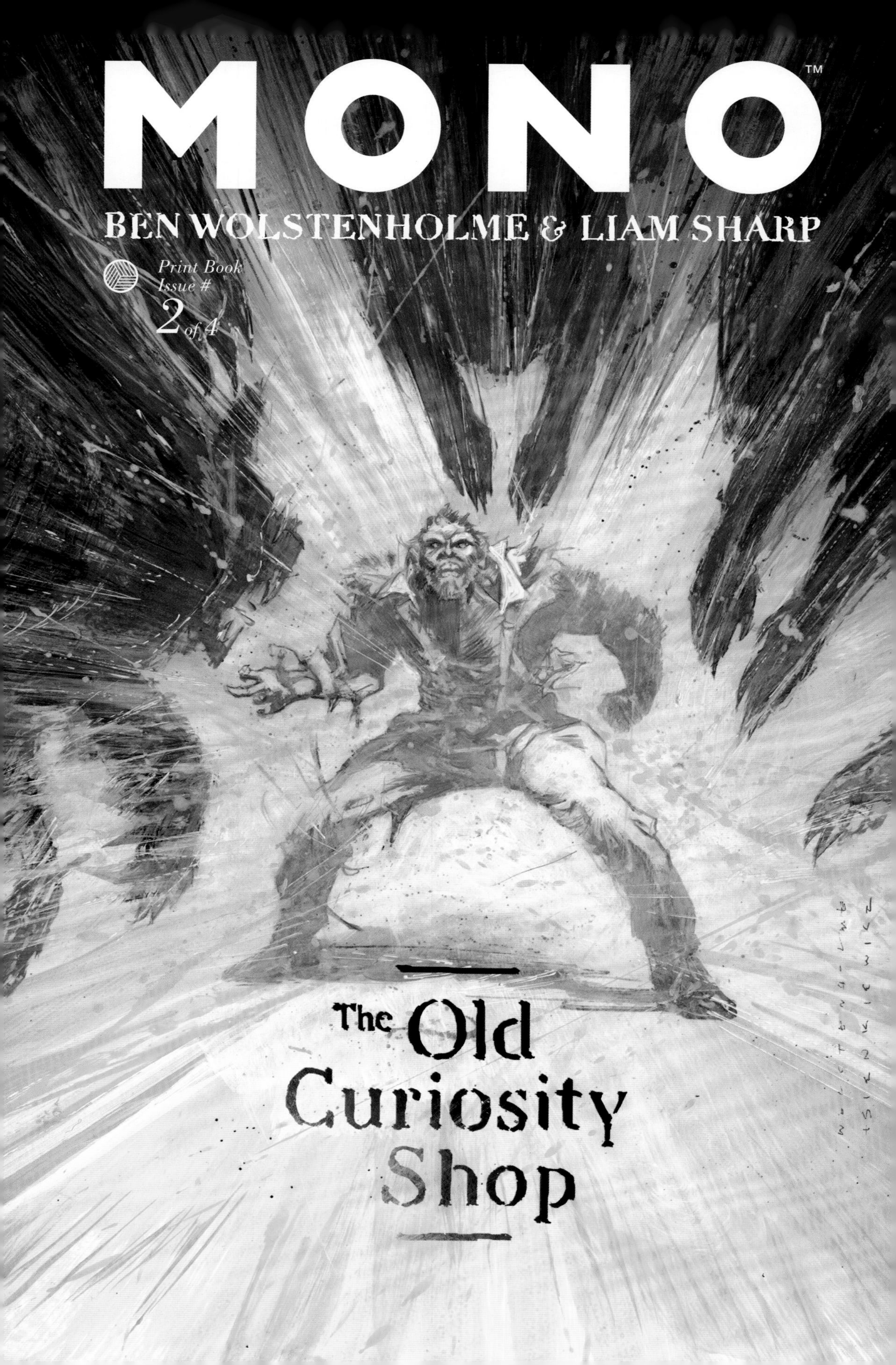
MONO™
BEN WOLSTENHOLME & LIAM SHARP
Print Book
Issue #
2 of 4
The Old
Curiosity
Shop

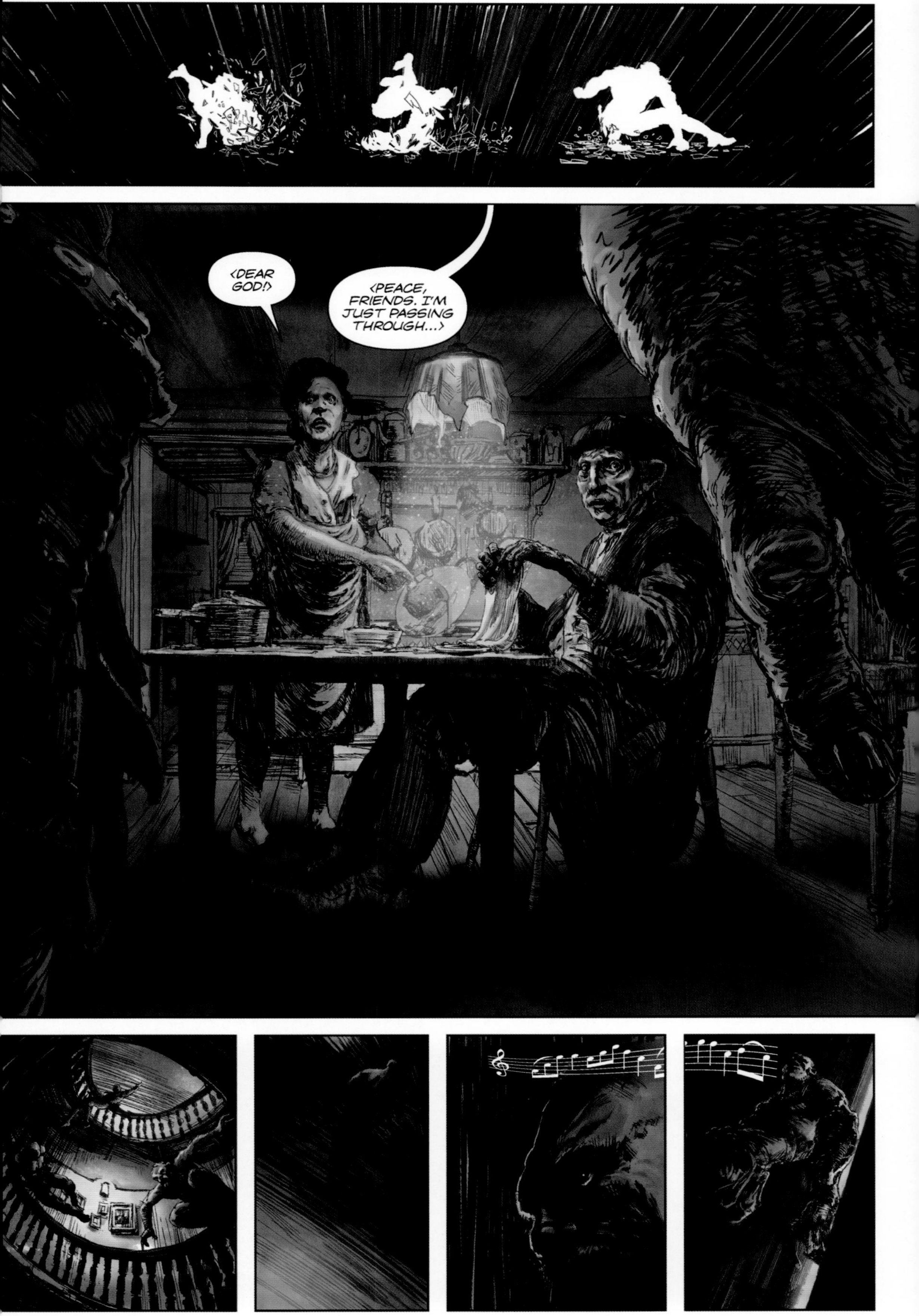
<DEAR GOD!>
<PEACE, FRIENDS. I'M JUST PASSING THROUGH...>

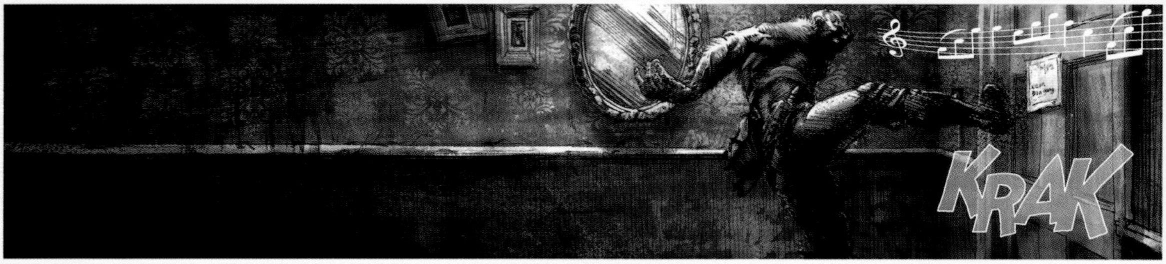
KRAK

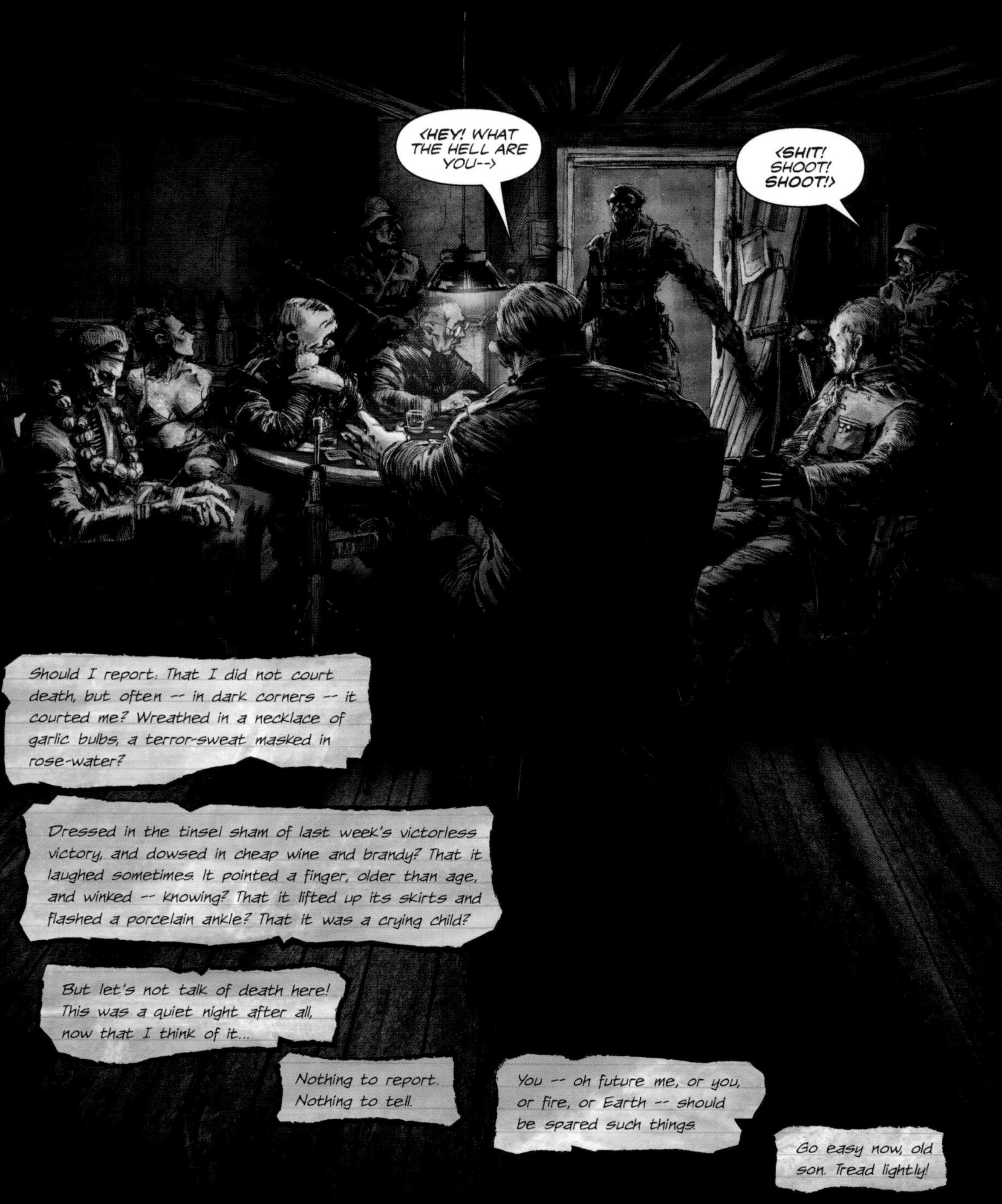
<HEY! WHAT THE HELL ARE YOU-->
<SHIT! SHOOT! SHOOT!>
Should I report: That I did not court death, but often -- in dark corners -- it courted me? Wreathed in a necklace of garlic bulbs, a terror-sweat masked in rose-water?
Dressed in the tinsel sham of last week's victorless victory, and dowsed in cheap wine and brandy? That it laughed sometimes. It pointed a finger, older than age, and winked -- knowing? That it lifted up its skirts and flashed a porcelain ankle? That it was a crying child?
But let's not talk of death here! This was a quiet night after all, now that I think of it...
Nothing to report. Nothing to tell.
You -- oh future me, or you, or fire, or Earth -- should be spared such things.
Go easy now, old son. Tread lightly!

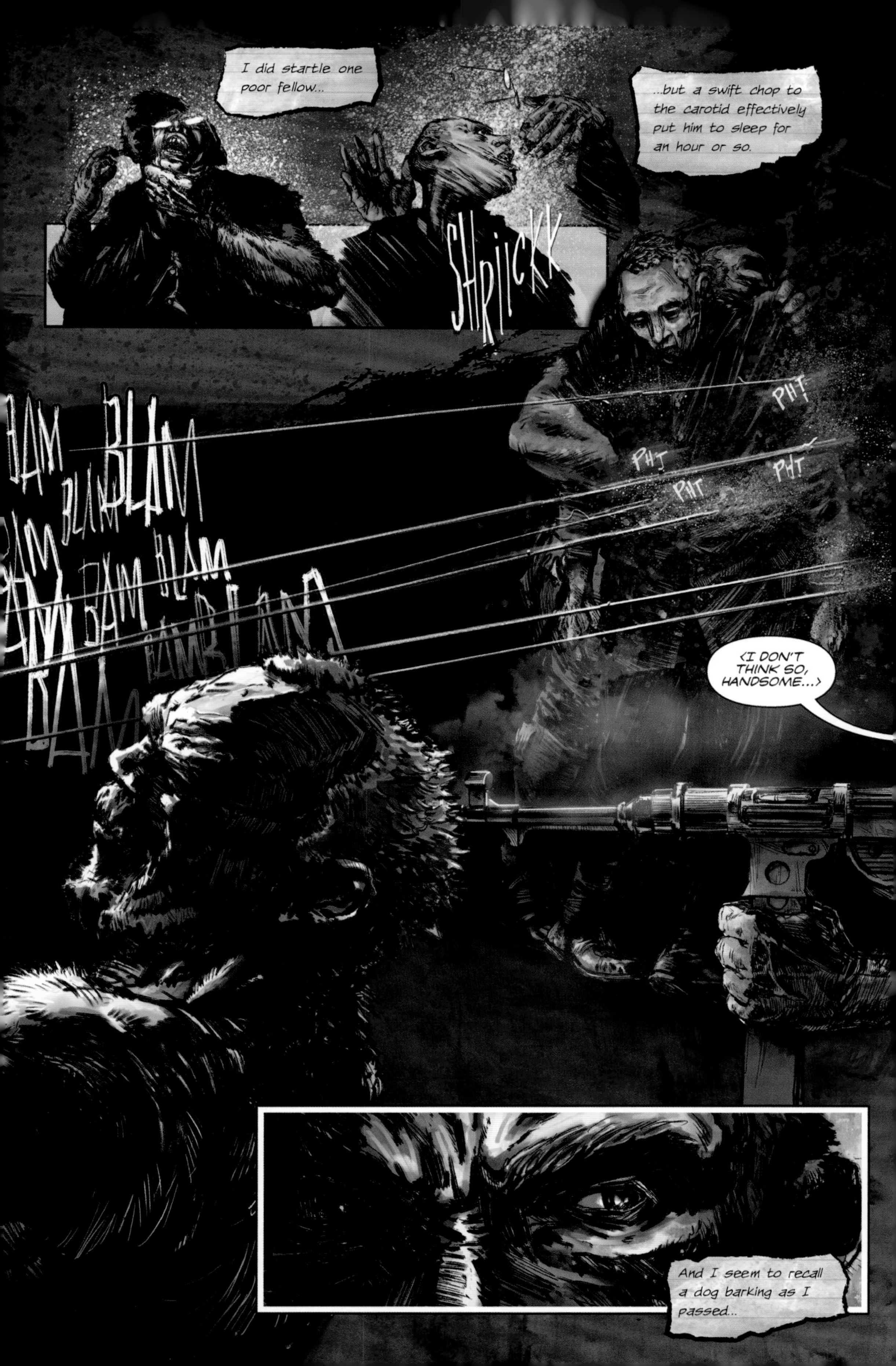
I did startle one poor fellow...
...but a swift chop to the carotid effectively put him to sleep for an hour or so.
SHRIICKK
BAM BLAM BLAM BLAM BAM BAM BLAM BAM BAM BLAM
PHT PHT PHT PHT
<I DON'T THINK SO, HANDSOME...>
And I seem to recall a dog barking as I passed...

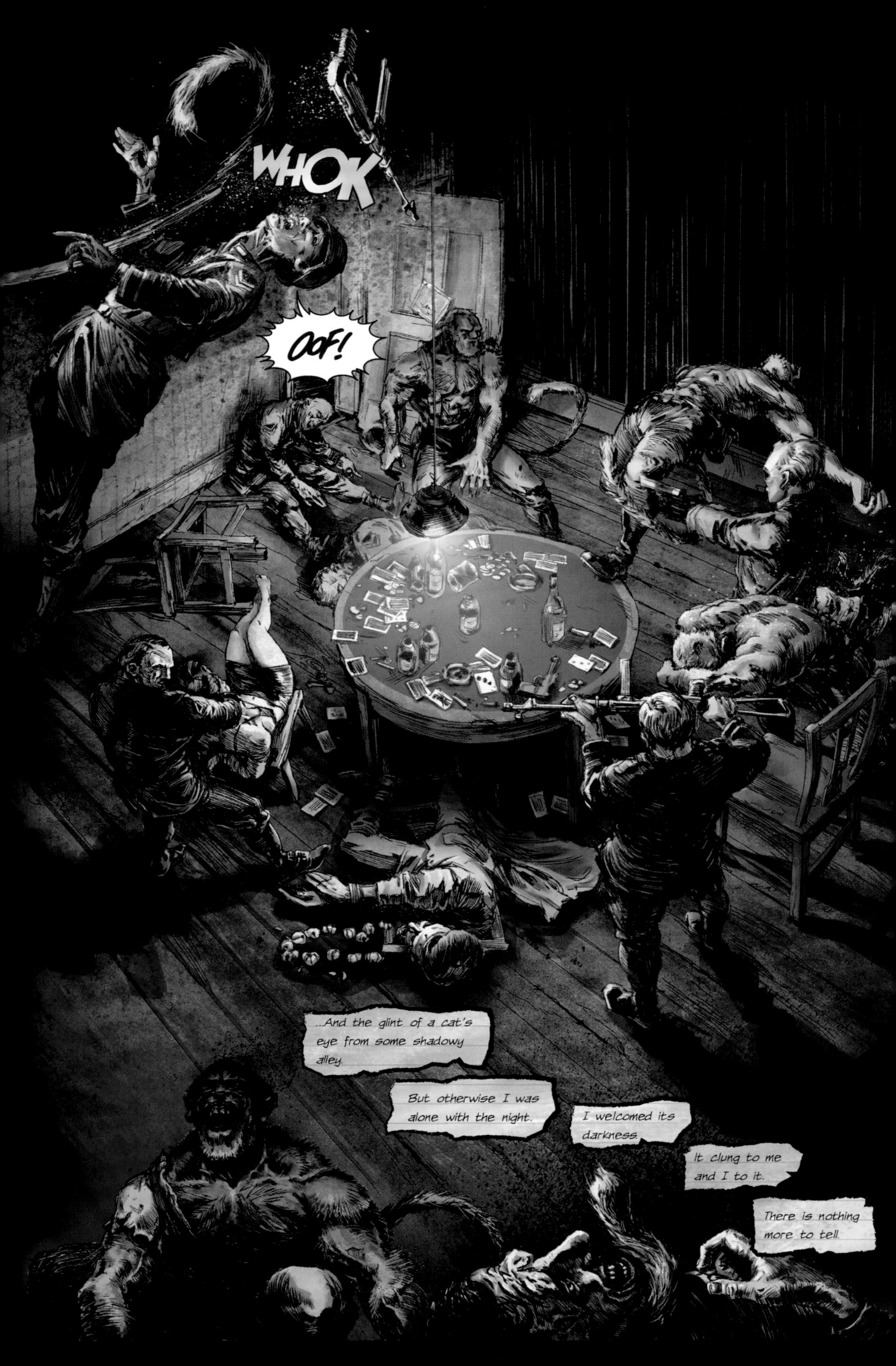
WHOK
OOF!
...And the glint of a cat's eye from some shadowy alley.
But otherwise I was alone with the night.
I welcomed its darkness.
It clung to me and I to it.
There is nothing more to tell.

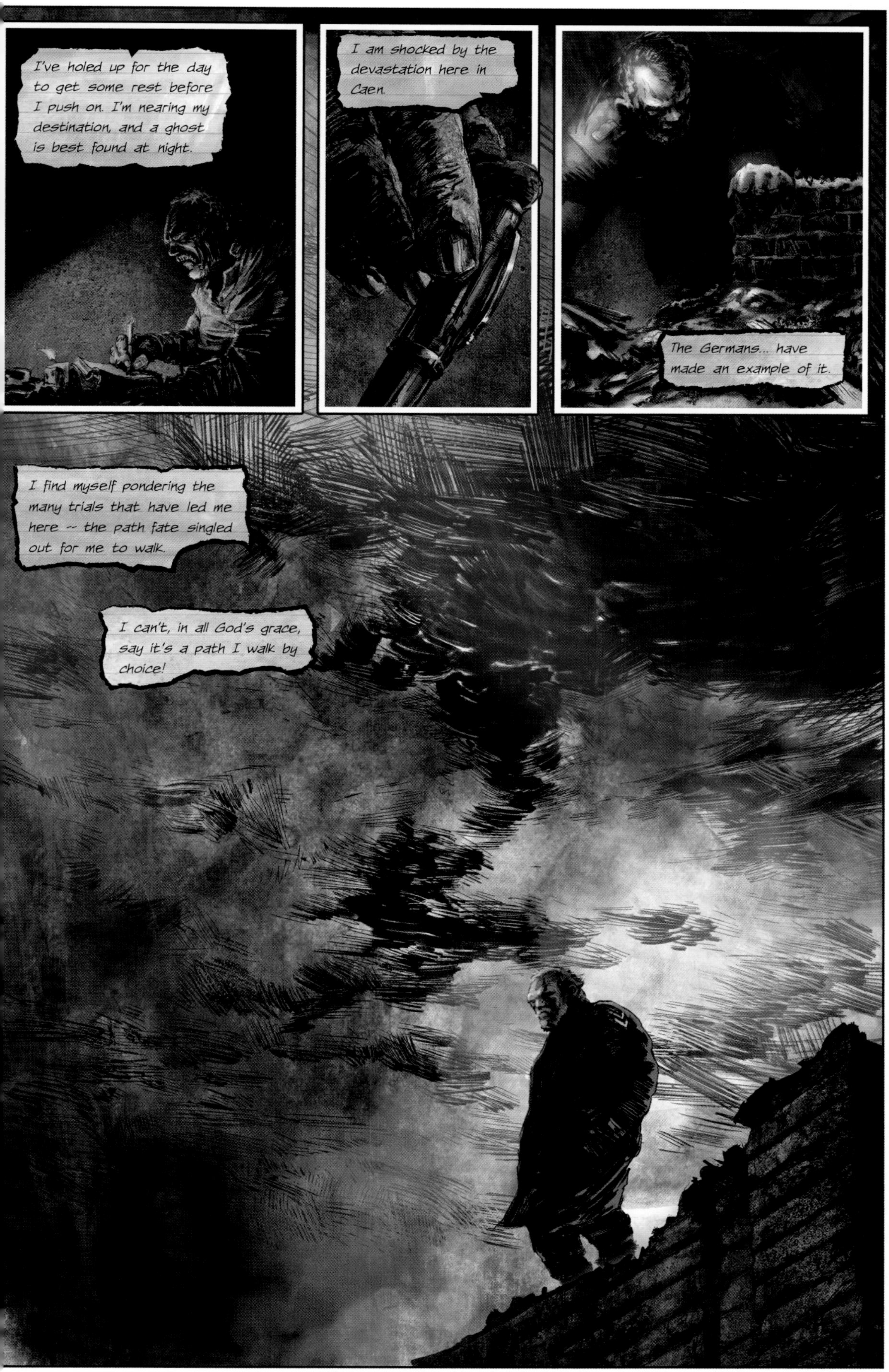
I've holed up for the day to get some rest before I push on. I'm nearing my destination, and a ghost is best found at night.
I am shocked by the devastation here in Caen.
The Germans... have made an example of it.
I find myself pondering the many trials that have led me here -- the path fate singled out for me to walk.
I can't, in all God's grace, say it's a path I walk by choice!

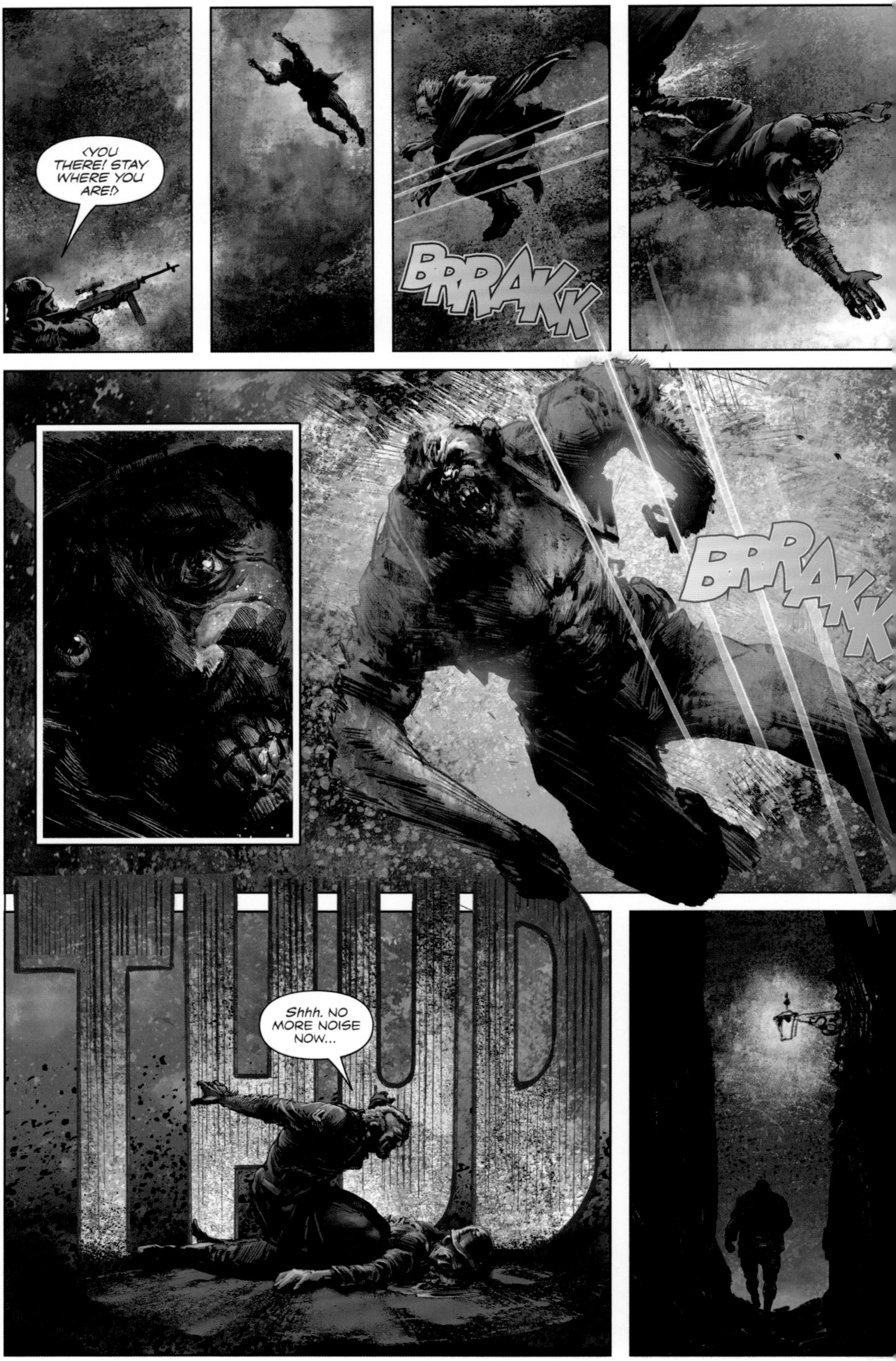

<YOU THERE! STAY WHERE YOU ARE!>
BRRAKK
BRRAKK
THUD
Shhh. NO MORE NOISE NOW...

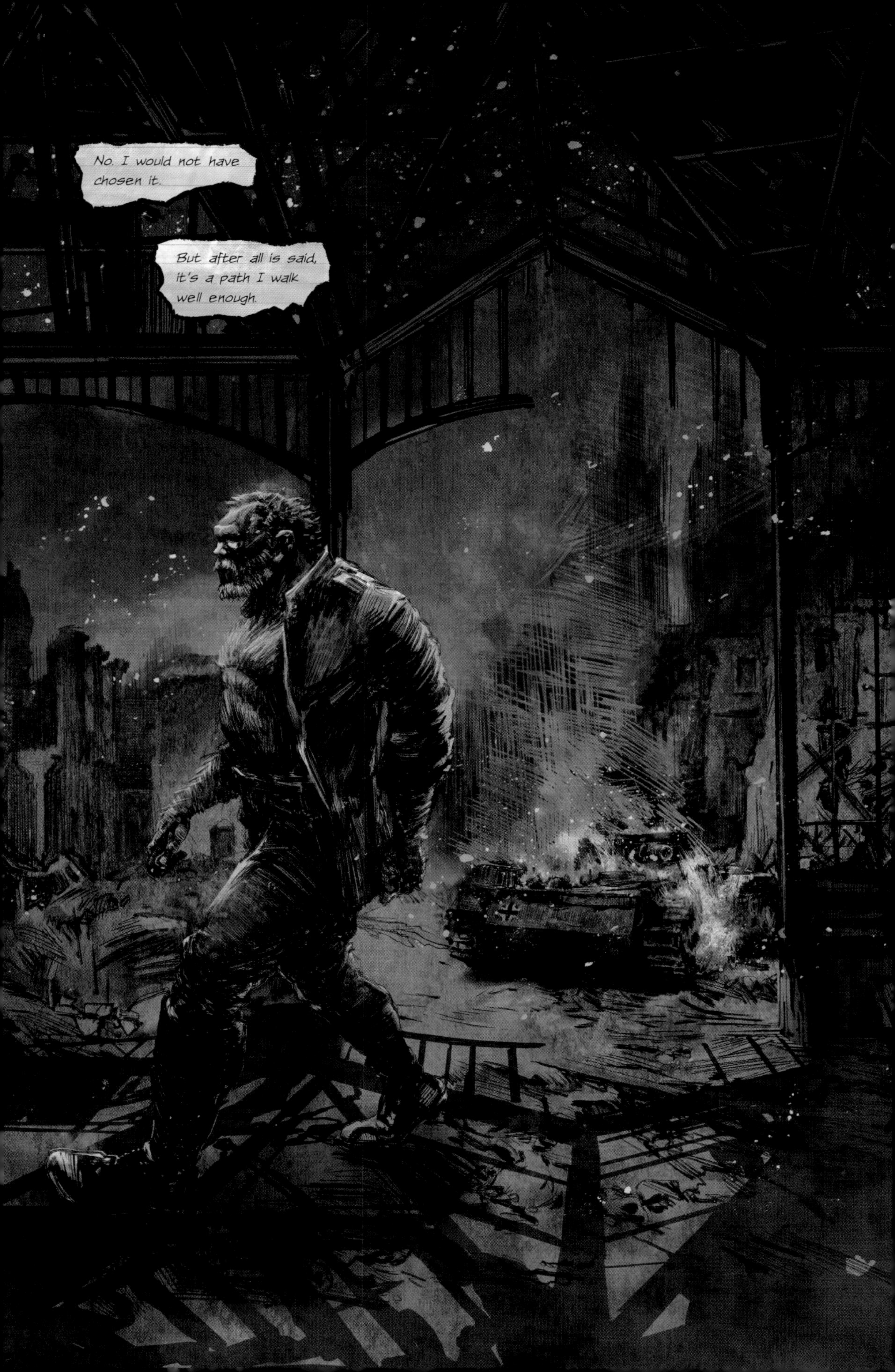
No. I would not have chosen it.
But after all is said, it's a path I walk well enough.

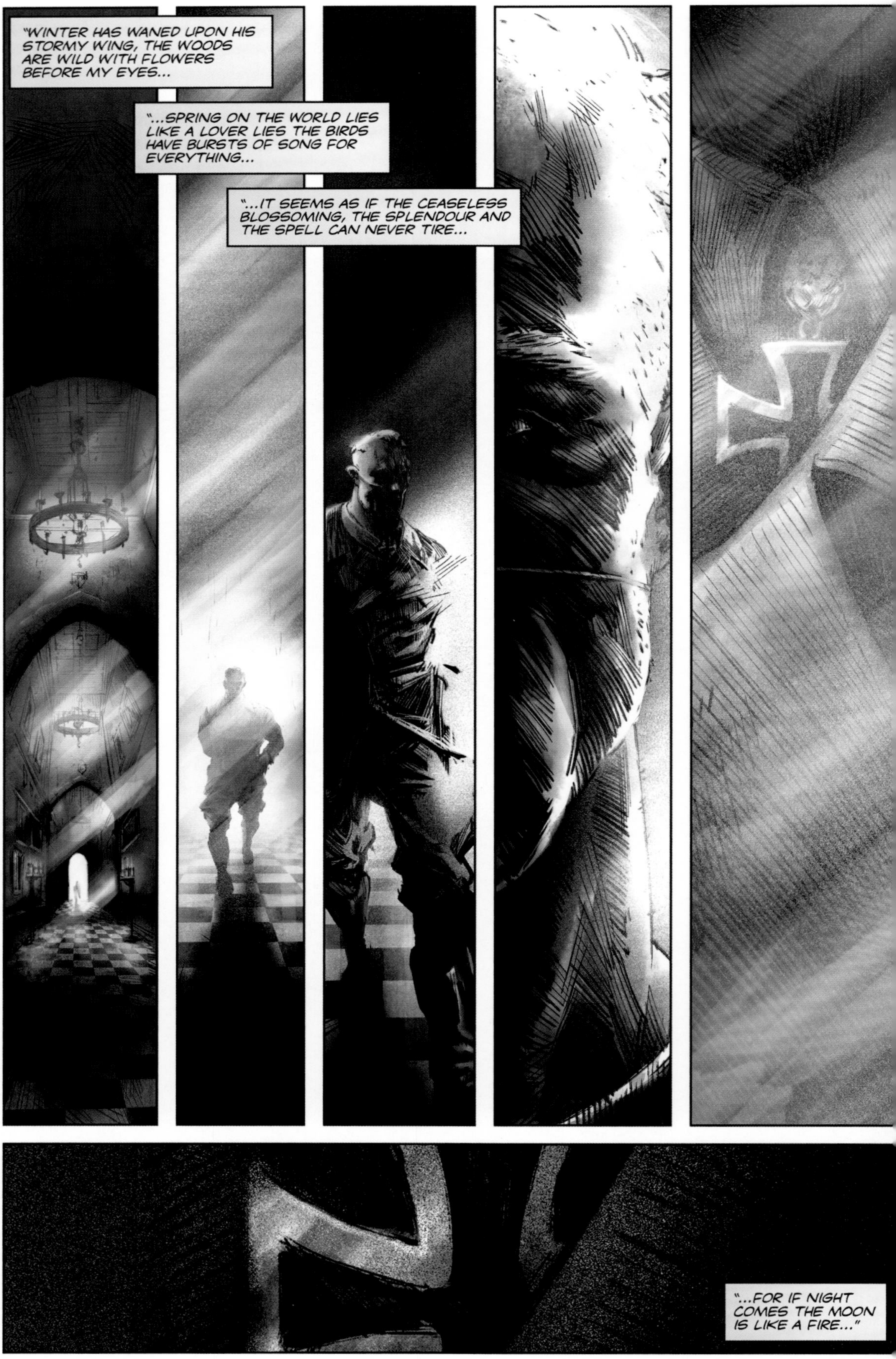
"WINTER HAS WANED UPON HIS STORMY WING, THE WOODS ARE WILD WITH FLOWERS BEFORE MY EYES...
"...SPRING ON THE WORLD LIES LIKE A LOVER LIES THE BIRDS HAVE BURSTS OF SONG FOR EVERYTHING...
"...IT SEEMS AS IF THE CEASELESS BLOSSOMING, THE SPLENDOUR AND THE SPELL CAN NEVER TIRE...
"...FOR IF NIGHT COMES THE MOON IS LIKE A FIRE..."

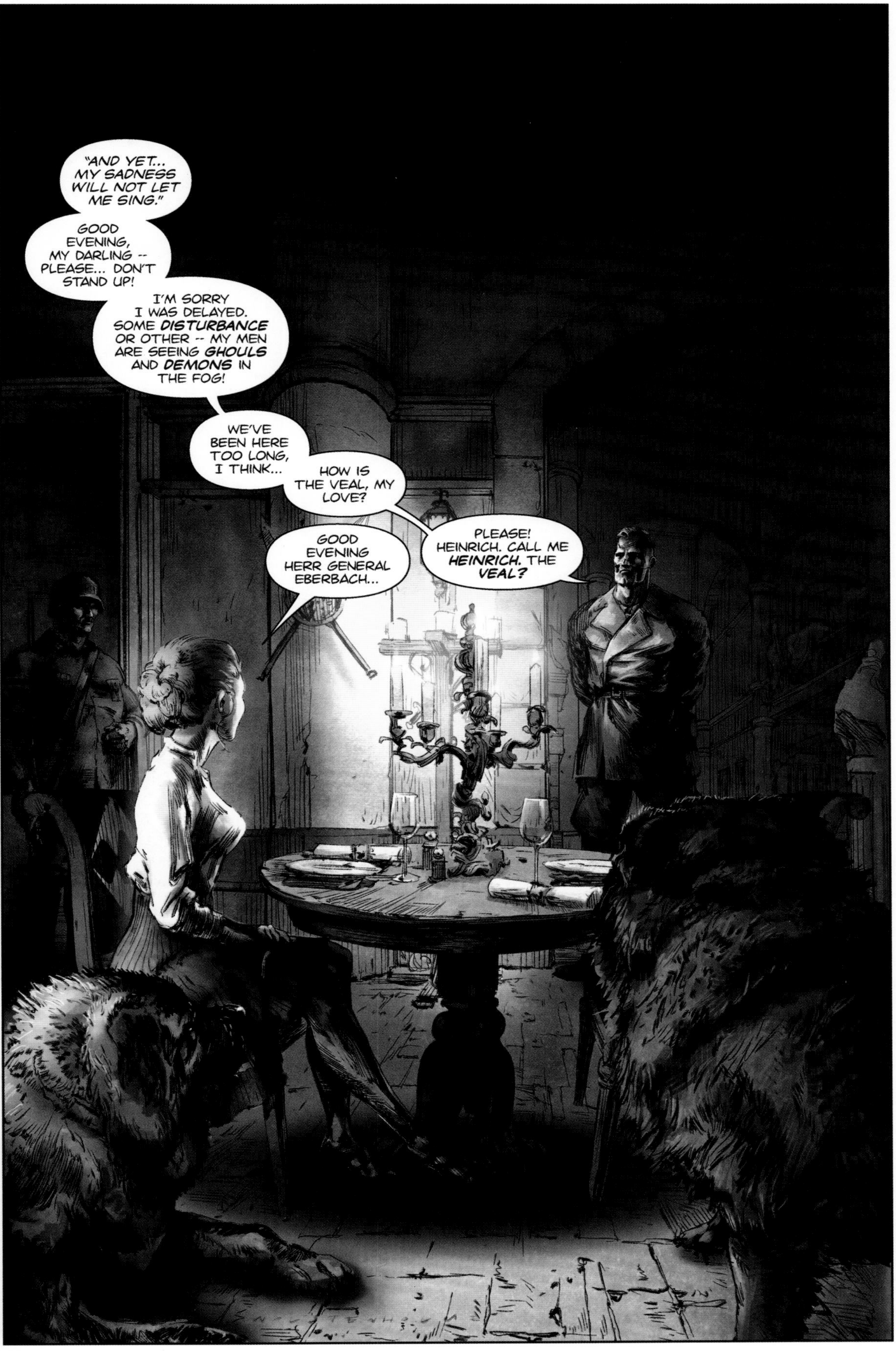
"AND YET... MY SADNESS WILL NOT LET ME SING."
GOOD EVENING, MY DARLING -- PLEASE... DON'T STAND UP!
I'M SORRY I WAS DELAYED. SOME DISTURBANCE OR OTHER -- MY MEN ARE SEEING GHOULS AND DEMONS IN THE FOG!
WE'VE BEEN HERE TOO LONG, I THINK...
HOW IS THE VEAL, MY LOVE?
GOOD EVENING HERR GENERAL EBERBACH...
PLEASE! HEINRICH. CALL ME HEINRICH. THE VEAL?

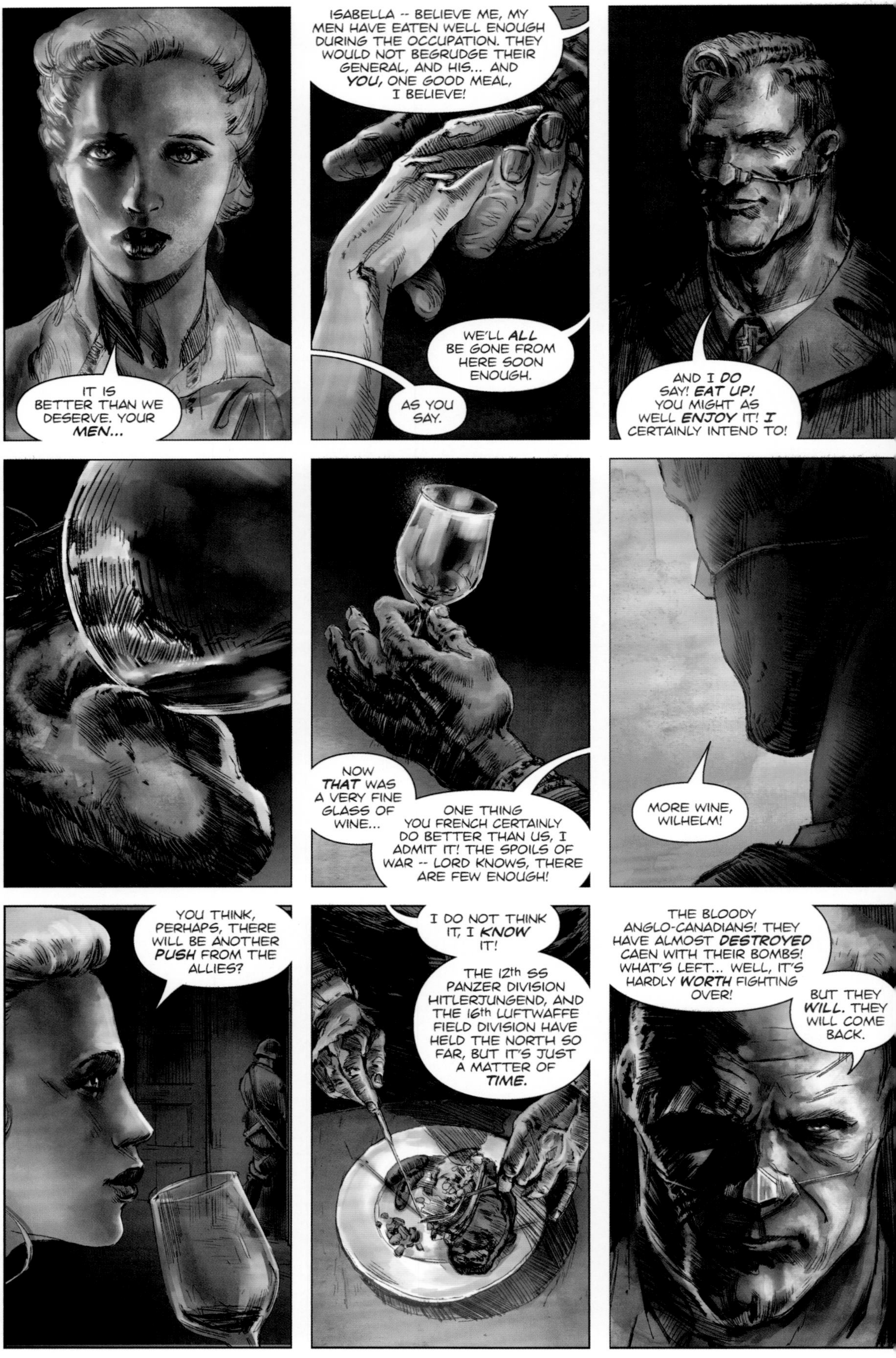
IT IS BETTER THAN WE DESERVE. YOUR MEN...
ISABELLA -- BELIEVE ME, MY MEN HAVE EATEN WELL ENOUGH DURING THE OCCUPATION. THEY WOULD NOT BEGRUDGE THEIR GENERAL, AND HIS... AND YOU, ONE GOOD MEAL, I BELIEVE!
AS YOU SAY.
WE'LL ALL BE GONE FROM HERE SOON ENOUGH.
AND I DO SAY! EAT UP! YOU MIGHT AS WELL ENJOY IT! I CERTAINLY INTEND TO!
NOW THAT WAS A VERY FINE GLASS OF WINE...
ONE THING YOU FRENCH CERTAINLY DO BETTER THAN US, I ADMIT IT! THE SPOILS OF WAR -- LORD KNOWS, THERE ARE FEW ENOUGH!
MORE WINE, WILHELM!
YOU THINK, PERHAPS, THERE WILL BE ANOTHER PUSH FROM THE ALLIES?
I DO NOT THINK IT, I KNOW IT!
THE 12th SS PANZER DIVISION HITLERJUNGEND, AND THE 16th LUFTWAFFE FIELD DIVISION HAVE HELD THE NORTH SO FAR, BUT IT'S JUST A MATTER OF TIME.
THE BLOODY ANGLO-CANADIANS! THEY HAVE ALMOST DESTROYED CAEN WITH THEIR BOMBS! WHAT'S LEFT... WELL, IT'S HARDLY WORTH FIGHTING OVER!
BUT THEY WILL. THEY WILL COME BACK.

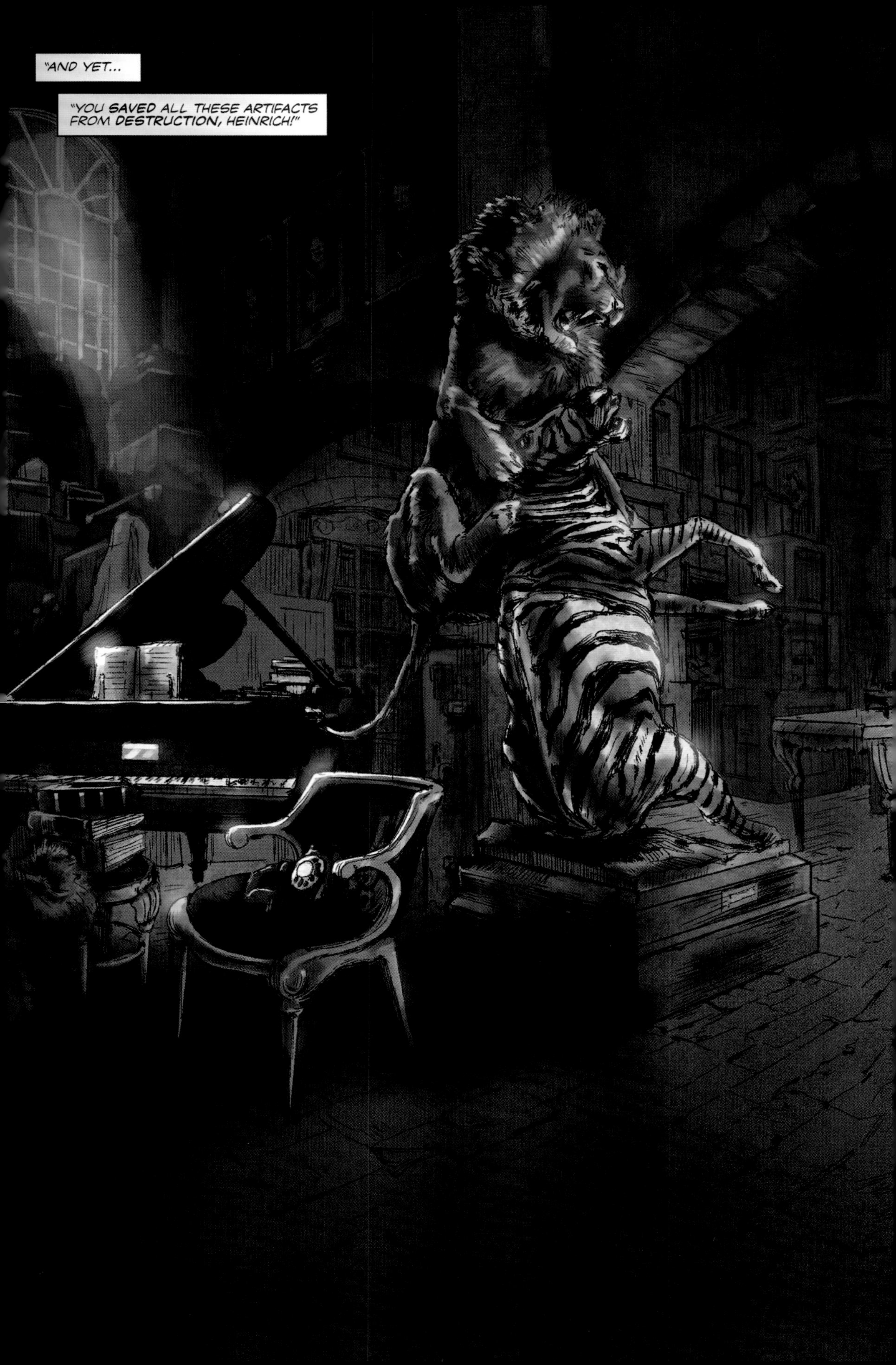
"AND YET...
"YOU SAVED ALL THESE ARTIFACTS FROM DESTRUCTION, HEINRICH!"

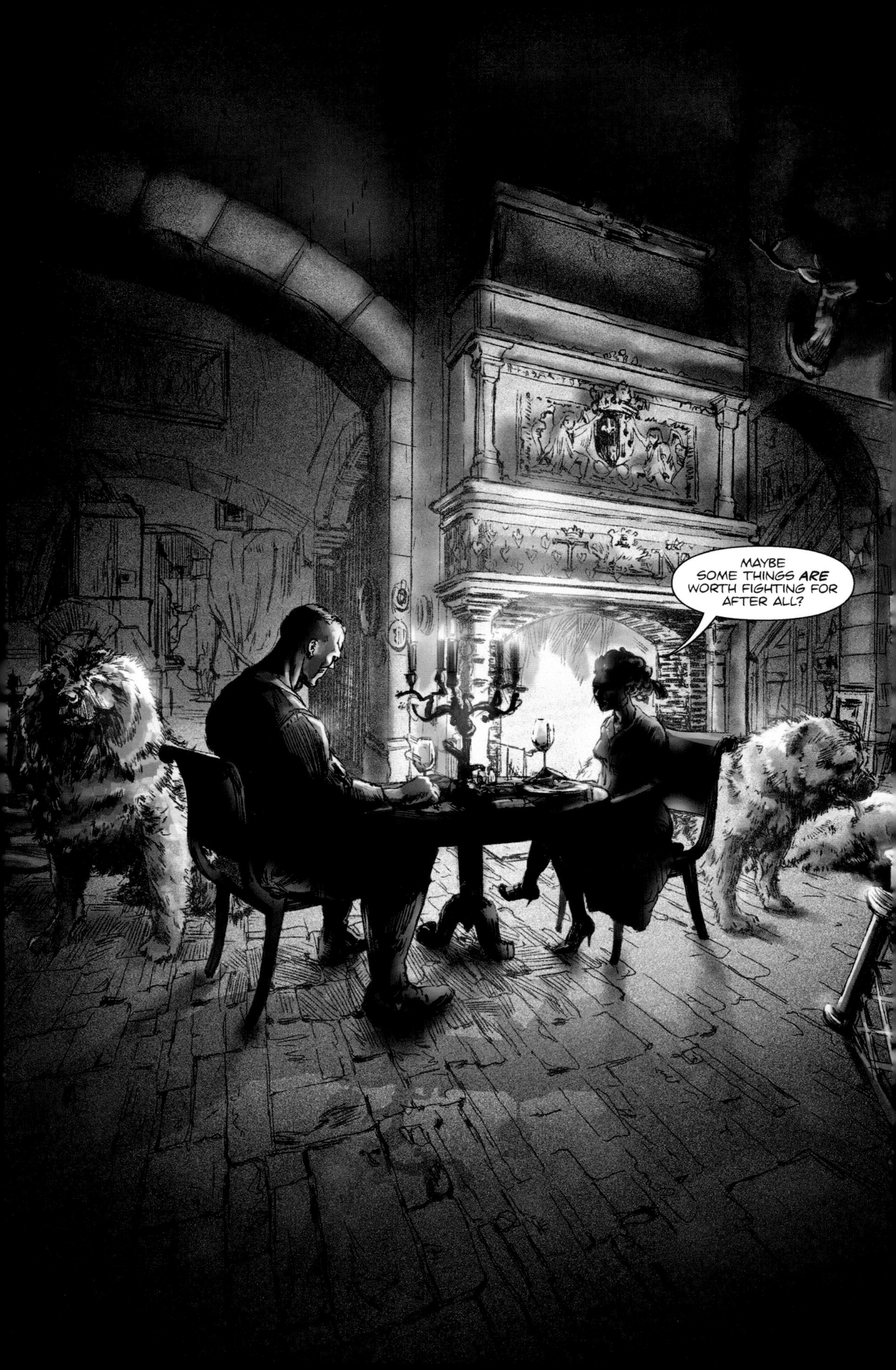
MAYBE SOME THINGS ARE WORTH FIGHTING FOR AFTER ALL?

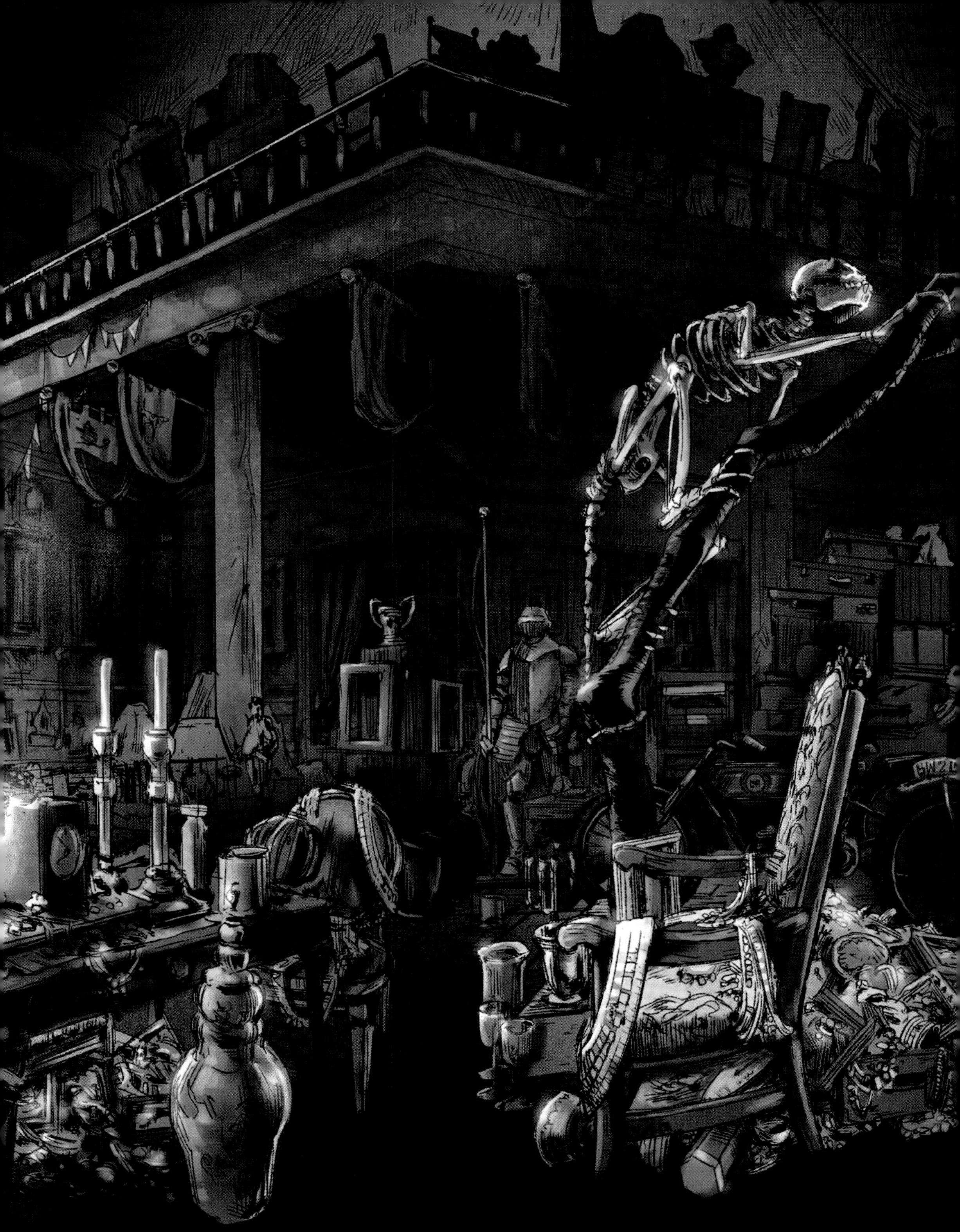

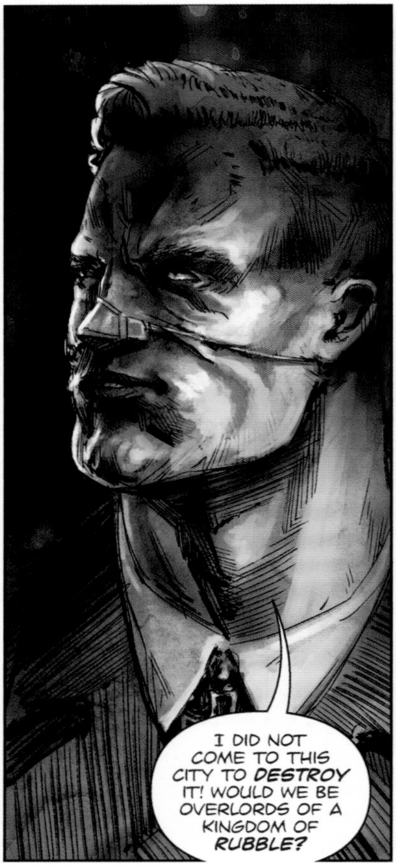
I DID NOT COME TO THIS CITY TO DESTROY IT! WOULD WE BE OVERLORDS OF A KINGDOM OF RUBBLE?

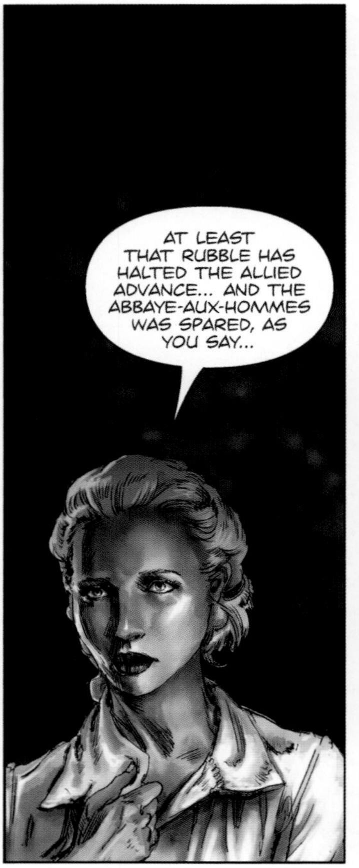
AT LEAST THAT RUBBLE HAS HALTED THE ALLIED ADVANCE... AND THE ABBAYE-AUX-HOMMES WAS SPARED, AS YOU SAY...

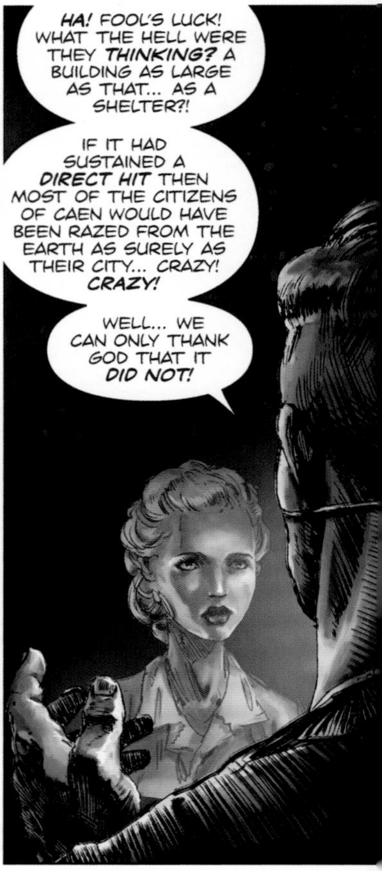
HA! FOOL'S LUCK! WHAT THE HELL WERE THEY THINKING? A BUILDING AS LARGE AS THAT... AS A SHELTER?!
IF IT HAD SUSTAINED A DIRECT HIT THEN MOST OF THE CITIZENS OF CAEN WOULD HAVE BEEN RAZED FROM THE EARTH AS SURELY AS THEIR CITY... CRAZY! CRAZY!
WELL... WE CAN ONLY THANK GOD THAT IT DID NOT!

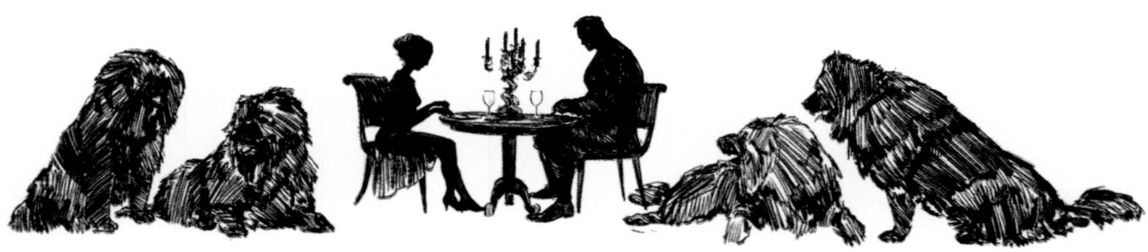

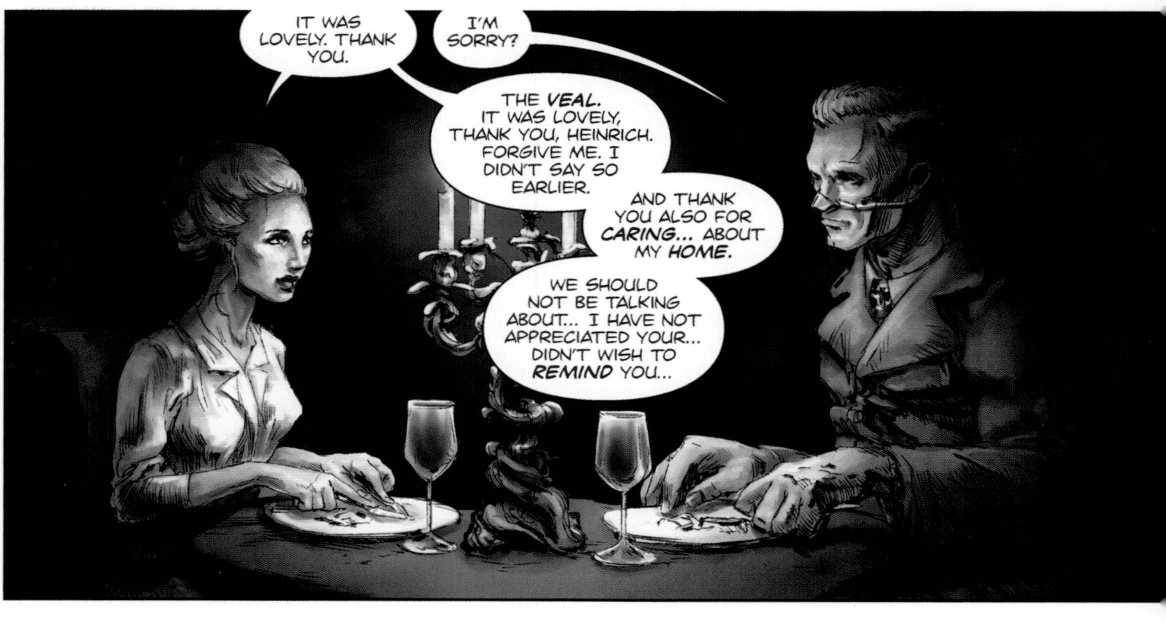
IT WAS LOVELY. THANK YOU.
I'M SORRY?
THE VEAL. IT WAS LOVELY, THANK YOU, HEINRICH. FORGIVE ME. I DIDN'T SAY SO EARLIER.
AND THANK YOU ALSO FOR CARING... ABOUT MY HOME.
WE SHOULD NOT BE TALKING ABOUT... I HAVE NOT APPRECIATED YOUR... DIDN'T WISH TO REMIND YOU...

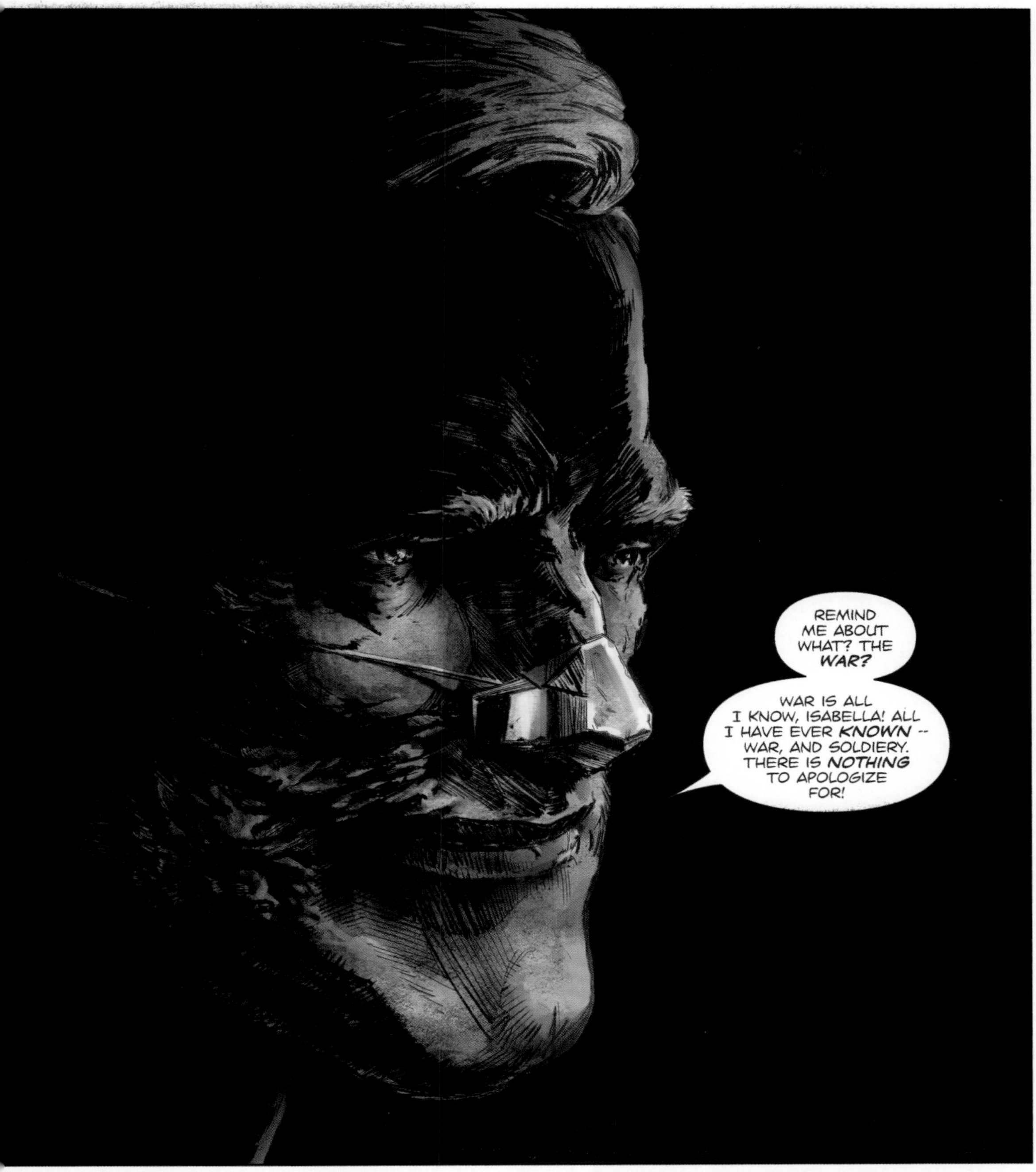
REMIND ME ABOUT WHAT? THE *WAR?*
WAR IS ALL I KNOW, ISABELLA! ALL I HAVE EVER *KNOWN* -- WAR, AND SOLDIERY. THERE IS *NOTHING* TO APOLOGIZE FOR!

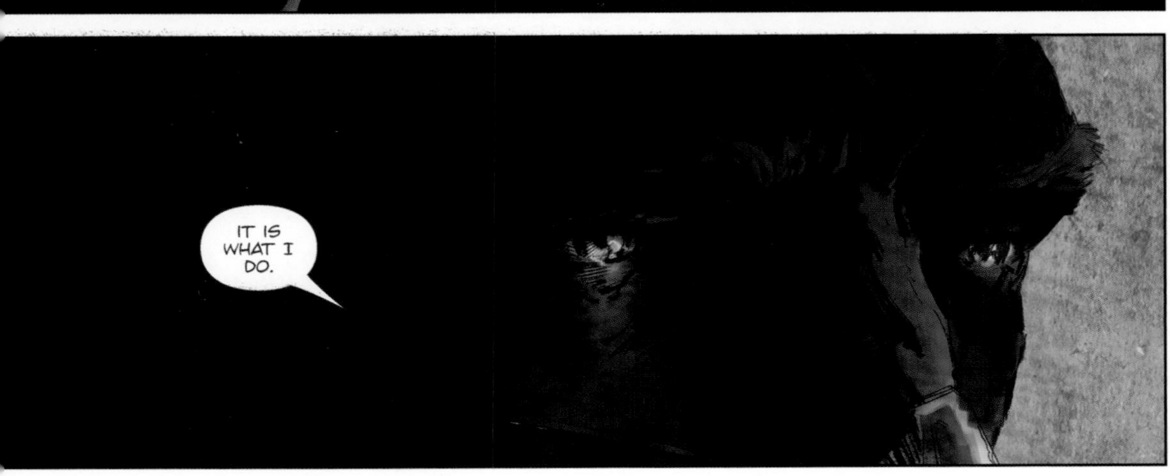
IT IS WHAT I DO.

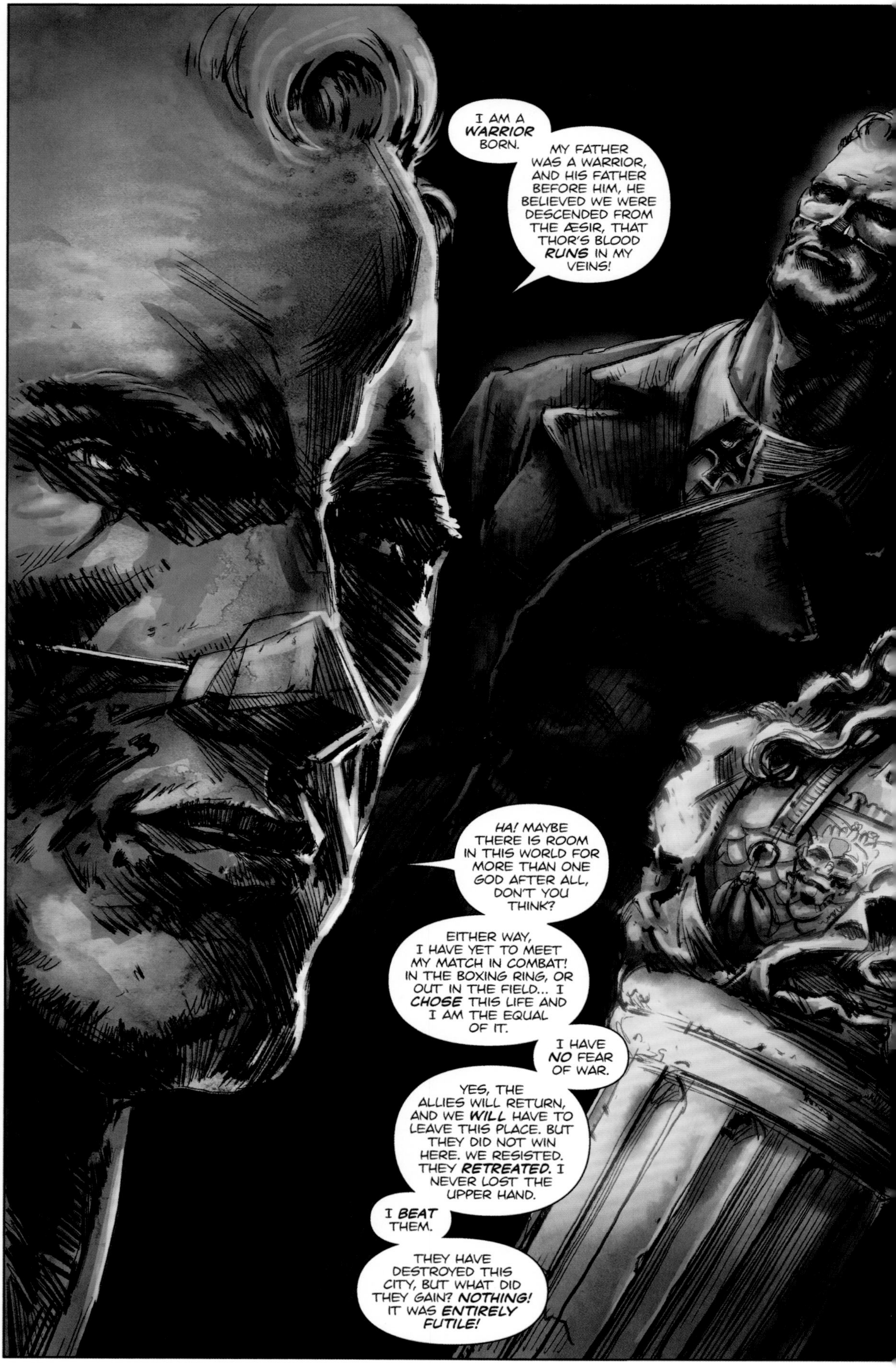
I AM A *WARRIOR* BORN.
MY FATHER WAS A WARRIOR, AND HIS FATHER BEFORE HIM, HE BELIEVED WE WERE DESCENDED FROM THE ÆSIR, THAT THOR'S BLOOD *RUNS* IN MY VEINS!
HA! MAYBE THERE IS ROOM IN THIS WORLD FOR MORE THAN ONE GOD AFTER ALL, DON'T YOU THINK?
EITHER WAY, I HAVE YET TO MEET MY MATCH IN COMBAT! IN THE BOXING RING, OR OUT IN THE FIELD... I *CHOSE* THIS LIFE AND I AM THE EQUAL OF IT.
I HAVE *NO* FEAR OF WAR.
YES, THE ALLIES WILL RETURN, AND WE *WILL* HAVE TO LEAVE THIS PLACE. BUT THEY DID NOT WIN HERE. WE RESISTED. THEY *RETREATED.* I NEVER LOST THE UPPER HAND.
I *BEAT* THEM.
THEY HAVE DESTROYED THIS CITY, BUT WHAT DID THEY GAIN? *NOTHING!* IT WAS *ENTIRELY FUTILE!*

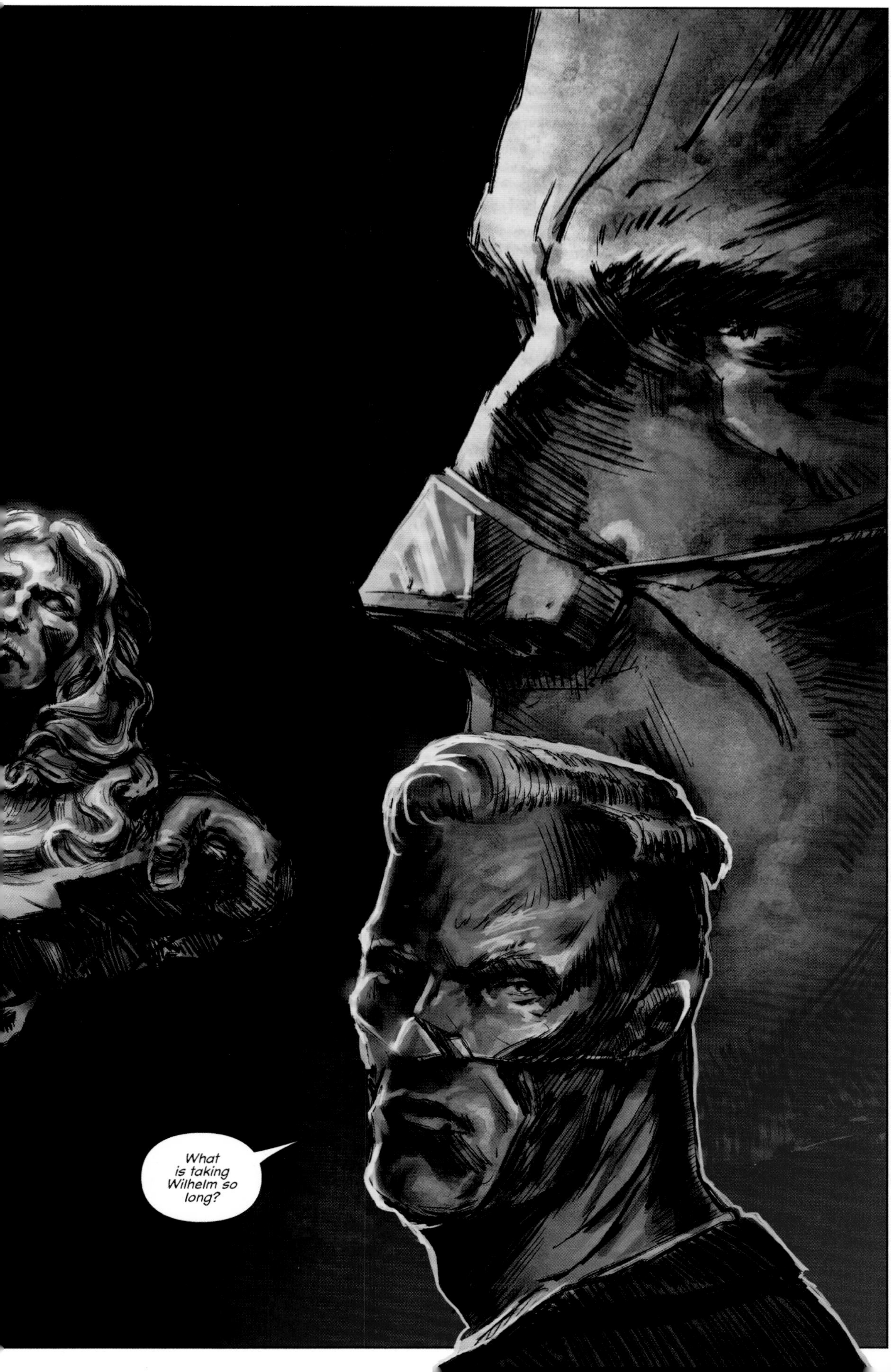
What is taking Wilhelm so long?

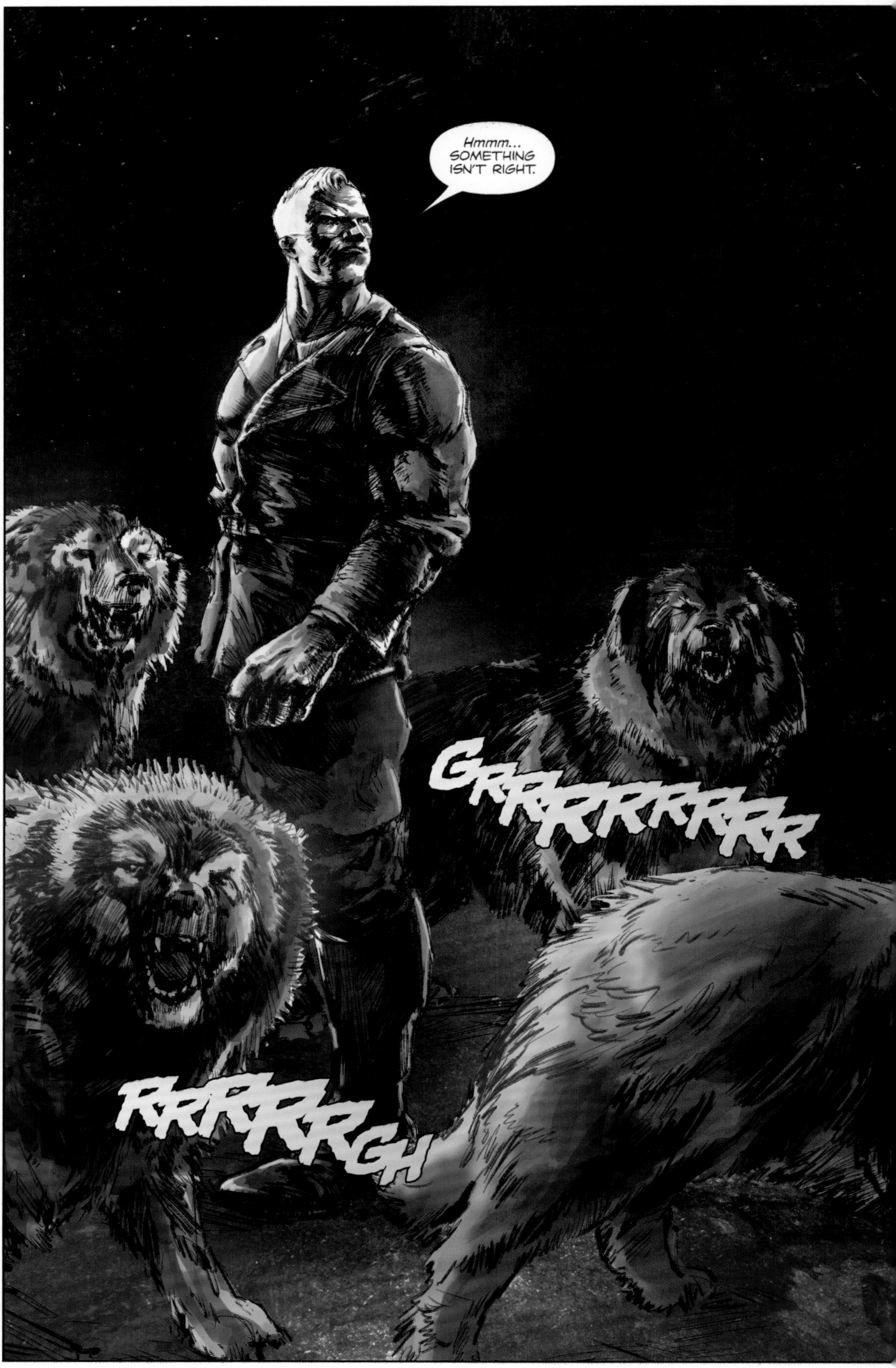
Hmmm... SOMETHING ISN'T RIGHT.
GRRRRRRRRR
RRRRRRGH

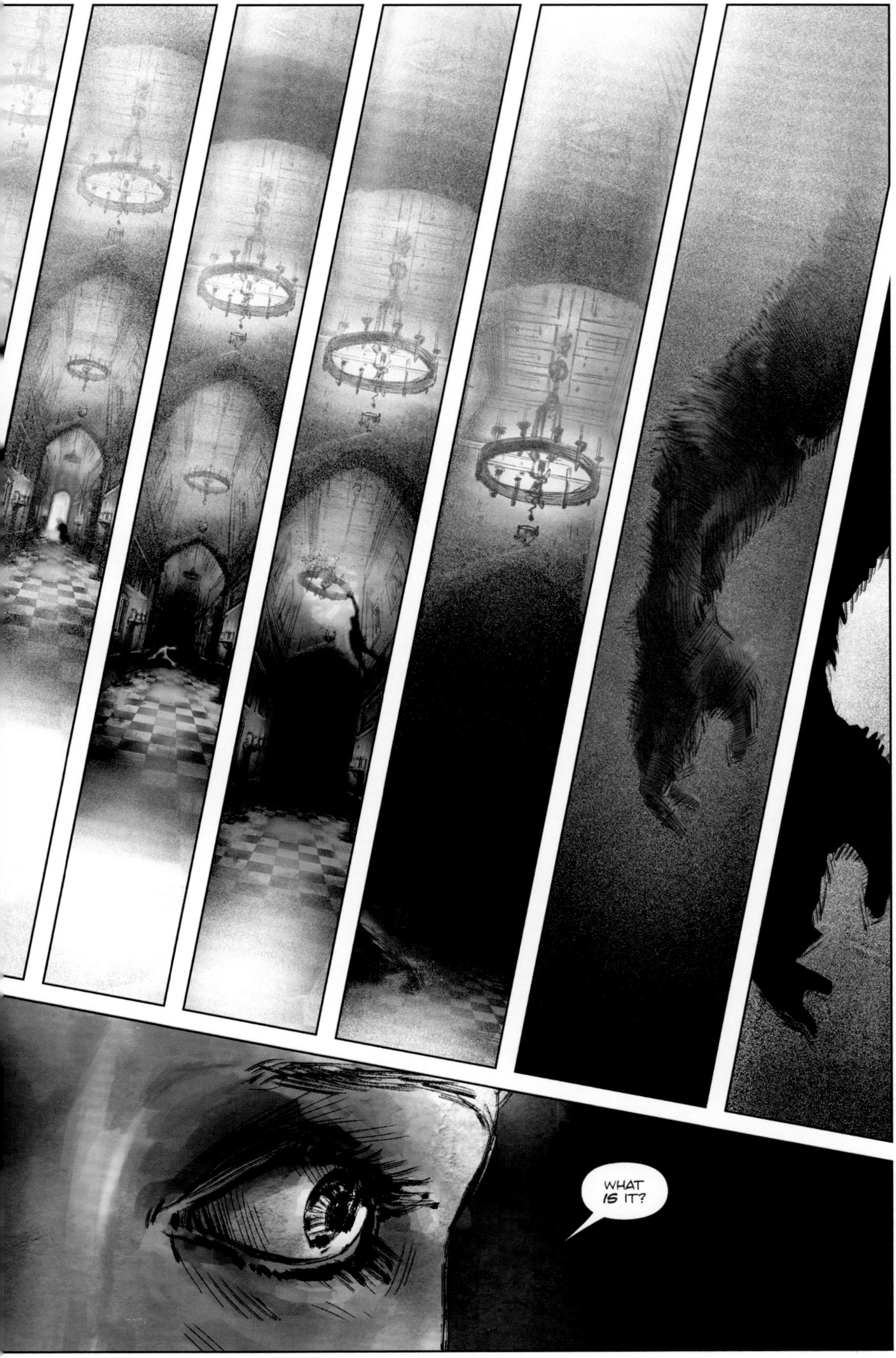
WHAT *IS* IT?

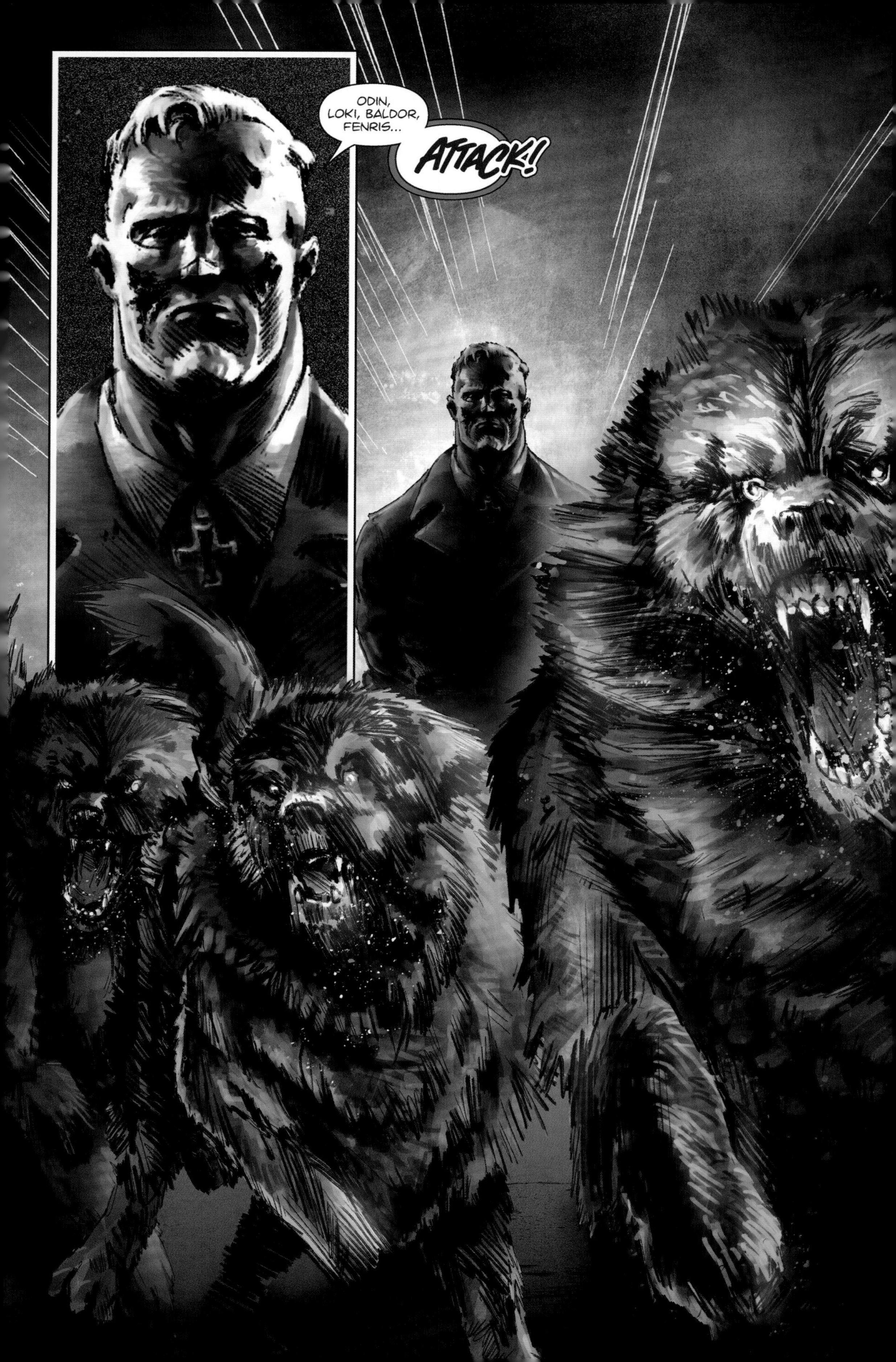
ODIN, LOKI, BALDOR, FENRIS...
ATTACK!

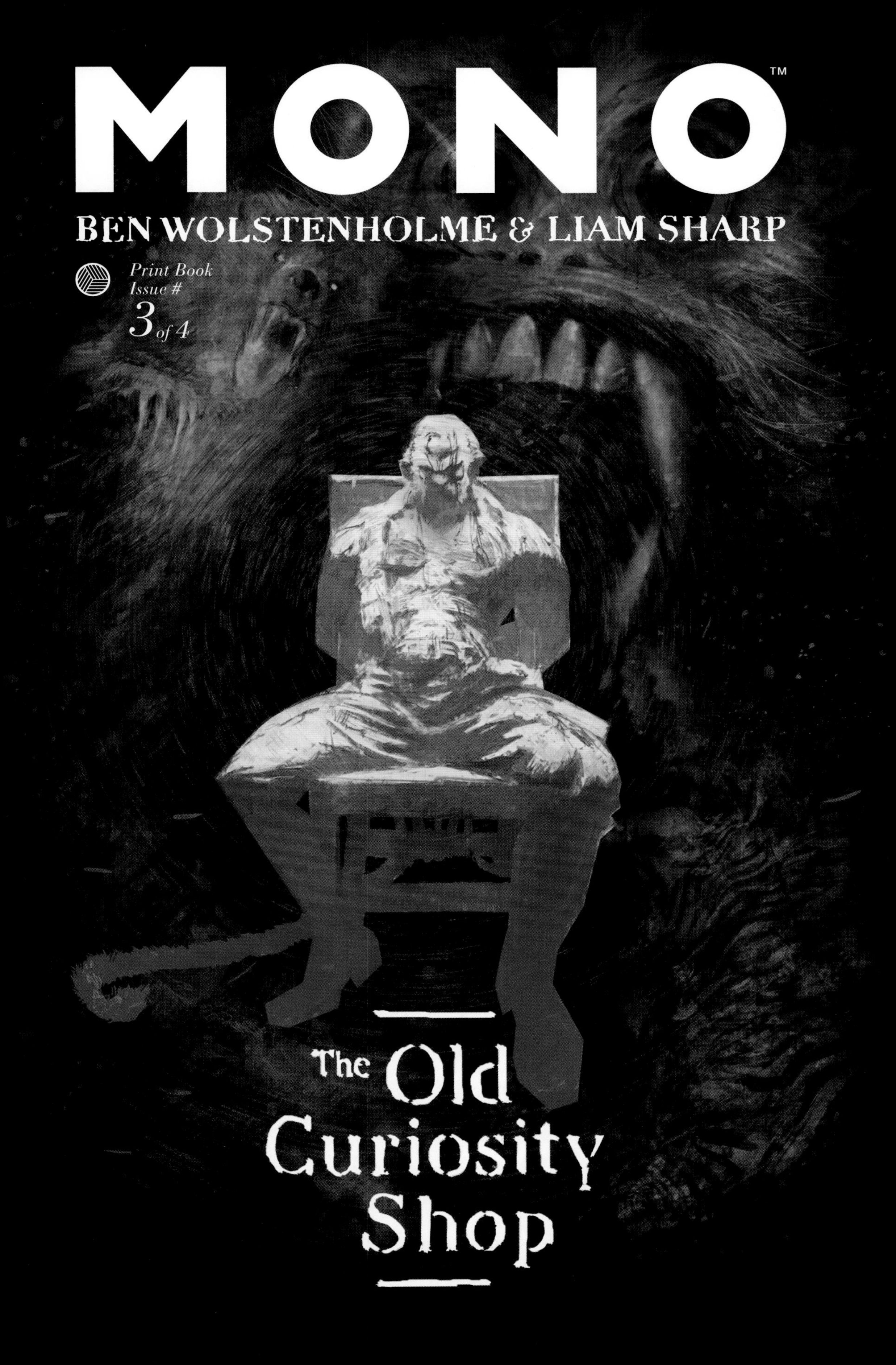

MONO™
BEN WOLSTENHOLME & LIAM SHARP
Print Book
Issue #
3 of 4
The Old
Curiosity
Shop

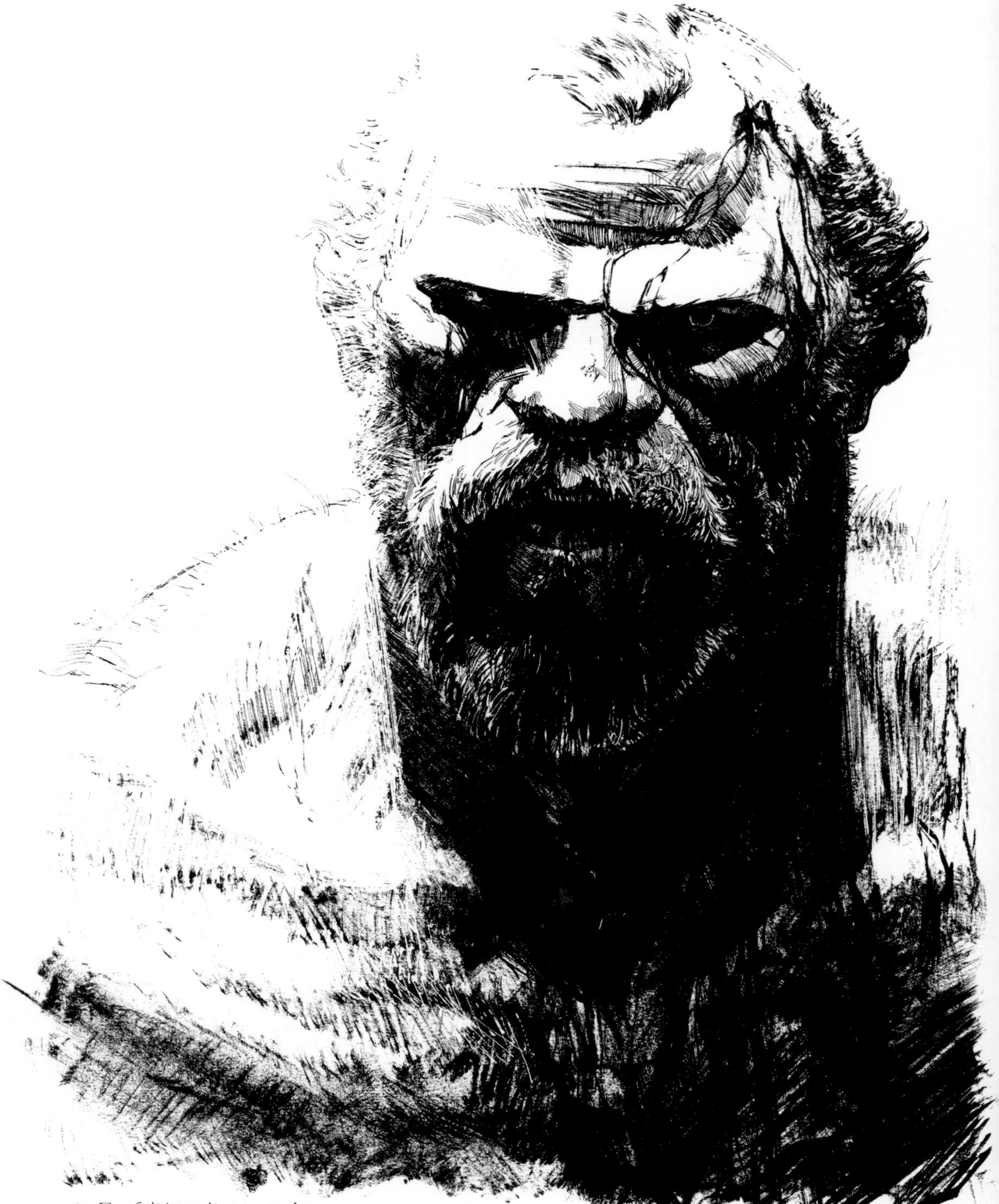

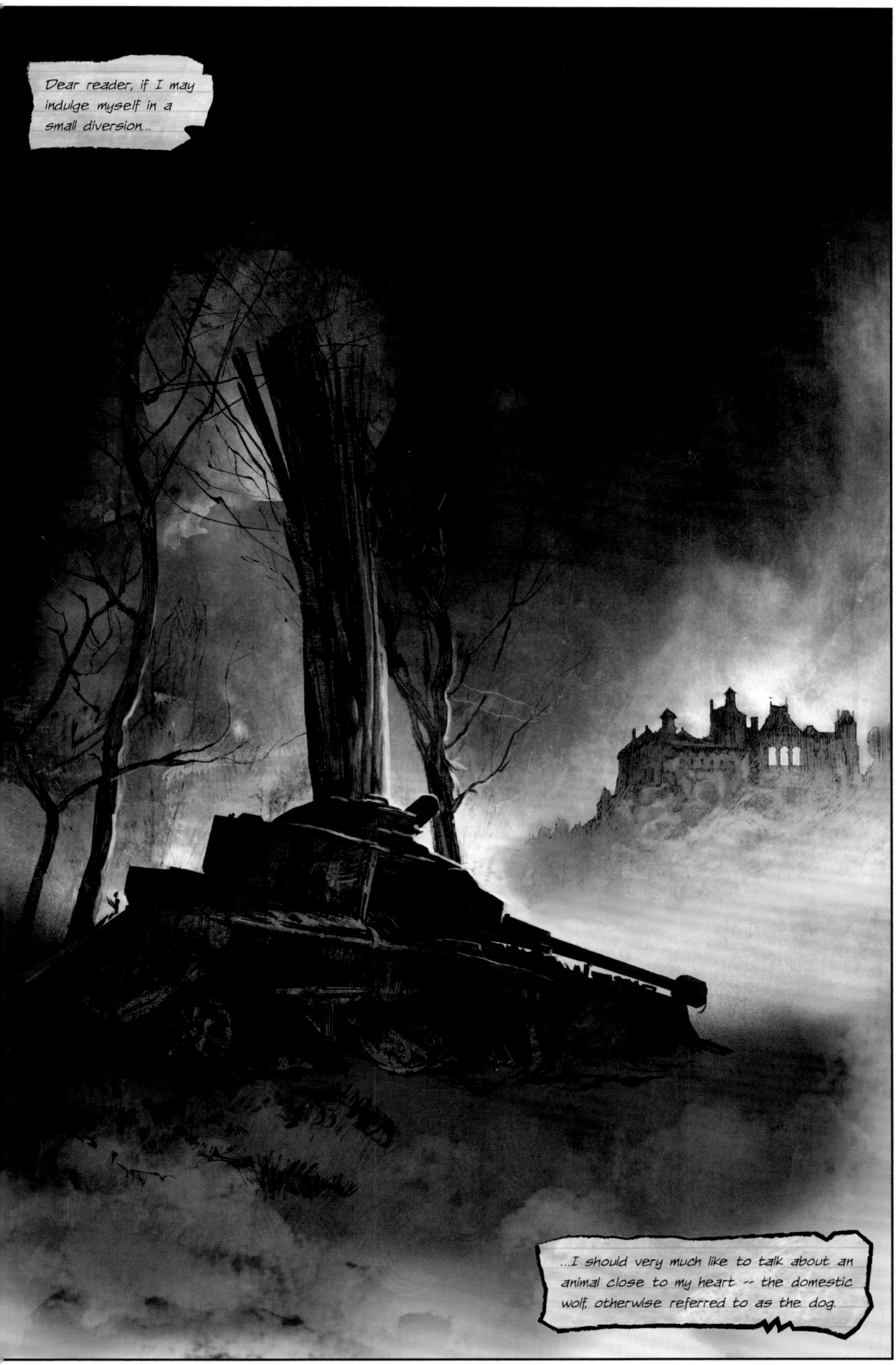
Dear reader, if I may indulge myself in a small diversion...
...I should very much like to talk about an animal close to my heart -- the domestic wolf, otherwise referred to as the dog.

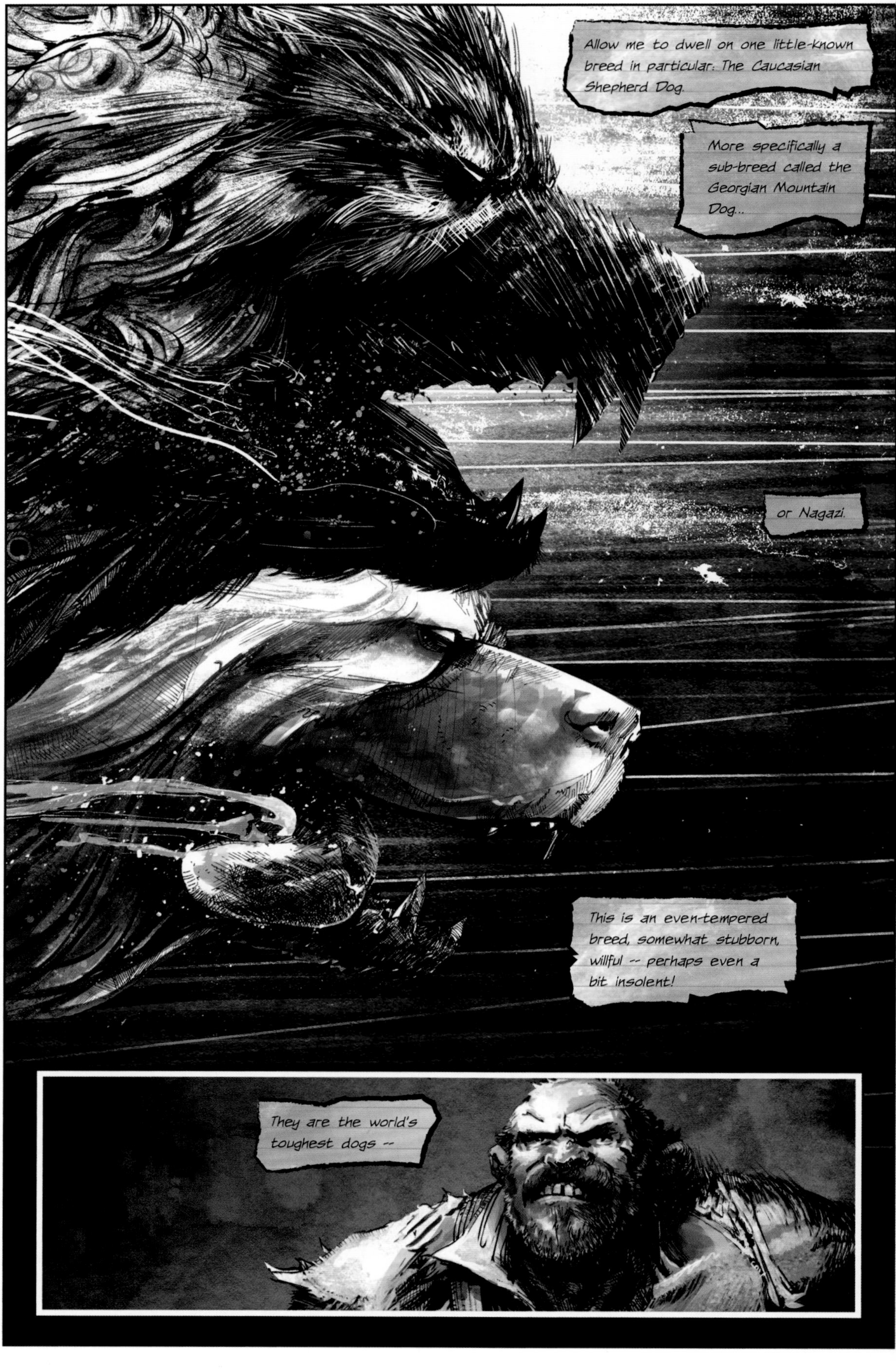
Allow me to dwell on one little-known breed in particular: The Caucasian Shepherd Dog.
More specifically a sub-breed called the Georgian Mountain Dog...
or Nagazi.
This is an even-tempered breed, somewhat stubborn, willful -- perhaps even a bit insolent!
They are the world's toughest dogs --

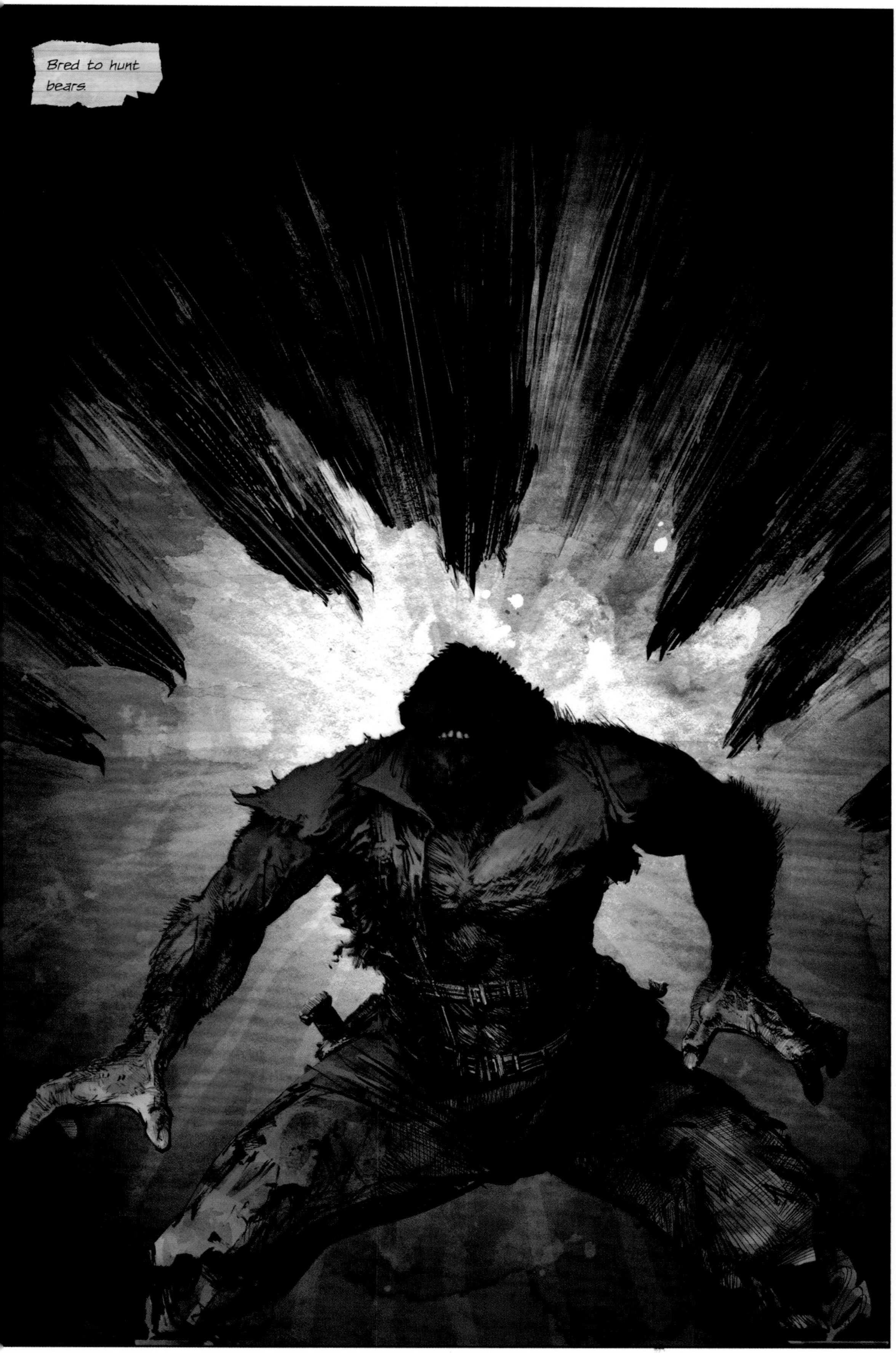
Bred to hunt bears.

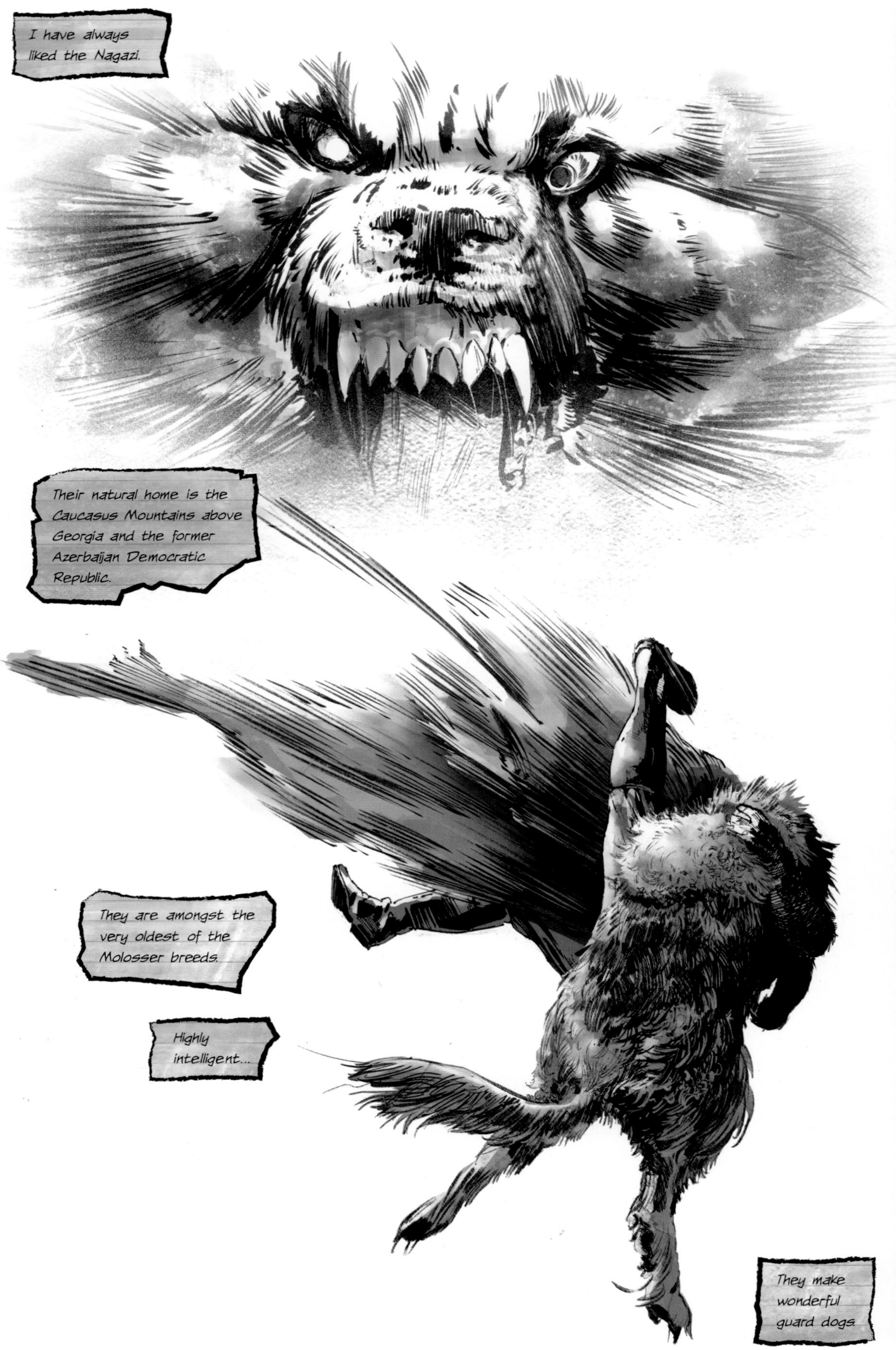
I have always liked the Nagazi.
Their natural home is the Caucasus Mountains above Georgia and the former Azerbaijan Democratic Republic.
They are amongst the very oldest of the Molosser breeds.
Highly intelligent...
They make wonderful guard dogs.

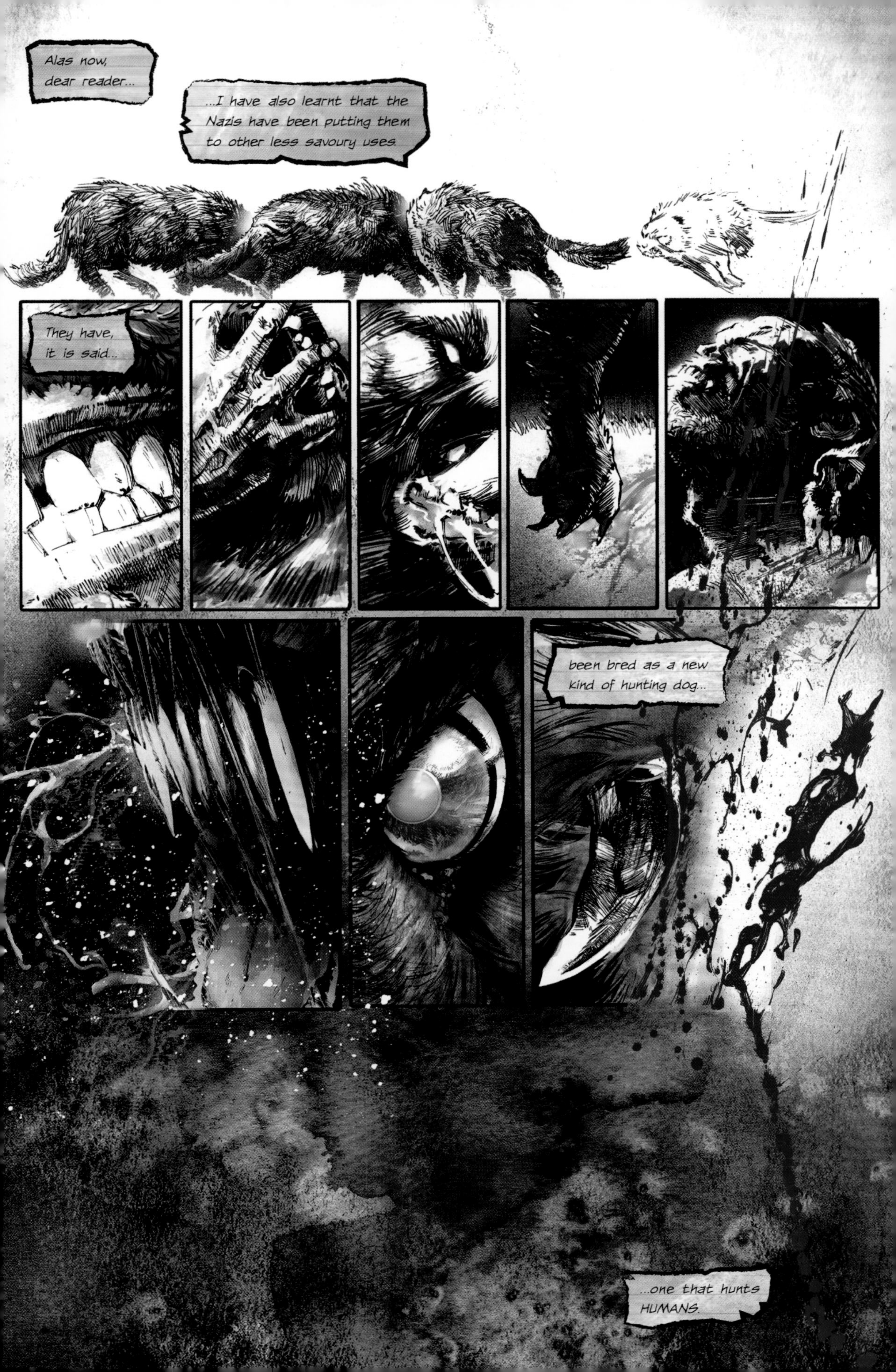
Alas now, dear reader...
...I have also learnt that the Nazis have been putting them to other less savoury uses.
They have, it is said...
been bred as a new kind of hunting dog...
...one that hunts HUMANS.

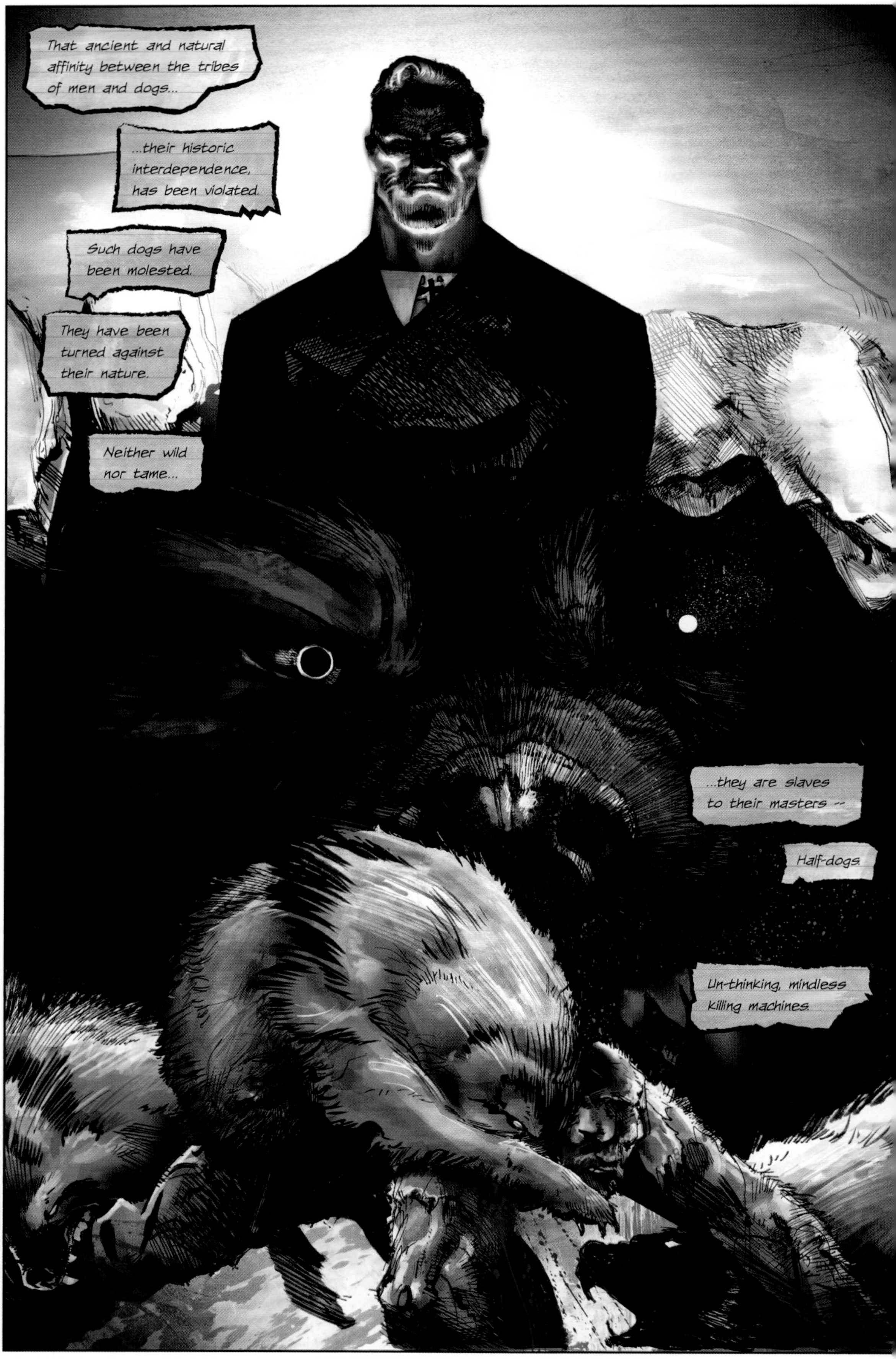
That ancient and natural affinity between the tribes of men and dogs...
...their historic interdependence, has been violated.
Such dogs have been molested.
They have been turned against their nature.
Neither wild nor tame...
...they are slaves to their masters --
Half-dogs.
Un-thinking, mindless killing machines.

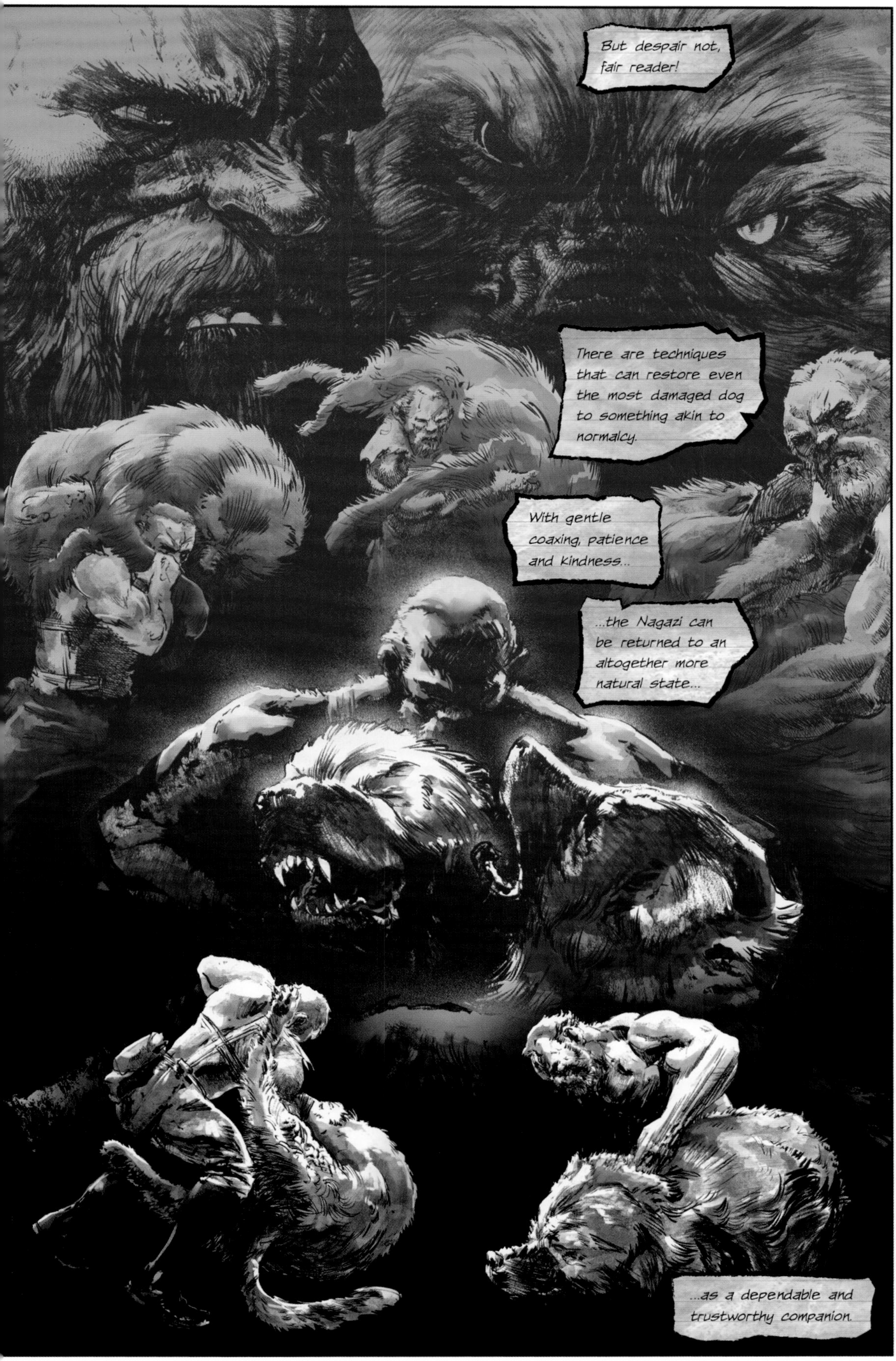
But despair not, fair reader!
There are techniques that can restore even the most damaged dog to something akin to normalcy.
With gentle coaxing, patience and kindness...
...the Nagazi can be returned to an altogether more natural state...
...as a dependable and trustworthy companion.

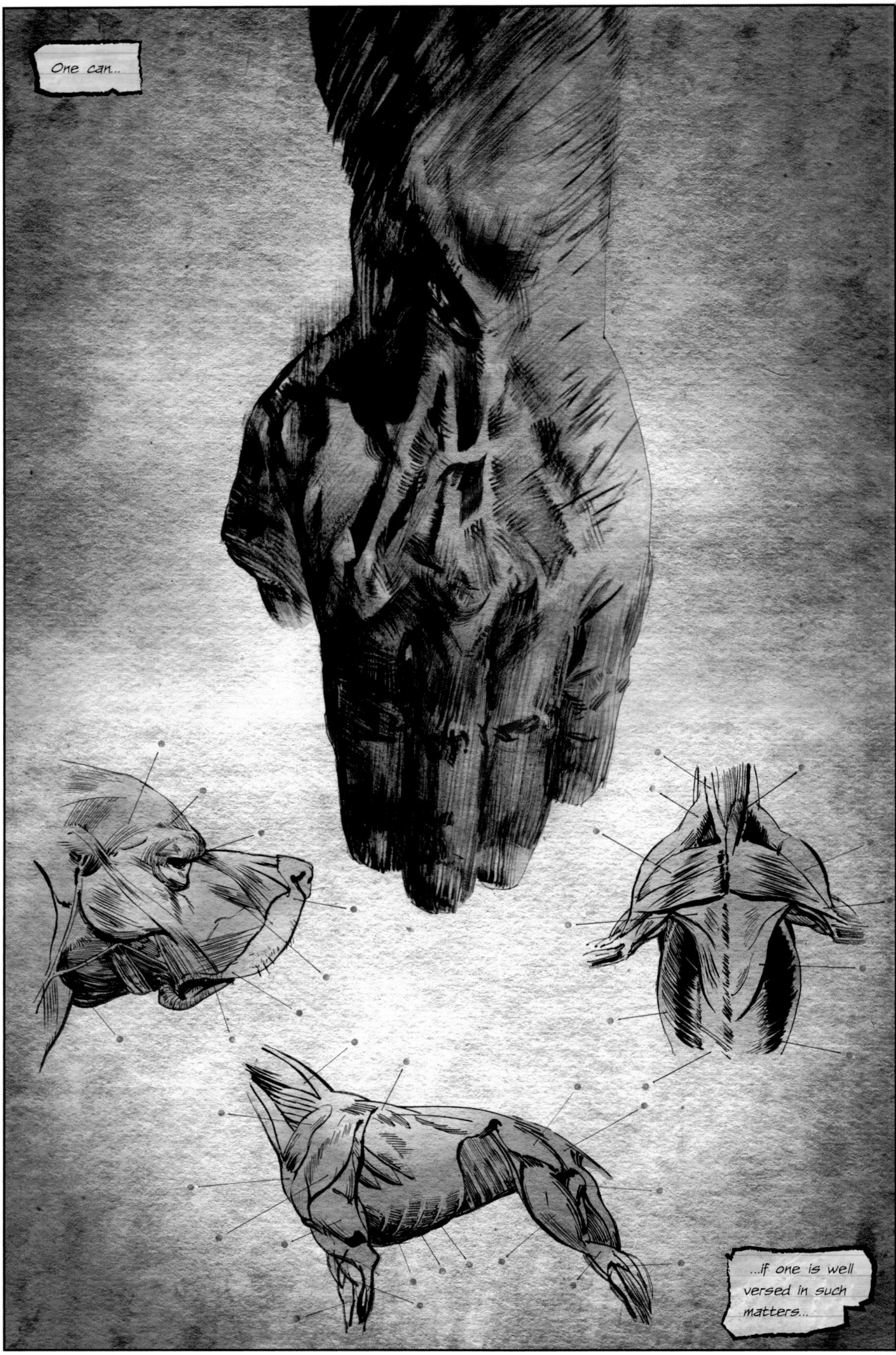
One can...
...if one is well versed in such matters...

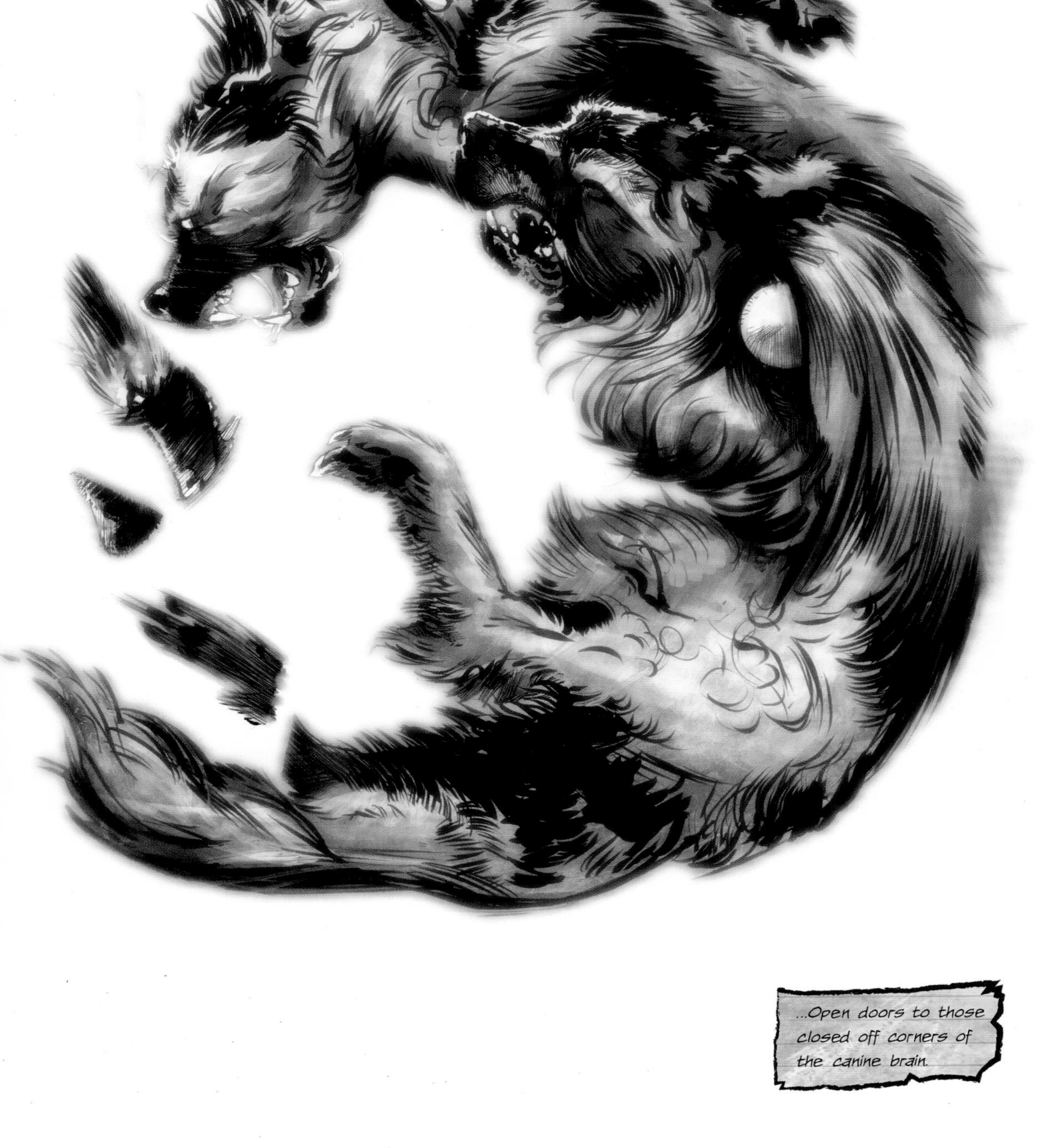
...Open doors to those closed off corners of the canine brain.

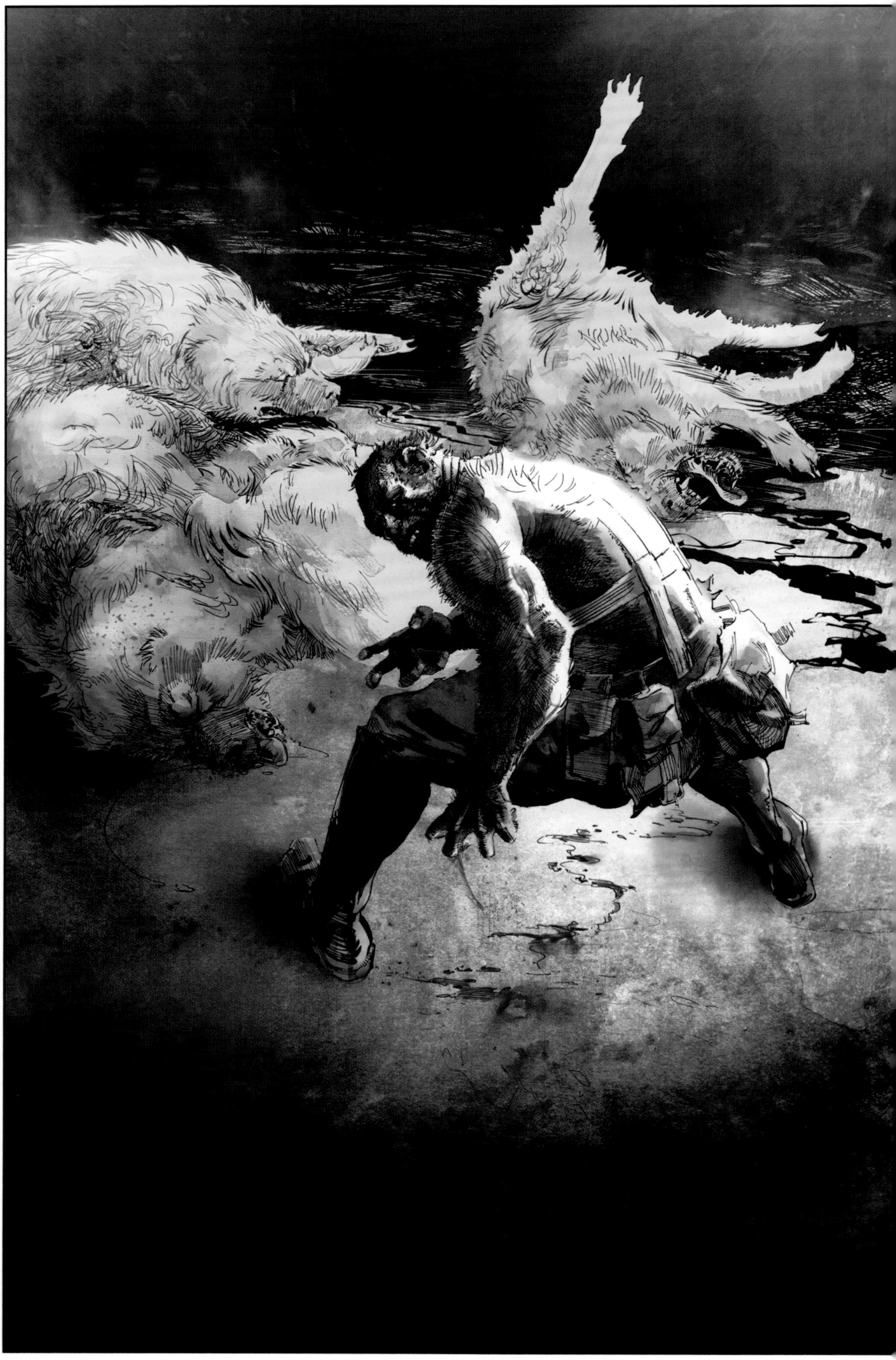

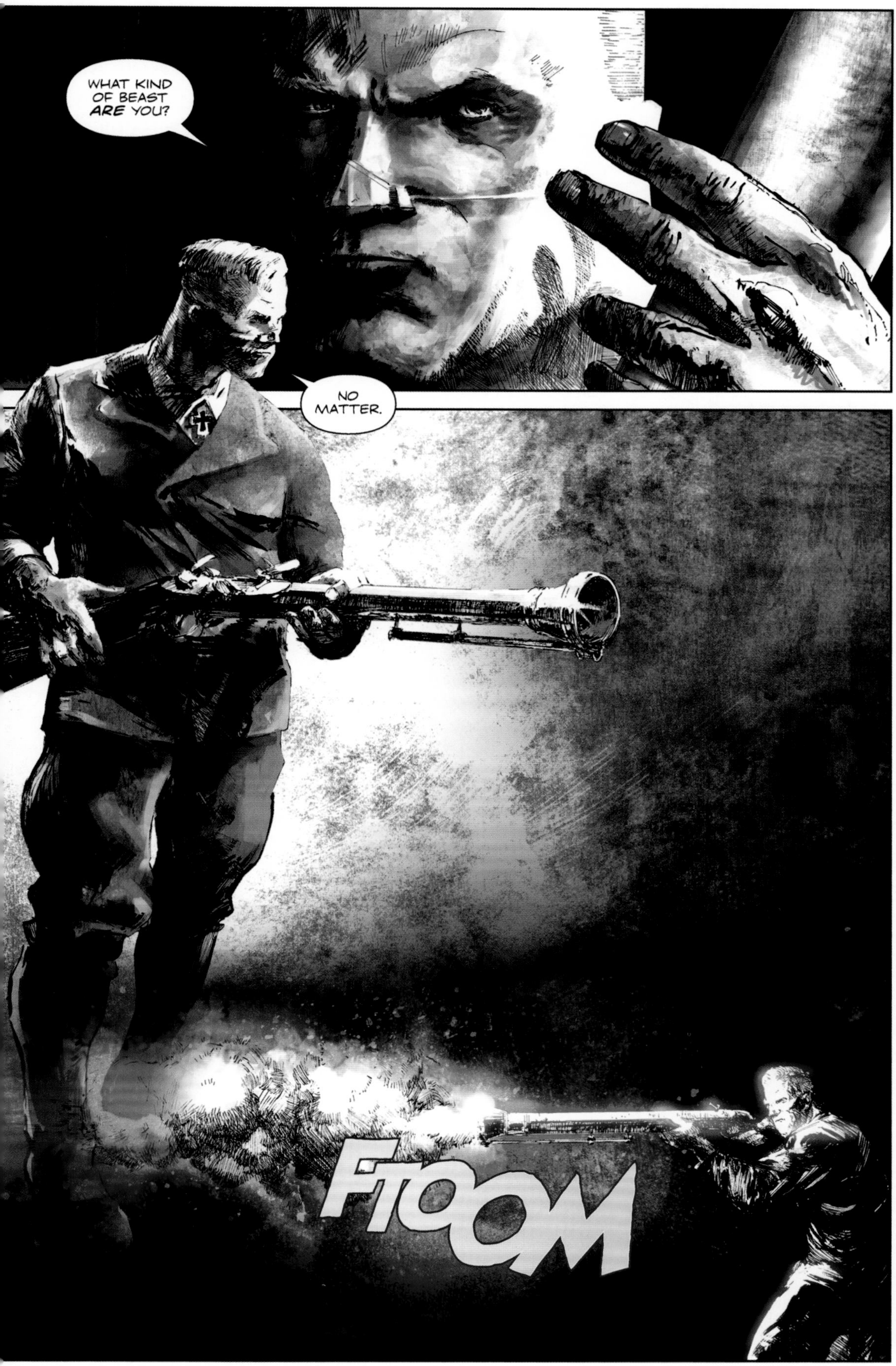
WHAT KIND OF BEAST ARE YOU?
NO MATTER.
FTOOM

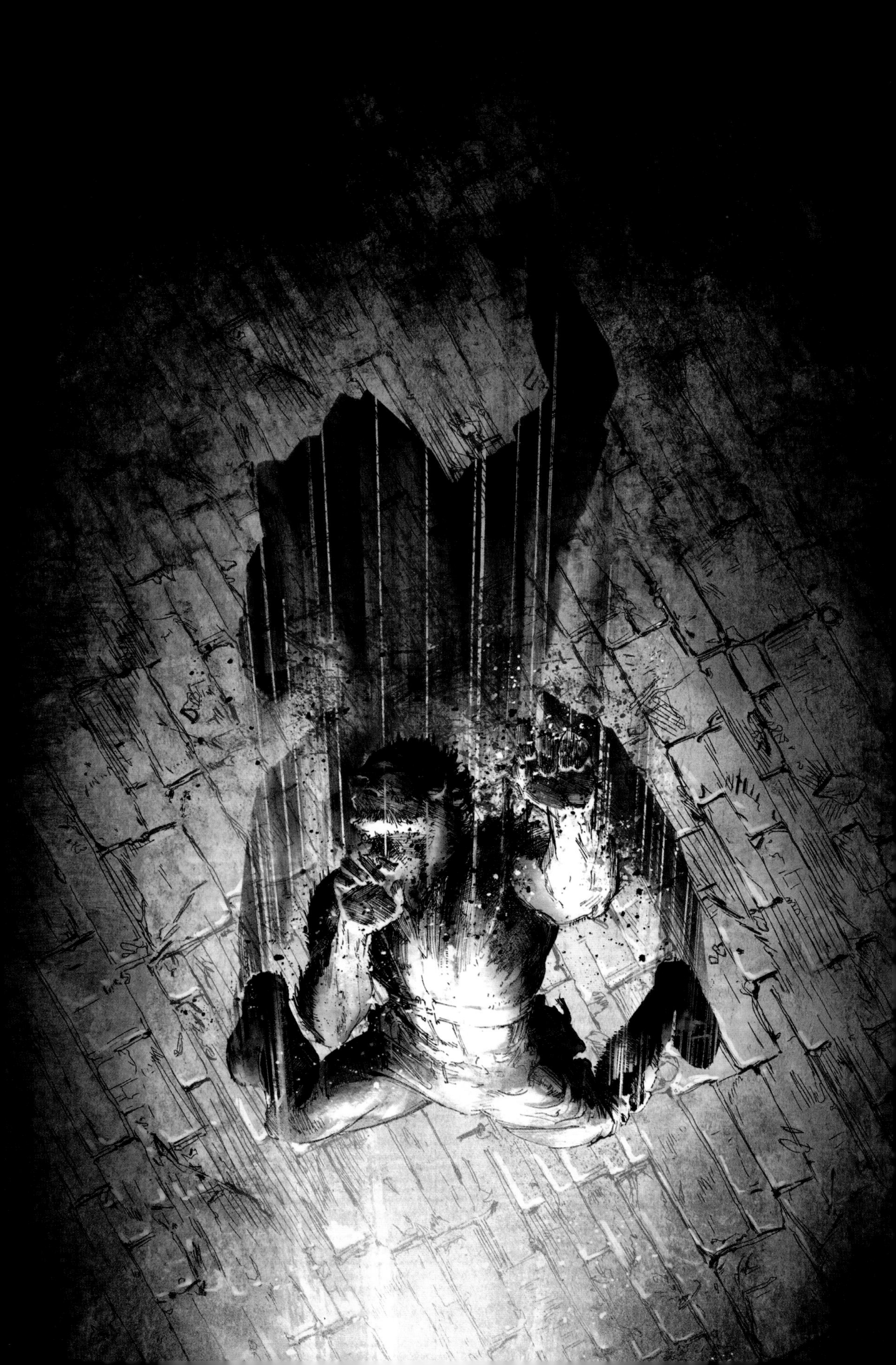

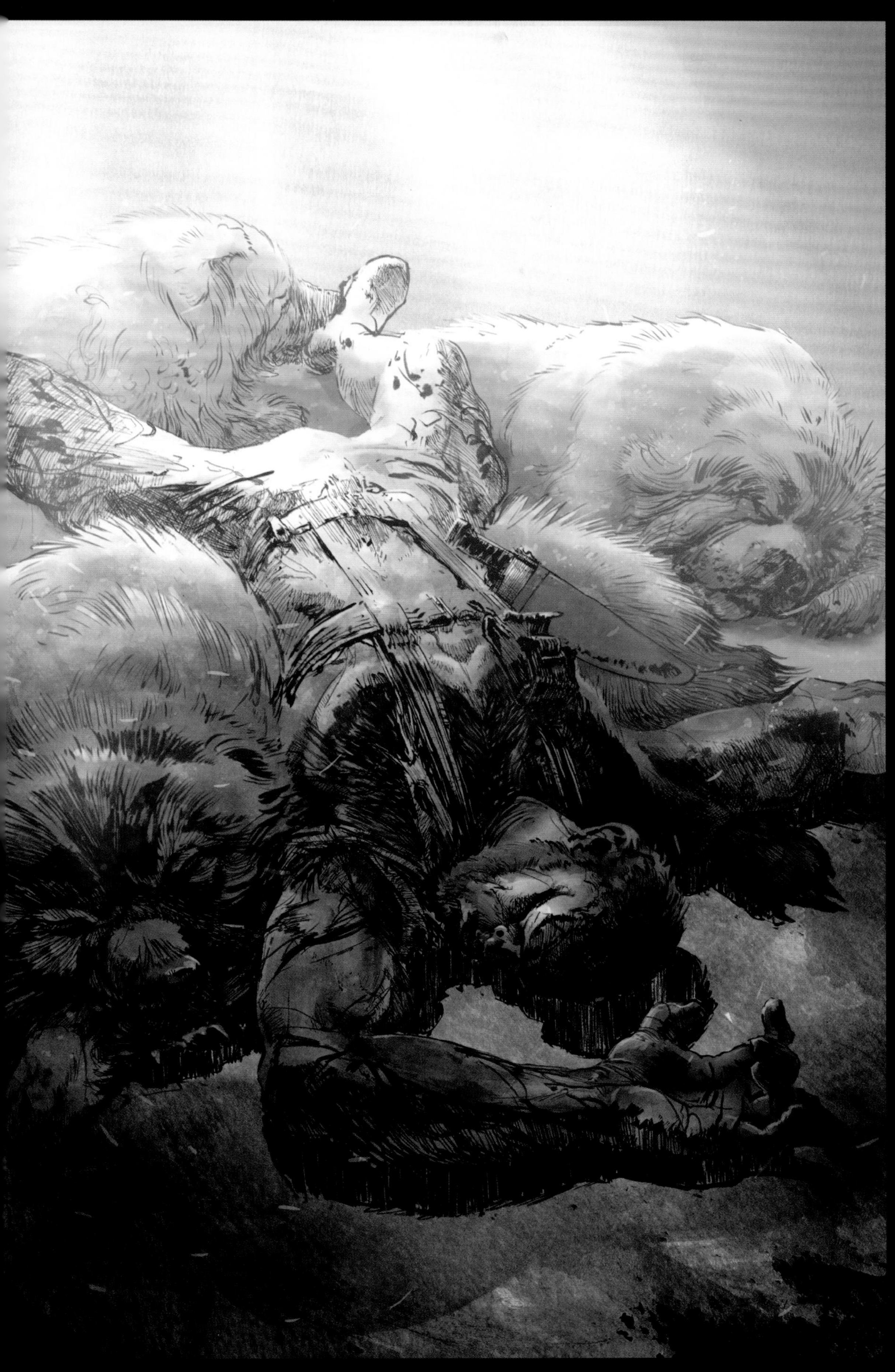

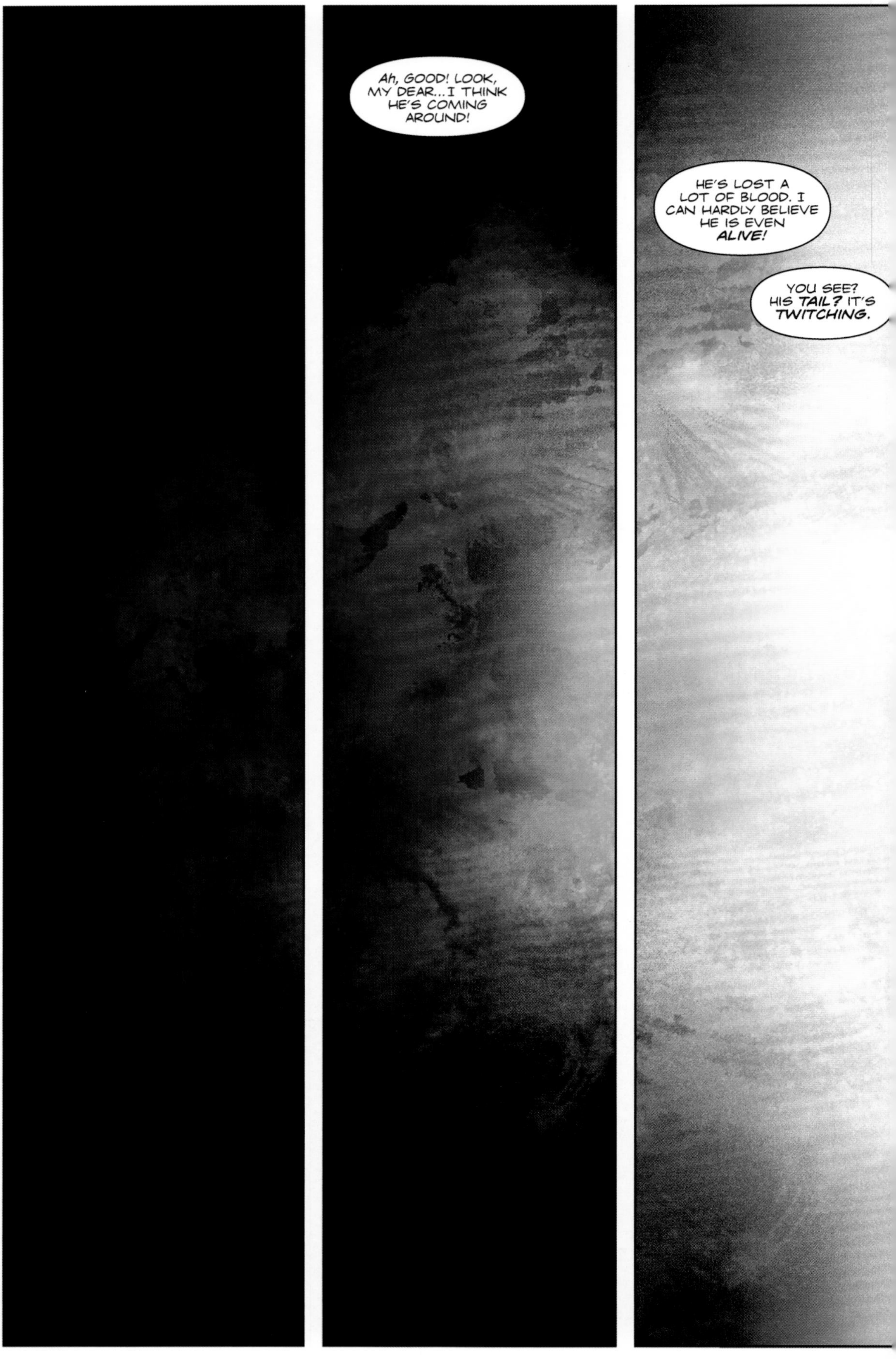
Ah, GOOD! LOOK, MY DEAR...I THINK HE'S COMING AROUND!
HE'S LOST A LOT OF BLOOD. I CAN HARDLY BELIEVE HE IS EVEN ALIVE!
YOU SEE? HIS TAIL? IT'S TWITCHING.

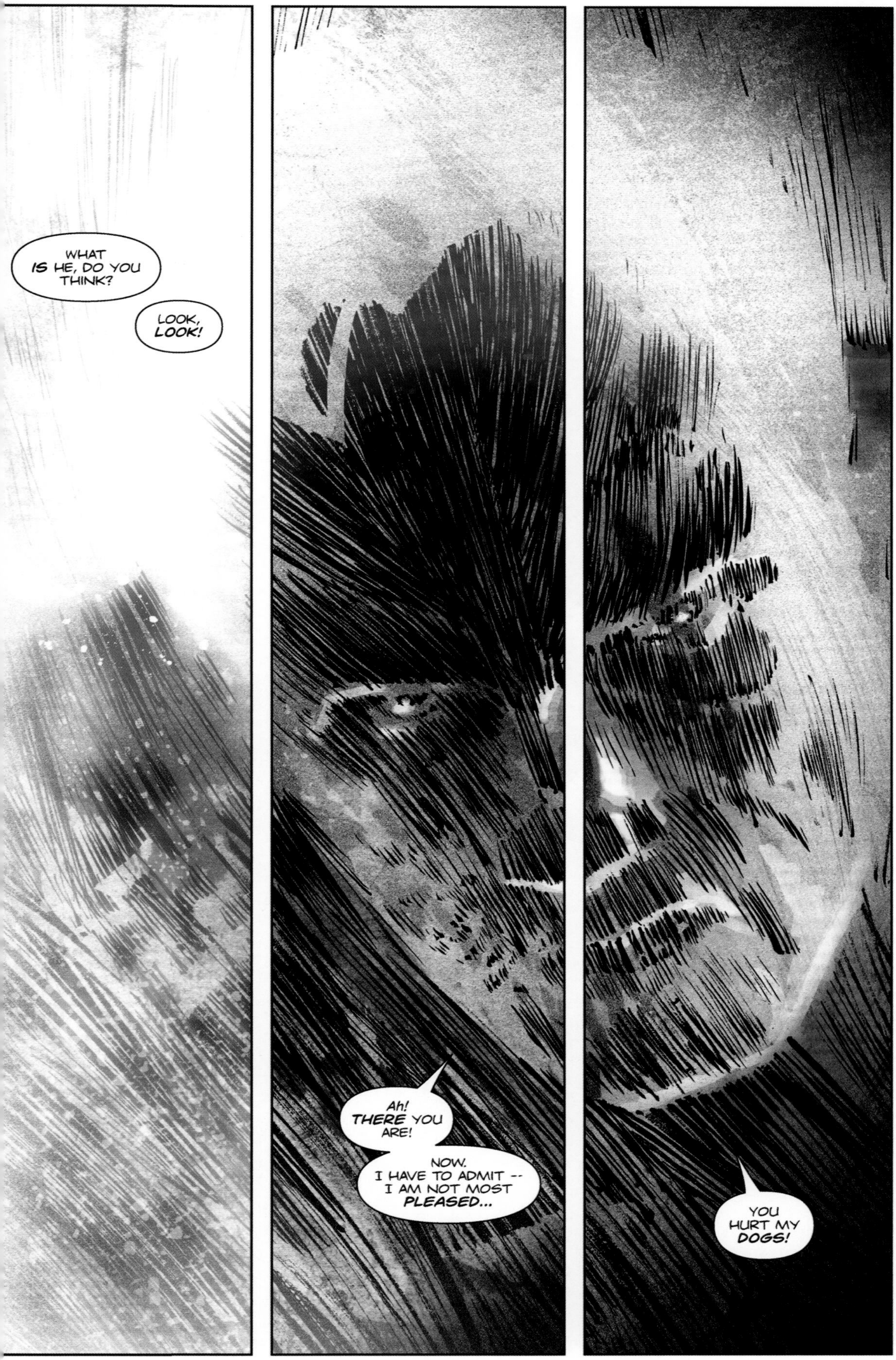
WHAT IS HE, DO YOU THINK?
LOOK, LOOK!
Ah! THERE YOU ARE!
NOW. I HAVE TO ADMIT -- I AM NOT MOST PLEASED...
YOU HURT MY DOGS!

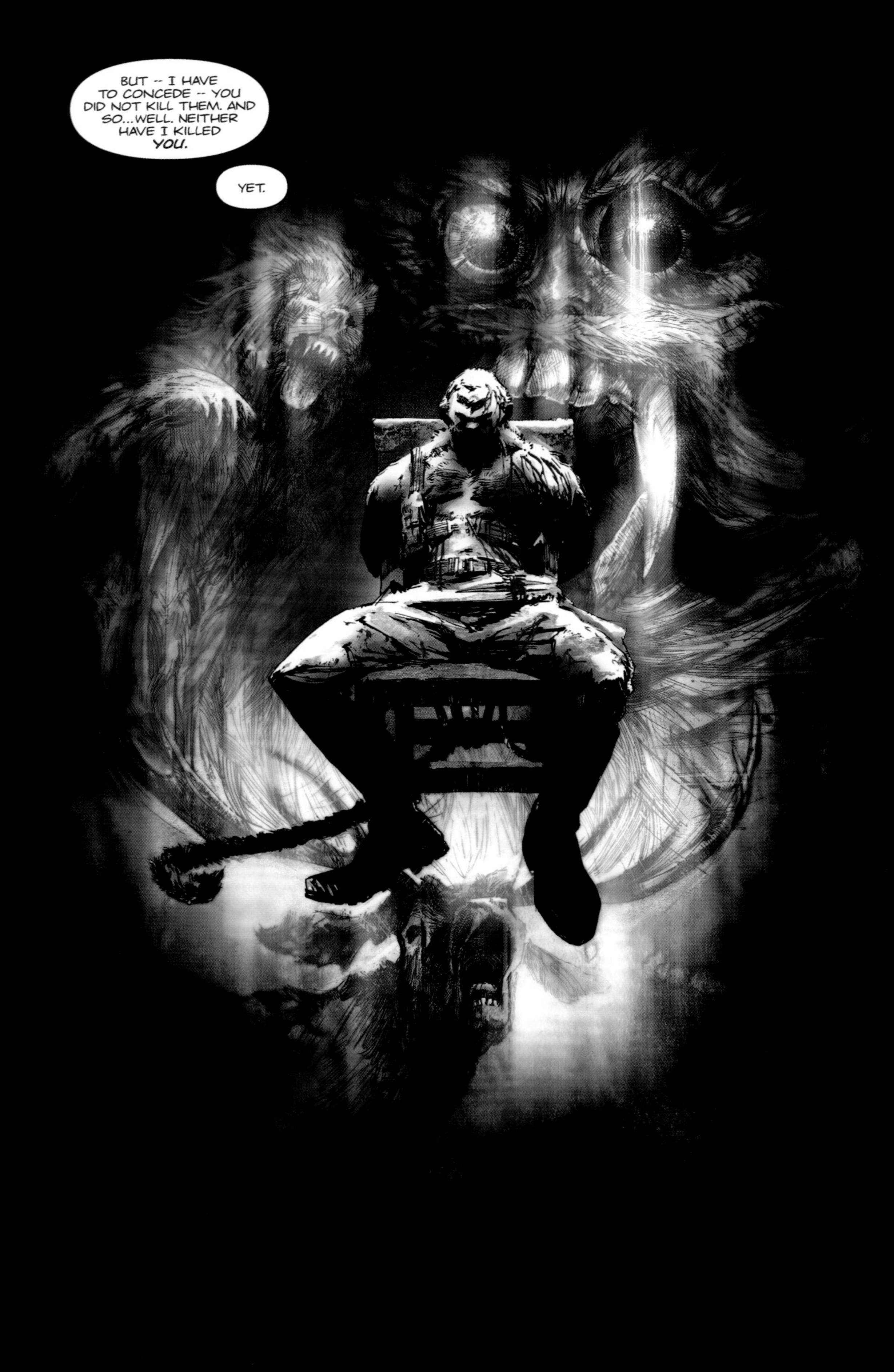
BUT -- I HAVE TO CONCEDE -- YOU DID NOT KILL THEM. AND SO...WELL. NEITHER HAVE I KILLED YOU.
YET.

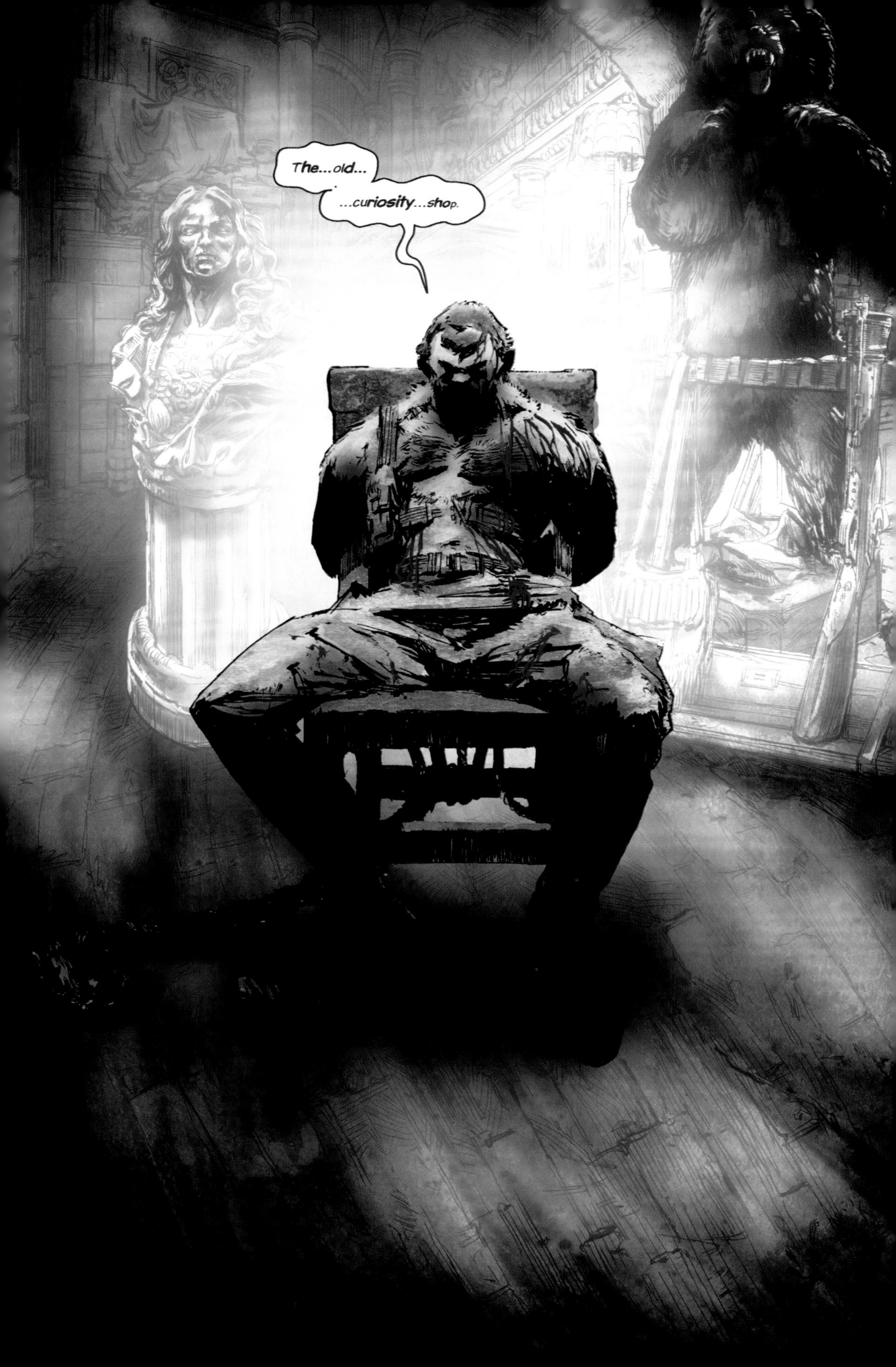
The...old...
...curiosity...shop.

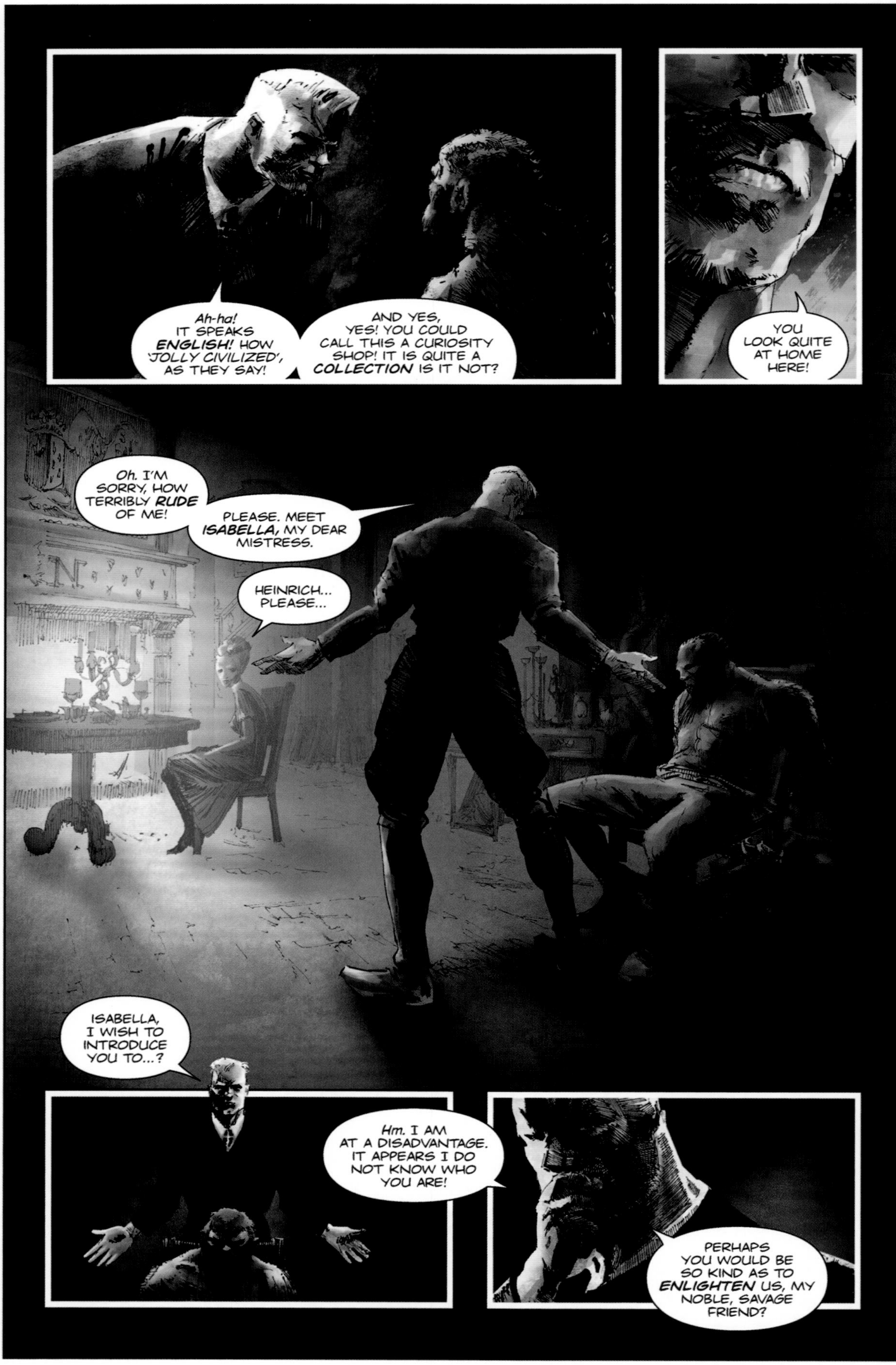

Ah-ha! IT SPEAKS ENGLISH! HOW 'JOLLY CIVILIZED', AS THEY SAY!
AND YES, YES! YOU COULD CALL THIS A CURIOSITY SHOP! IT IS QUITE A COLLECTION IS IT NOT?
YOU LOOK QUITE AT HOME HERE!
Oh. I'M SORRY, HOW TERRIBLY RUDE OF ME!
PLEASE. MEET ISABELLA, MY DEAR MISTRESS.
HEINRICH... PLEASE...
ISABELLA, I WISH TO INTRODUCE YOU TO...?
Hm. I AM AT A DISADVANTAGE. IT APPEARS I DO NOT KNOW WHO YOU ARE!
PERHAPS YOU WOULD BE SO KIND AS TO ENLIGHTEN US, MY NOBLE, SAVAGE FRIEND?

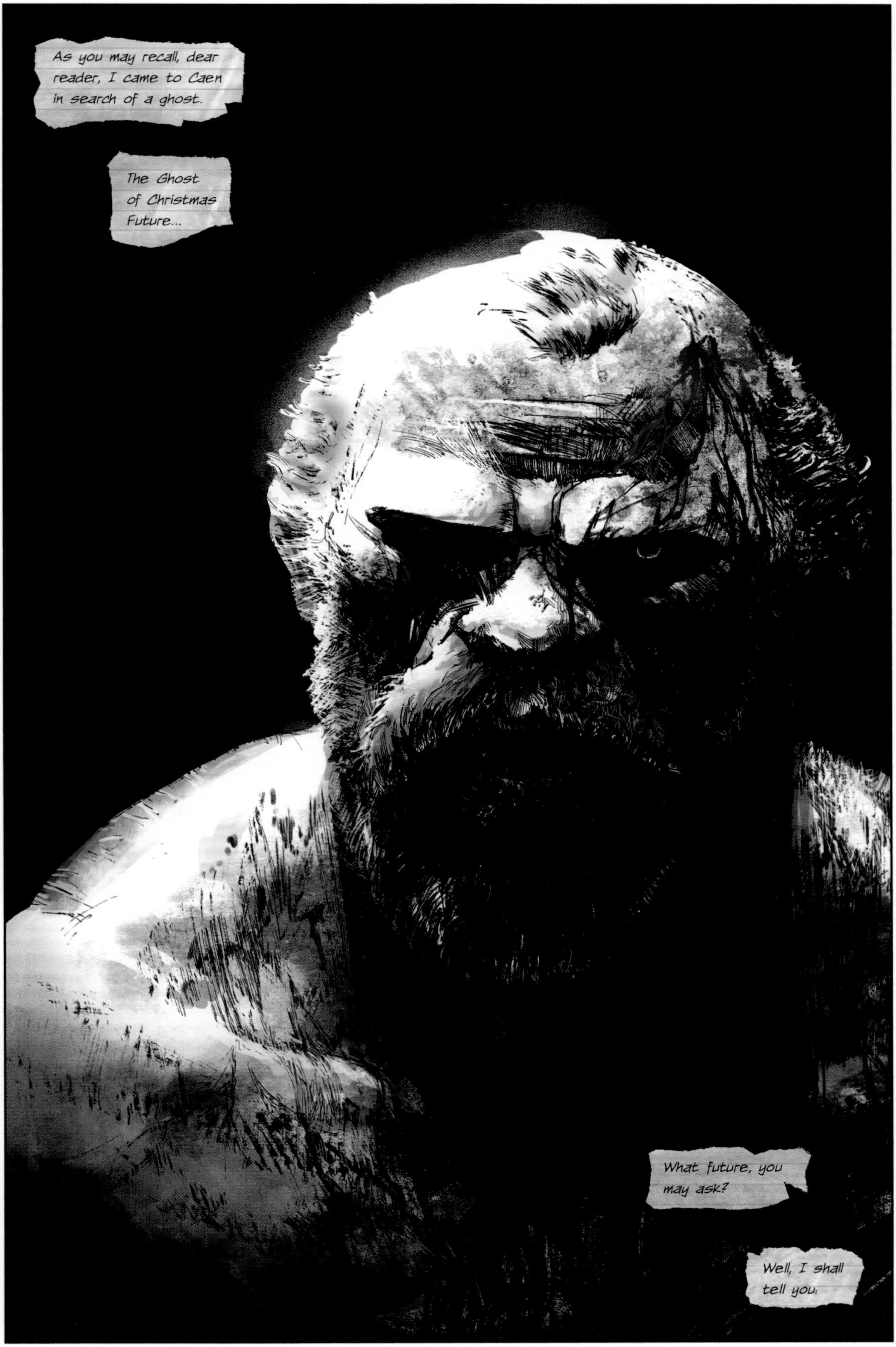
As you may recall, dear reader, I came to Caen in search of a ghost.
The Ghost of Christmas Future...
What future, you may ask?
Well, I shall tell you.

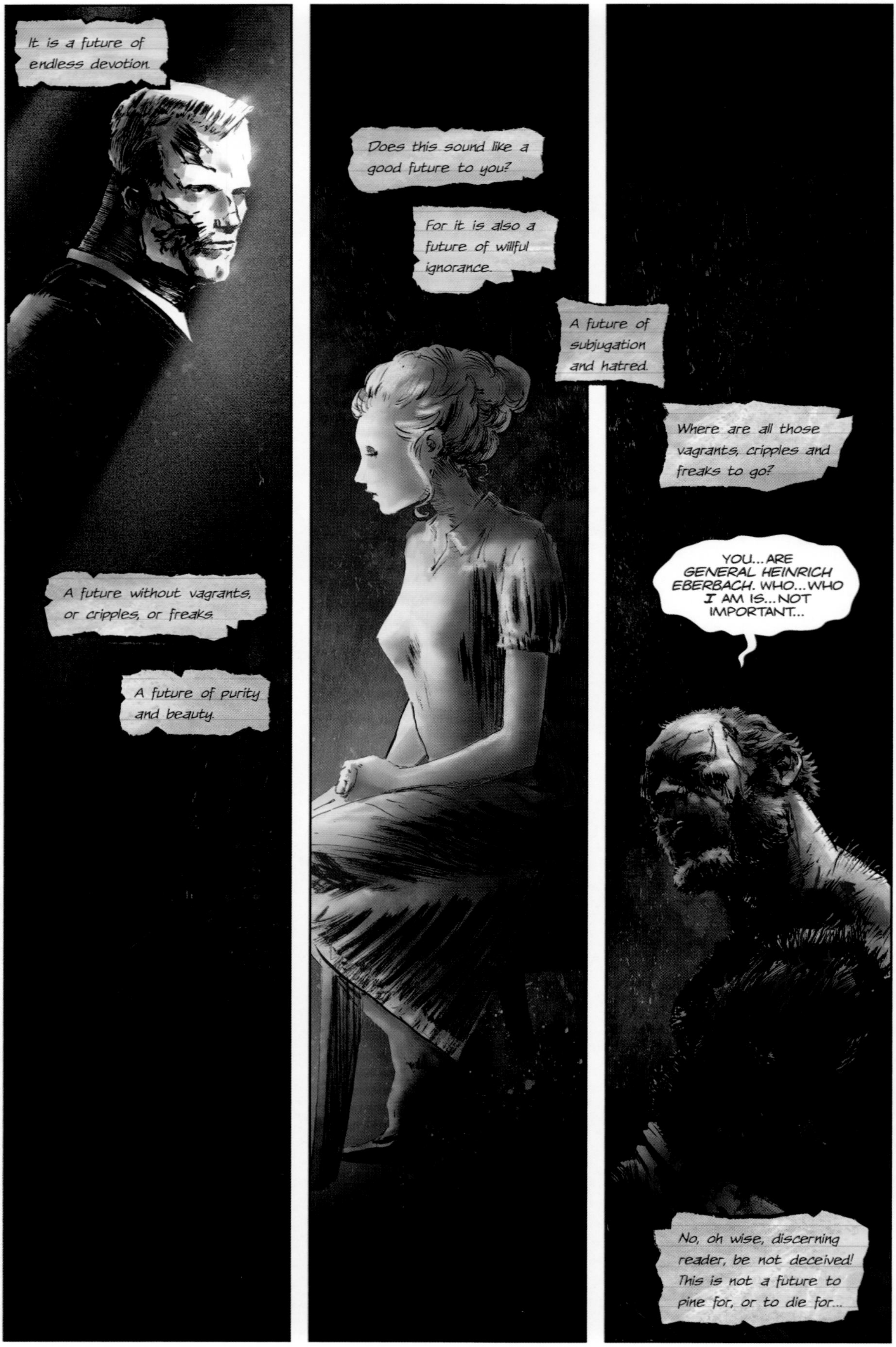
It is a future of endless devotion.
A future without vagrants, or cripples, or freaks.
A future of purity and beauty.
Does this sound like a good future to you?
For it is also a future of willful ignorance.
A future of subjugation and hatred.
Where are all those vagrants, cripples and freaks to go?
YOU... ARE GENERAL HEINRICH EBERBACH. WHO... WHO I AM IS... NOT IMPORTANT...
No, oh wise, discerning reader, be not deceived! This is not a future to pine for, or to die for...

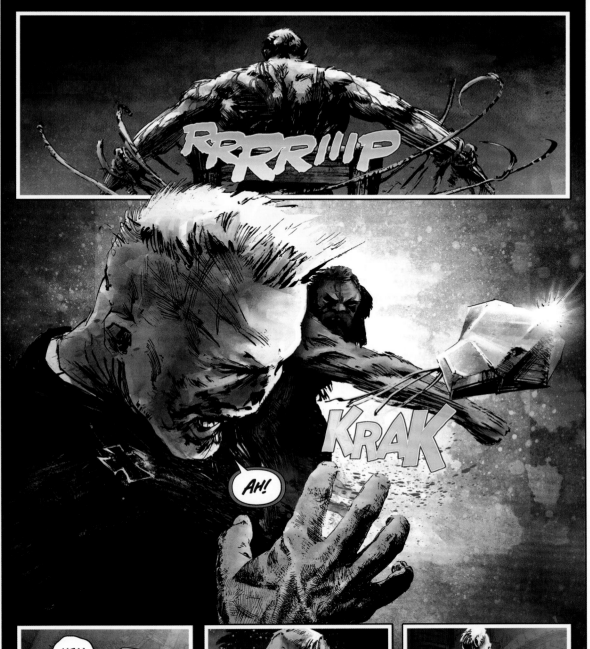

RRRRIIIIP

KRAK

AH!

UGH. I...

I WAS SENT HERE TO KILL YOU....

ARE... ARE YOU ALL RIGHT, HEINRICH?

YES. YES, I'M FINE. STAND ASIDE NOW...

KILL ME YOU SAY? HA! AND HOW DO YOU PROPOSE TO DO THAT?

YOU HAVE A GOOD RIGHT HOOK, I'LL GRANT YOU!

BUT IT WON'T DO YOU ANY GOOD.

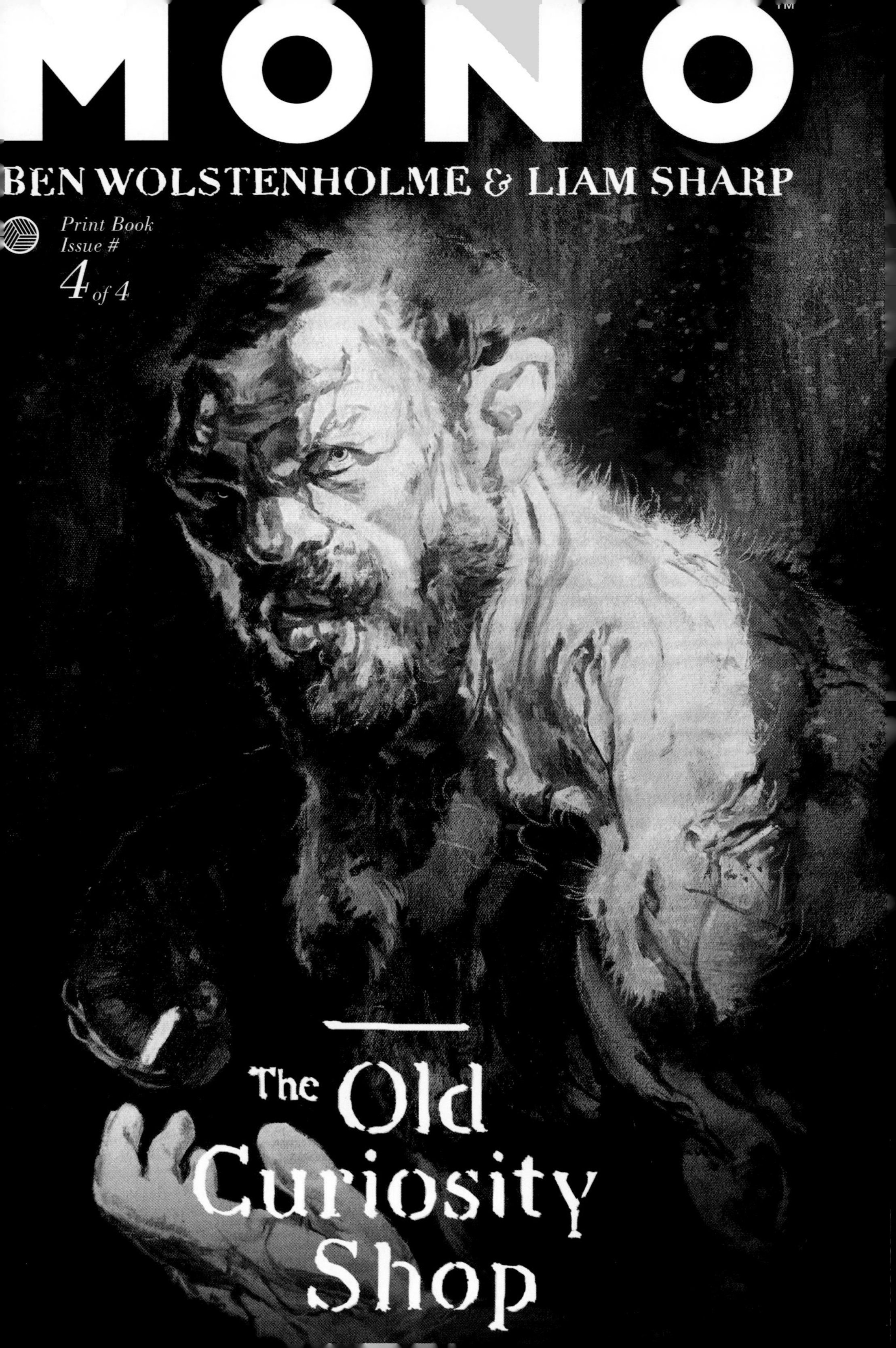
MONO™
BEN WOLSTENHOLME & LIAM SHARP
Print Book
Issue #
4 of 4
The Old Curiosity Shop

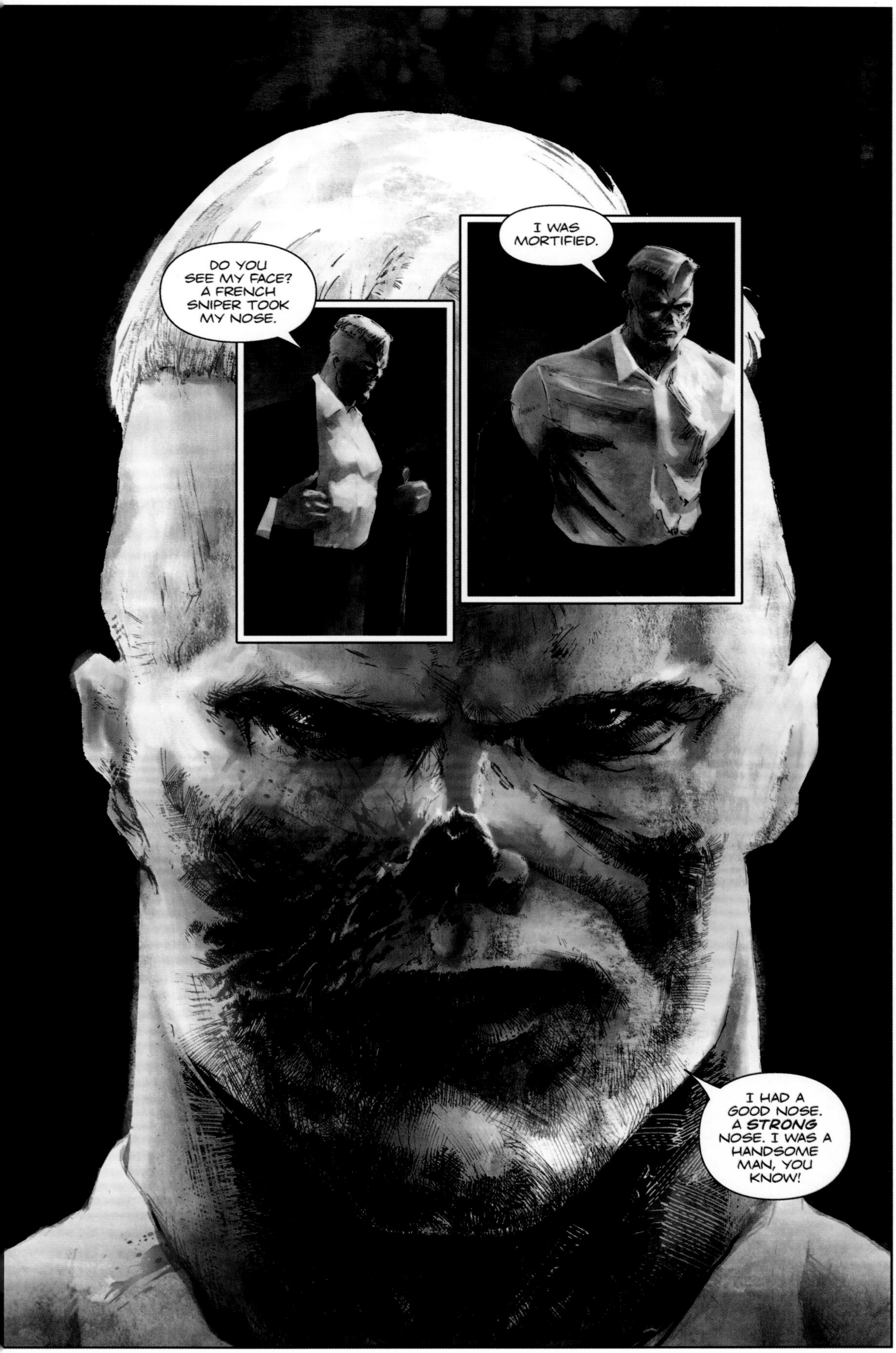
DO YOU SEE MY FACE? A FRENCH SNIPER TOOK MY NOSE.
I WAS MORTIFIED.
I HAD A GOOD NOSE. A STRONG NOSE. I WAS A HANDSOME MAN, YOU KNOW!

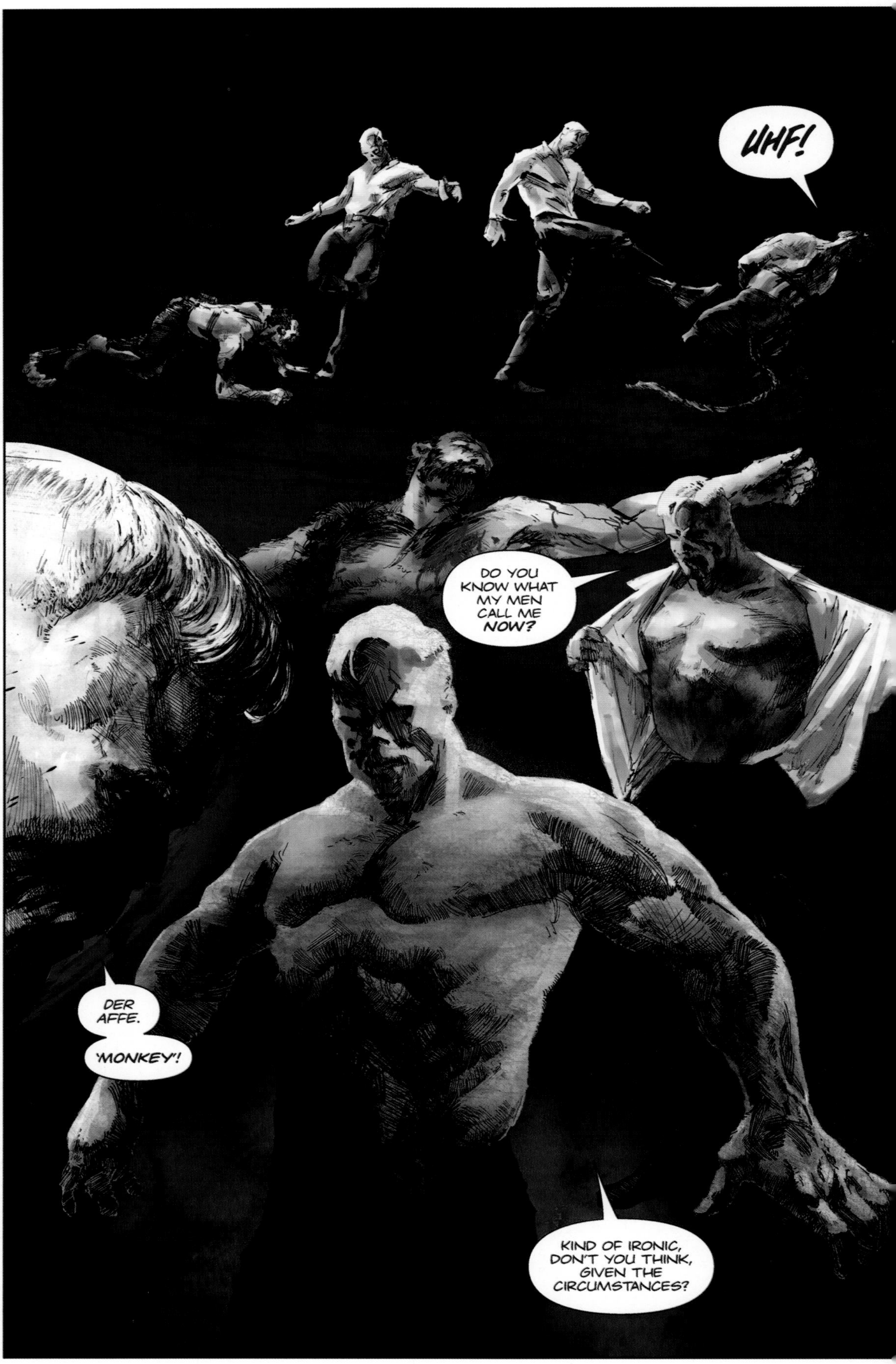
UHF!
DO YOU KNOW WHAT MY MEN CALL ME NOW?
DER AFFE.
'MONKEY'!
KIND OF IRONIC, DON'T YOU THINK, GIVEN THE CIRCUMSTANCES?

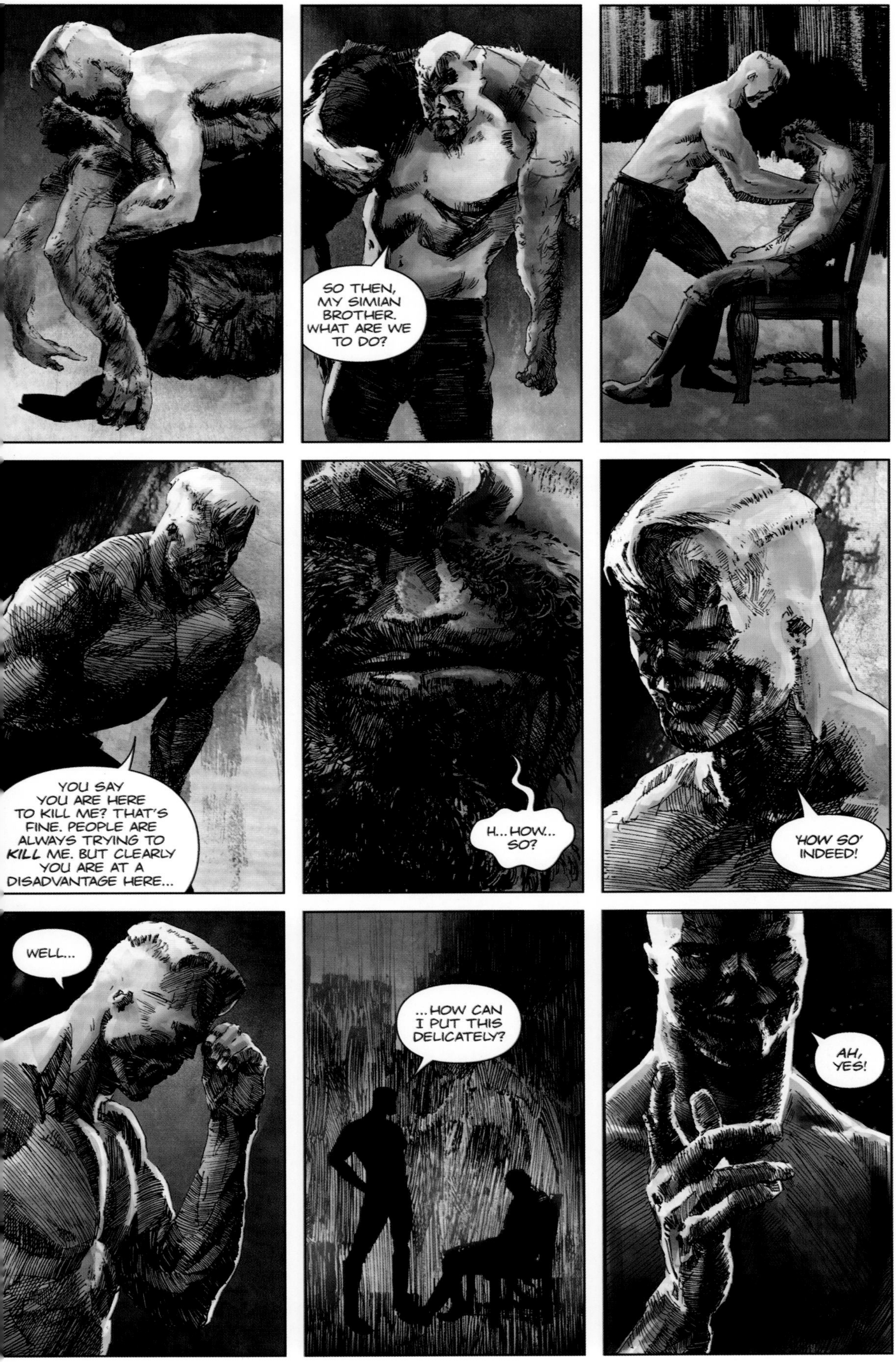
SO THEN, MY SIMIAN BROTHER. WHAT ARE WE TO DO?
YOU SAY YOU ARE HERE TO KILL ME? THAT'S FINE. PEOPLE ARE ALWAYS TRYING TO KILL ME. BUT CLEARLY YOU ARE AT A DISADVANTAGE HERE...
H...HOW... SO?
'HOW SO' INDEED!
WELL...
...HOW CAN I PUT THIS DELICATELY?
AH, YES!

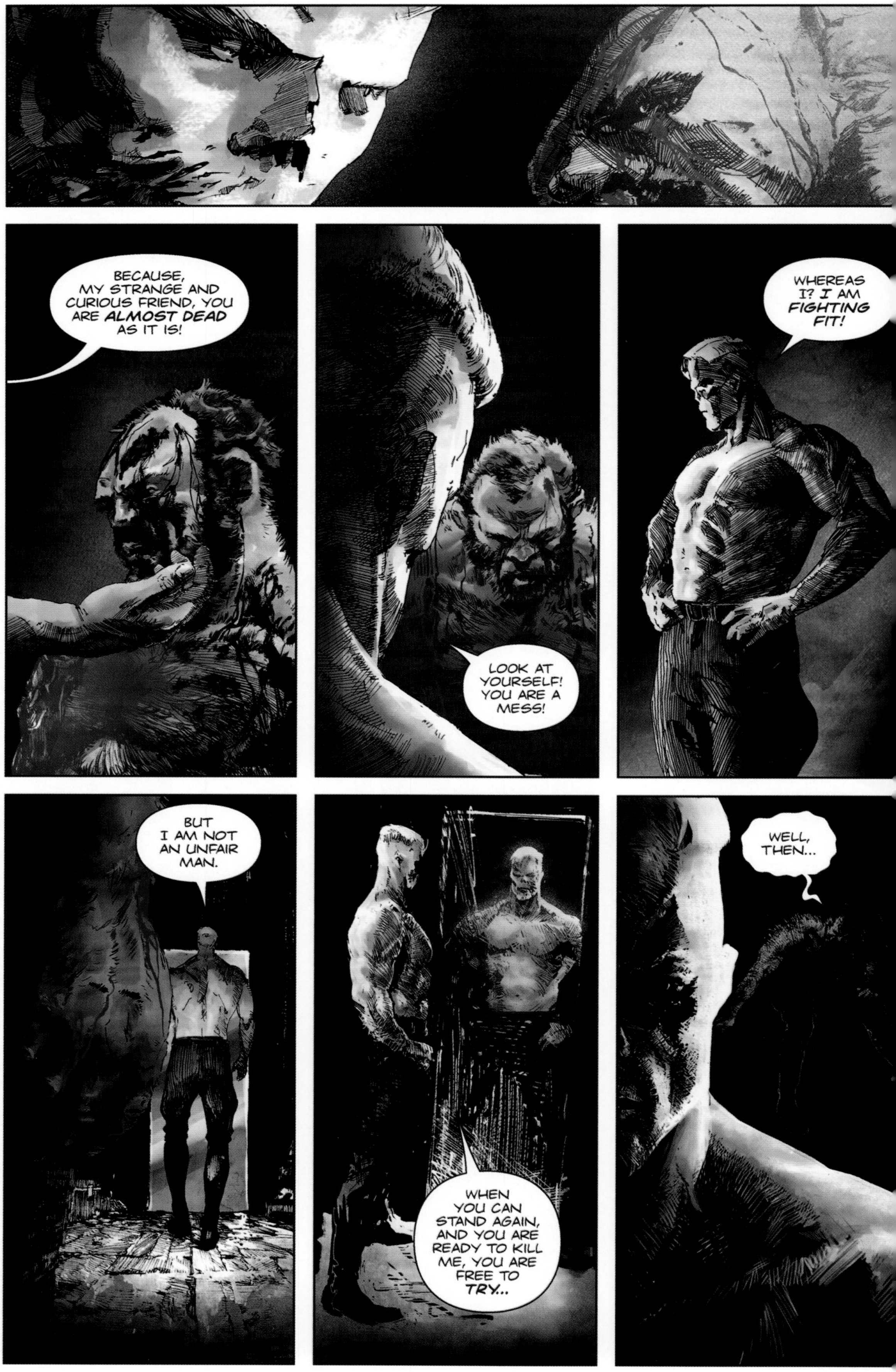
BECAUSE, MY STRANGE AND CURIOUS FRIEND, YOU ARE **ALMOST DEAD** AS IT IS!
LOOK AT YOURSELF! YOU ARE A MESS!
WHEREAS I? *I AM* ***FIGHTING FIT!***
BUT I AM NOT AN UNFAIR MAN.
WHEN YOU CAN STAND AGAIN, AND YOU ARE READY TO KILL ME, YOU ARE FREE TO ***TRY...***
WELL, THEN...

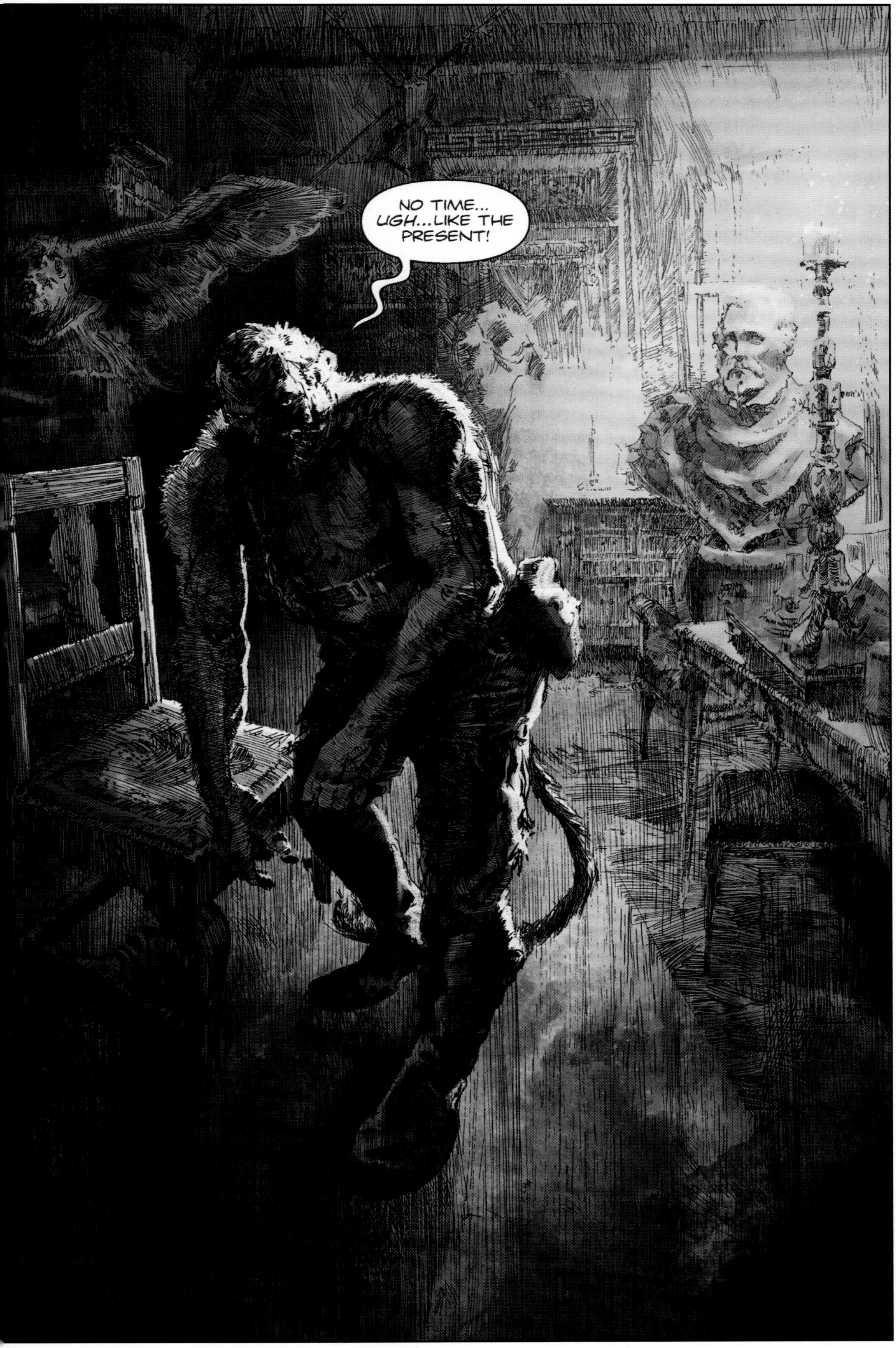
NO TIME... UGH...LIKE THE PRESENT!

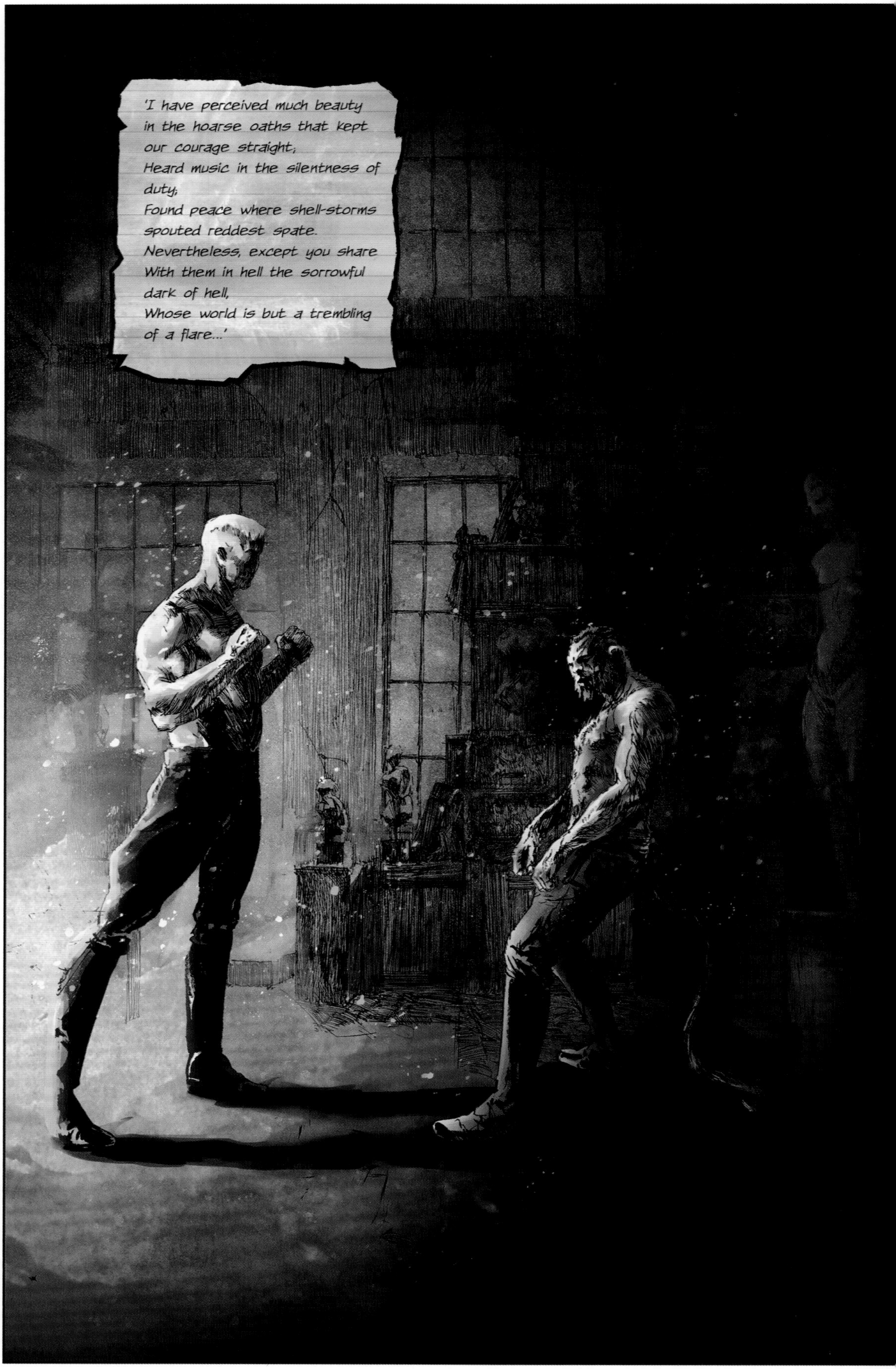
'I have perceived much beauty
in the hoarse oaths that kept
our courage straight;
Heard music in the silentness of
duty;
Found peace where shell-storms
spouted reddest spate.
Nevertheless, except you share
With them in hell the sorrowful
dark of hell,
Whose world is but a trembling
of a flare...'

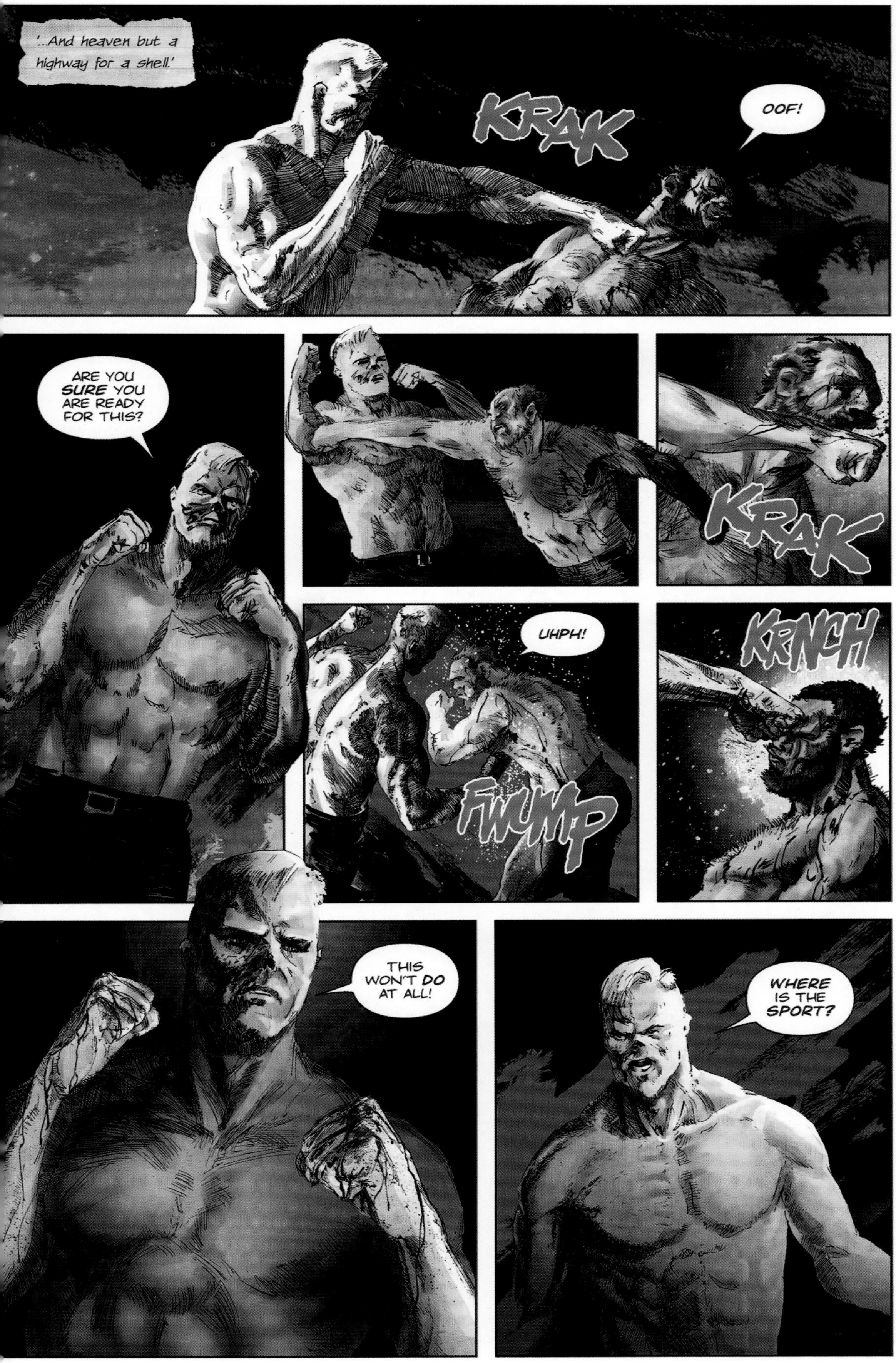
'..And heaven but a highway for a shell.'
KRAK
OOF!
ARE YOU SURE YOU ARE READY FOR THIS?
KRAK
UHPH!
FWUMP
KRNCH
THIS WON'T DO AT ALL!
WHERE IS THE SPORT?

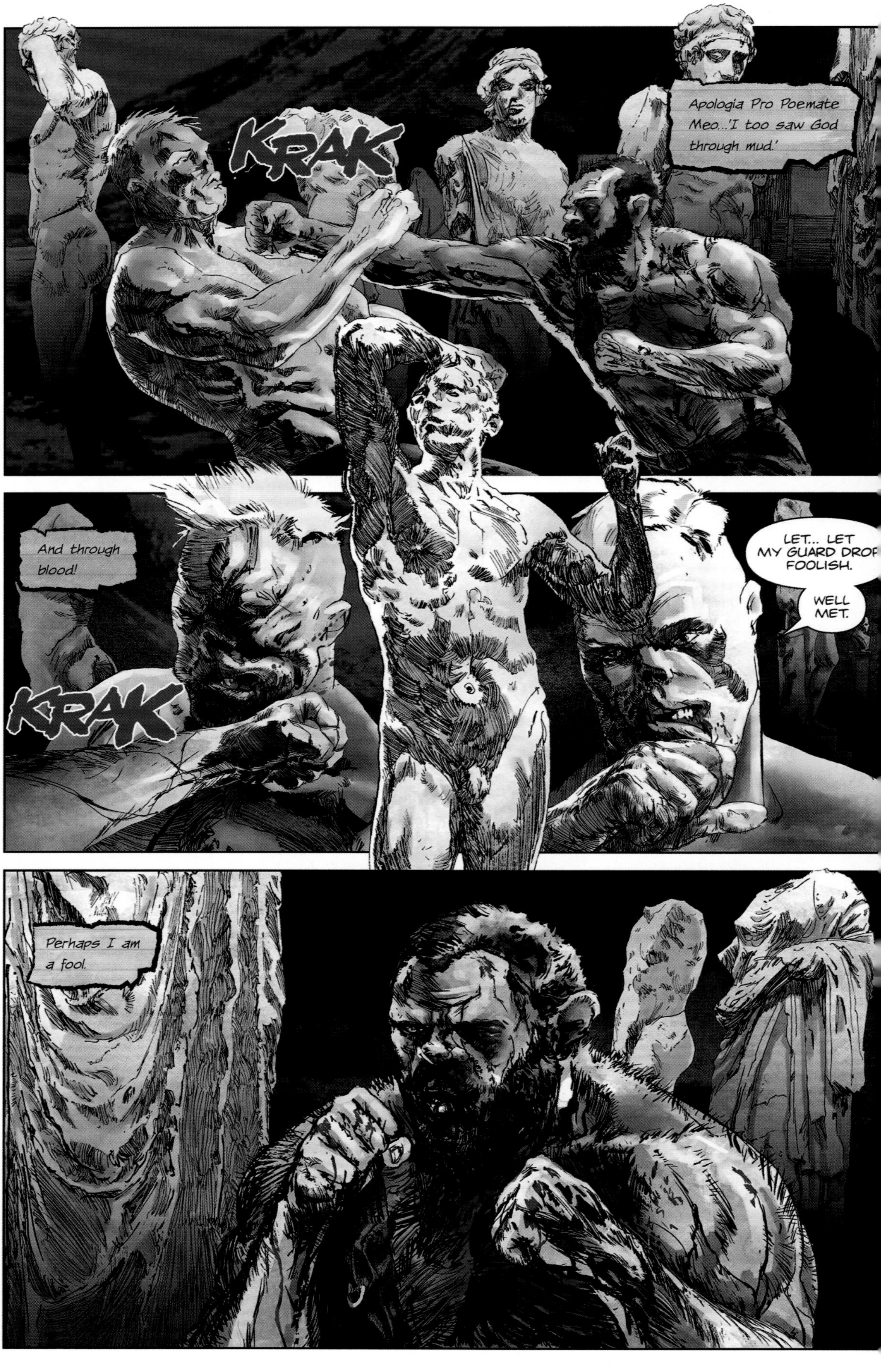
KRAK
Apologia Pro Poemate Meo...'I too saw God through mud.'
And through blood!
KRAK
LET... LET MY GUARD DROP. FOOLISH.
WELL MET.
Perhaps I am a fool.

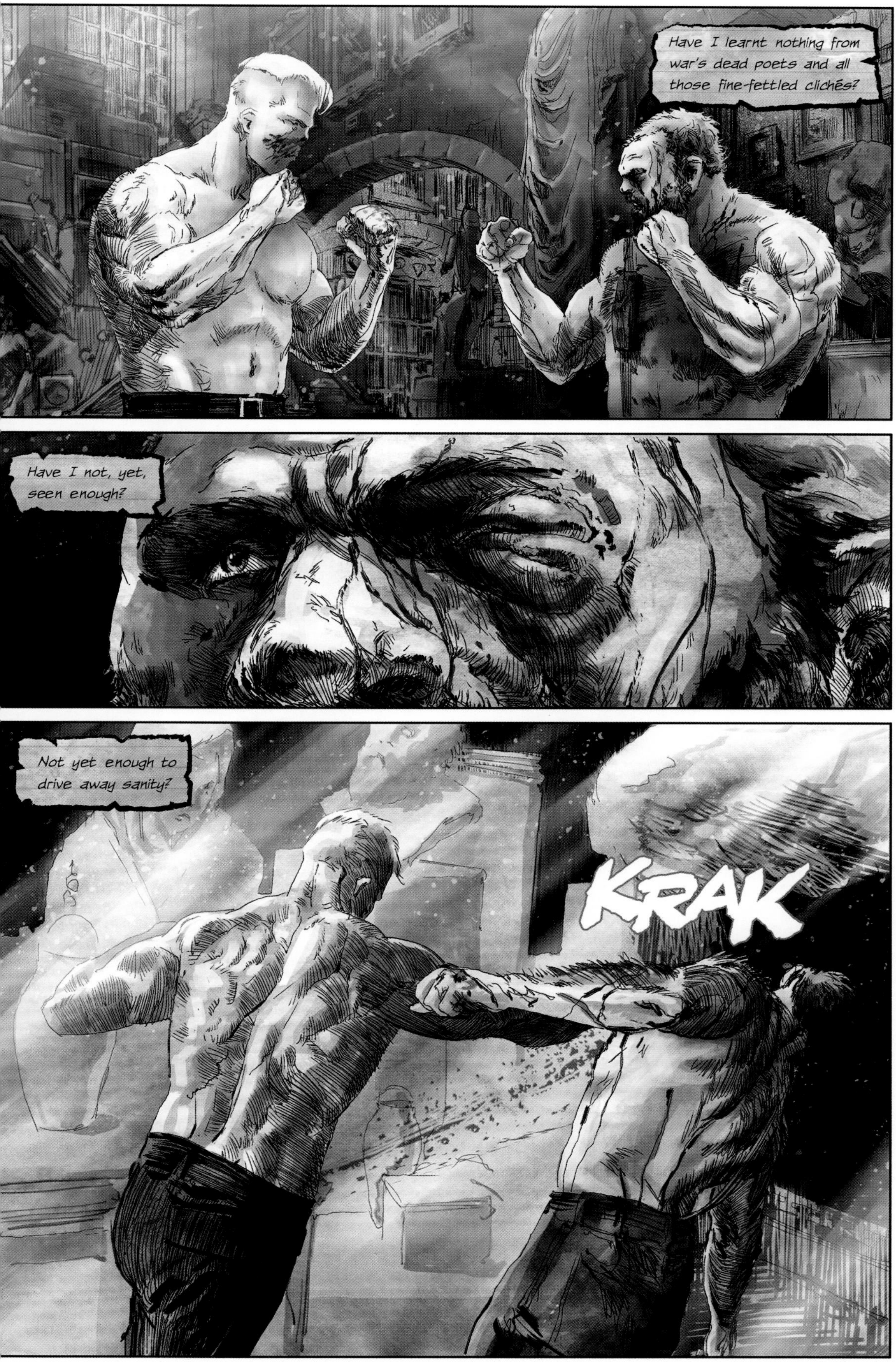
Have I learnt nothing from war's dead poets and all those fine-fettled clichés?
Have I not, yet, seen enough?
Not yet enough to drive away sanity?
KRAK

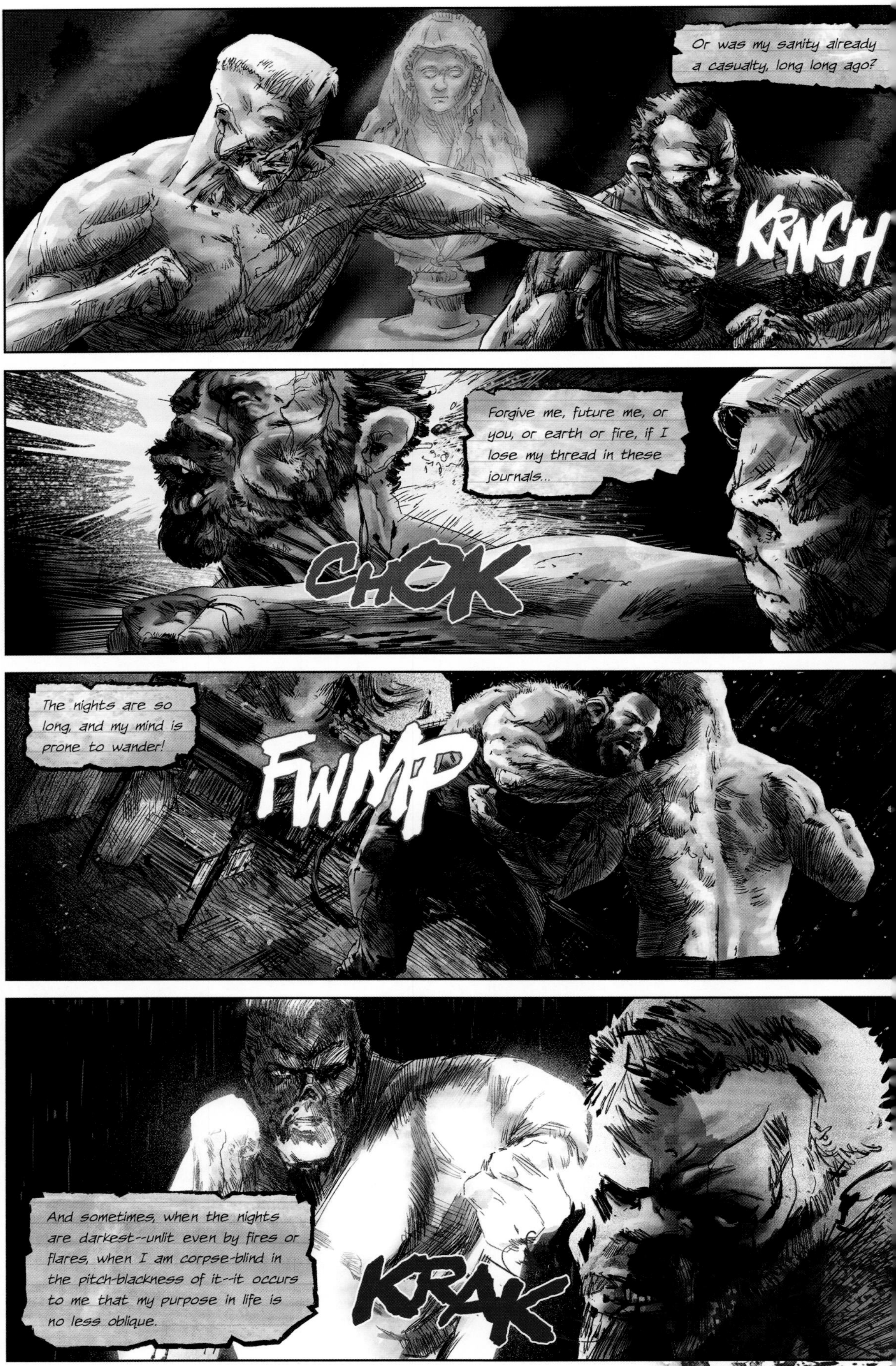
Or was my sanity already a casualty, long long ago?
KRNCH
Forgive me, future me, or you, or earth or fire, if I lose my thread in these journals...
CHOK
The nights are so long, and my mind is prone to wander!
FWMP
And sometimes, when the nights are darkest--unlit even by fires or flares, when I am corpse-blind in the pitch-blackness of it--it occurs to me that my purpose in life is no less oblique.
KRAK

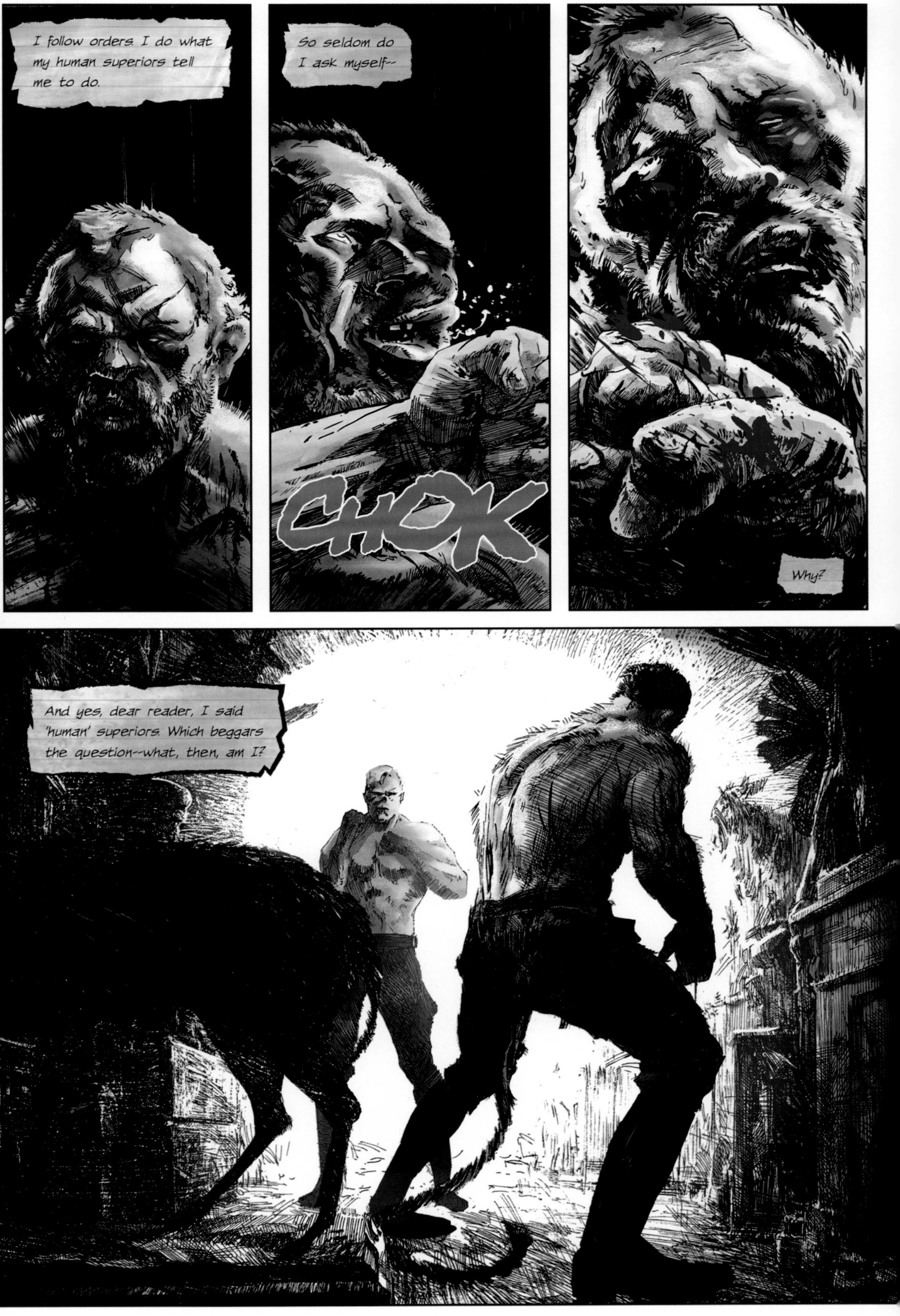

I follow orders. I do what my human superiors tell me to do.
So seldom do I ask myself--
CHOK
Why?
And yes, dear reader, I said 'human' superiors. Which beggars the question--what, then, am I?

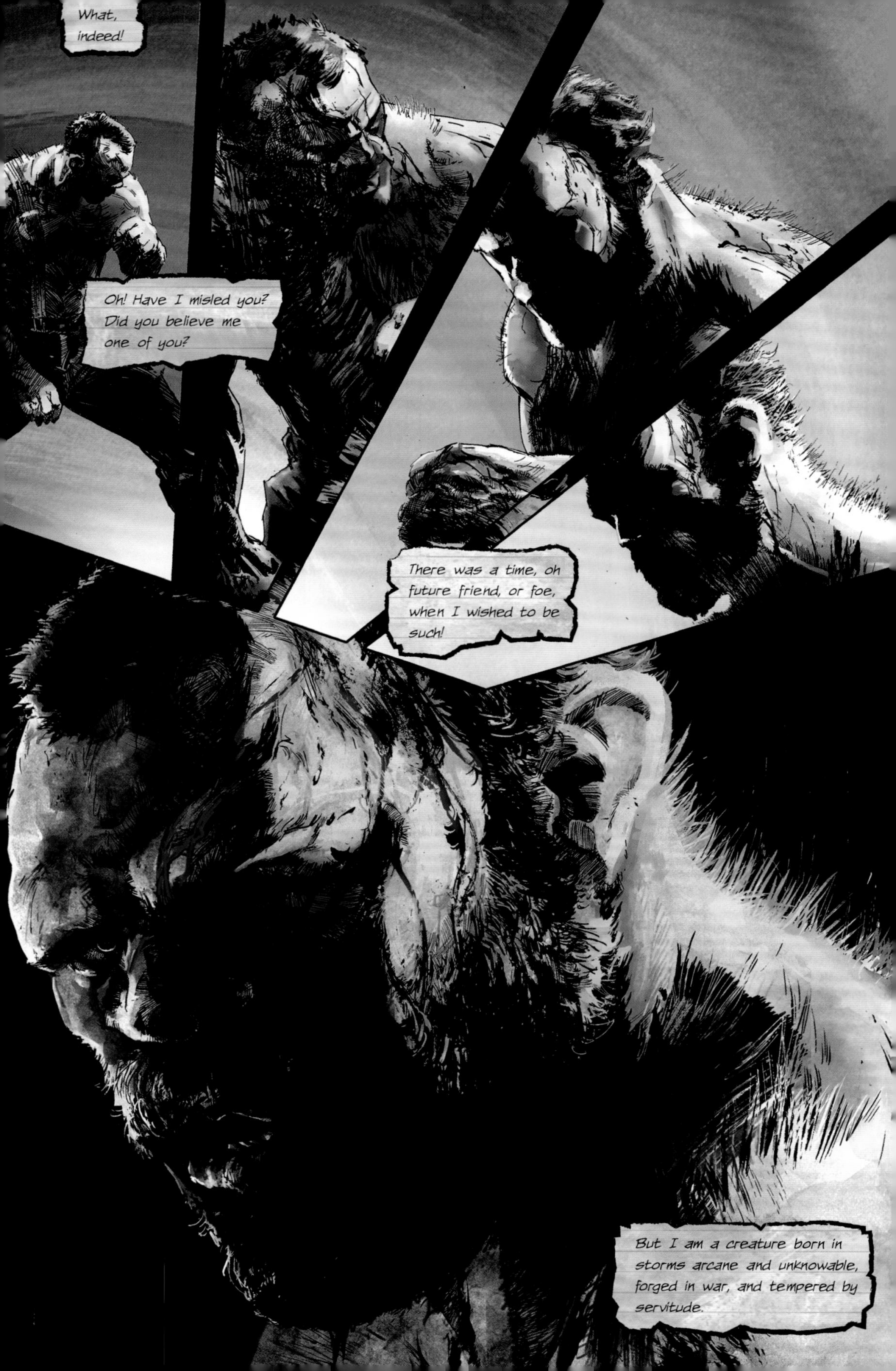
What, indeed!
Oh! Have I misled you? Did you believe me one of you?
There was a time, oh future friend, or foe, when I wished to be such!
But I am a creature born in storms arcane and unknowable, forged in war, and tempered by servitude.

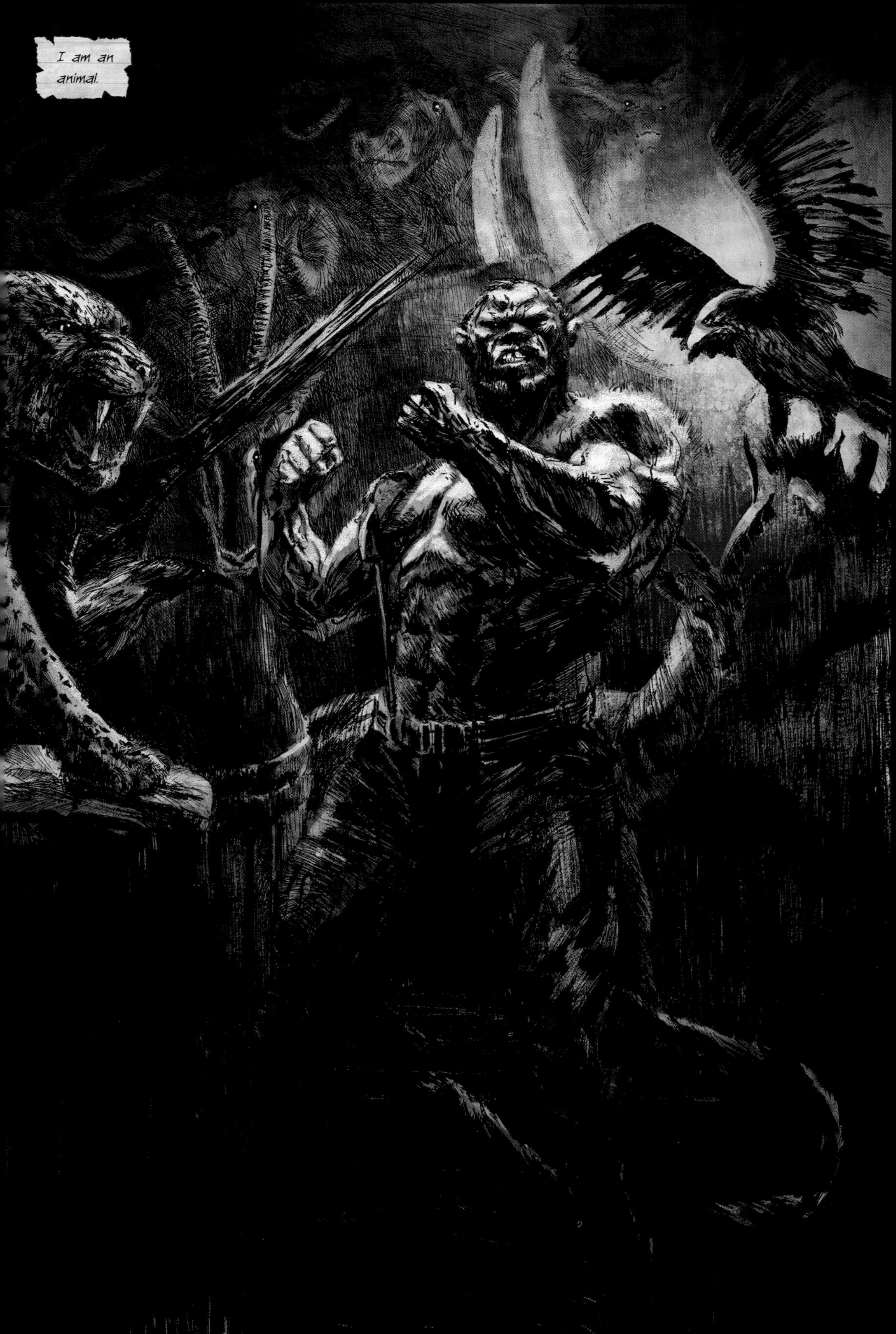
I am an animal.

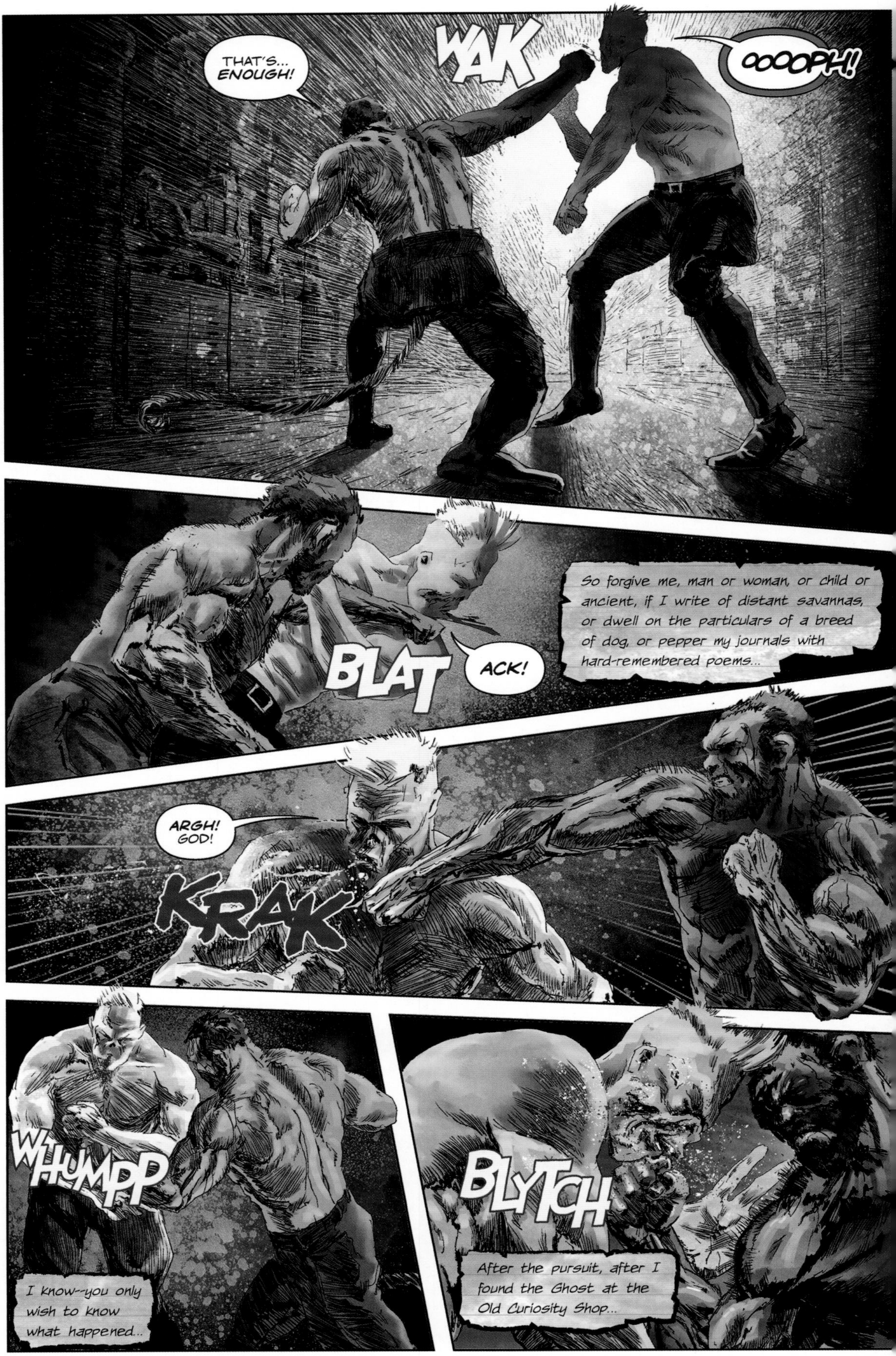
THAT'S... ENOUGH!
WAK
OOOOPH!
BLAT
ACK!
So forgive me, man or woman, or child or ancient, if I write of distant savannas, or dwell on the particulars of a breed of dog, or pepper my journals with hard-remembered poems...
ARGH! GOD!
KRAK
WHUMPP
I know--you only wish to know what happened...
BLYTCH
After the pursuit, after I found the Ghost at the Old Curiosity Shop...

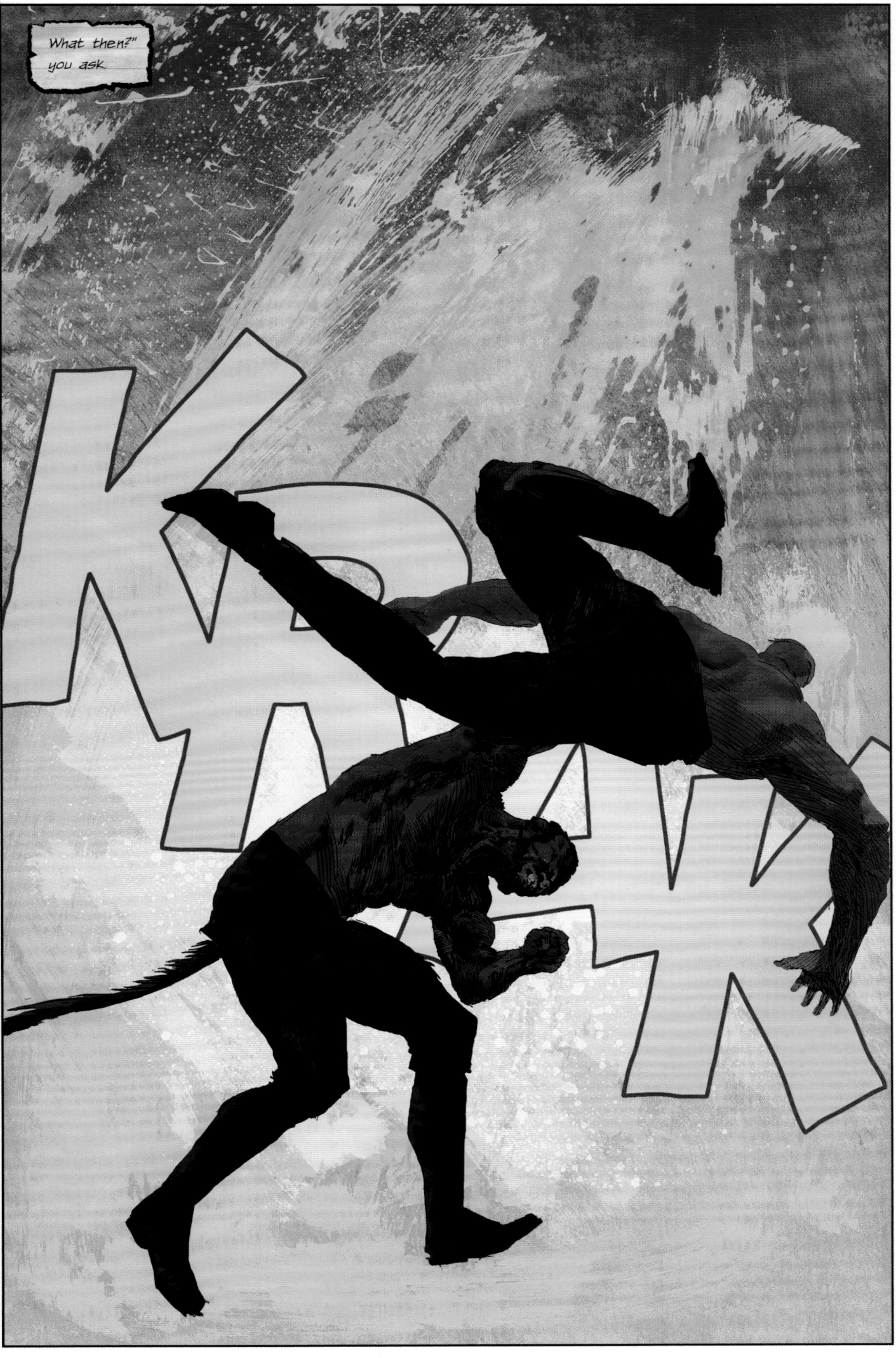
What then?" you ask.

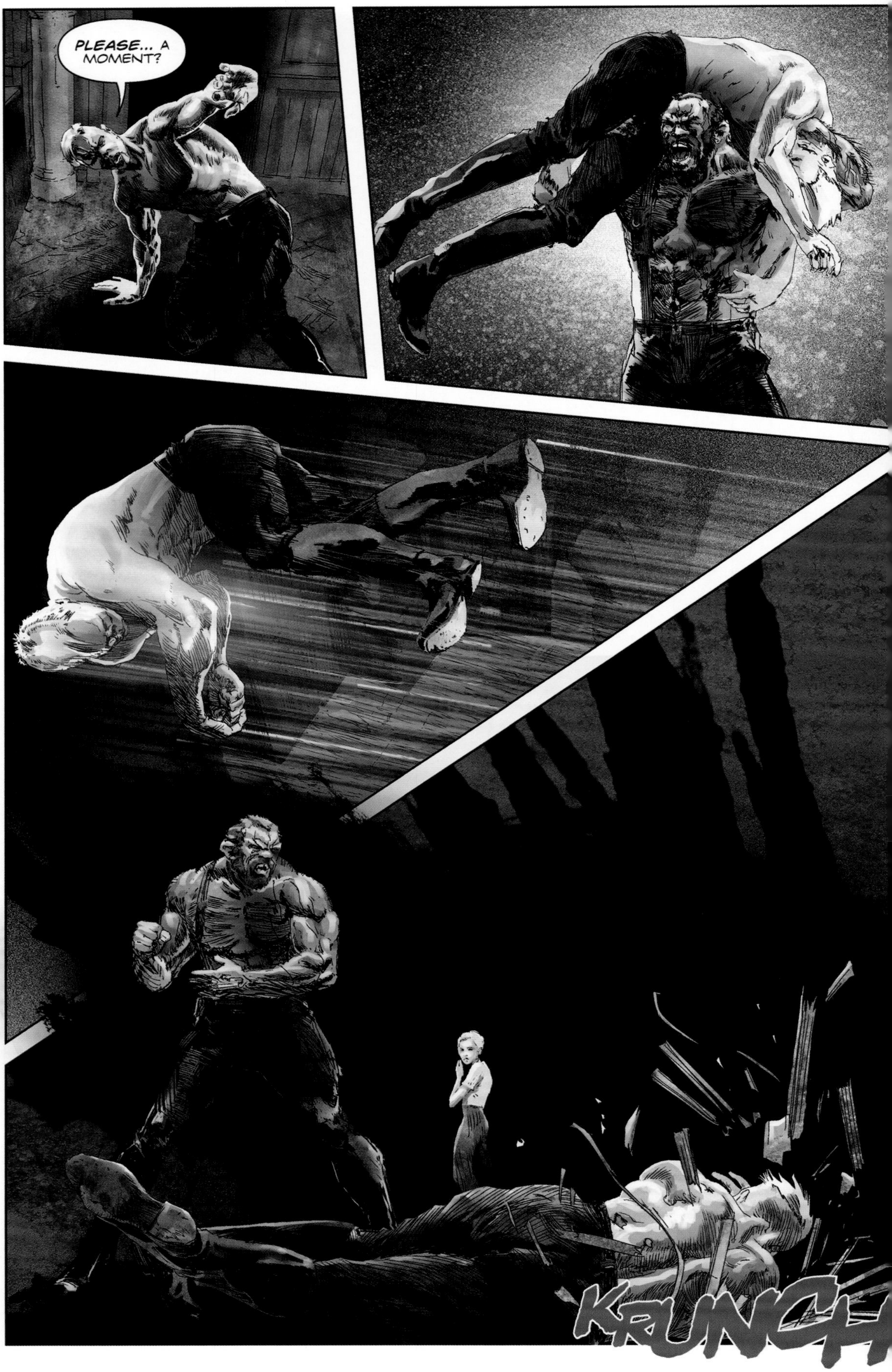
PLEASE... A MOMENT?
KRUNCH

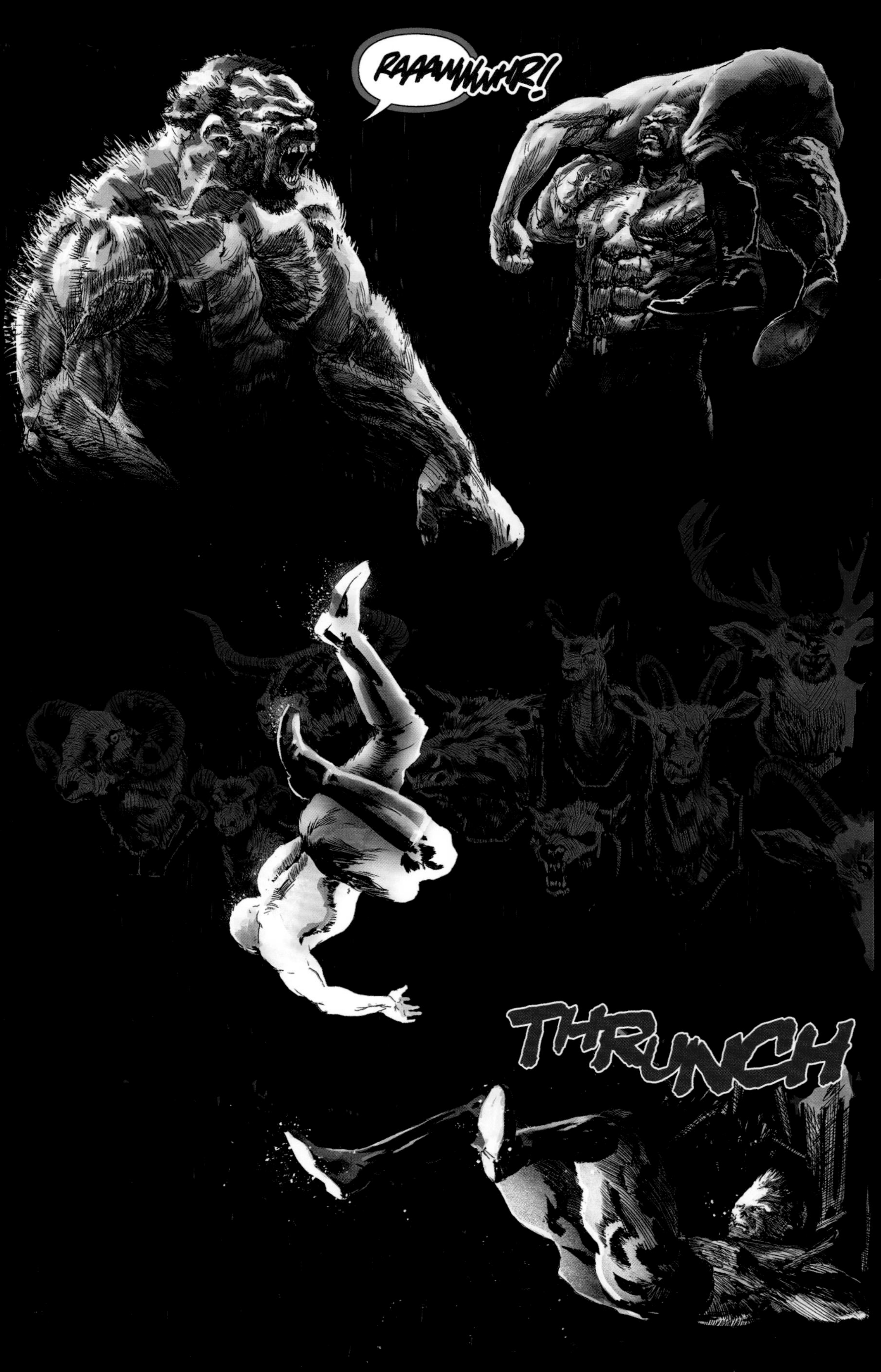
RAAAWWHR!
THRUNCH

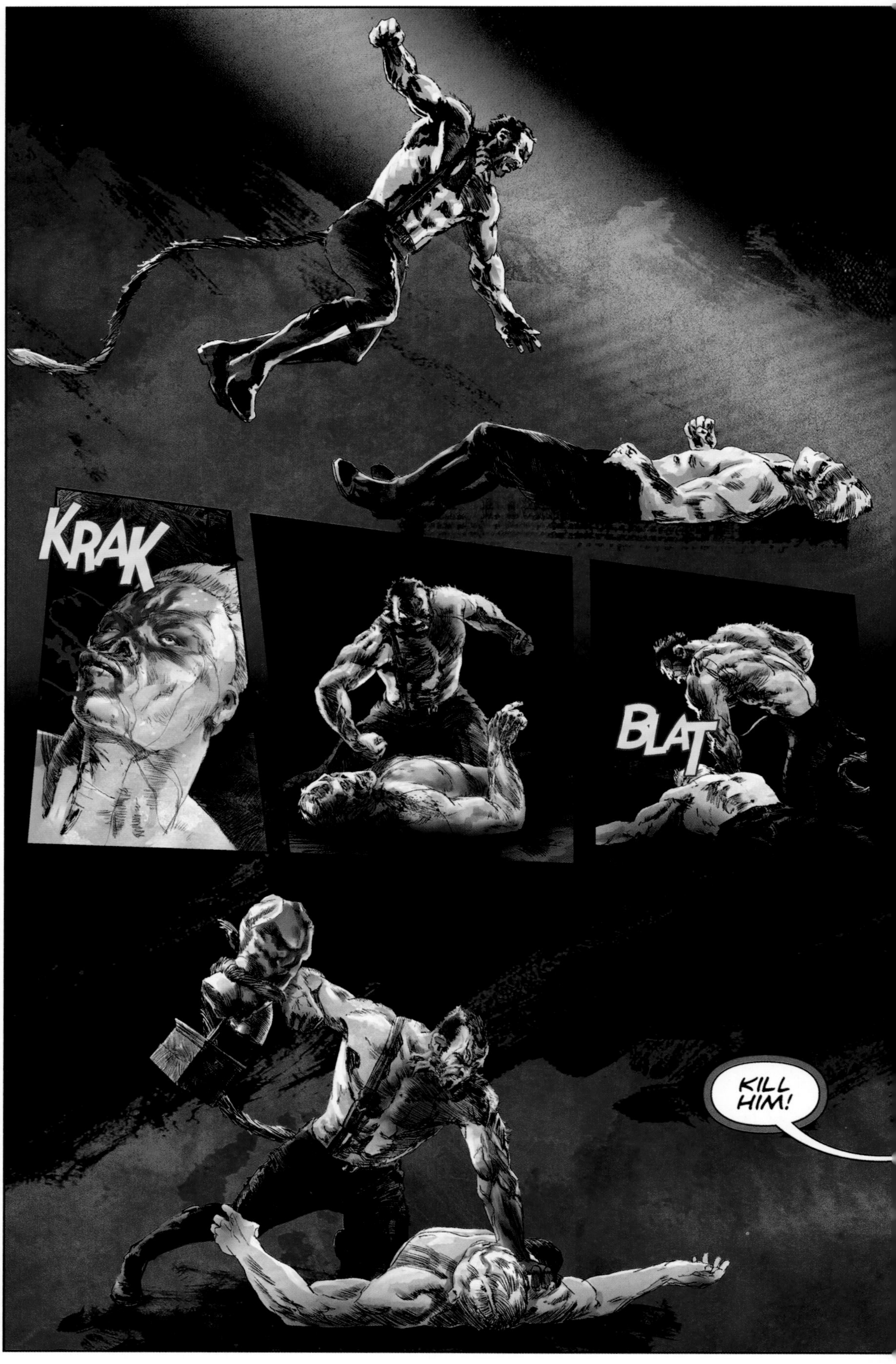
KRAK
BLAT
KILL HIM!

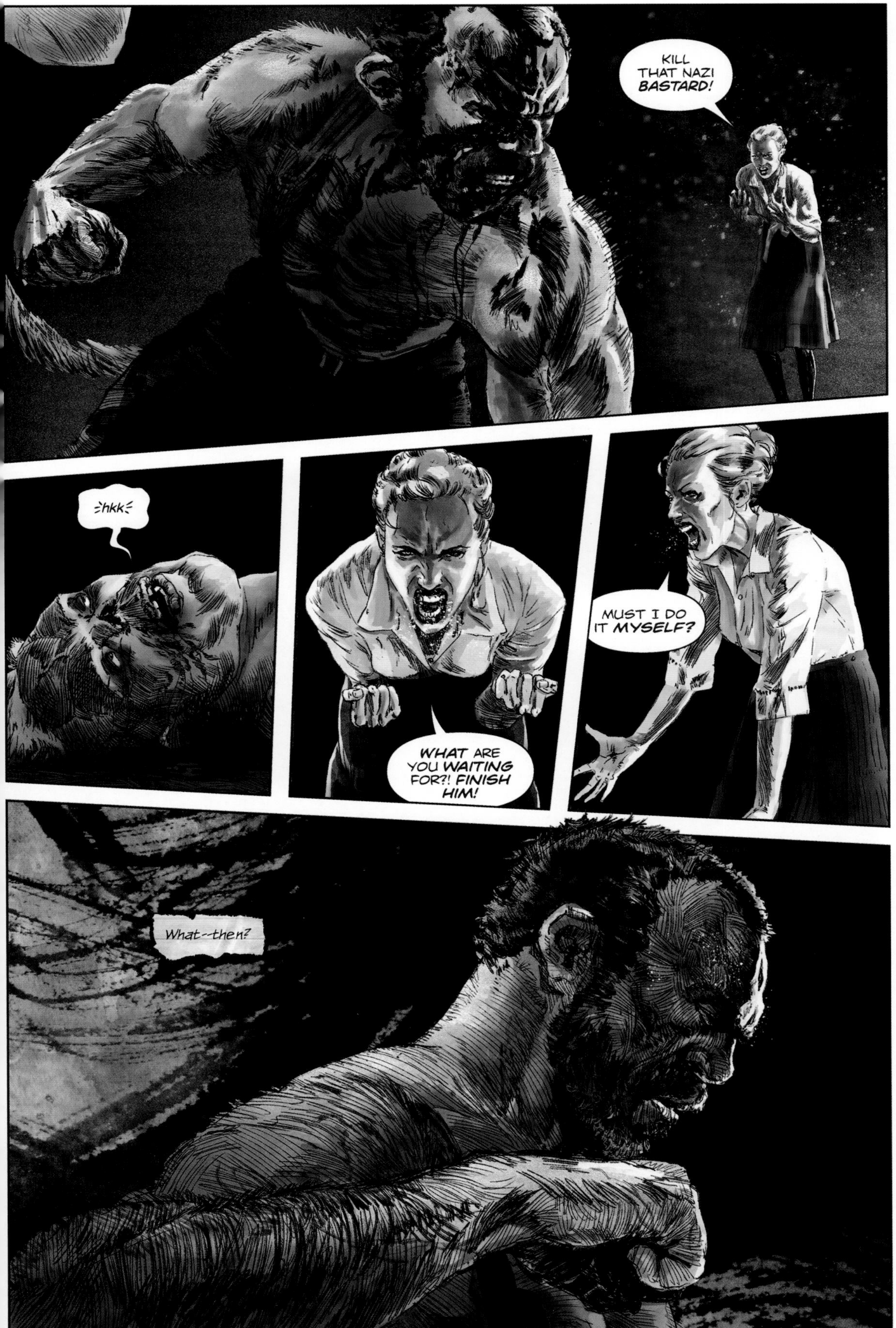
KILL THAT NAZI BASTARD!
hkk
WHAT ARE YOU WAITING FOR?! FINISH HIM!
MUST I DO IT MYSELF?
What--then?

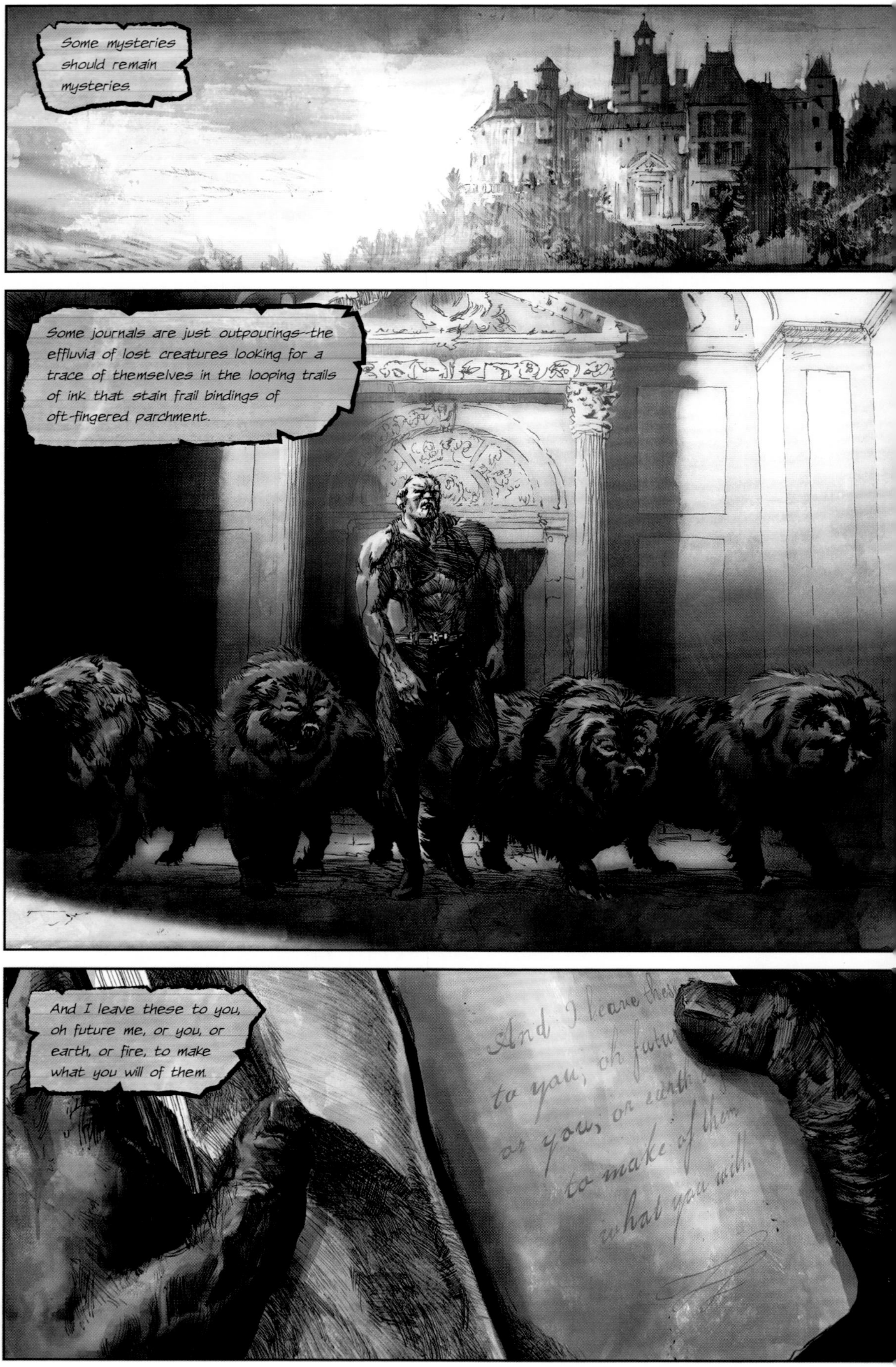
Some mysteries should remain mysteries.
Some journals are just outpourings--the effluvia of lost creatures looking for a trace of themselves in the looping trails of ink that stain frail bindings of oft-fingered parchment.
And I leave these to you, oh future me, or you, or earth, or fire, to make what you will of them.

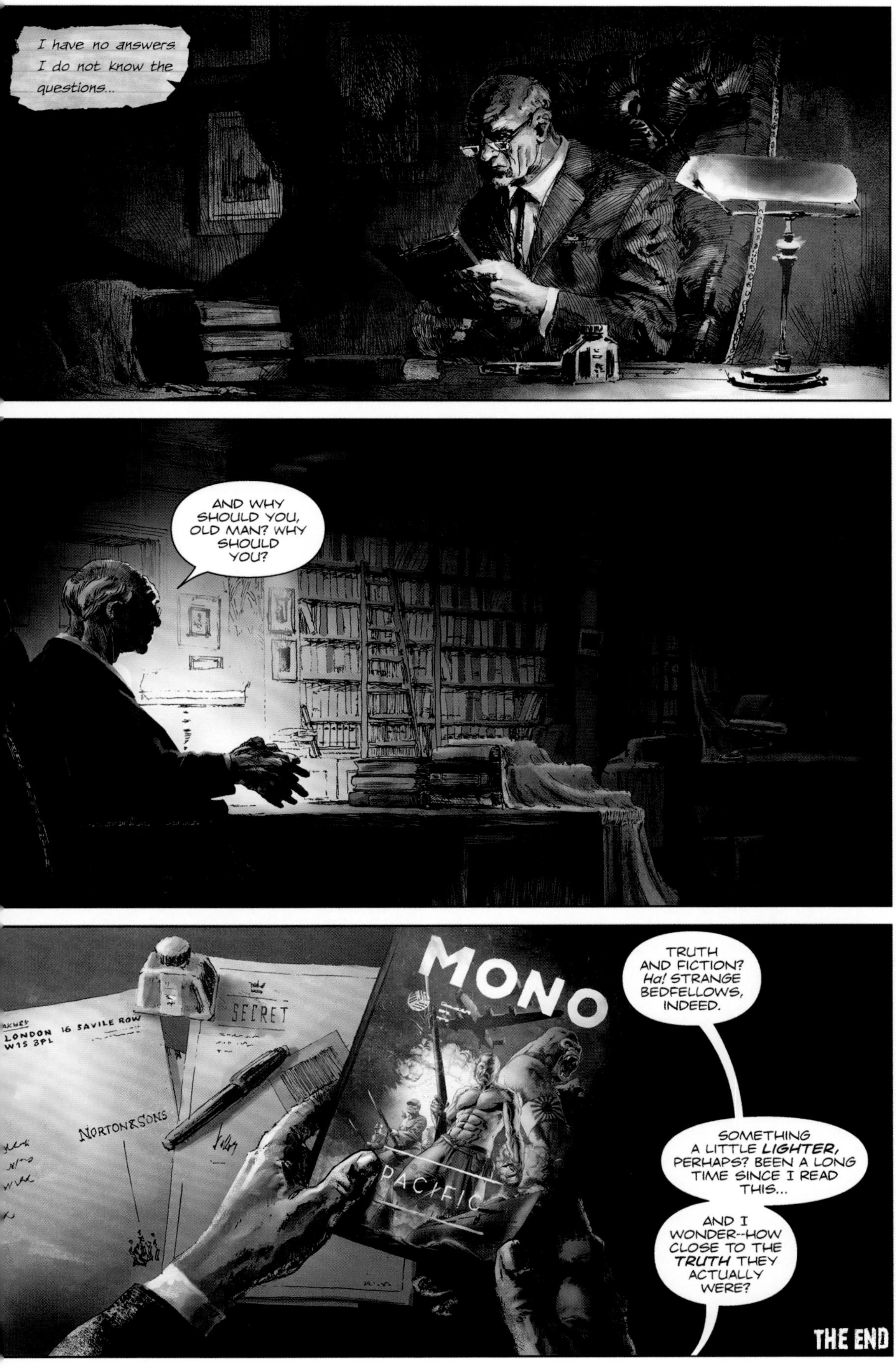
I have no answers. I do not know the questions...
AND WHY SHOULD YOU, OLD MAN? WHY SHOULD YOU?
16 SAVILE ROW
LONDON W1S 3PL
SECRET
NORTON & SONS
MONO
PACIFIC
TRUTH AND FICTION? *Ha!* STRANGE BEDFELLOWS, INDEED.
SOMETHING A LITTLE ***LIGHTER,*** PERHAPS? BEEN A LONG TIME SINCE I READ THIS...
AND I WONDER--HOW CLOSE TO THE ***TRUTH*** THEY ACTUALLY WERE?
THE END

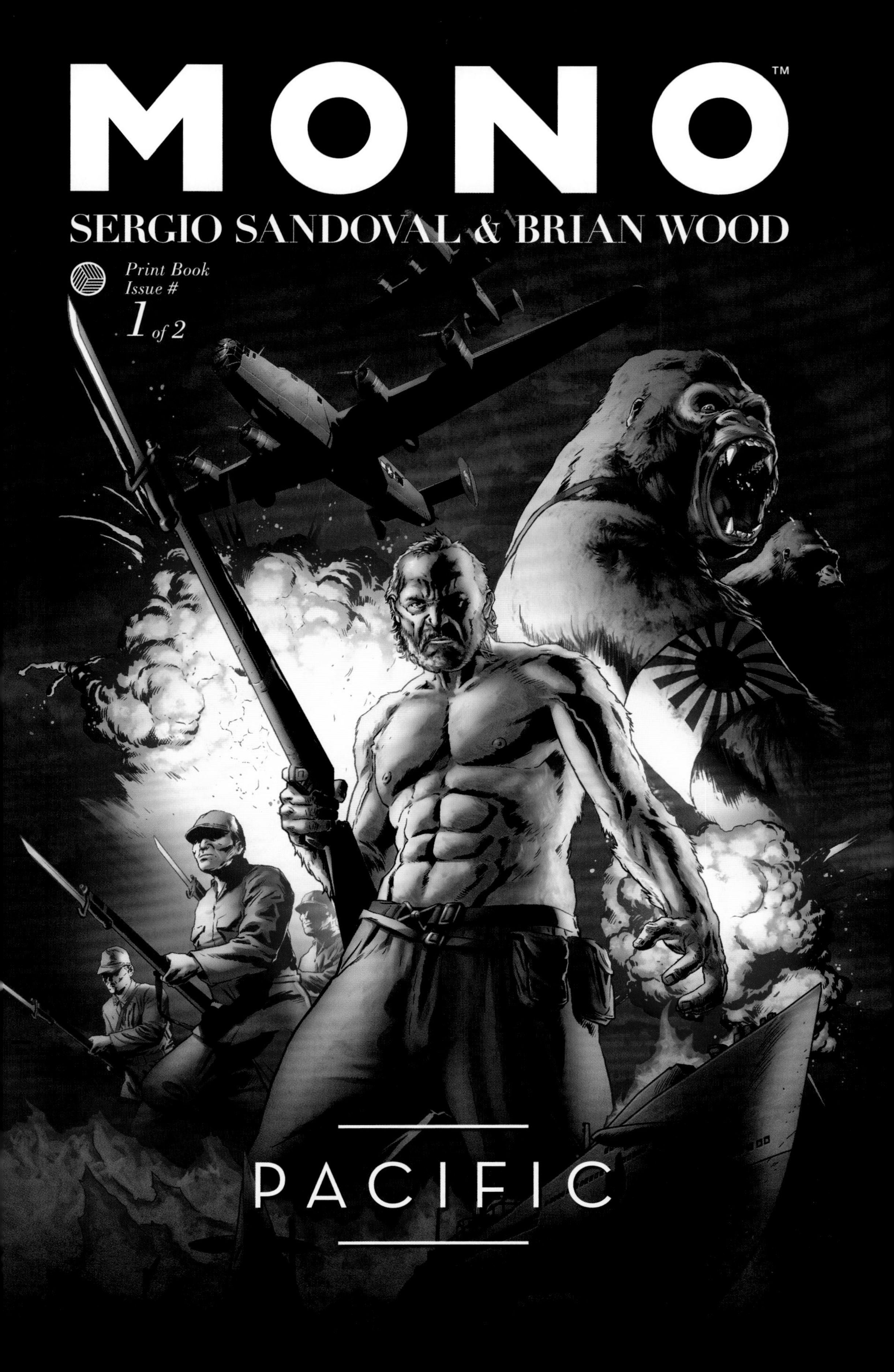
MONO™
SERGIO SANDOVAL & BRIAN WOOD
Print Book
Issue #
1 of 2
PACIFIC

MONO: PACIFIC

It's 1945 and World War II is nearing its apocalyptic conclusion.

In the Pacific Theater, the Japanese are preparing for one final, deadly gambit... and all that stands between annihilation of the American fleet is the British ape-human secret agent MONO!

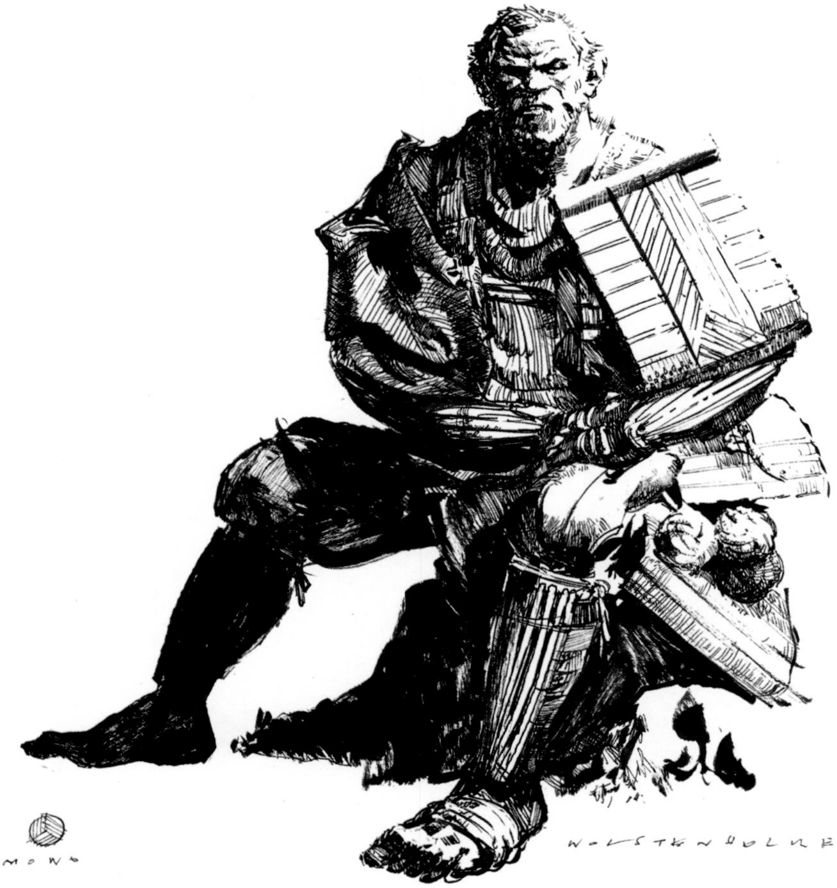
MONO
WOLSTENHOLME

Art Sergio Sandoval **Script** Brian Wood **Colors** Diego Rodriguez
Letters Jim Campbell **Cover by** Sergio Sandoval & Diego Rodriguez
MONO Created by Ben Wolstenholme

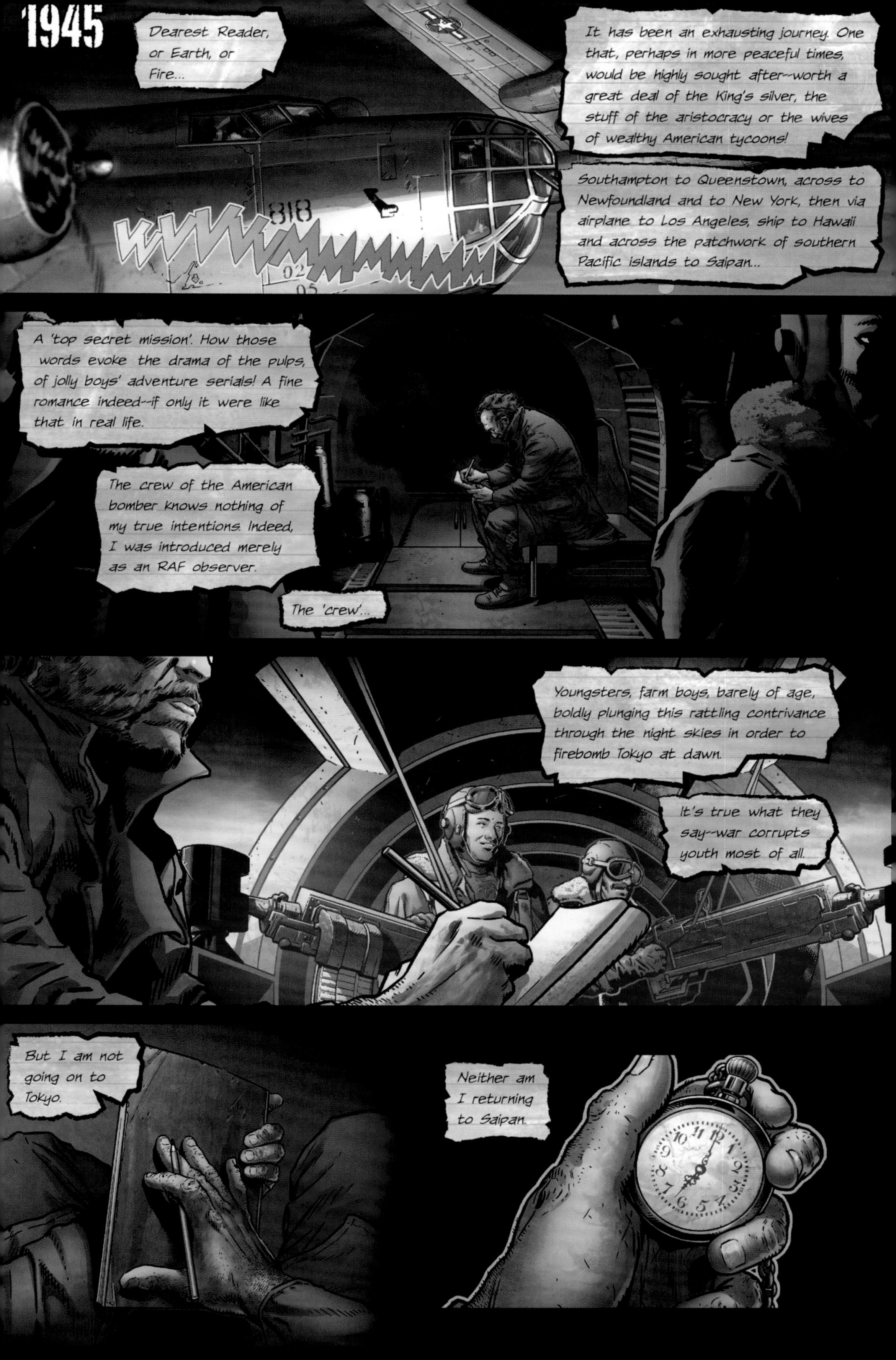
1945
Dearest Reader, or Earth, or Fire...
It has been an exhausting journey. One that, perhaps in more peaceful times, would be highly sought after--worth a great deal of the King's silver, the stuff of the aristocracy or the wives of wealthy American tycoons!
Southampton to Queenstown, across to Newfoundland and to New York, then via airplane to Los Angeles, ship to Hawaii and across the patchwork of southern Pacific islands to Saipan...
KVVVKMMMMM
818
A 'top secret mission'. How those words evoke the drama of the pulps, of jolly boys' adventure serials! A fine romance indeed--if only it were like that in real life.
The crew of the American bomber knows nothing of my true intentions. Indeed, I was introduced merely as an RAF observer.
The 'crew'...
Youngsters, farm boys, barely of age, boldly plunging this rattling contrivance through the night skies in order to firebomb Tokyo at dawn.
It's true what they say--war corrupts youth most of all.
But I am not going on to Tokyo.
Neither am I returning to Saipan.

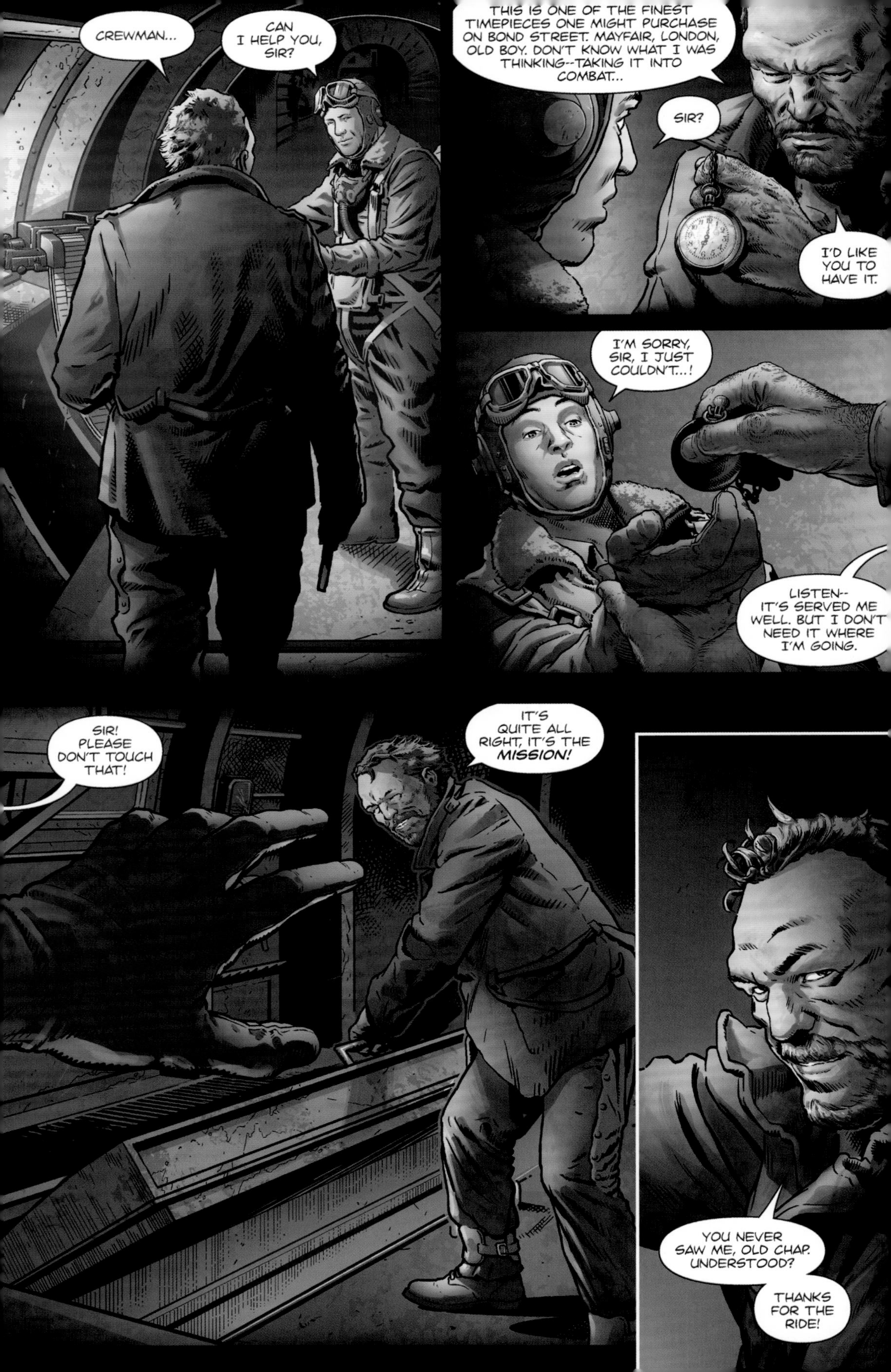
CREWMAN...
CAN I HELP YOU, SIR?
THIS IS ONE OF THE FINEST TIMEPIECES ONE MIGHT PURCHASE ON BOND STREET. MAYFAIR, LONDON, OLD BOY. DON'T KNOW WHAT I WAS THINKING--TAKING IT INTO COMBAT...
SIR?
I'D LIKE YOU TO HAVE IT.
I'M SORRY, SIR, I JUST COULDN'T...!
LISTEN-- IT'S SERVED ME WELL. BUT I DON'T NEED IT WHERE I'M GOING.
SIR! PLEASE DON'T TOUCH THAT!
IT'S QUITE ALL RIGHT, IT'S THE *MISSION!*
YOU NEVER SAW ME, OLD CHAP. UNDERSTOOD?
THANKS FOR THE RIDE!

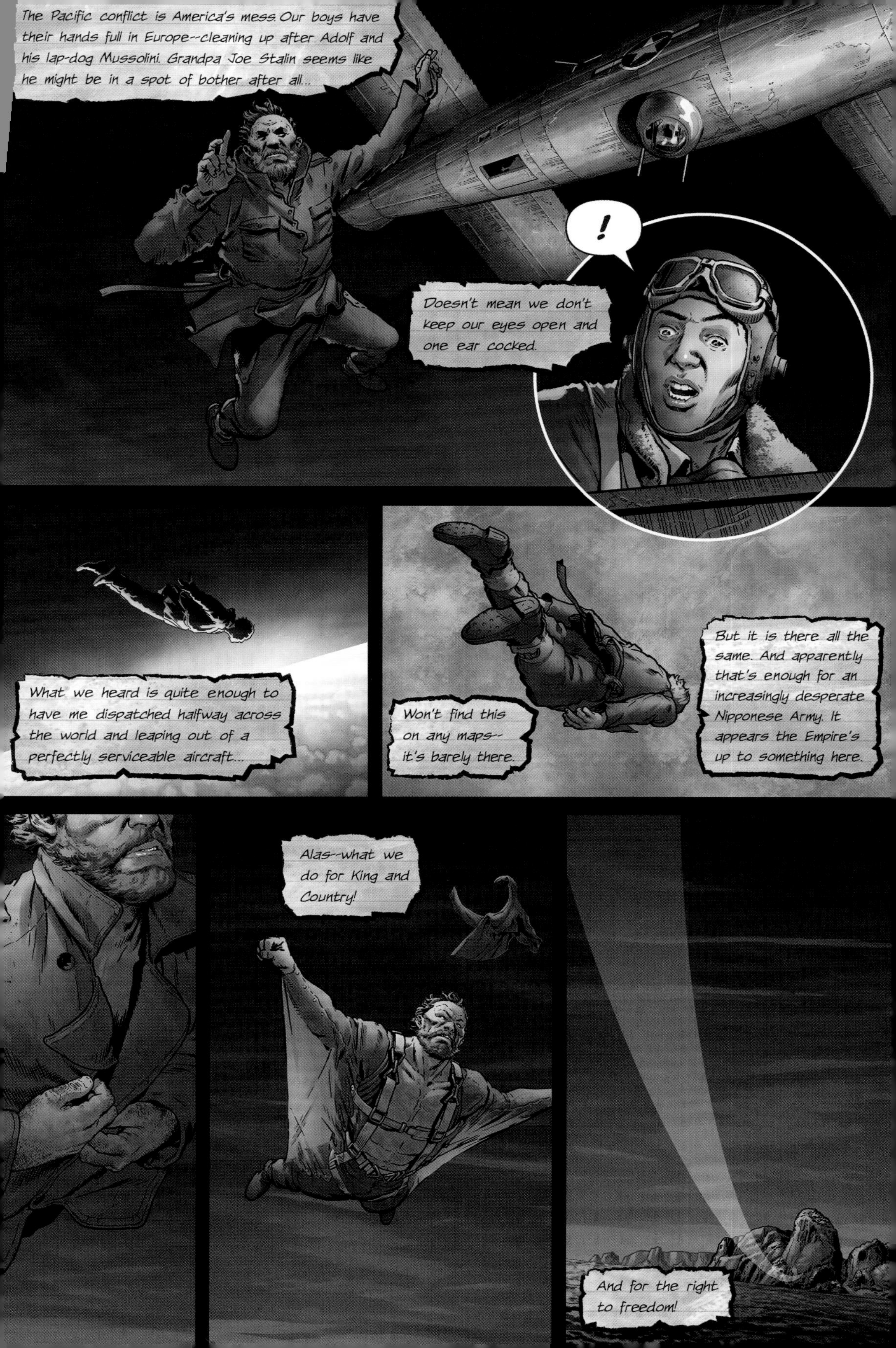
The Pacific conflict is America's mess. Our boys have their hands full in Europe--cleaning up after Adolf and his lap-dog Mussolini. Grandpa Joe Stalin seems like he might be in a spot of bother after all...
!
Doesn't mean we don't keep our eyes open and one ear cocked.
What we heard is quite enough to have me dispatched halfway across the world and leaping out of a perfectly serviceable aircraft...
Won't find this on any maps-- it's barely there.
But it is there all the same. And apparently that's enough for an increasingly desperate Nipponese Army. It appears the Empire's up to something here.
Alas--what we do for King and Country!
And for the right to freedom!

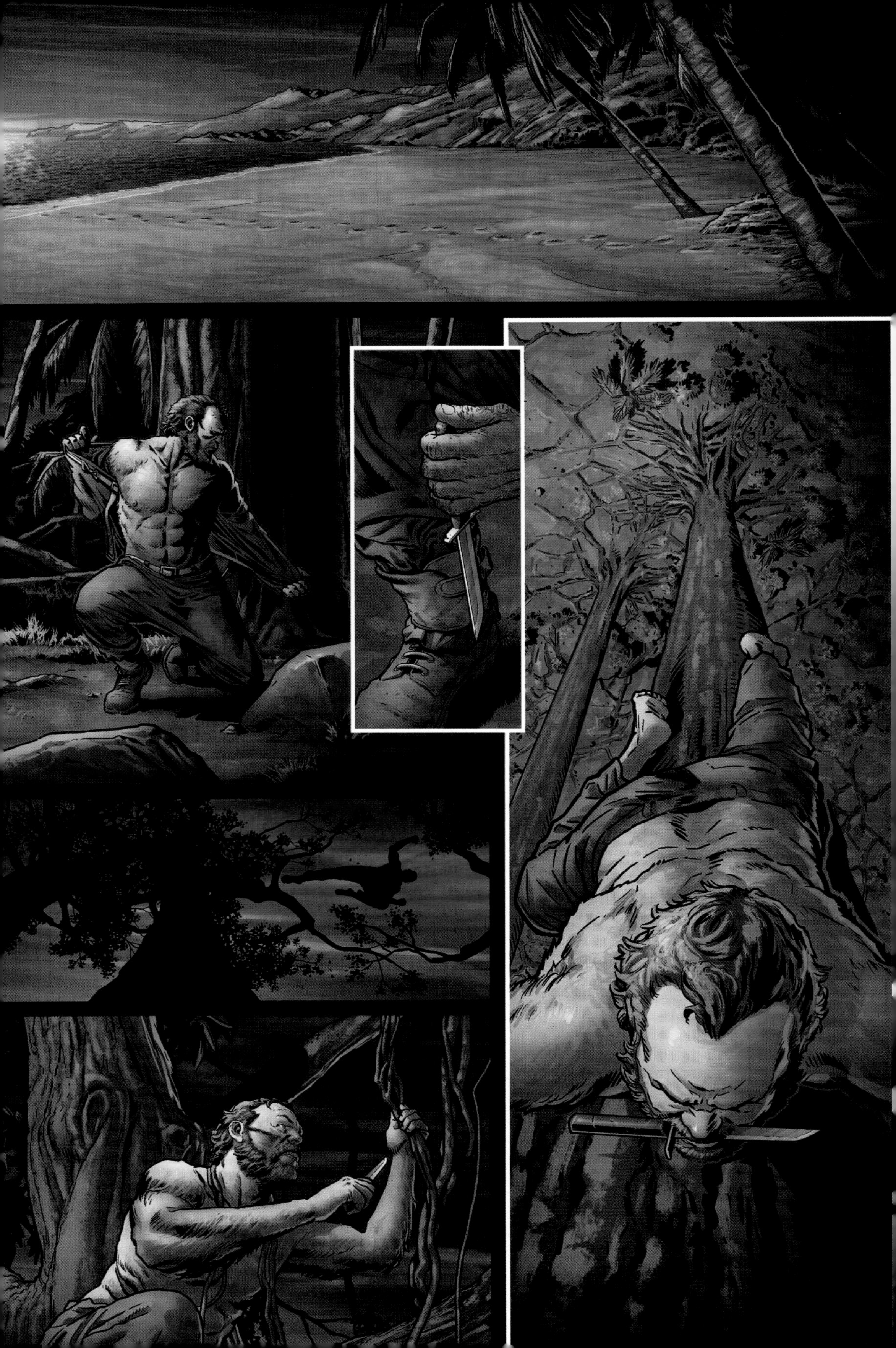

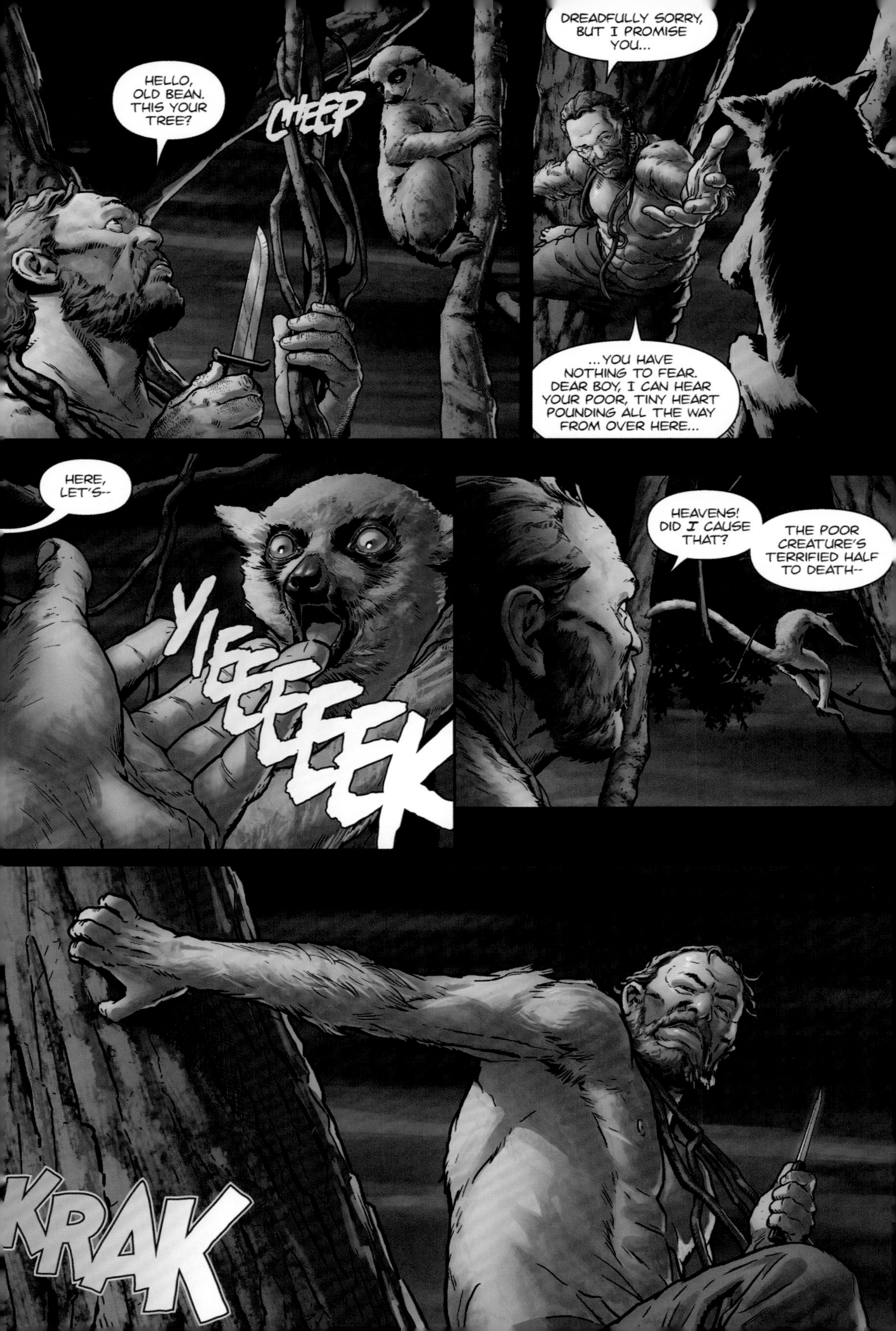
HELLO, OLD BEAN. THIS YOUR TREE?
CHEEP
DREADFULLY SORRY, BUT I PROMISE YOU...
...YOU HAVE NOTHING TO FEAR. DEAR BOY, I CAN HEAR YOUR POOR, TINY HEART POUNDING ALL THE WAY FROM OVER HERE...
HERE, LET'S--
YIEEEEEK
HEAVENS! DID I CAUSE THAT?
THE POOR CREATURE'S TERRIFIED HALF TO DEATH--
KRAK

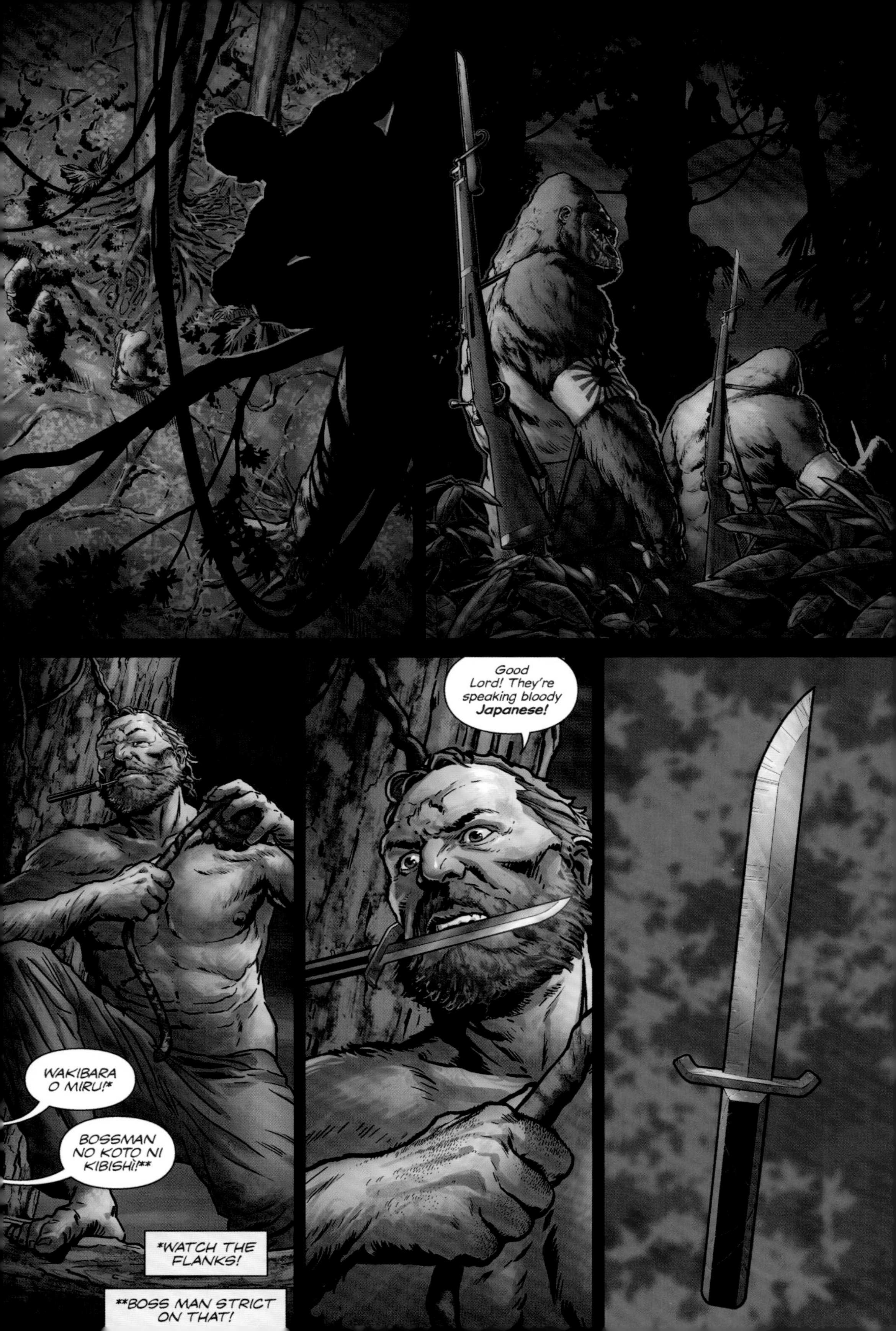
WAKIBARA O MIRU!*
BOSSMAN NO KOTO NI KIBISHI!**
*WATCH THE FLANKS!
**BOSS MAN STRICT ON THAT!
Good Lord! They're speaking bloody Japanese!

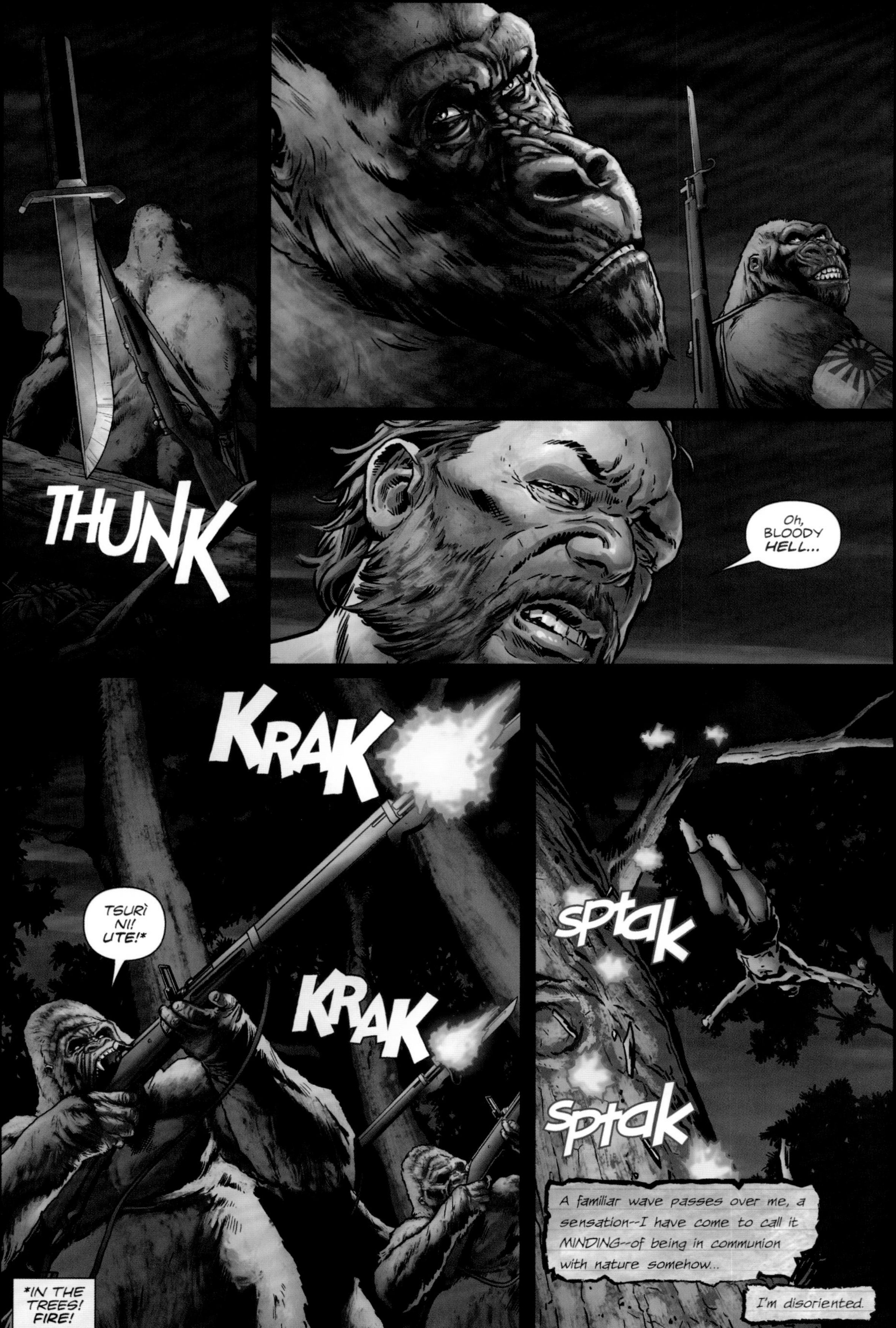
THUNK
Oh, BLOODY HELL...
KRAK
TSURÌ NI! UTE!*
KRAK
*IN THE TREES! FIRE!
sptak
sptak
A familiar wave passes over me, a sensation--I have come to call it MINDING--of being in communion with nature somehow...
I'm disoriented.

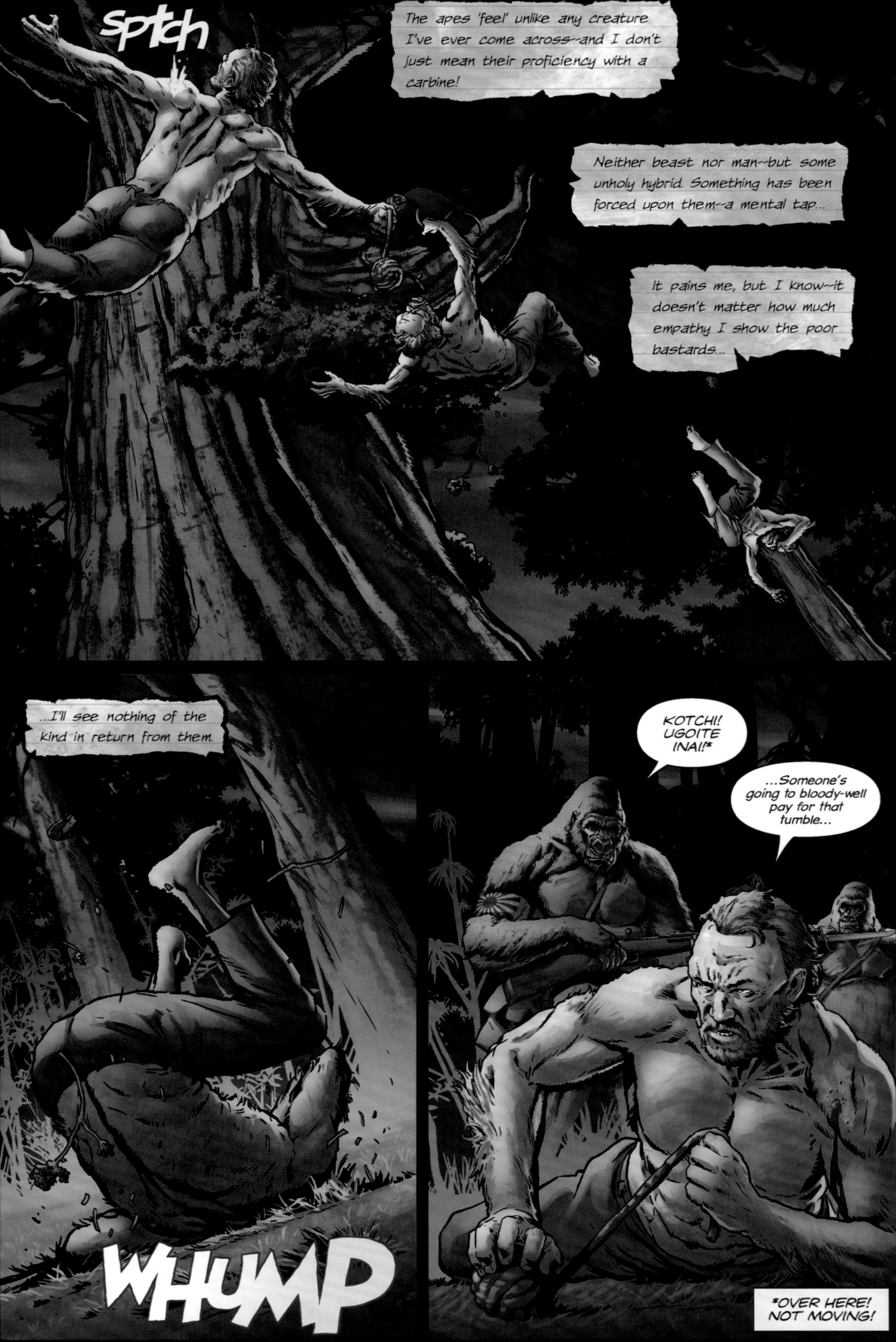
sptch
The apes 'feel' unlike any creature I've ever come across--and I don't just mean their proficiency with a carbine!
Neither beast nor man--but some unholy hybrid. Something has been forced upon them--a mental tap...
It pains me, but I know--it doesn't matter how much empathy I show the poor bastards...
...I'll see nothing of the kind in return from them.
WHUMP
KOTCHI! UGOITE INAI!*
...Someone's going to bloody-well pay for that tumble...
*OVER HERE! NOT MOVING!

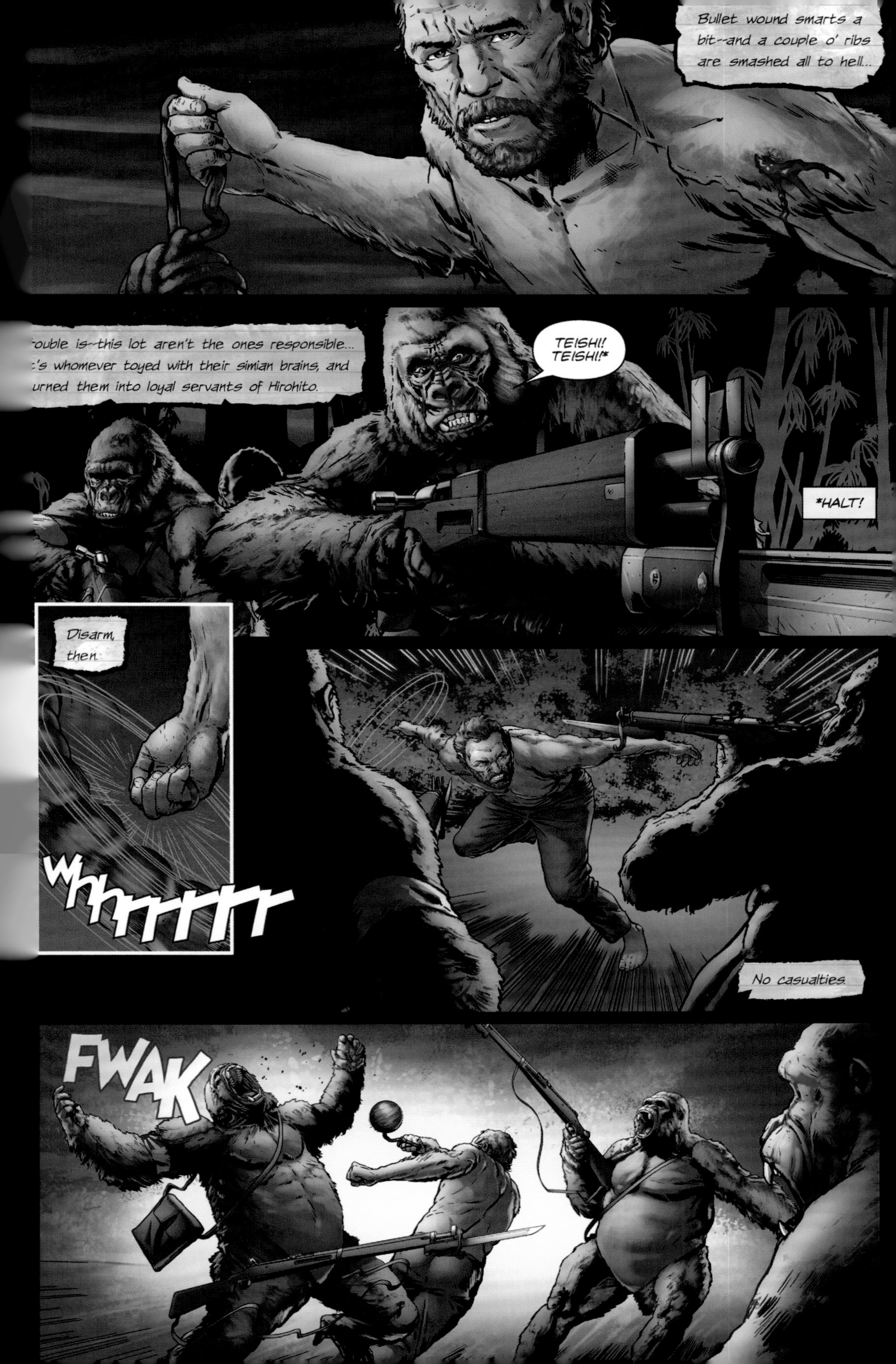

Bullet wound smarts a bit--and a couple o' ribs are smashed all to hell...
rouble is--this lot aren't the ones responsible...
's whomever toyed with their simian brains, and
urned them into loyal servants of Hirohito.
TEISHI! TEISHI!*
*HALT!
Disarm, then.
WHRRRRRRR
No casualties.
FWAK

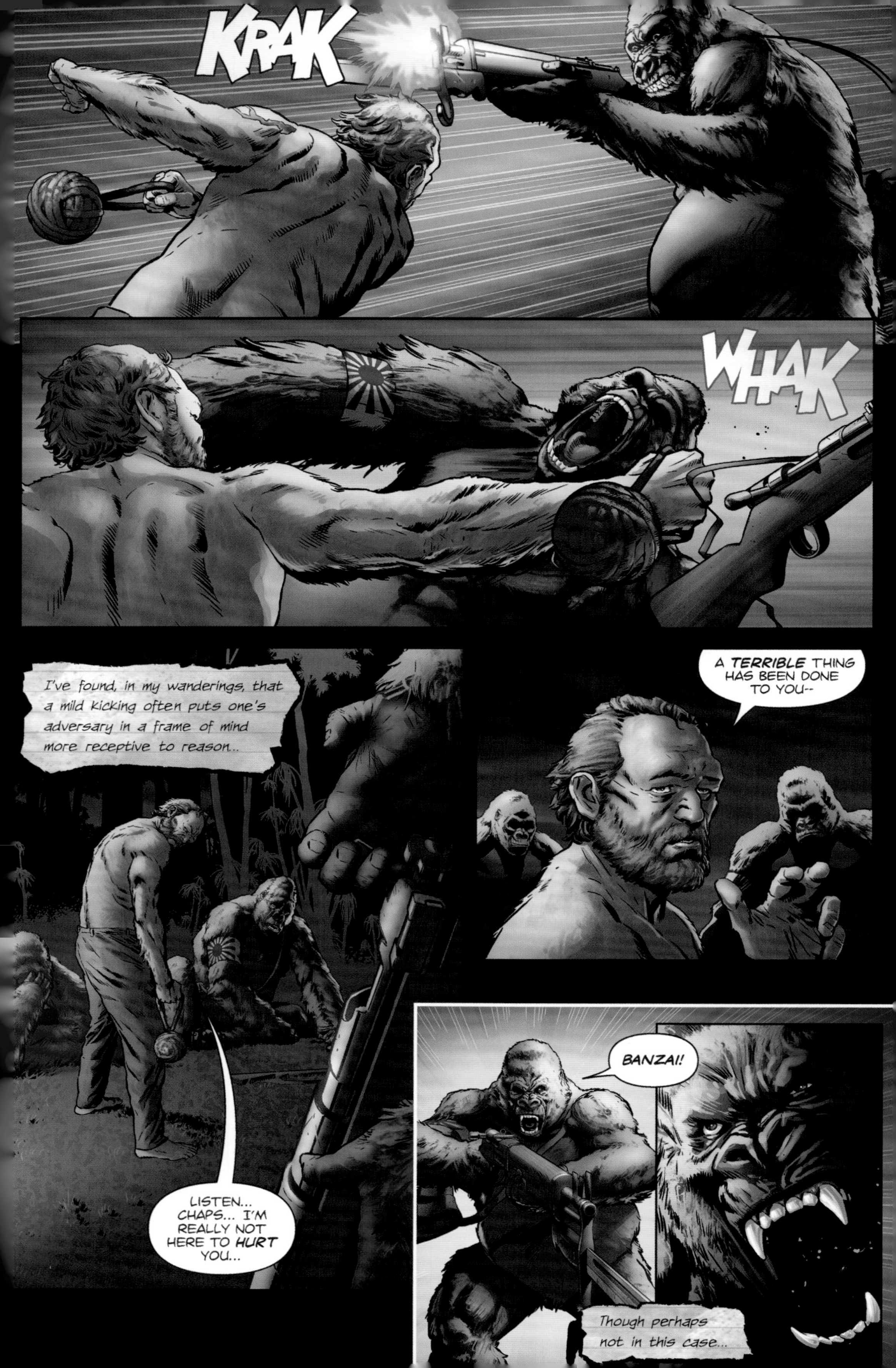
KRAK
WHAK
I've found, in my wanderings, that a mild kicking often puts one's adversary in a frame of mind more receptive to reason...
A TERRIBLE THING HAS BEEN DONE TO YOU--
LISTEN... CHAPS... I'M REALLY NOT HERE TO HURT YOU...
BANZAI!
Though perhaps not in this case...

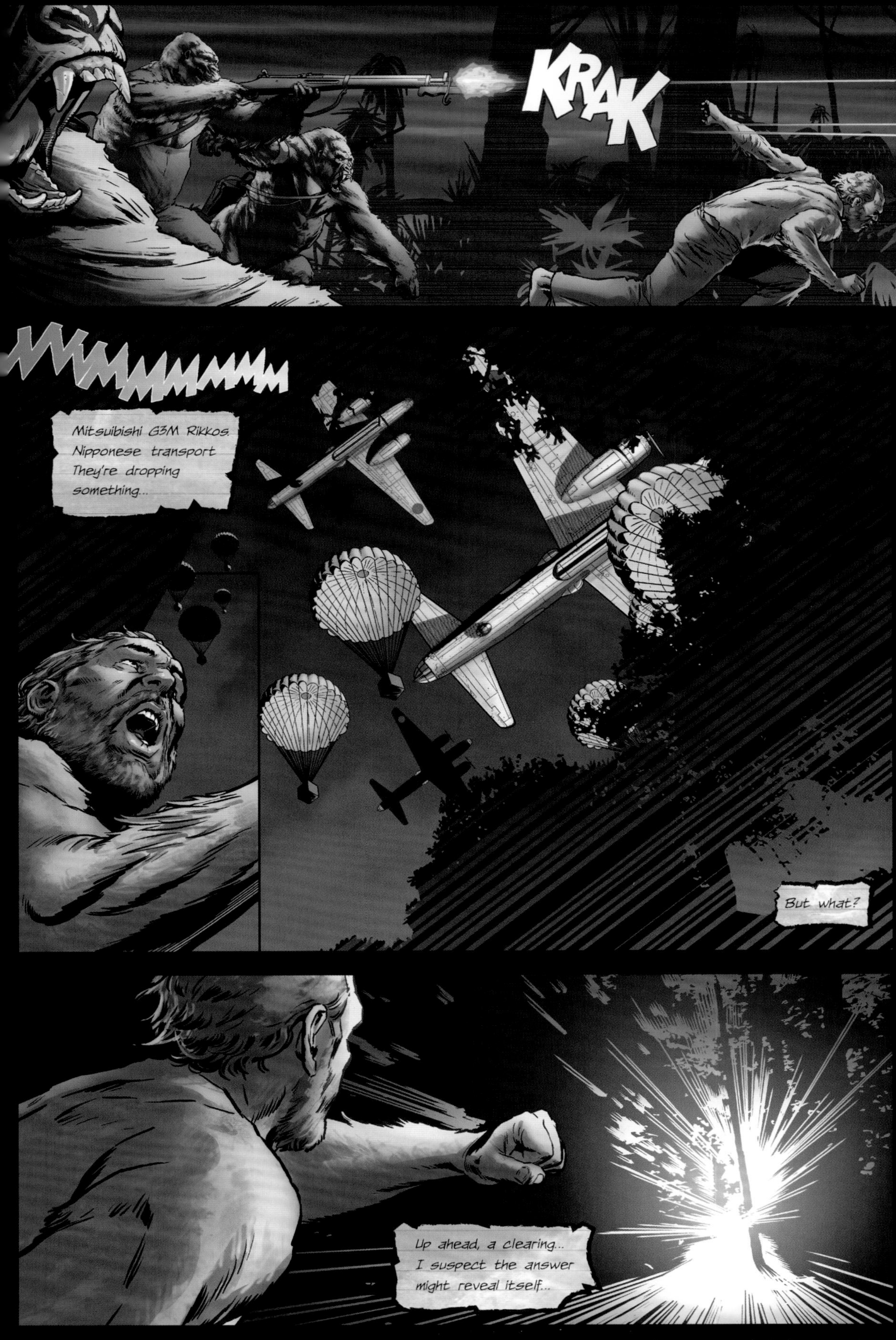
KRAK
WMMMMMMMMM
Mitsuibishi G3M Rikkos. Nipponese transport They're dropping something...
But what?
Up ahead, a clearing... I suspect the answer might reveal itself...

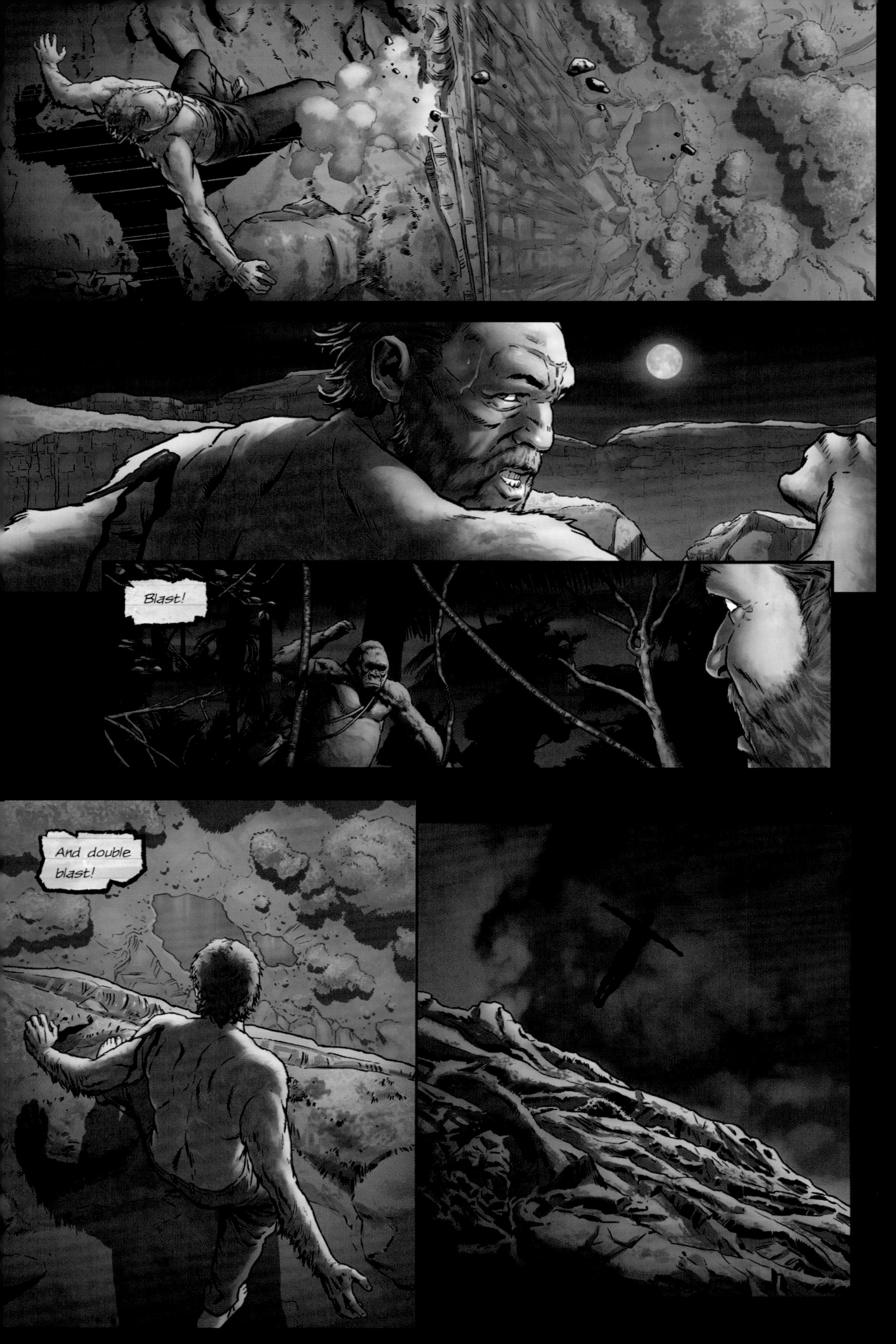
Blast!
And double blast!

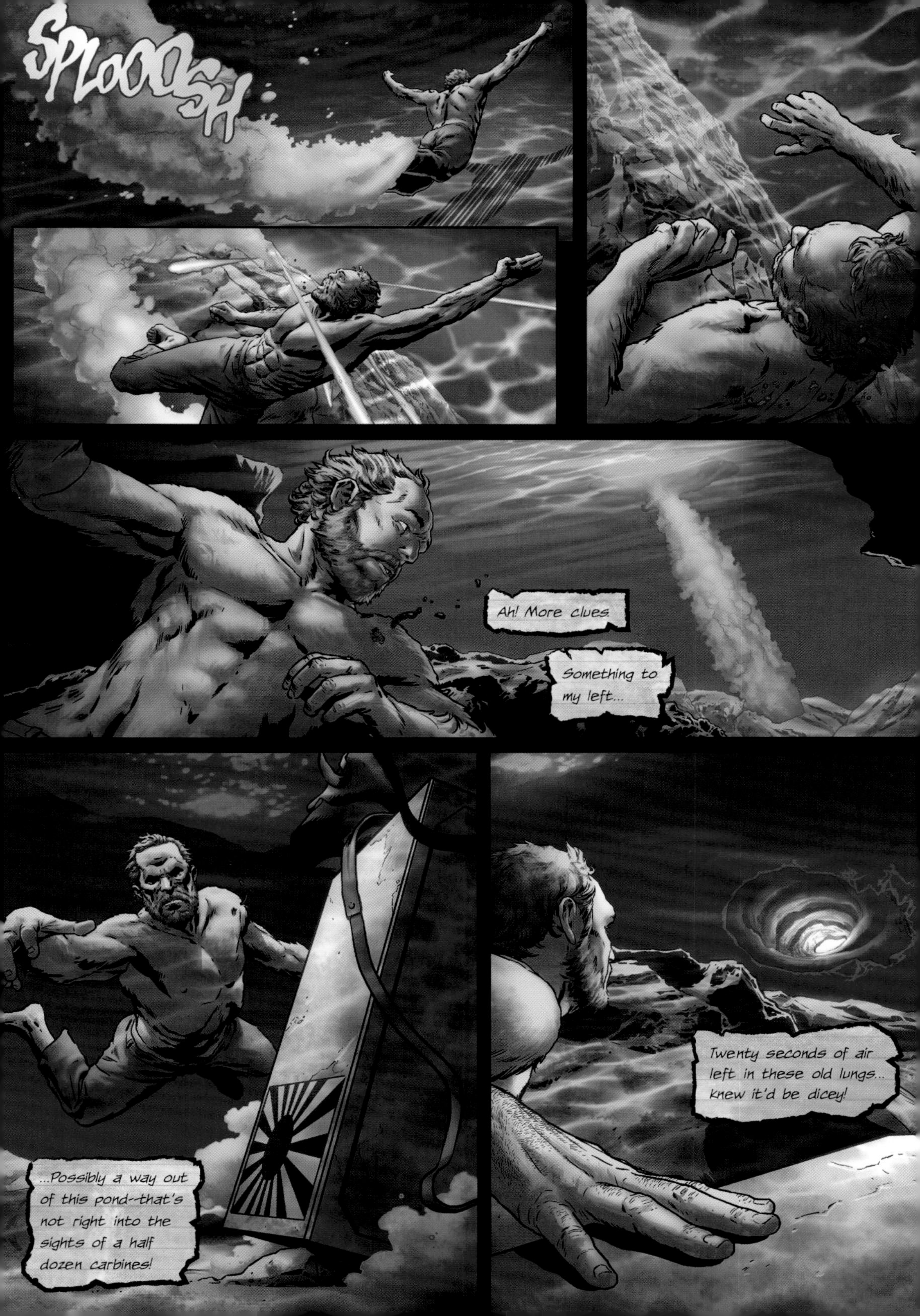
SPLOOOSH
Ah! More clues.
Something to my left...
...Possibly a way out of this pond--that's not right into the sights of a half dozen carbines!
Twenty seconds of air left in these old lungs... knew it'd be dicey!

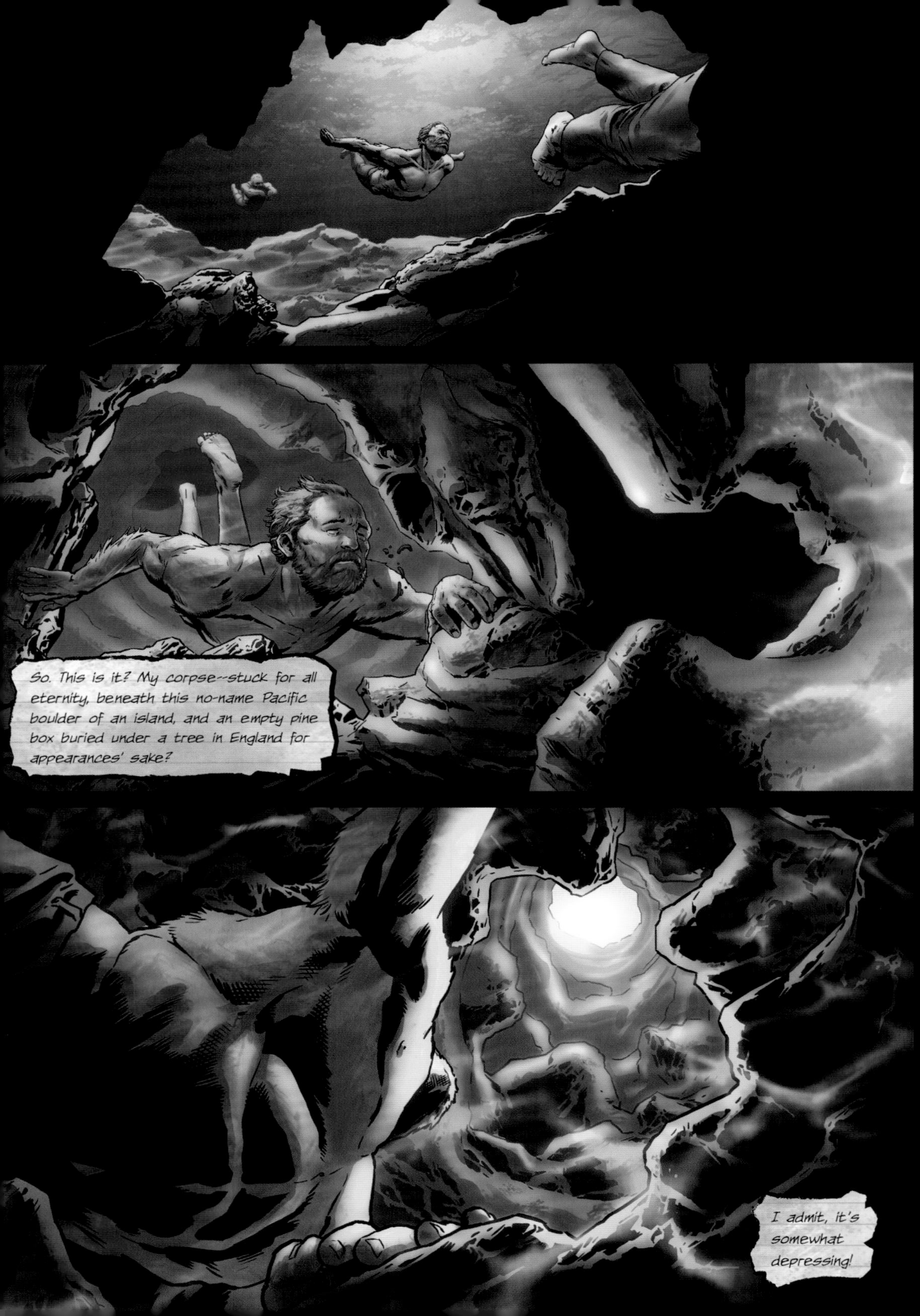
So. This is it? My corpse--stuck for all eternity, beneath this no-name Pacific boulder of an island, and an empty pine box buried under a tree in England for appearances' sake?
I admit, it's somewhat depressing!

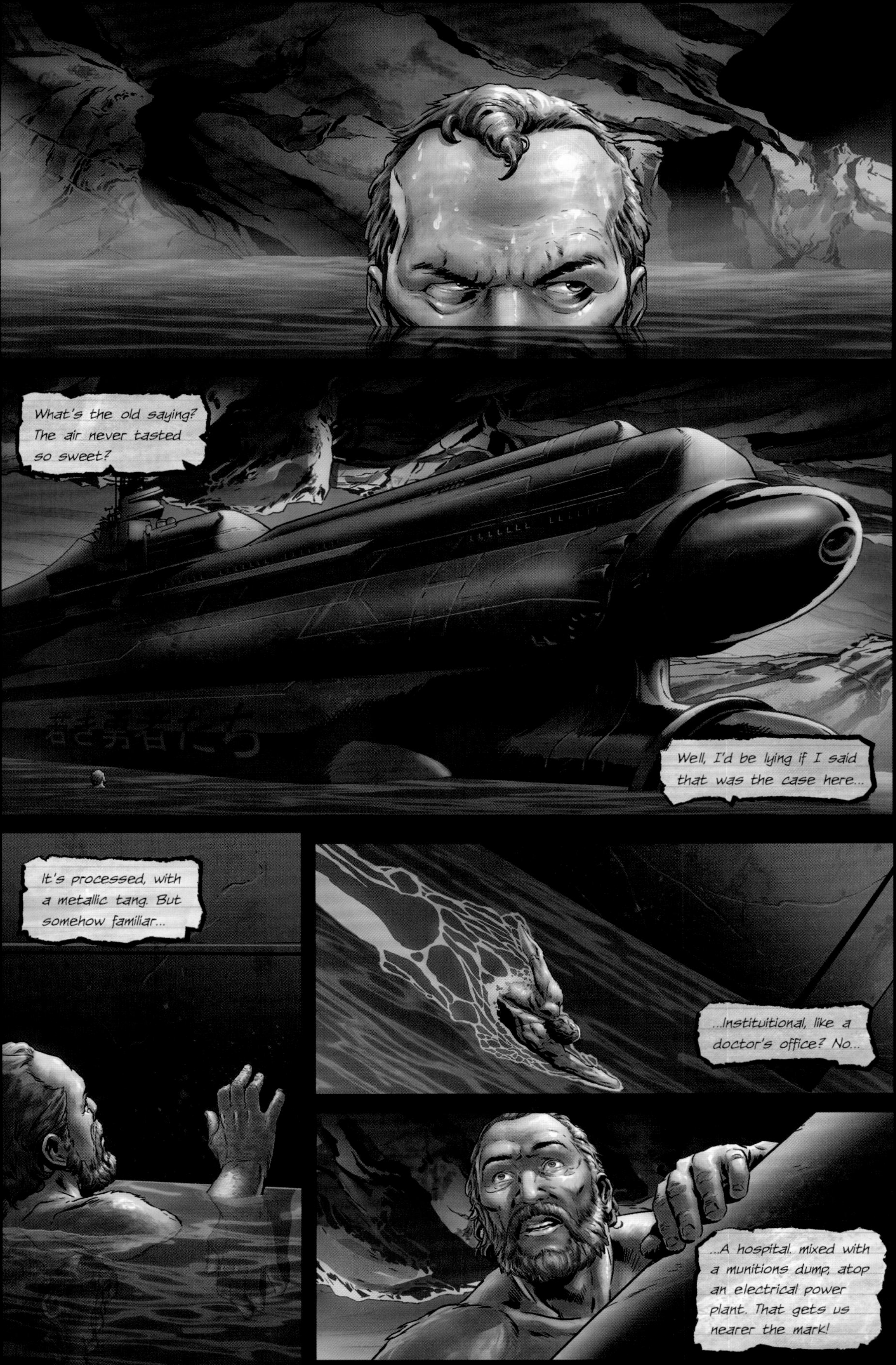
What's the old saying? The air never tasted so sweet?
Well, I'd be lying if I said that was the case here...
It's processed, with a metallic tang. But somehow familiar...
...Instituitional, like a doctor's office? No...
...A hospital, mixed with a munitions dump, atop an electrical power plant. That gets us nearer the mark!

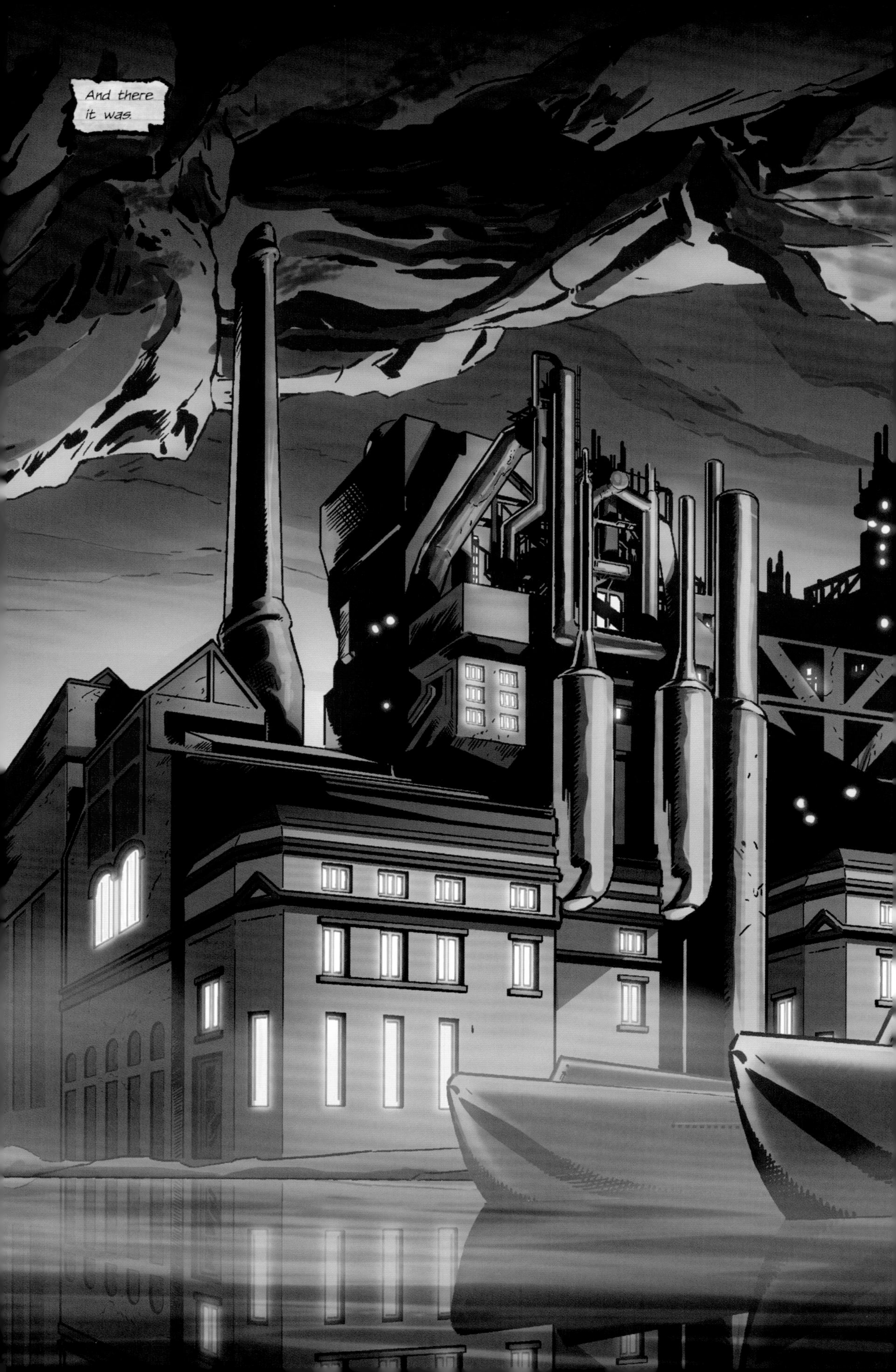
And there it was.

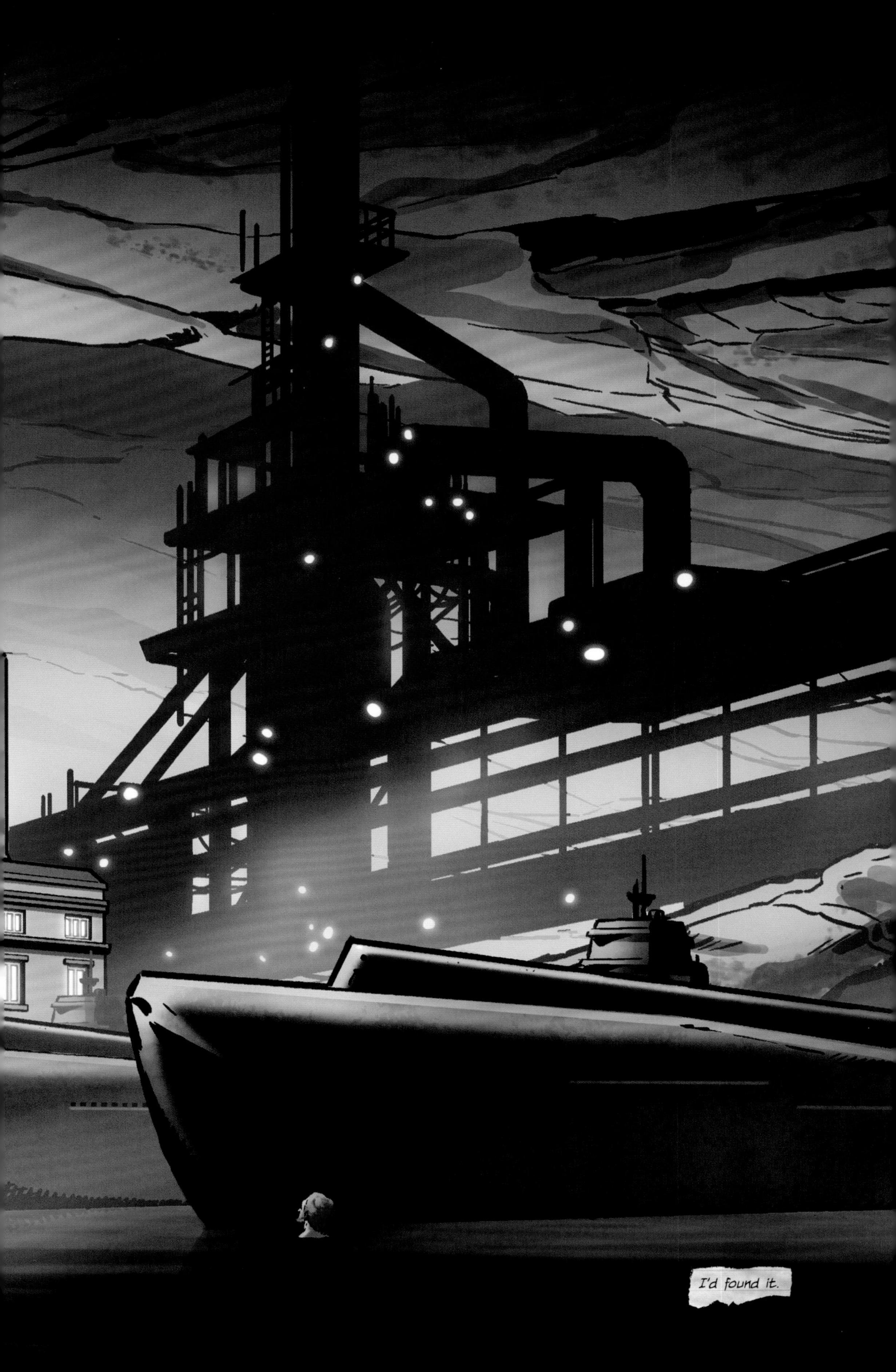
I'd found it.

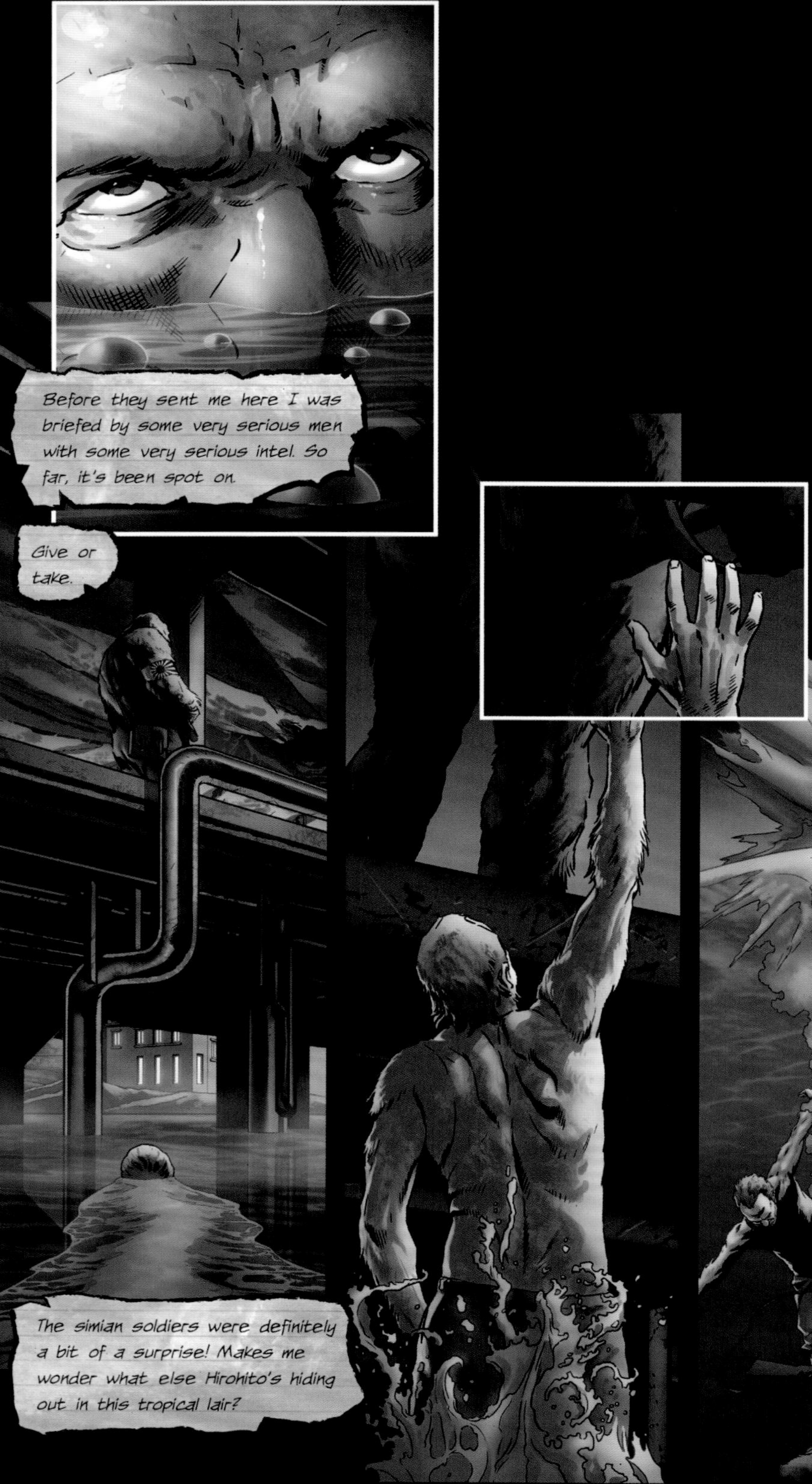
Before they sent me here I was briefed by some very serious men with some very serious intel. So far, it's been spot on.
Give or take.
The simian soldiers were definitely a bit of a surprise! Makes me wonder what else Hirohito's hiding out in this tropical lair?

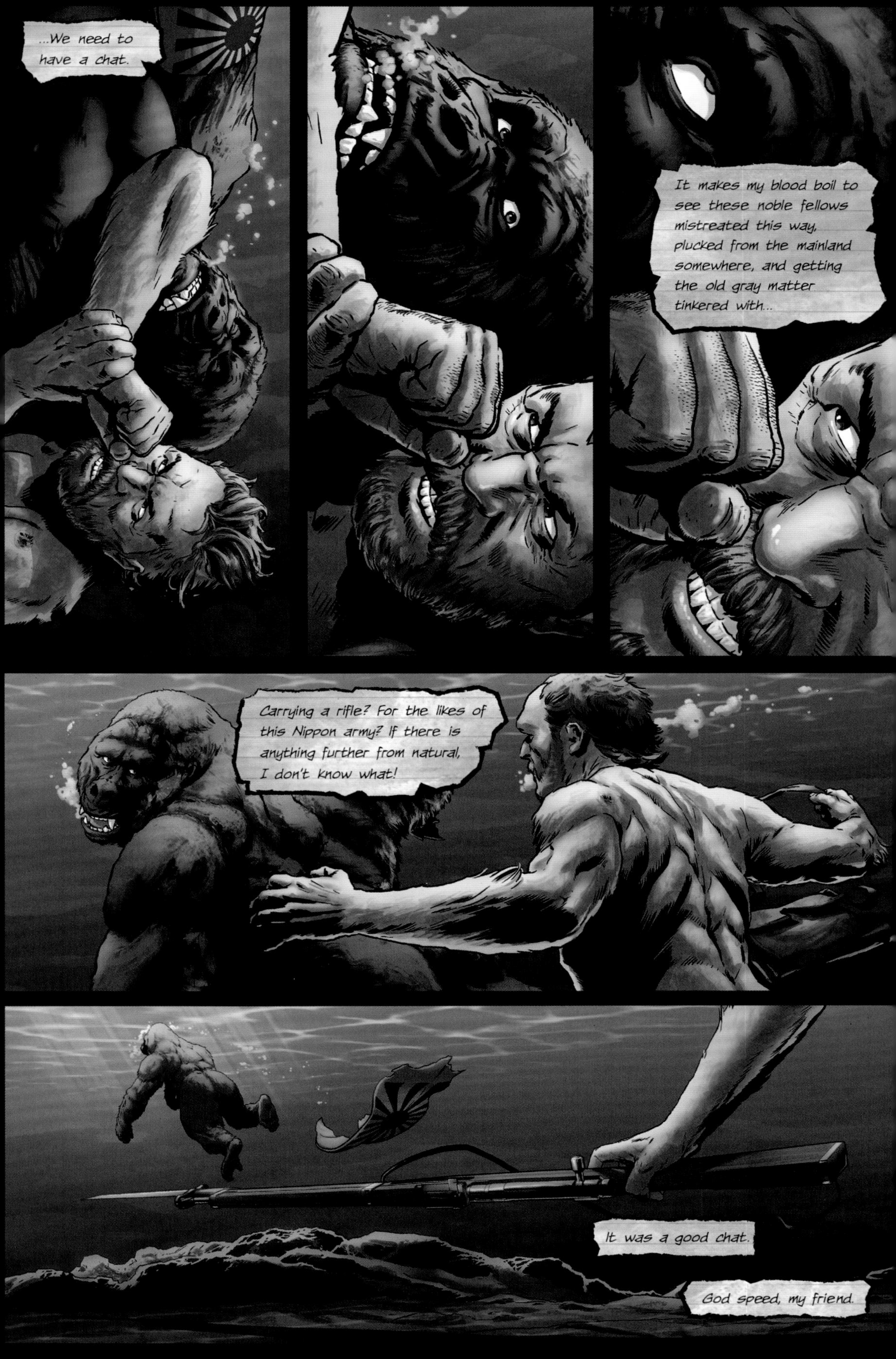

...We need to have a chat.
It makes my blood boil to see these noble fellows mistreated this way, plucked from the mainland somewhere, and getting the old gray matter tinkered with...
Carrying a rifle? For the likes of this Nippon army? If there is anything further from natural, I don't know what!
It was a good chat.
God speed, my friend.

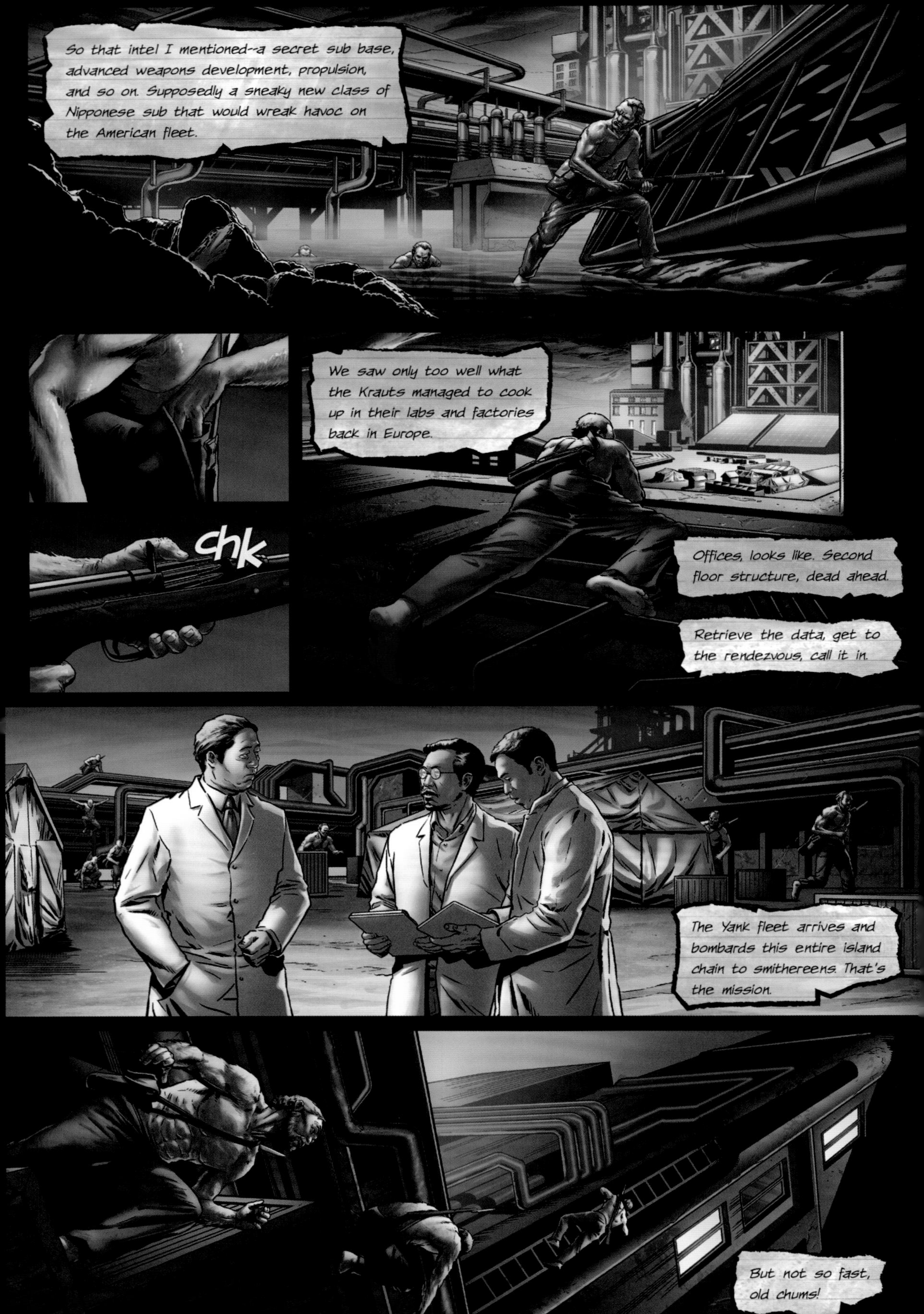
So that intel I mentioned--a secret sub base, advanced weapons development, propulsion, and so on. Supposedly a sneaky new class of Nipponese sub that would wreak havoc on the American fleet.
We saw only too well what the Krauts managed to cook up in their labs and factories back in Europe.
CHK
Offices, looks like. Second floor structure, dead ahead.
Retrieve the data, get to the rendezvous, call it in.
The Yank fleet arrives and bombards this entire island chain to smithereens. That's the mission.
But not so fast, old chums!

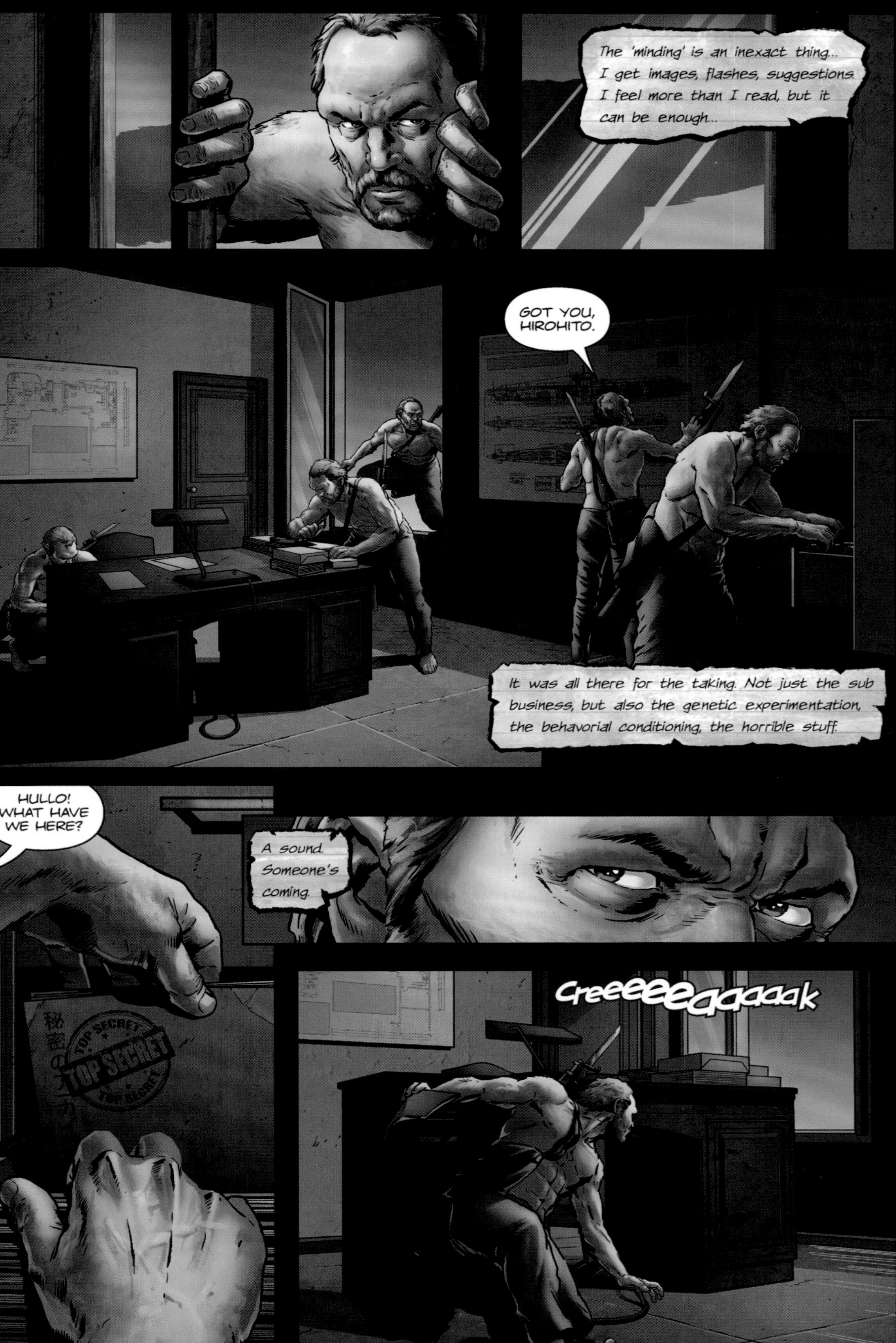
The 'minding' is an inexact thing... I get images, flashes, suggestions. I feel more than I read, but it can be enough...
GOT YOU, HIROHITO.
It was all there for the taking. Not just the sub business, but also the genetic experimentation, the behavorial conditioning, the horrible stuff.
HULLO! WHAT HAVE WE HERE?
TOP SECRET
A sound. Someone's coming.
Creeeeeeaaaaak

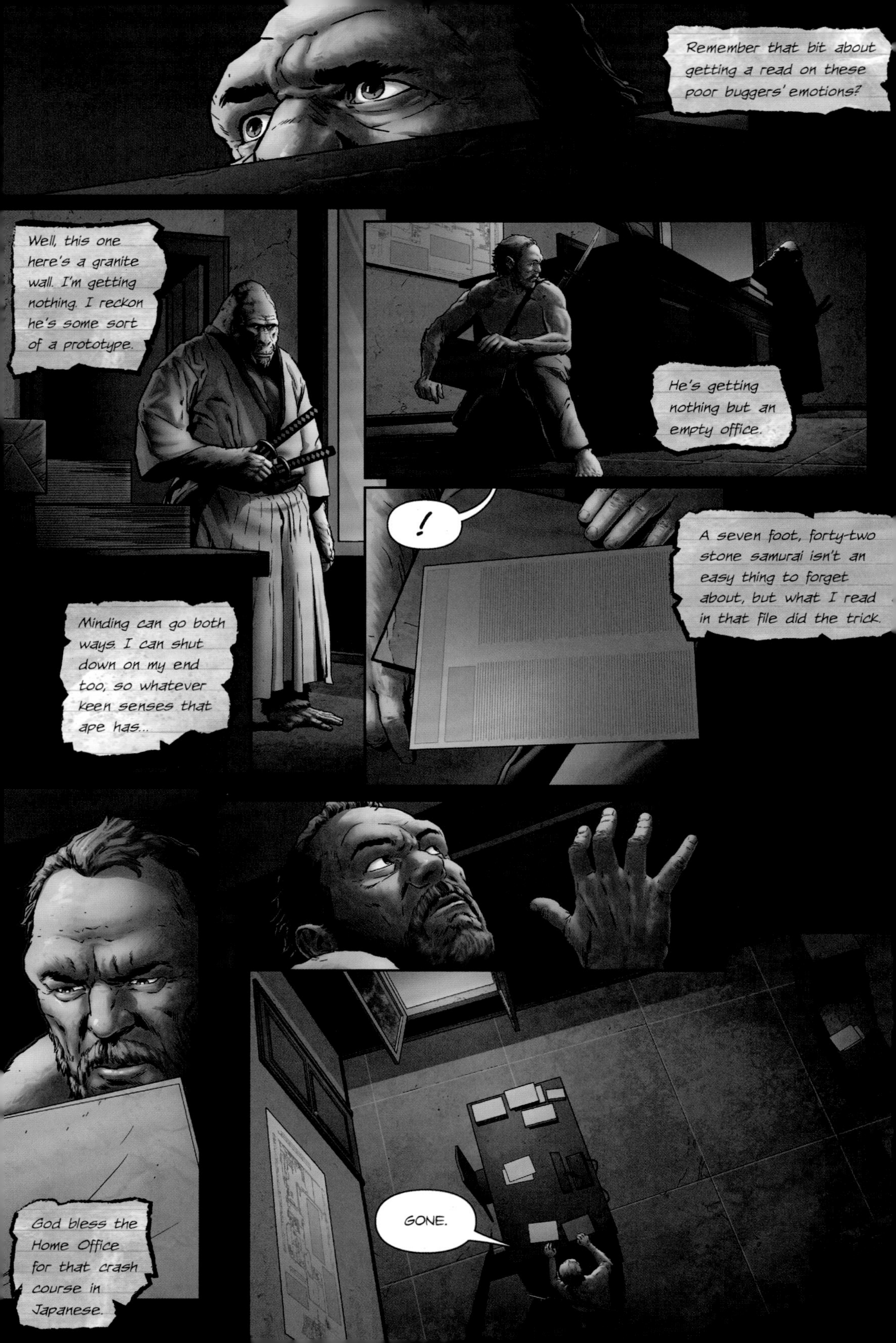
Remember that bit about getting a read on these poor buggers' emotions?
Well, this one here's a granite wall. I'm getting nothing. I reckon he's some sort of a prototype.
He's getting nothing but an empty office.
Minding can go both ways. I can shut down on my end too, so whatever keen senses that ape has...
!
A seven foot, forty-two stone samurai isn't an easy thing to forget about, but what I read in that file did the trick.
God bless the Home Office for that crash course in Japanese.
GONE.

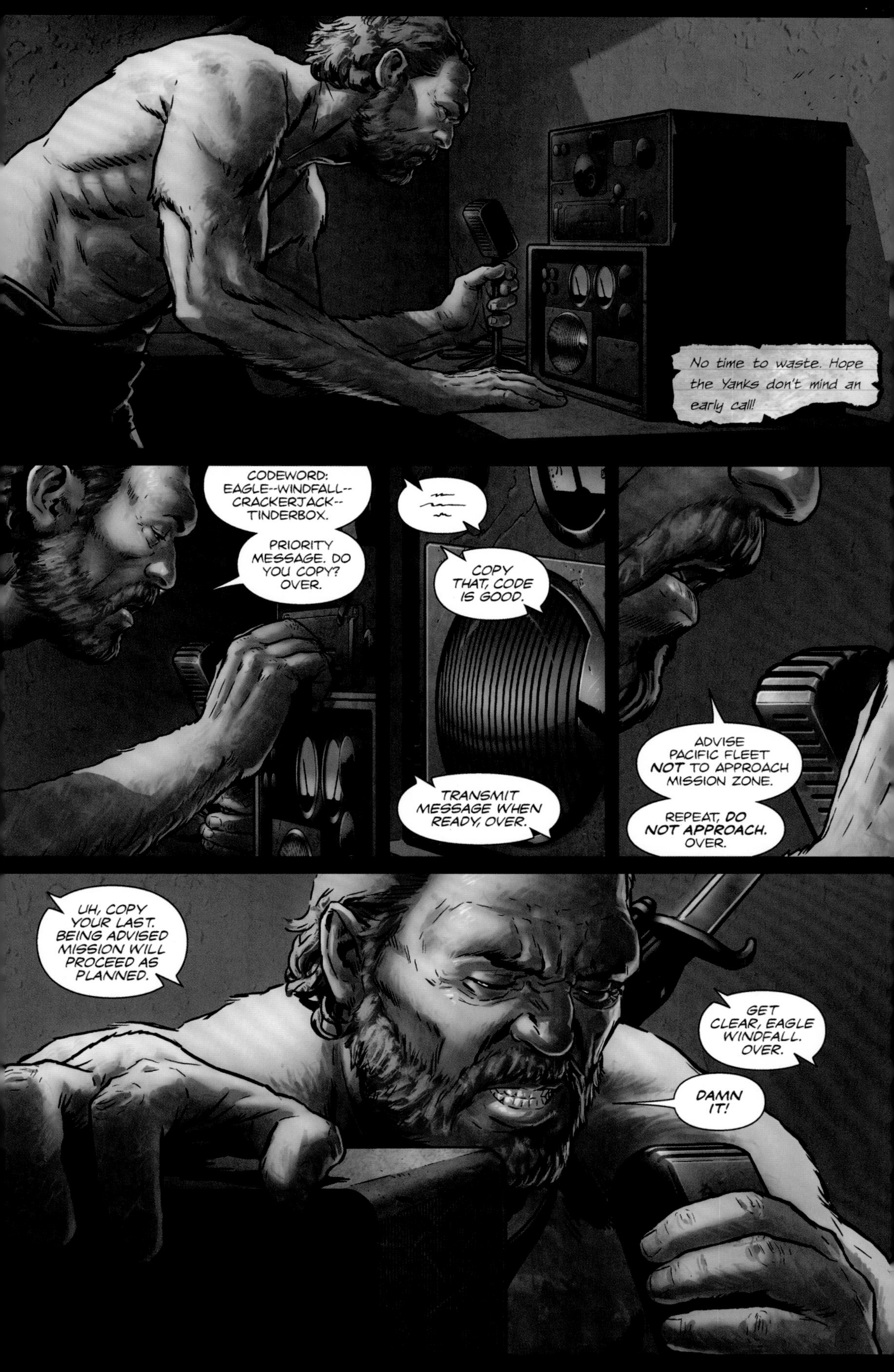
No time to waste. Hope the Yanks don't mind an early call!
CODEWORD: EAGLE--WINDFALL--CRACKERJACK--TINDERBOX.
PRIORITY MESSAGE. DO YOU COPY? OVER.
COPY THAT, CODE IS GOOD.
TRANSMIT MESSAGE WHEN READY, OVER.
ADVISE PACIFIC FLEET NOT TO APPROACH MISSION ZONE.
REPEAT, DO NOT APPROACH. OVER.
UH, COPY YOUR LAST. BEING ADVISED MISSION WILL PROCEED AS PLANNED.
GET CLEAR, EAGLE WINDFALL. OVER.
DAMN IT!

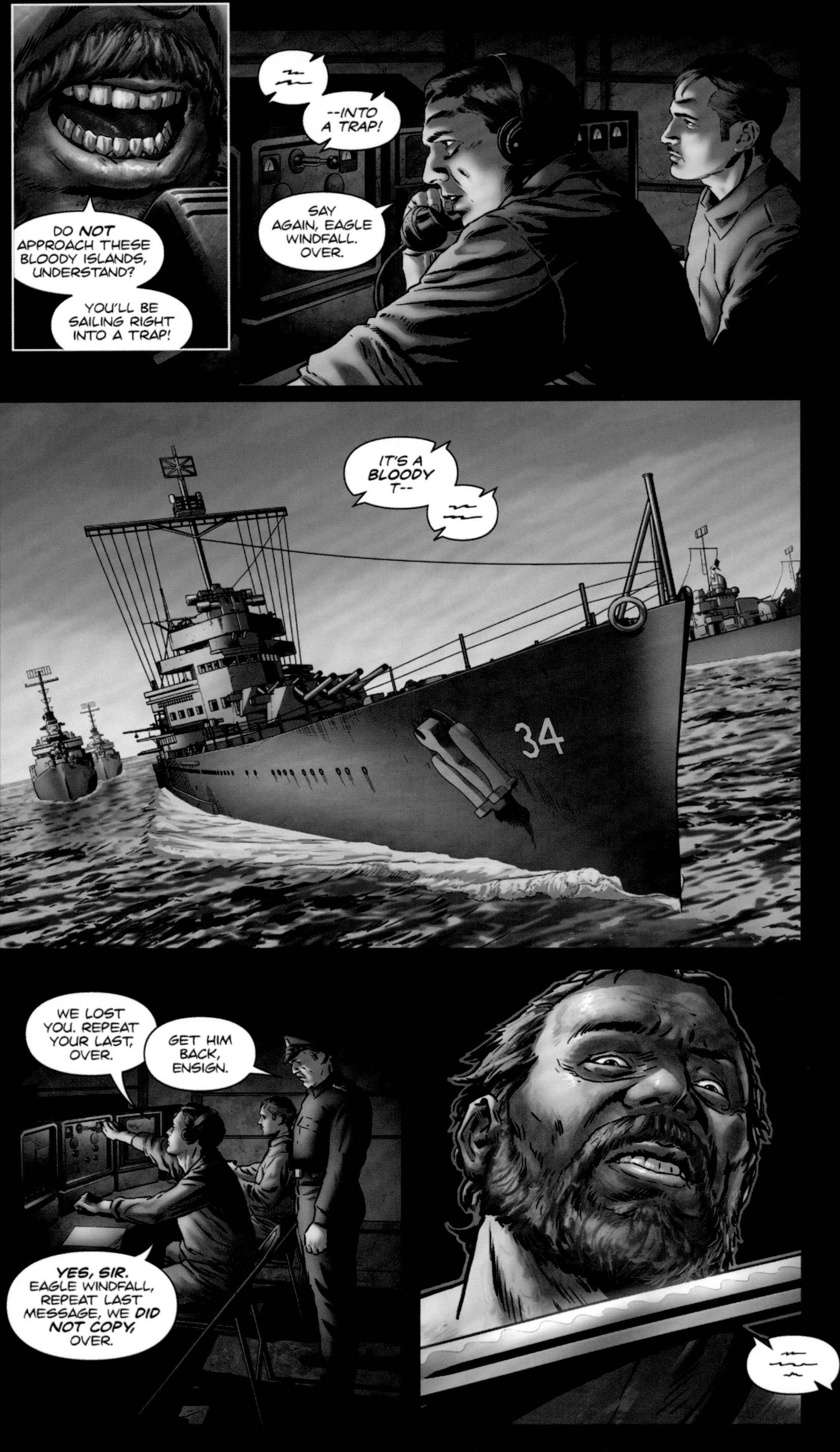
DO NOT APPROACH THESE BLOODY ISLANDS, UNDERSTAND?
YOU'LL BE SAILING RIGHT INTO A TRAP!
--INTO A TRAP!
SAY AGAIN, EAGLE WINDFALL. OVER.
IT'S A BLOODY T--
WE LOST YOU. REPEAT YOUR LAST, OVER.
GET HIM BACK, ENSIGN.
YES, SIR. EAGLE WINDFALL, REPEAT LAST MESSAGE, WE DID NOT COPY, OVER.

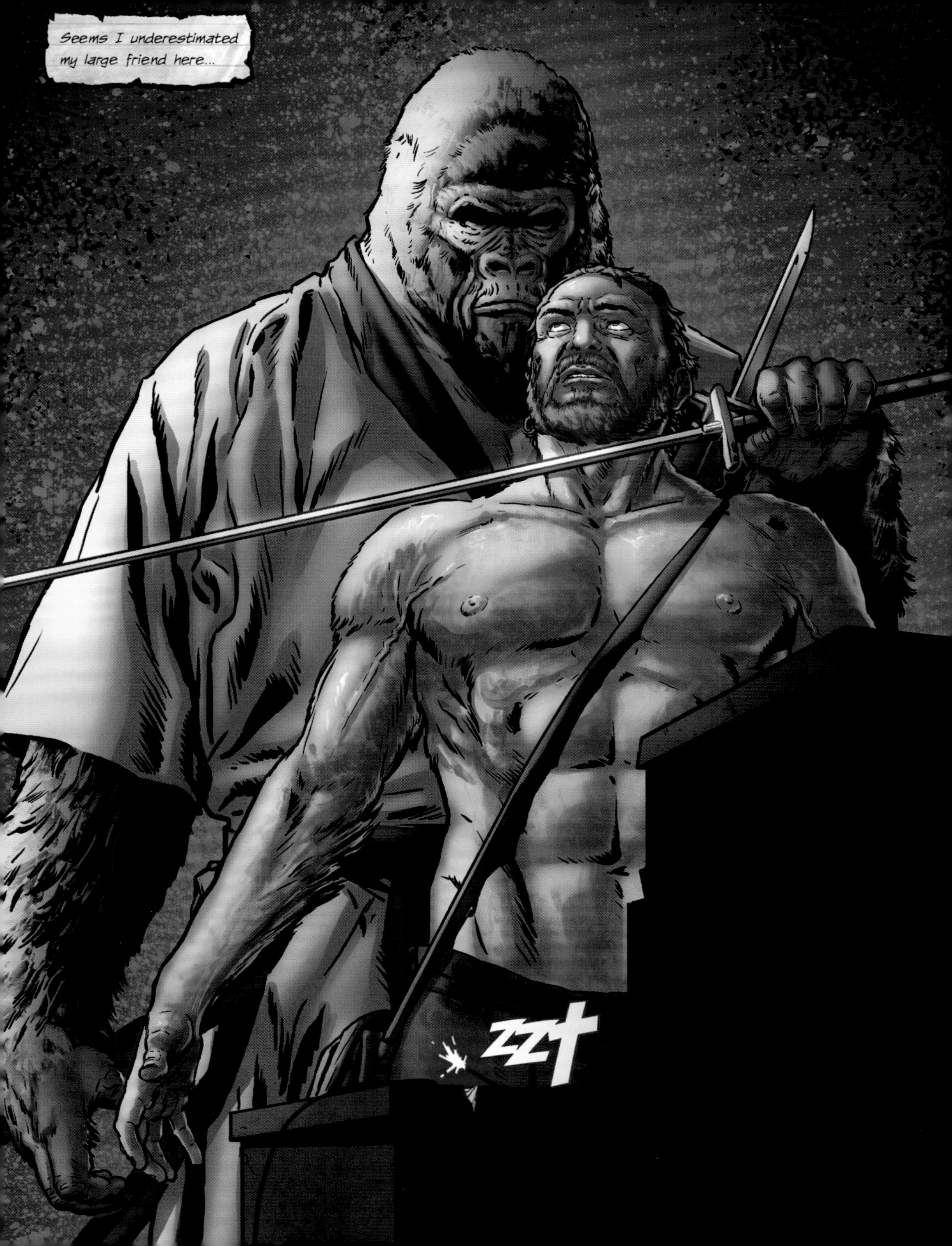
Seems I underestimated my large friend here...
ZZT

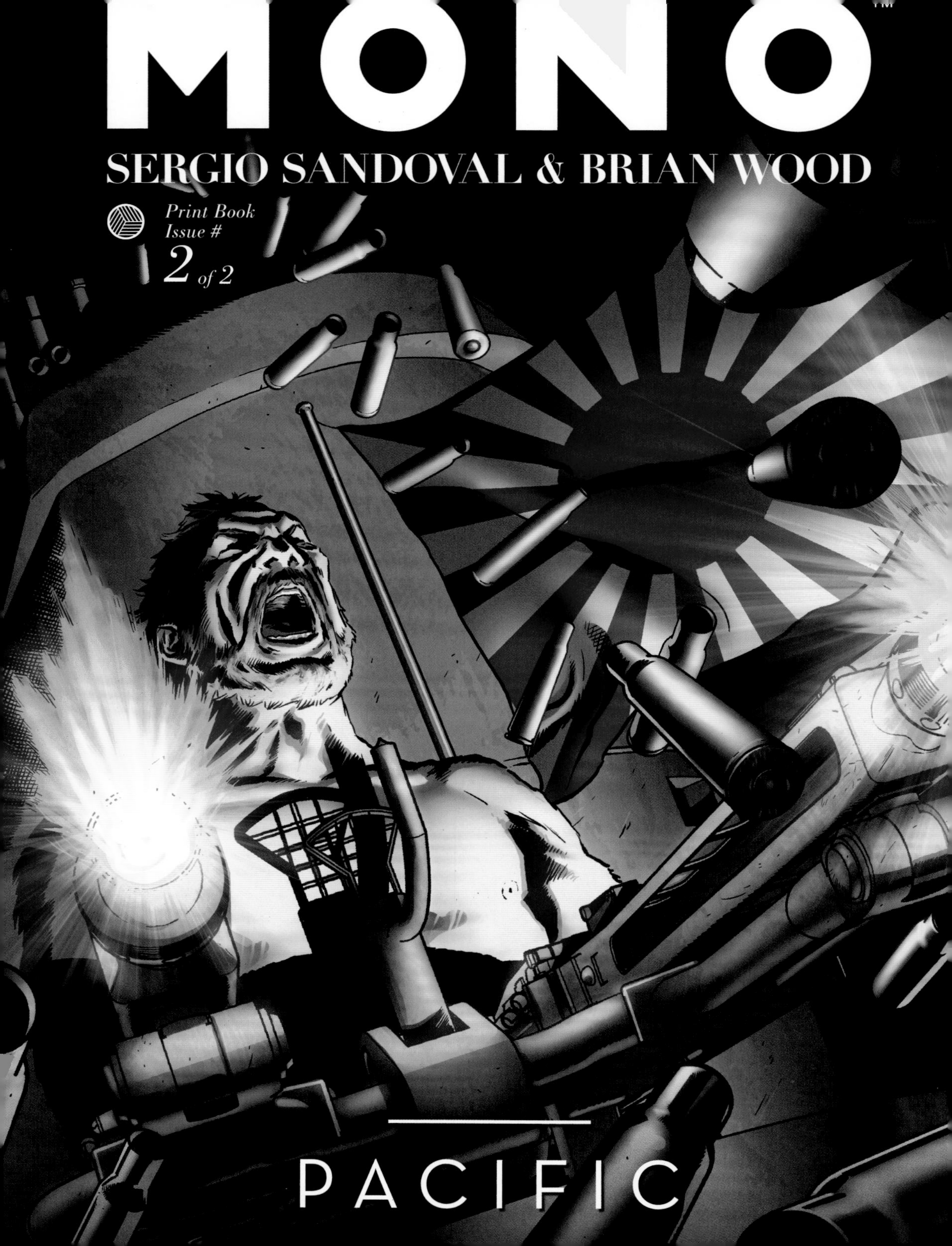
MONO™
SERGIO SANDOVAL & BRIAN WOOD
Print Book
Issue #
2 of 2
PACIFIC

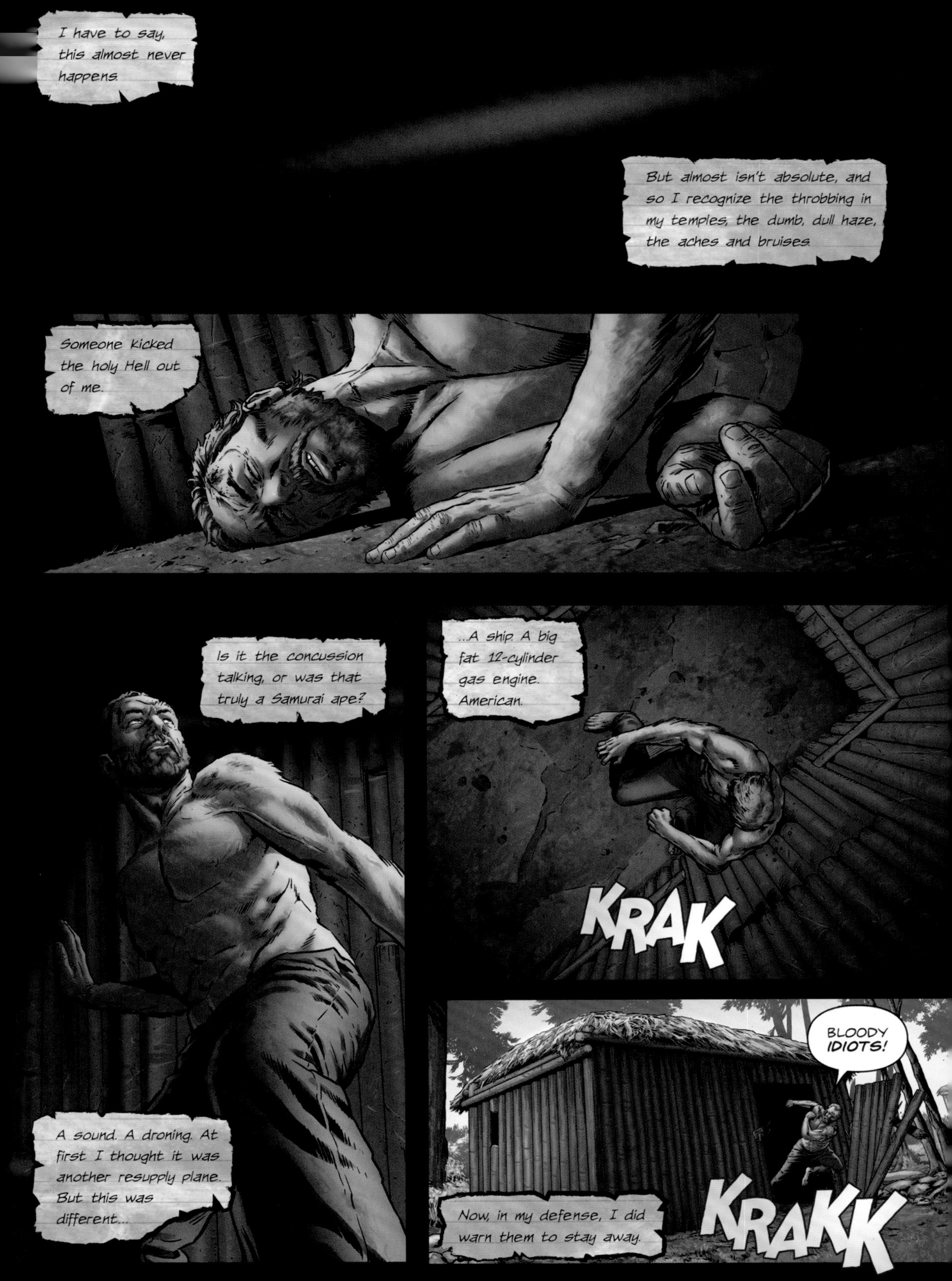
I have to say, this almost never happens.
But almost isn't absolute, and so I recognize the throbbing in my temples, the dumb, dull haze, the aches and bruises.
Someone kicked the holy Hell out of me.
Is it the concussion talking, or was that truly a Samurai ape?
A sound. A droning. At first I thought it was another resupply plane. But this was different...
...A ship. A big fat 12-cylinder gas engine. American.
KRAK
BLOODY IDIOTS!
Now, in my defense, I did warn them to stay away.
KRAKK

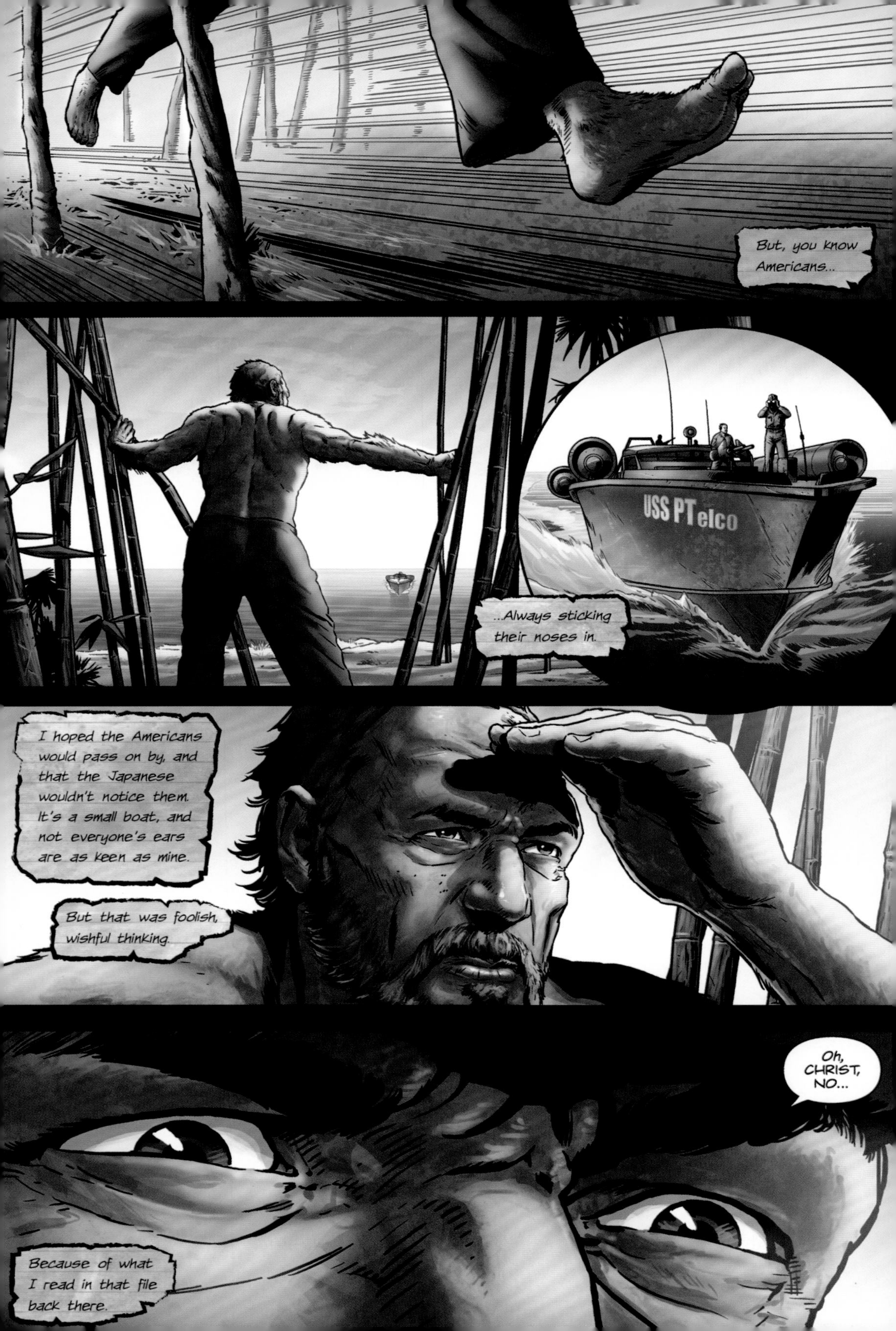
But, you know Americans...
USS PTelco
...Always sticking their noses in.
I hoped the Americans would pass on by, and that the Japanese wouldn't notice them. It's a small boat, and not everyone's ears are as keen as mine.
But that was foolish, wishful thinking.
Oh, CHRIST, NO...
Because of what I read in that file back there.

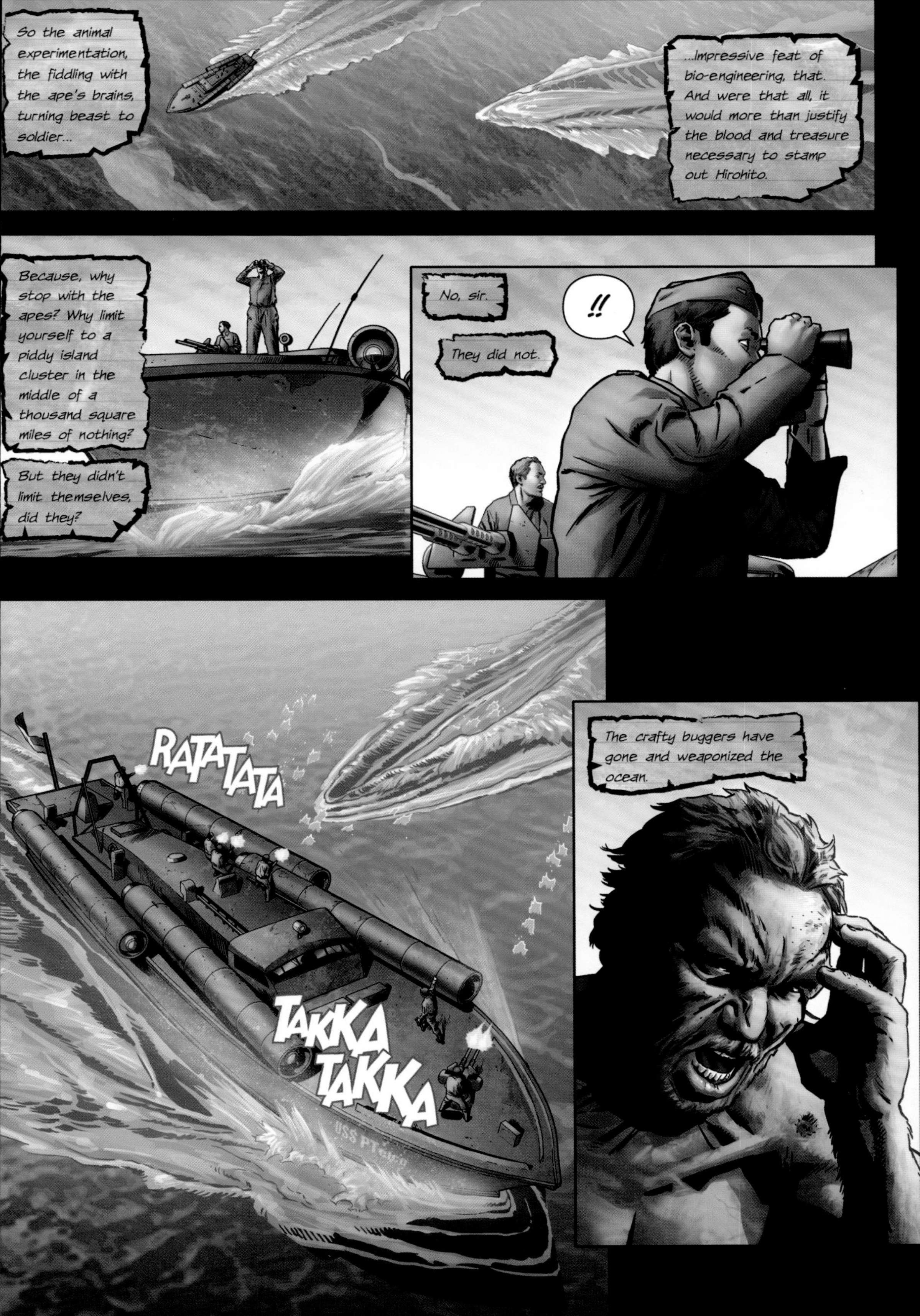
So the animal experimentation, the fiddling with the ape's brains, turning beast to soldier...
...Impressive feat of bio-engineering, that. And were that all, it would more than justify the blood and treasure necessary to stamp out Hirohito.
Because, why stop with the apes? Why limit yourself to a piddy island cluster in the middle of a thousand square miles of nothing?
But they didn't limit themselves, did they?
No, sir.
They did not.
!!
RATATATA
TAKKA TAKKA
The crafty buggers have gone and weaponized the ocean.

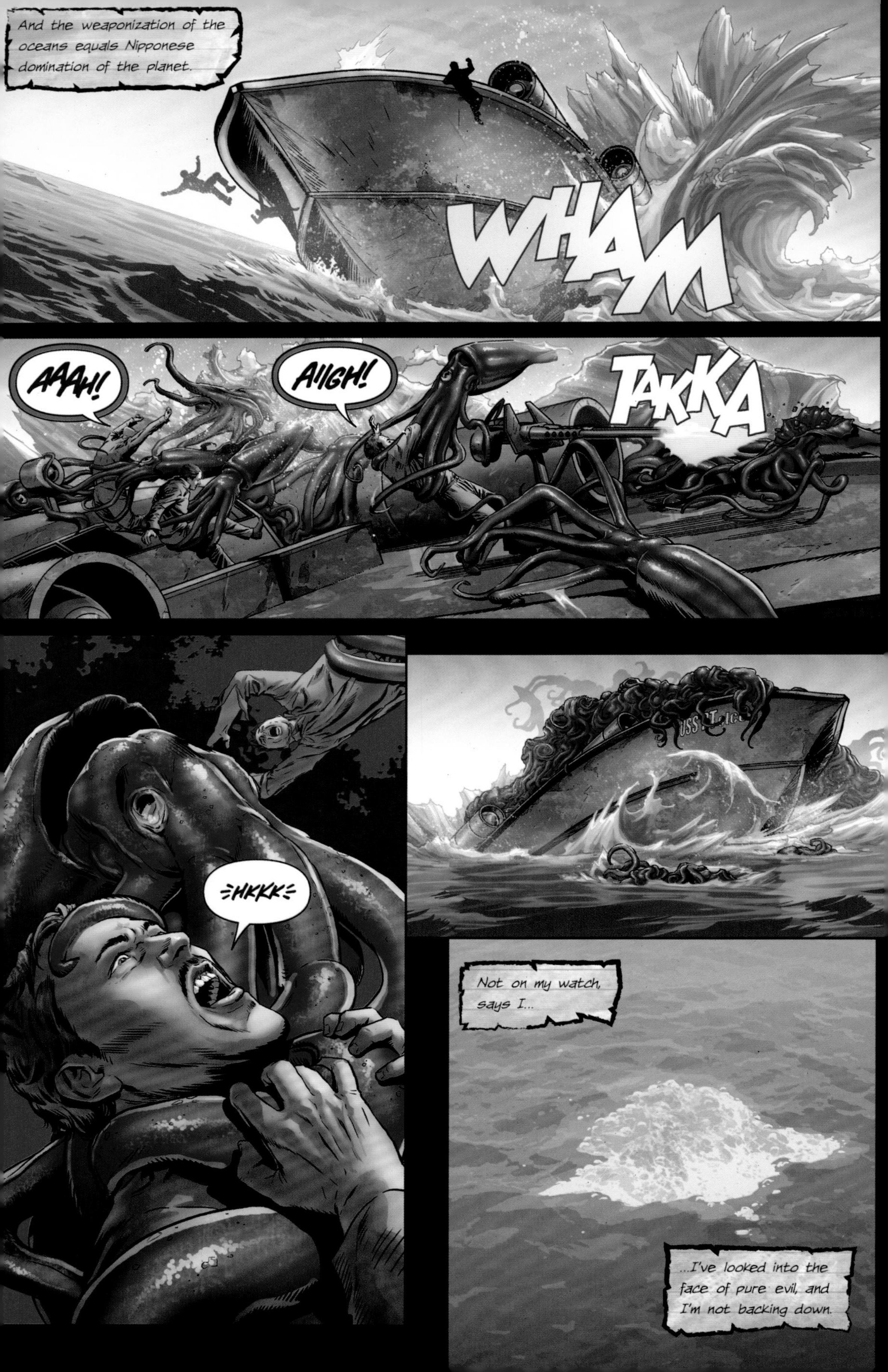

And the weaponization of the oceans equals Nipponese domination of the planet.
WHAM
AAAH!
AIIGH!
TAKKA
HKKK
Not on my watch, says I…
…I've looked into the face of pure evil, and I'm not backing down.

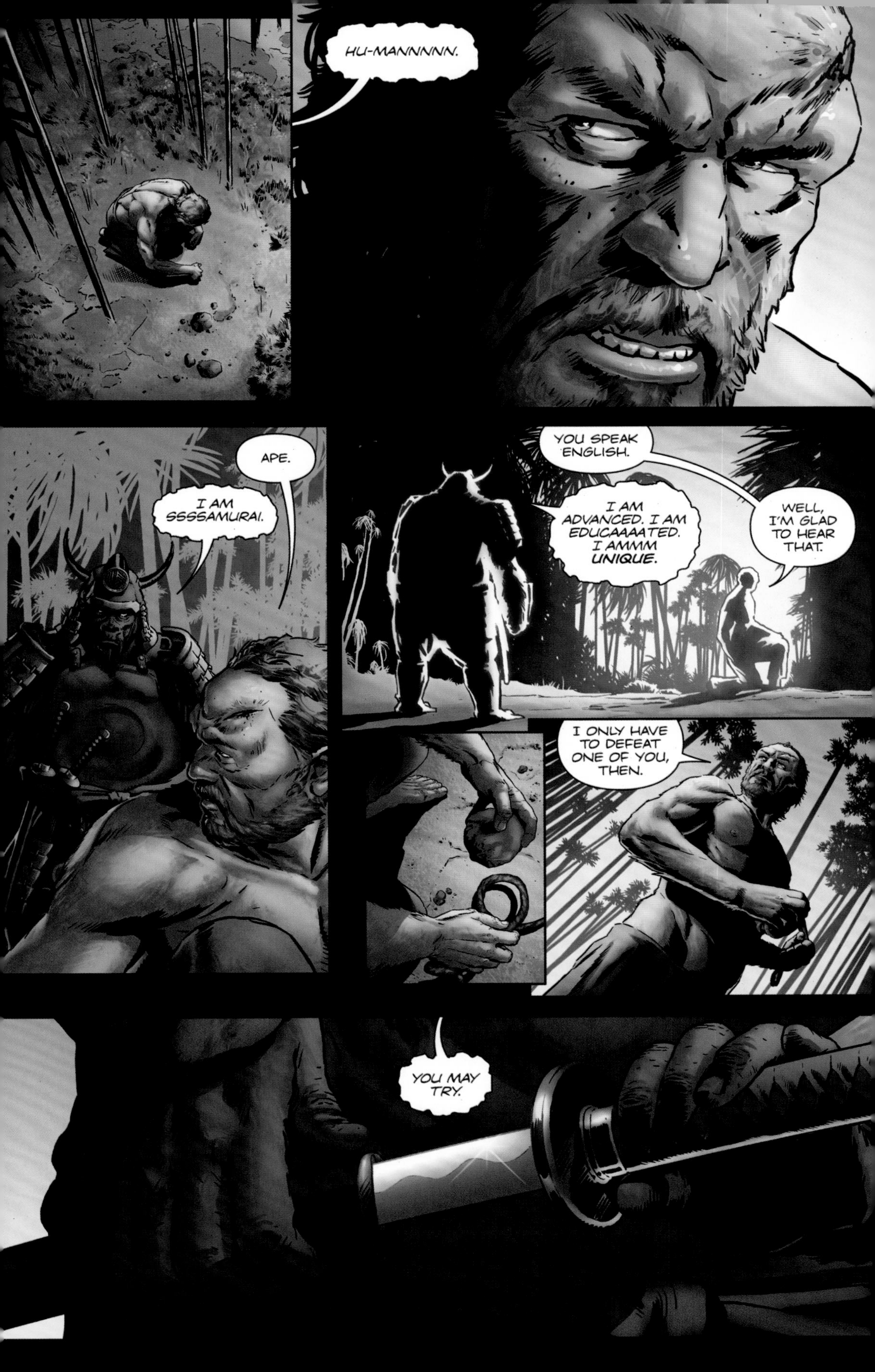
HU-MANNNNN.
APE.
I AM SSSSAMURAI.
YOU SPEAK ENGLISH.
I AM ADVANCED. I AM EDUCAAAATED. I AMMM **UNIQUE.**
WELL, I'M GLAD TO HEAR THAT.
I ONLY HAVE TO DEFEAT ONE OF YOU, THEN.
YOU MAY TRY.

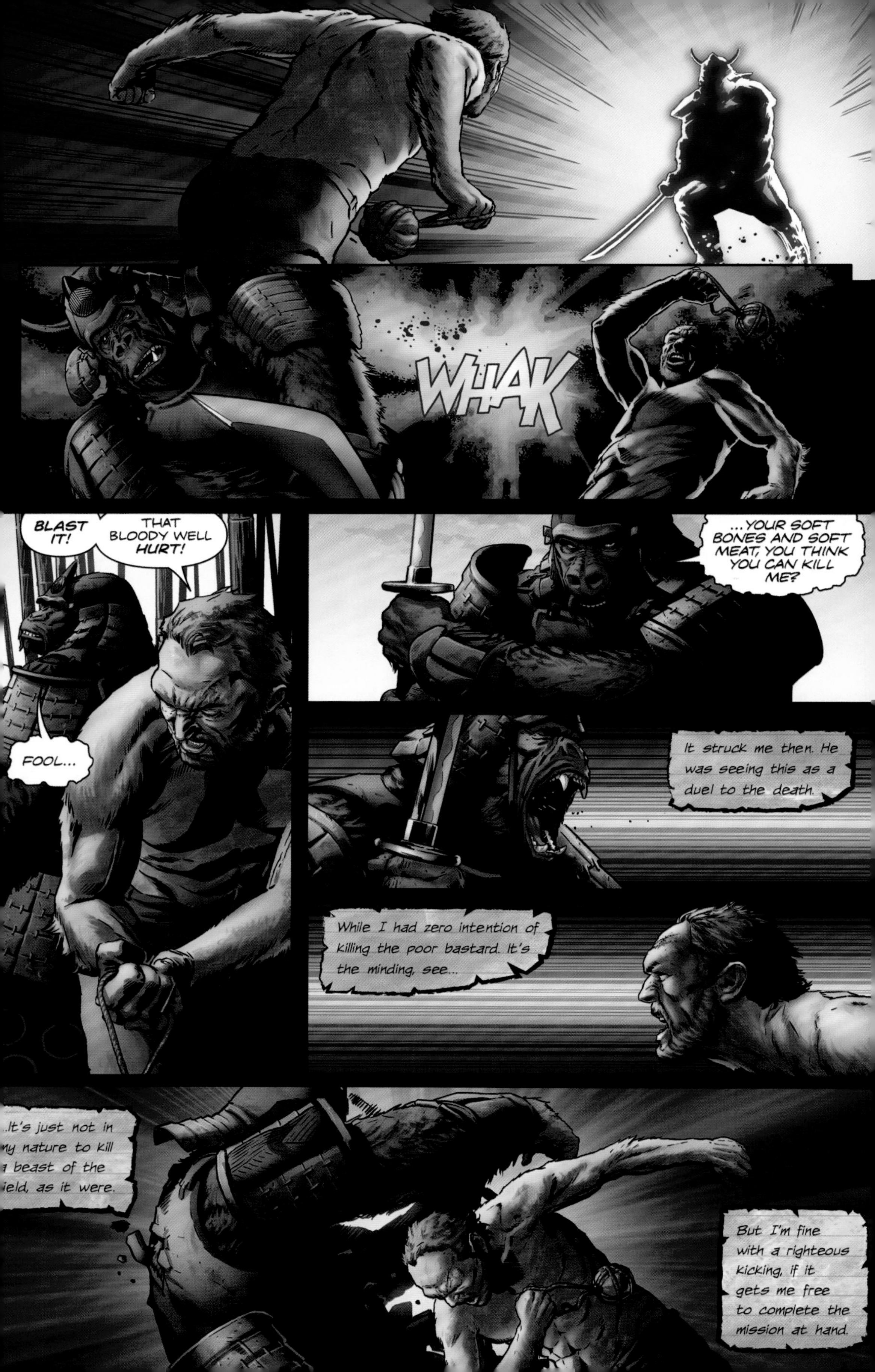

WHAK
BLAST IT!
THAT BLOODY WELL HURT!
FOOL...
...YOUR SOFT BONES AND SOFT MEAT, YOU THINK YOU CAN KILL ME?
It struck me then. He was seeing this as a duel to the death.
While I had zero intention of killing the poor bastard. It's the minding, see...
.It's just not in
my nature to kill
a beast of the
ield, as it were.
But I'm fine with a righteous kicking, if it gets me free to complete the mission at hand.

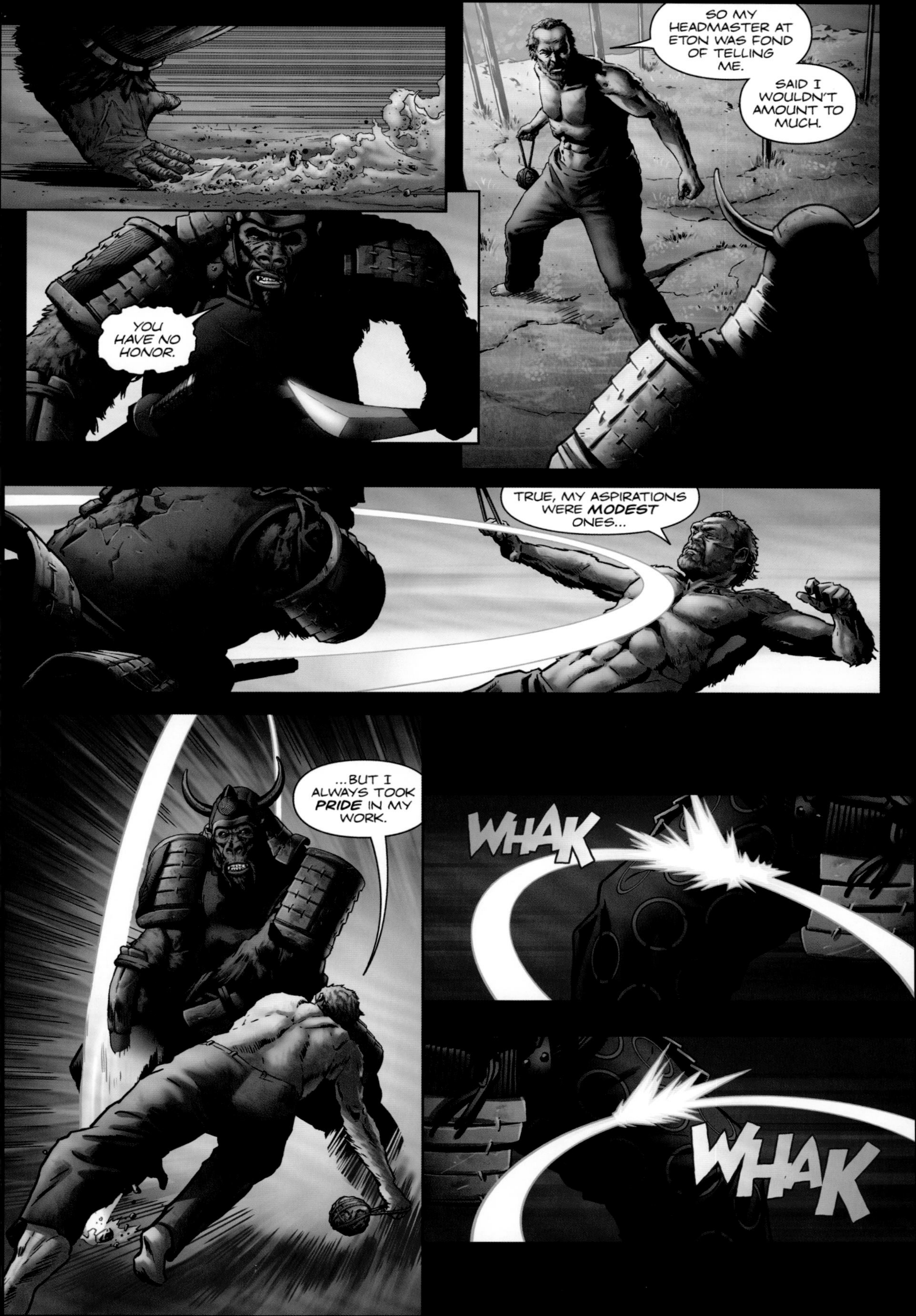
SO MY HEADMASTER AT ETON WAS FOND OF TELLING ME.
SAID I WOULDN'T AMOUNT TO MUCH.
YOU HAVE NO HONOR.
TRUE, MY ASPIRATIONS WERE MODEST ONES...
...BUT I ALWAYS TOOK PRIDE IN MY WORK.
WHAK
WHAK

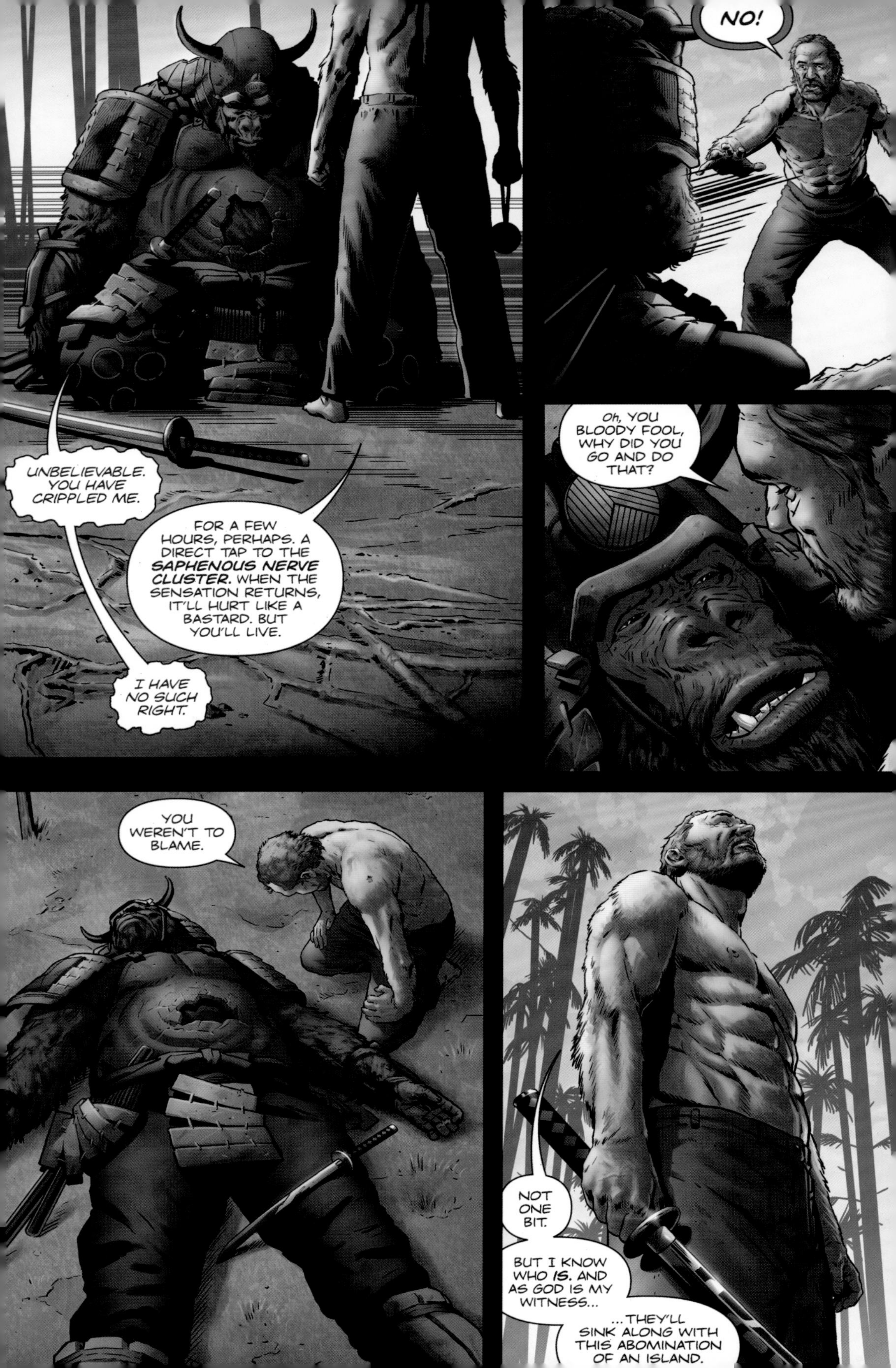
NO!
UNBELIEVABLE. YOU HAVE CRIPPLED ME.
FOR A FEW HOURS, PERHAPS. A DIRECT TAP TO THE SAPHENOUS NERVE CLUSTER. WHEN THE SENSATION RETURNS, IT'LL HURT LIKE A BASTARD. BUT YOU'LL LIVE.
I HAVE NO SUCH RIGHT.
Oh, YOU BLOODY FOOL, WHY DID YOU GO AND DO THAT?
YOU WEREN'T TO BLAME.
NOT ONE BIT.
BUT I KNOW WHO IS. AND AS GOD IS MY WITNESS...
...THEY'LL SINK ALONG WITH THIS ABOMINATION OF AN ISLAND.

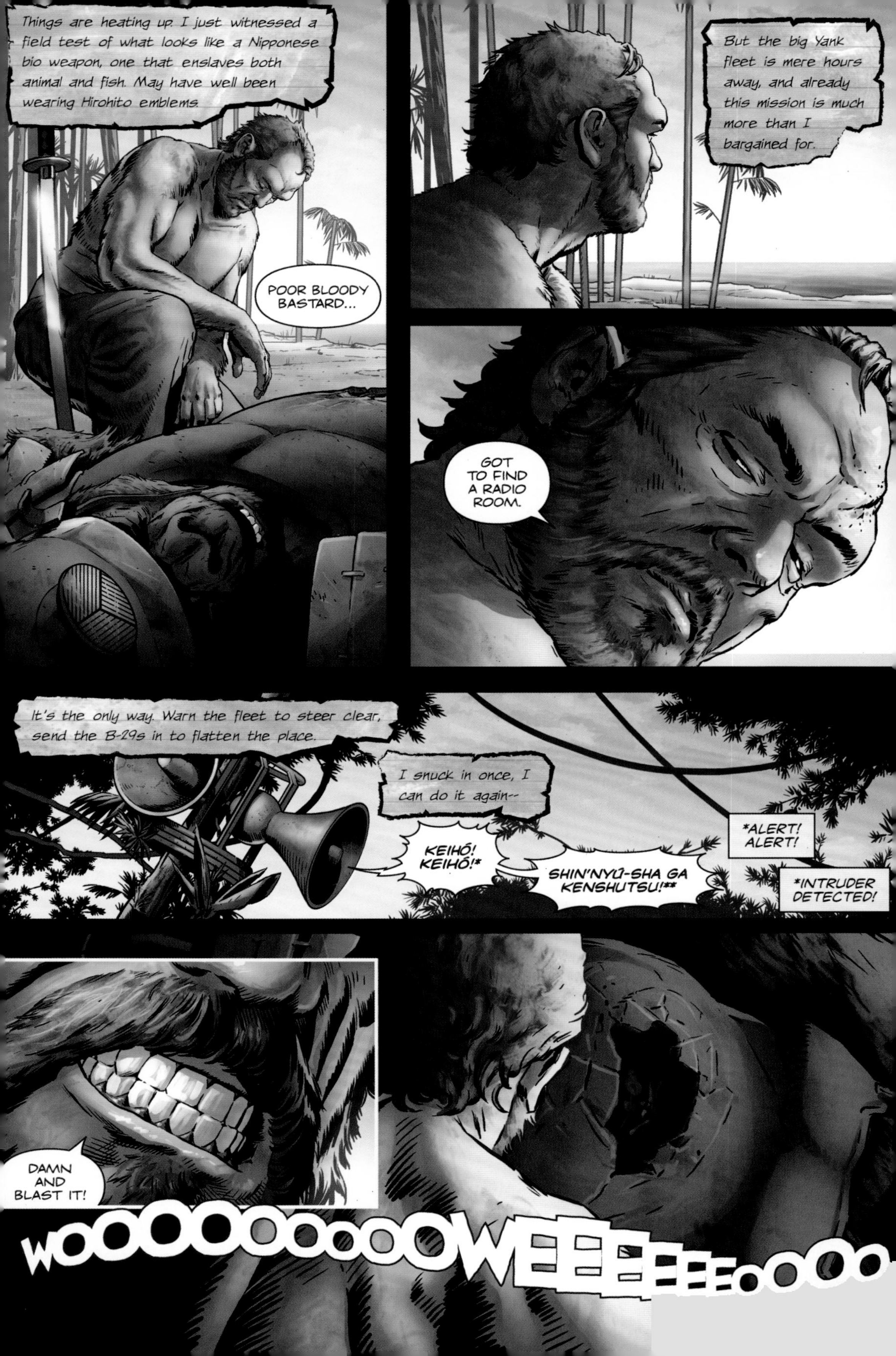
Things are heating up. I just witnessed a field test of what looks like a Nipponese bio weapon, one that enslaves both animal and fish. May have well been wearing Hirohito emblems.
POOR BLOODY BASTARD...
But the big Yank fleet is mere hours away, and already this mission is much more than I bargained for.
GOT TO FIND A RADIO ROOM.
It's the only way. Warn the fleet to steer clear, send the B-29s in to flatten the place.
I snuck in once, I can do it again--
KEIHŌ! KEIHŌ!*
SHIN'NYŪ-SHA GA KENSHUTSU!**
*ALERT! ALERT!
*INTRUDER DETECTED!
DAMN AND BLAST IT!
WOOOOOOOOOOWEEEEEEE.OOOO

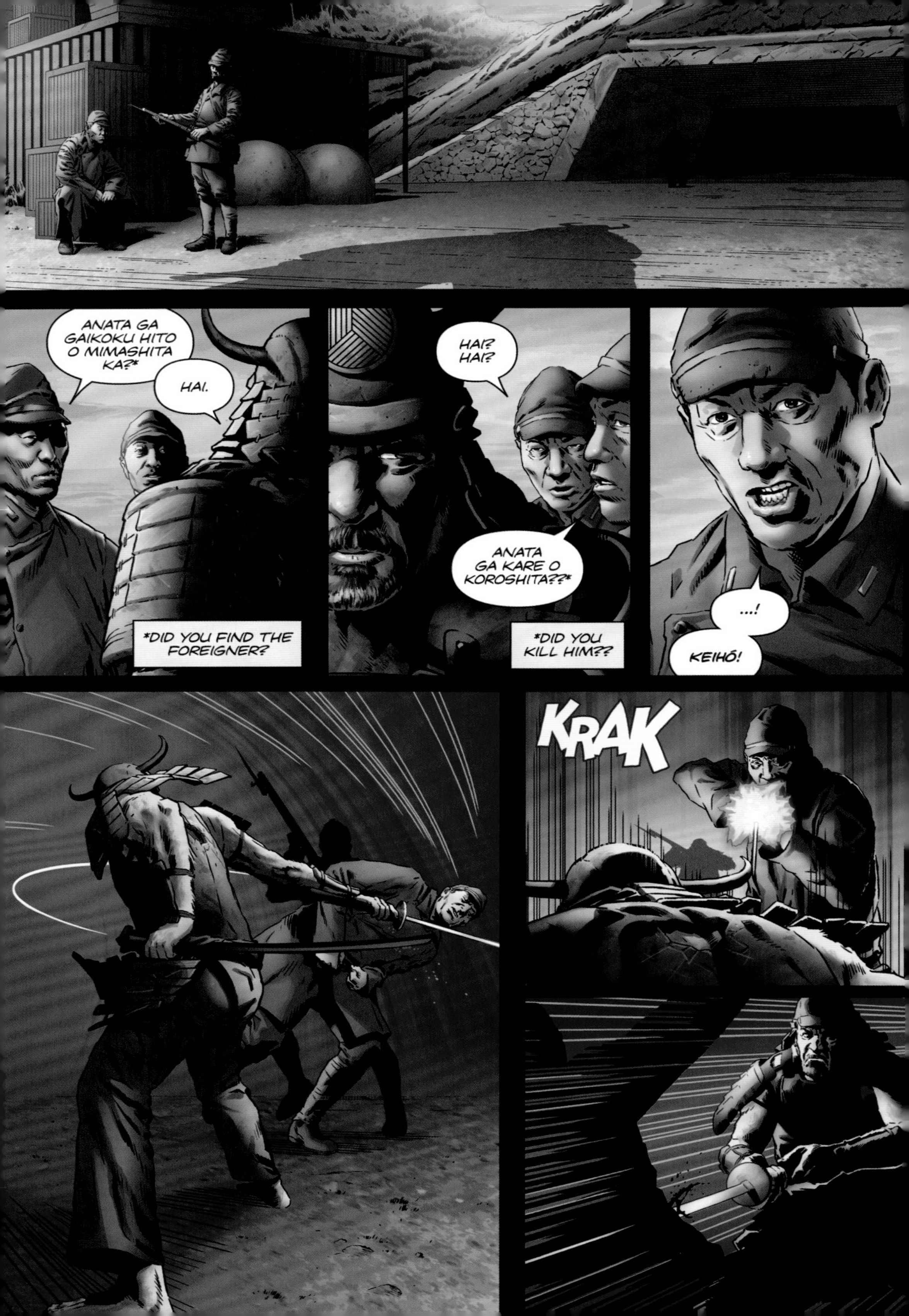
ANATA GA GAIKOKU HITO O MIMASHITA KA?*
HAI.
*DID YOU FIND THE FOREIGNER?
HAI? HAI?
ANATA GA KARE O KOROSHITA??*
*DID YOU KILL HIM??
...!
KEIHŌ!
KRAK

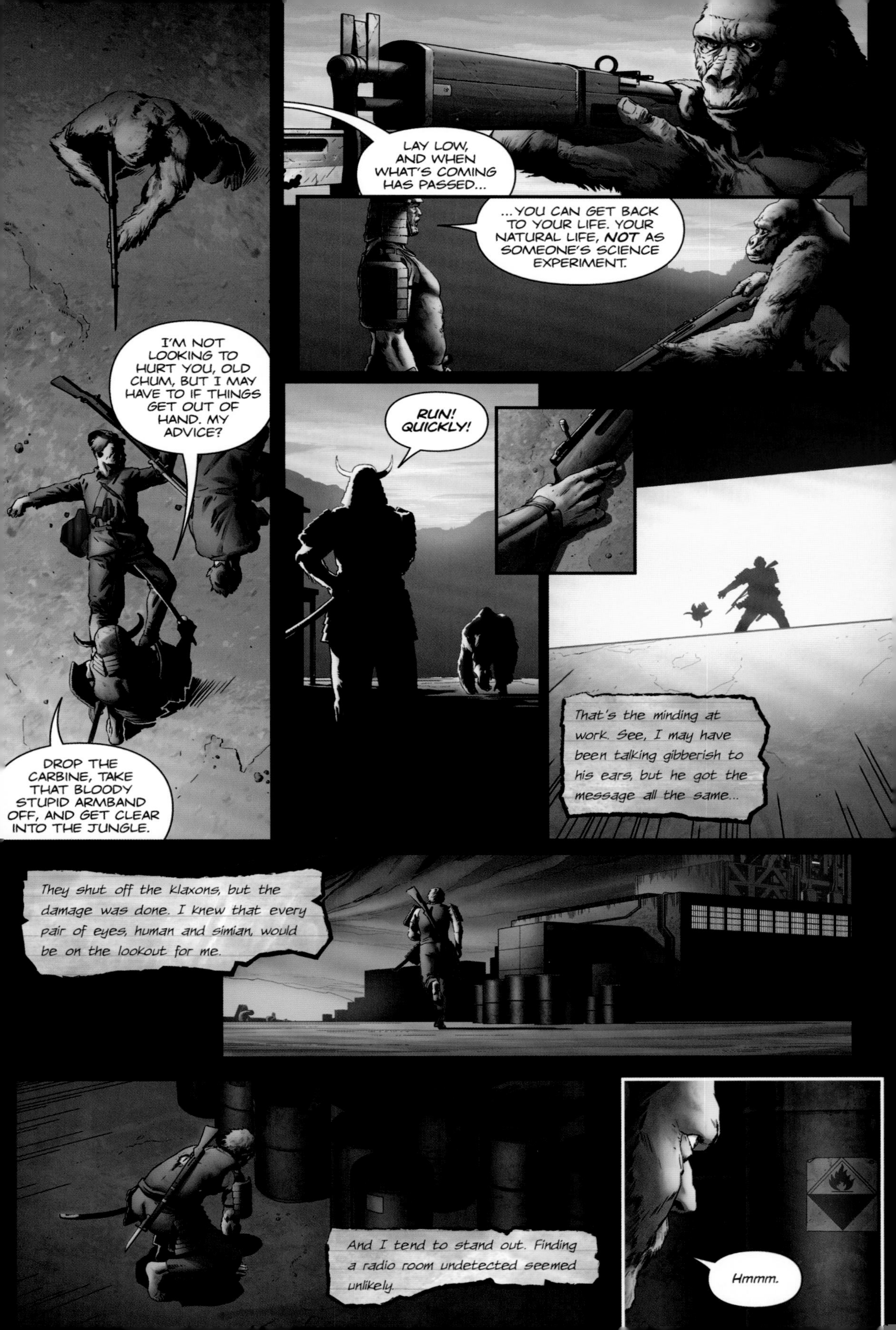

LAY LOW, AND WHEN WHAT'S COMING HAS PASSED...
...YOU CAN GET BACK TO YOUR LIFE. YOUR NATURAL LIFE, NOT AS SOMEONE'S SCIENCE EXPERIMENT.
I'M NOT LOOKING TO HURT YOU, OLD CHUM, BUT I MAY HAVE TO IF THINGS GET OUT OF HAND. MY ADVICE?
DROP THE CARBINE, TAKE THAT BLOODY STUPID ARMBAND OFF, AND GET CLEAR INTO THE JUNGLE.
RUN! QUICKLY!
That's the minding at work. See, I may have been talking gibberish to his ears, but he got the message all the same...
They shut off the klaxons, but the damage was done. I knew that every pair of eyes, human and simian, would be on the lookout for me.
And I tend to stand out. Finding a radio room undetected seemed unlikely.
Hmmm.

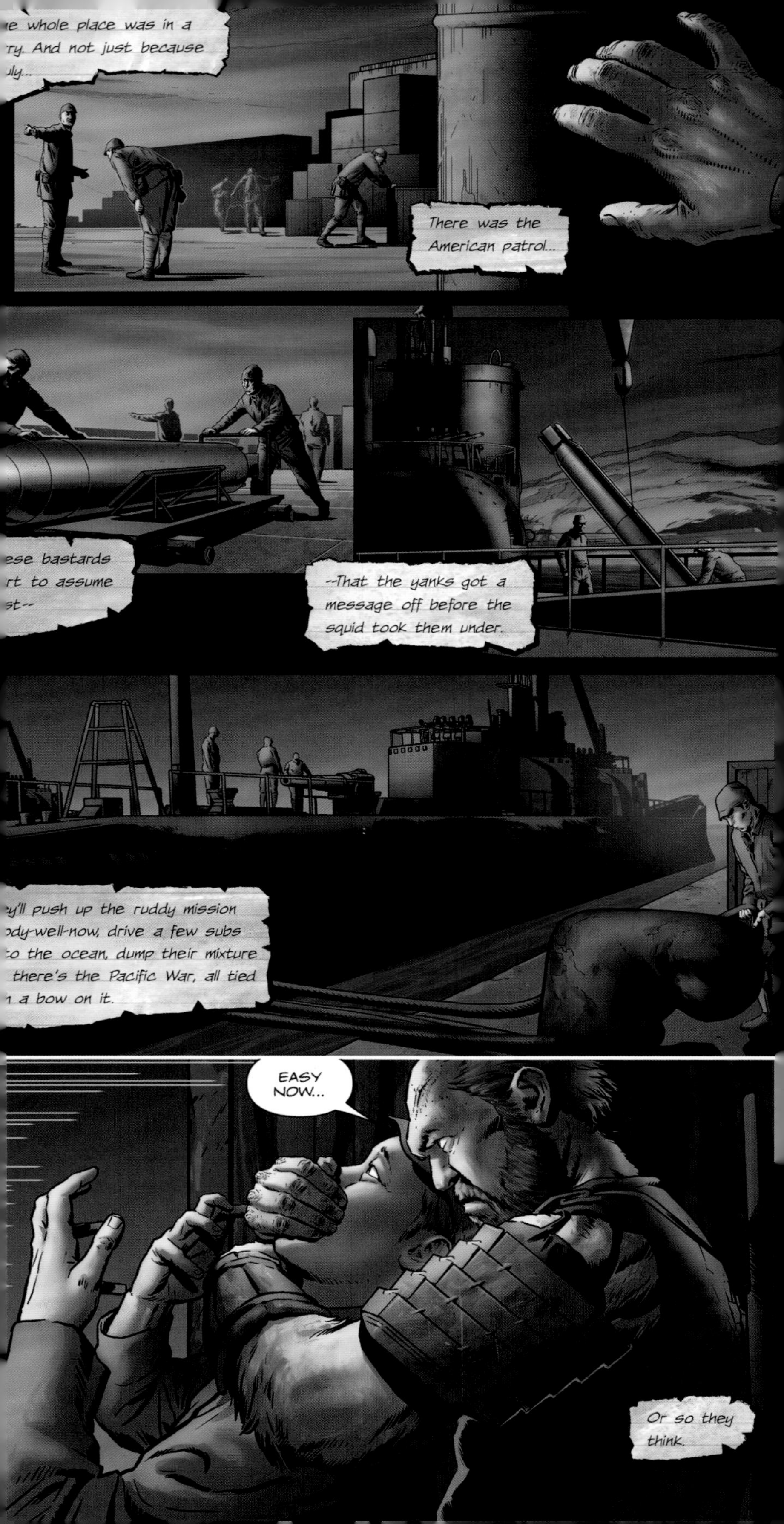
e whole place was in a ry. And not just because uly...
There was the American patrol...
ese bastards rt to assume st--
--That the yanks got a message off before the squid took them under.
y'll push up the ruddy mission ody-well-now, drive a few subs to the ocean, dump their mixture there's the Pacific War, all tied a bow on it.
EASY NOW...
Or so they think.

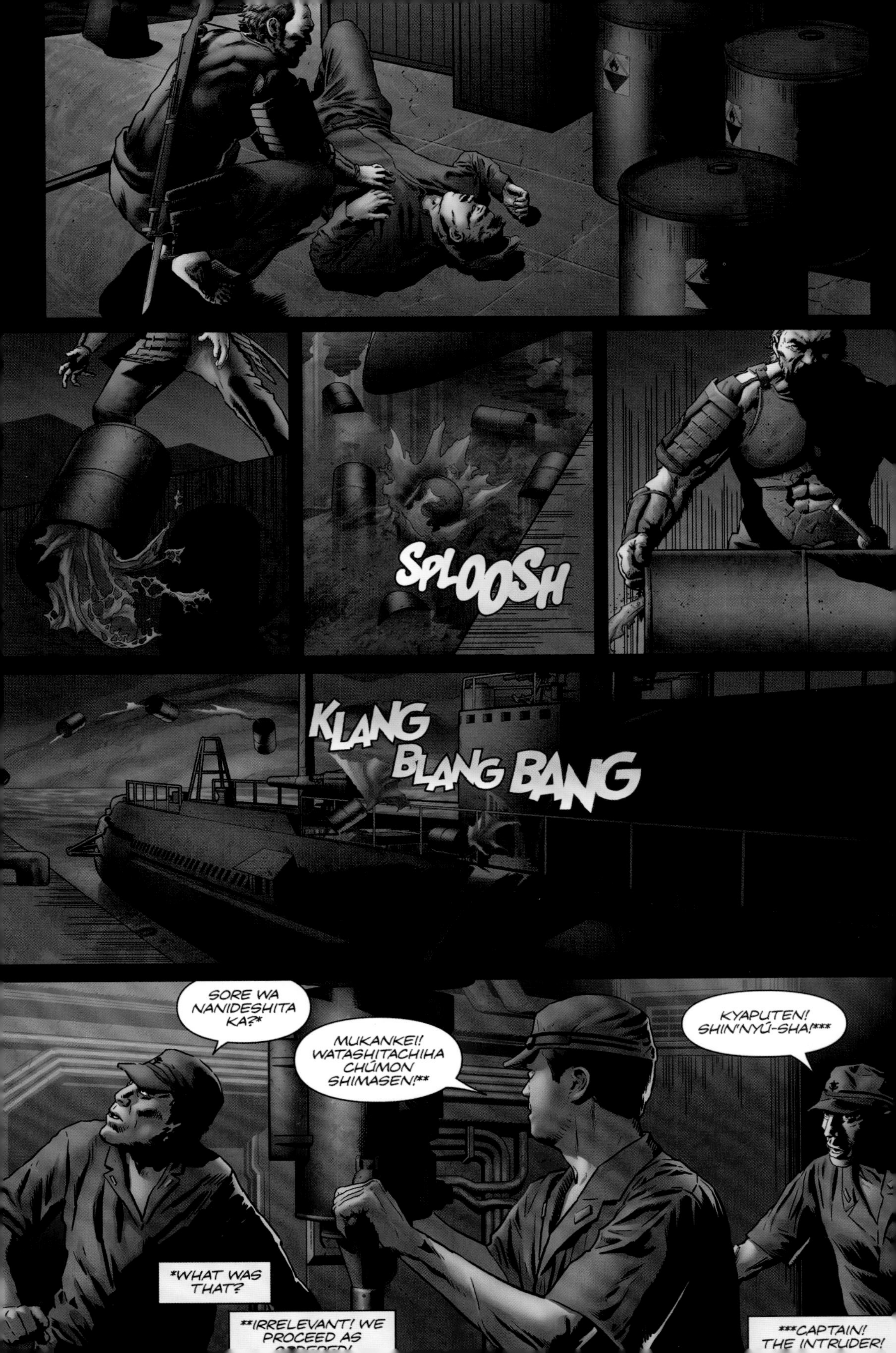
SPLOOSH
KLANG
BLANG BANG
SORE WA NANIDESHITA KA?*
MUKANKEI! WATASHITACHIHA CHŪMON SHIMASEN!**
KYAPUTEN! SHIN'NYŪ-SHA!***
*WHAT WAS THAT?
**IRRELEVANT! WE PROCEED AS
***CAPTAIN! THE INTRUDER!

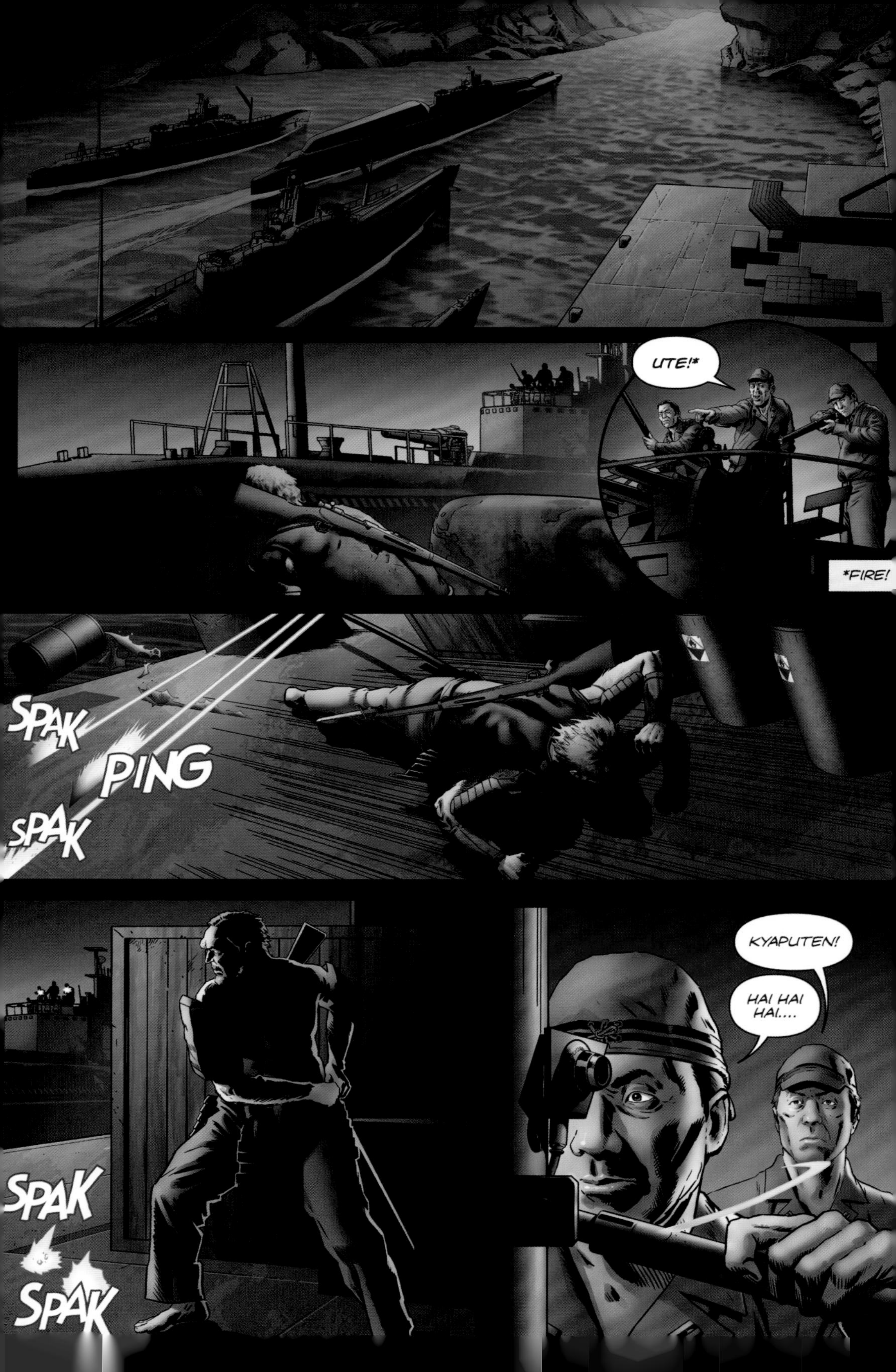
UTE!*
*FIRE!
SPAK
PING
SPAK
SPAK
SPAK
KYAPUTEN!
HAI HAI HAI....

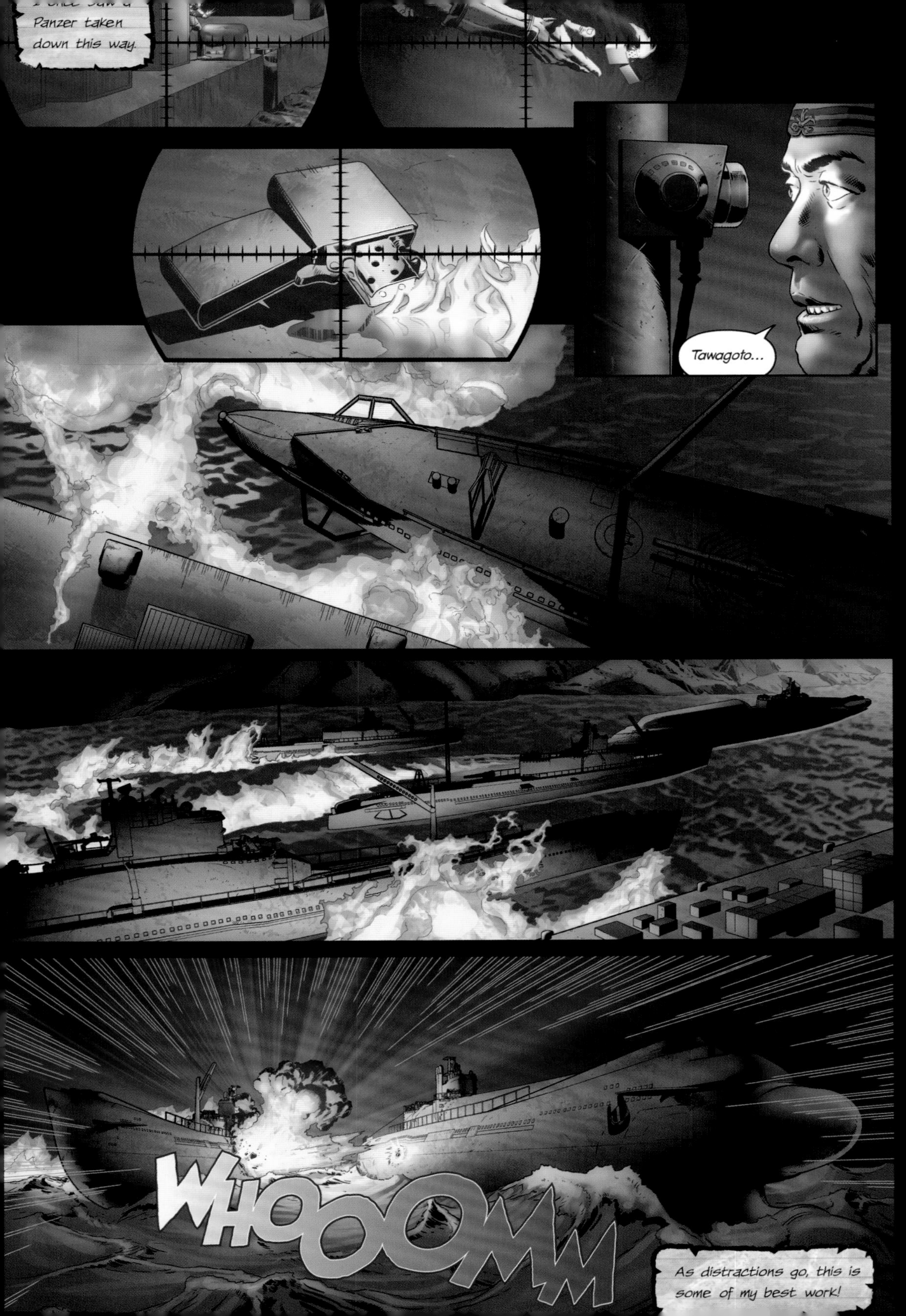
Panzer taken down this way.
Tawagoto...
WHOOOOMM
As distractions go, this is some of my best work!

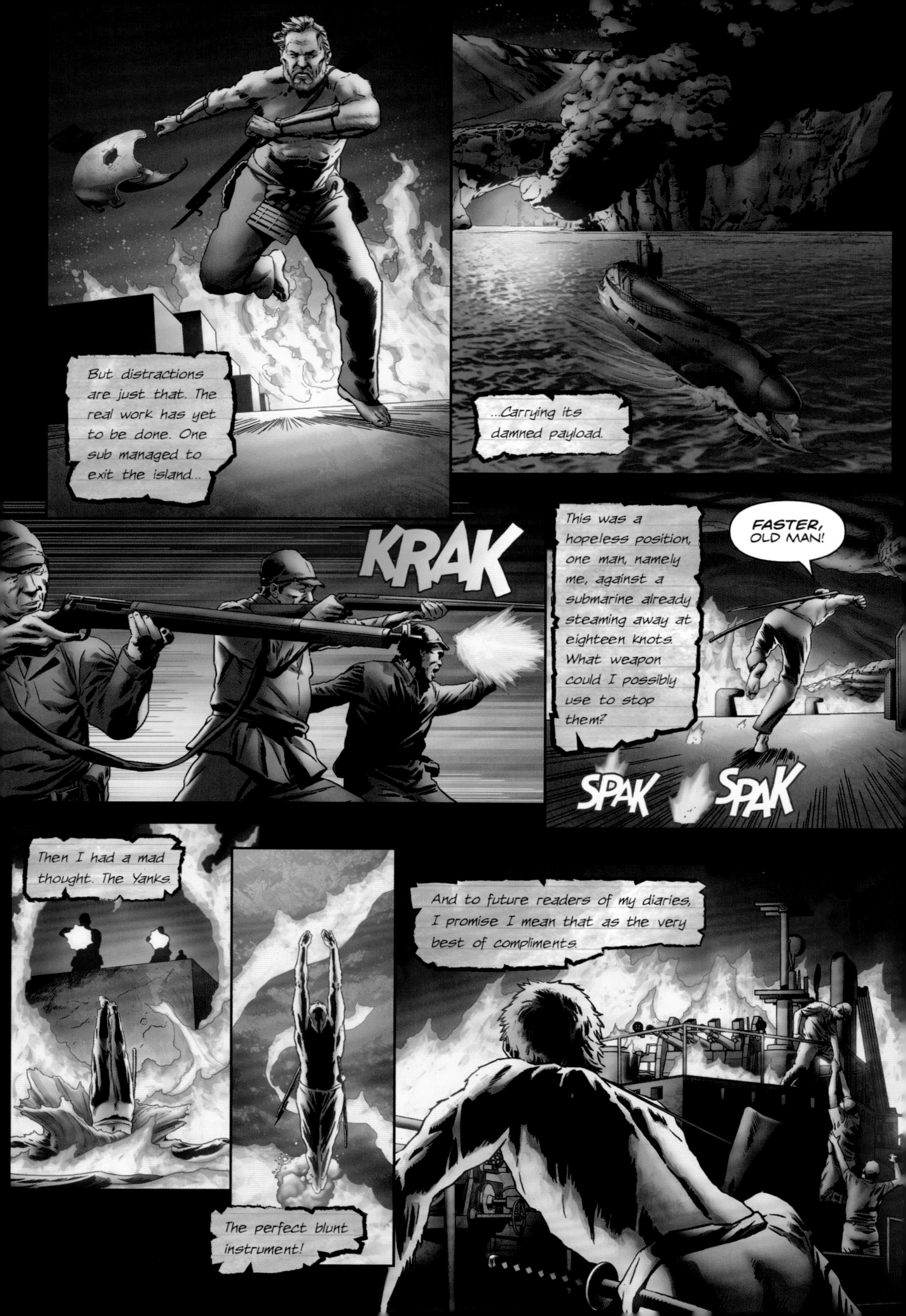
But distractions are just that. The real work has yet to be done. One sub managed to exit the island...
...Carrying its damned payload.
KRAK
This was a hopeless position, one man, namely me, against a submarine already steaming away at eighteen knots. What weapon could I possibly use to stop them?
FASTER, OLD MAN!
SPAK SPAK
Then I had a mad thought. The Yanks.
The perfect blunt instrument!
And to future readers of my diaries, I promise I mean that as the very best of compliments.

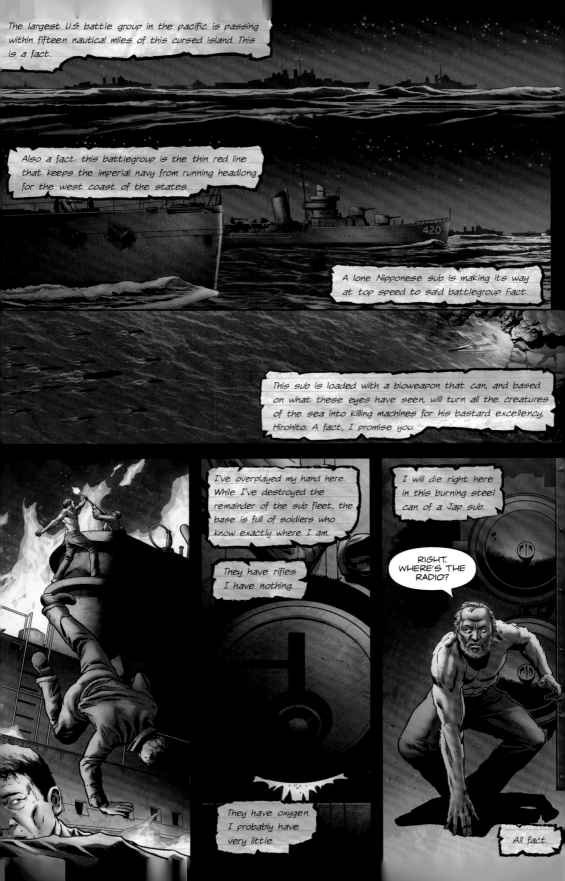

The largest U.S. battle group in the pacific is passing within fifteen nautical miles of this cursed island. This is a fact.

Also a fact: this battlegroup is the thin red line that keeps the imperial navy from running headlong for the west coast of the states.

A lone Nipponese sub is making its way at top speed to said battlegroup. Fact.

This sub is loaded with a bioweapon that can, and based on what these eyes have seen, will turn all the creatures of the sea into killing machines for his bastard excellency, Hirohito. A fact, I promise you.

I've overplayed my hand here. While I've destroyed the remainder of the sub fleet, the base is full of soldiers who know exactly where I am.

They have rifles. I have nothing.

They have oxygen. I probably have very little.

I will die right here in this burning steel can of a Jap sub.

RIGHT. WHERE'S THE RADIO?

All fact.

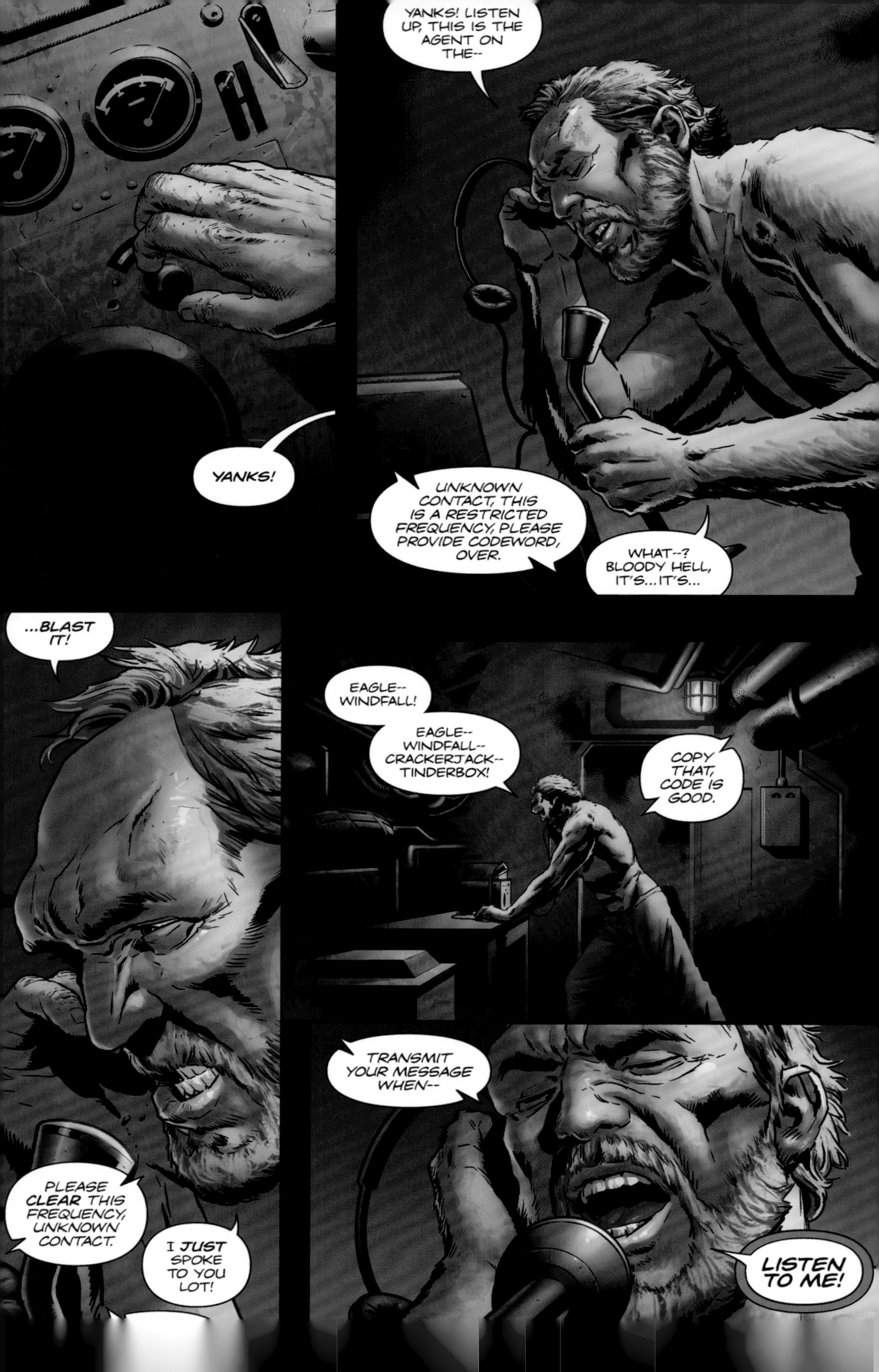

YANKS!
YANKS! LISTEN UP, THIS IS THE AGENT ON THE--
UNKNOWN CONTACT, THIS IS A RESTRICTED FREQUENCY, PLEASE PROVIDE CODEWORD, OVER.
WHAT--? BLOODY HELL, IT'S...IT'S...
...BLAST IT!
EAGLE-- WINDFALL!
EAGLE-- WINDFALL-- CRACKERJACK-- TINDERBOX!
COPY THAT, CODE IS GOOD.
PLEASE CLEAR THIS FREQUENCY, UNKNOWN CONTACT.
I JUST SPOKE TO YOU LOT!
TRANSMIT YOUR MESSAGE WHEN--
LISTEN TO ME!

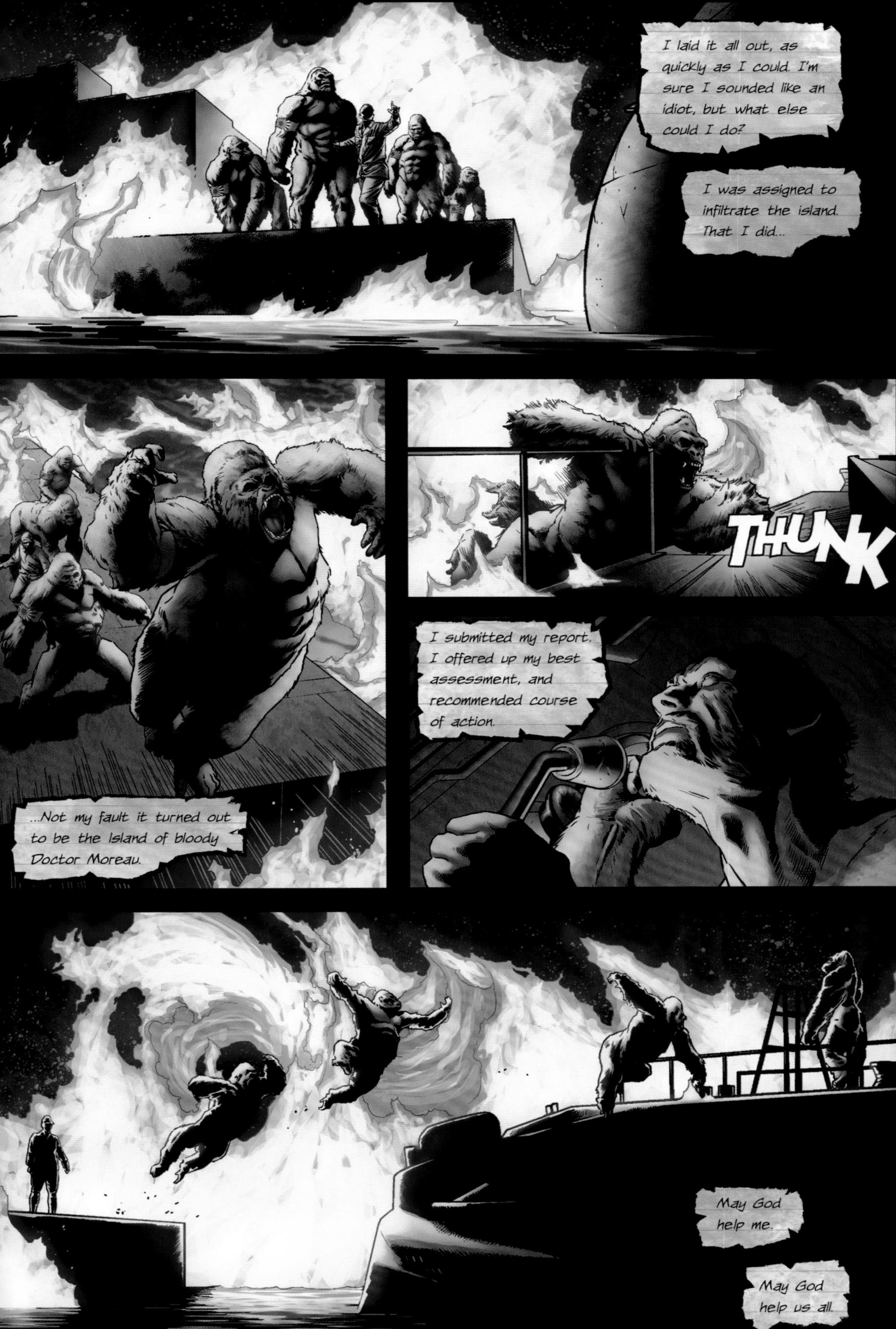
I laid it all out, as quickly as I could. I'm sure I sounded like an idiot, but what else could I do?
I was assigned to infiltrate the island. That I did...
...Not my fault it turned out to be the Island of bloody Doctor Moreau.
THUNK
I submitted my report. I offered up my best assessment, and recommended course of action.
May God help me.
May God help us all.

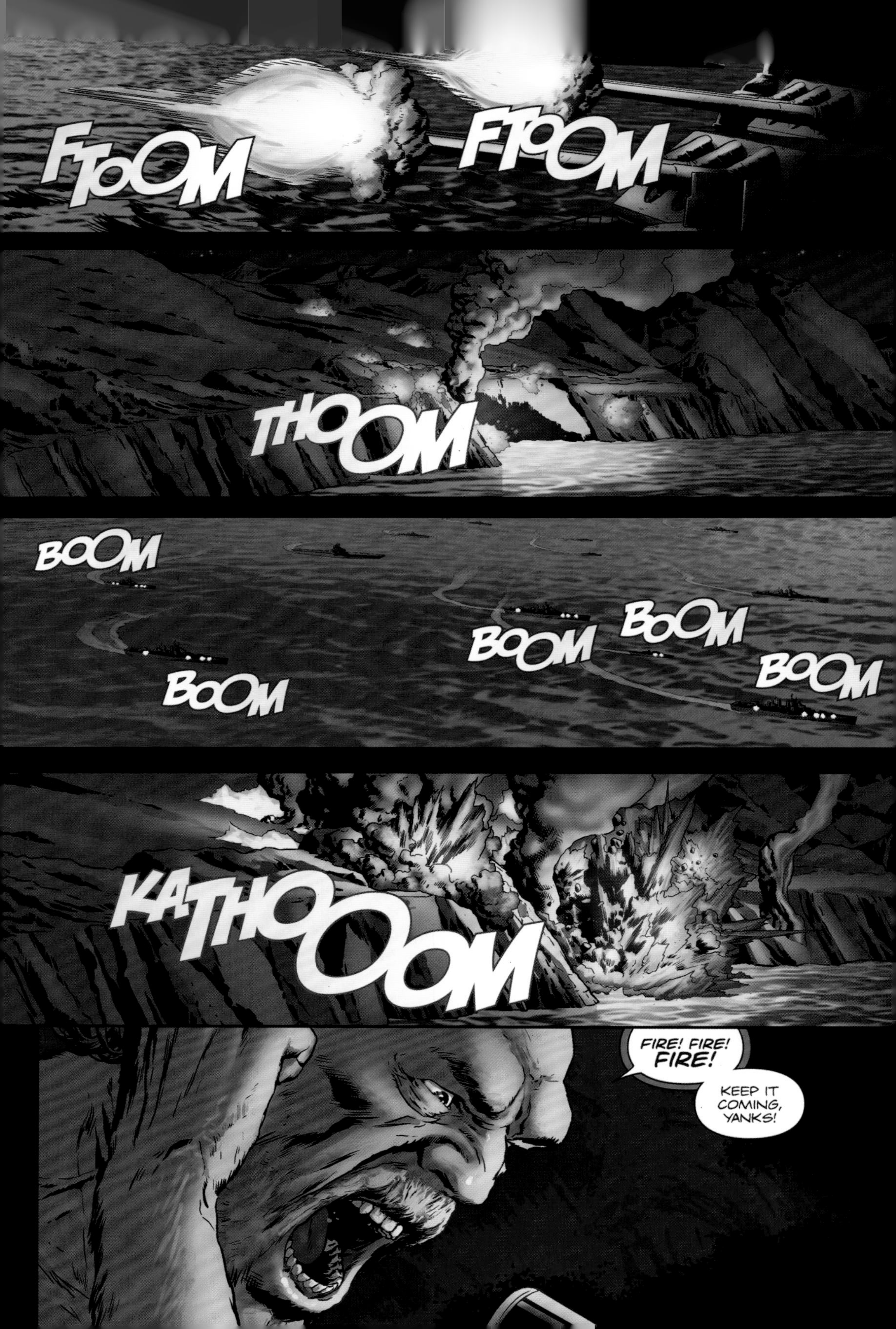
FTOOM
FTOOM
THOOM
BOOM
BOOM
BOOM
BOOM
BOOM
KATHOOOOM
FIRE! FIRE! FIRE!
KEEP IT COMING, YANKS!

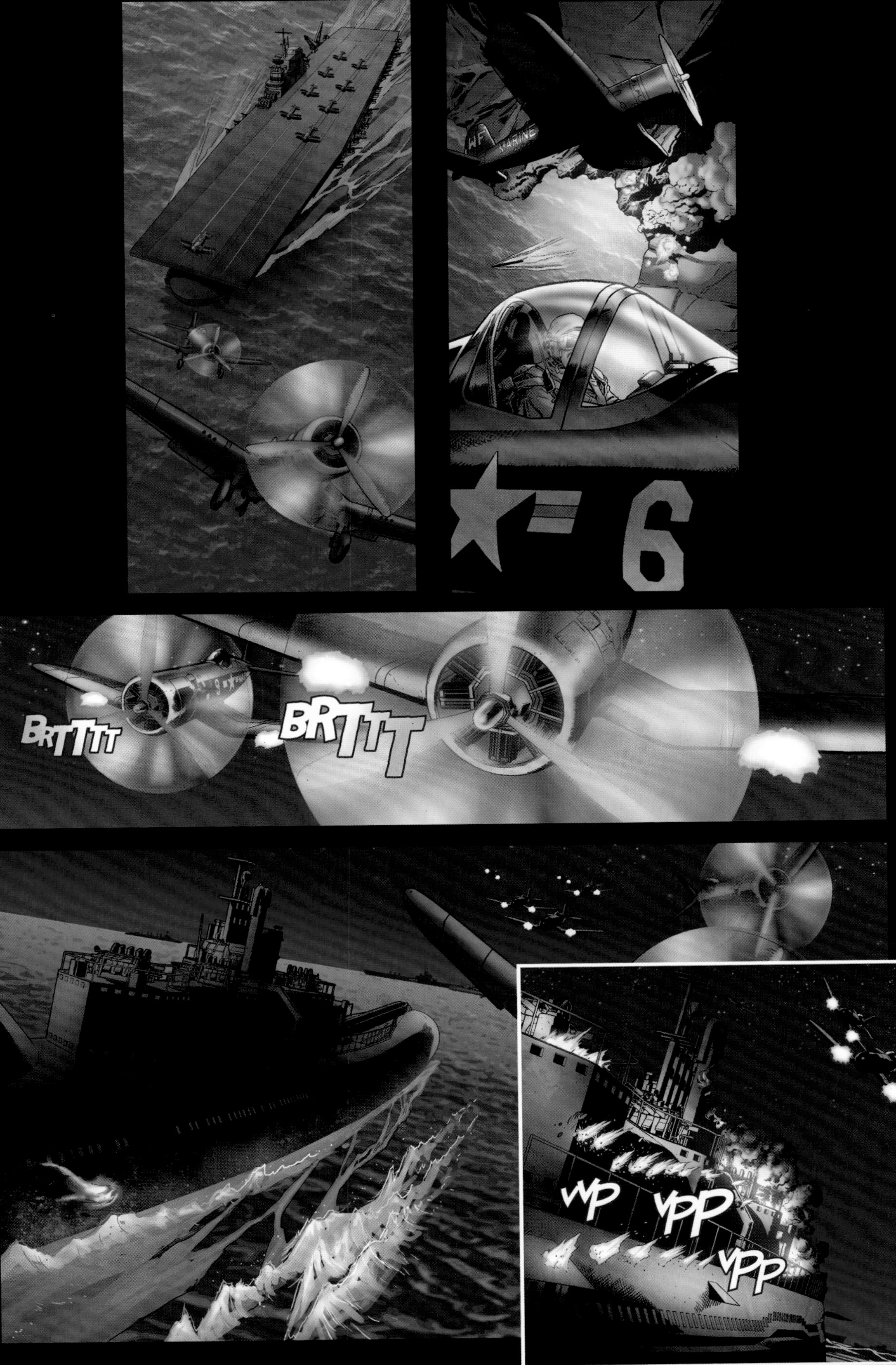
WF
MARINE
6
BRTTTT
BRTTT
VVP
VPP
VPP

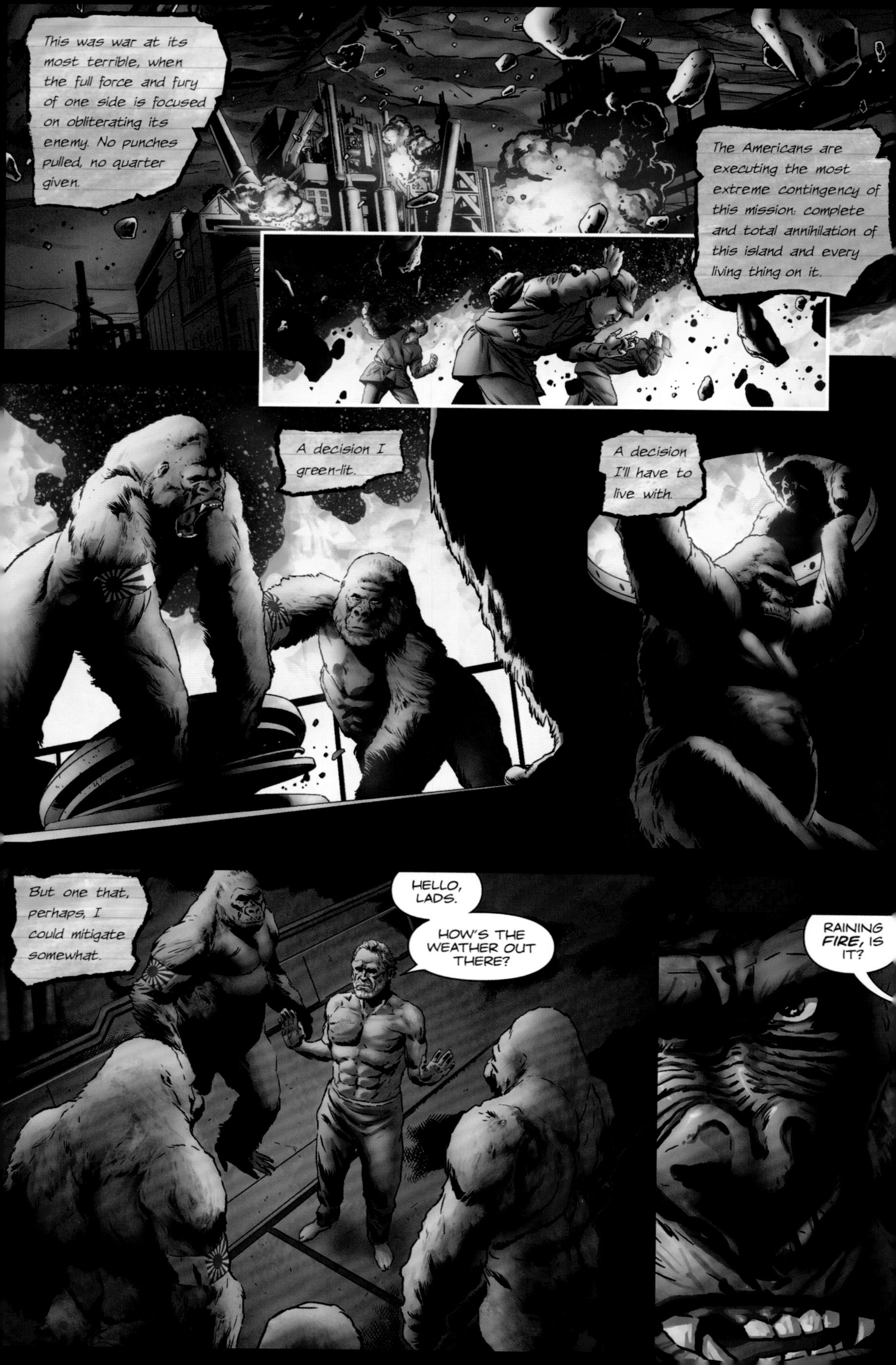
This was war at its most terrible, when the full force and fury of one side is focused on obliterating its enemy. No punches pulled, no quarter given.
The Americans are executing the most extreme contingency of this mission: complete and total annihilation of this island and every living thing on it.
A decision I green-lit.
A decision I'll have to live with.
But one that, perhaps, I could mitigate somewhat.
HELLO, LADS.
HOW'S THE WEATHER OUT THERE?
RAINING FIRE, IS IT?

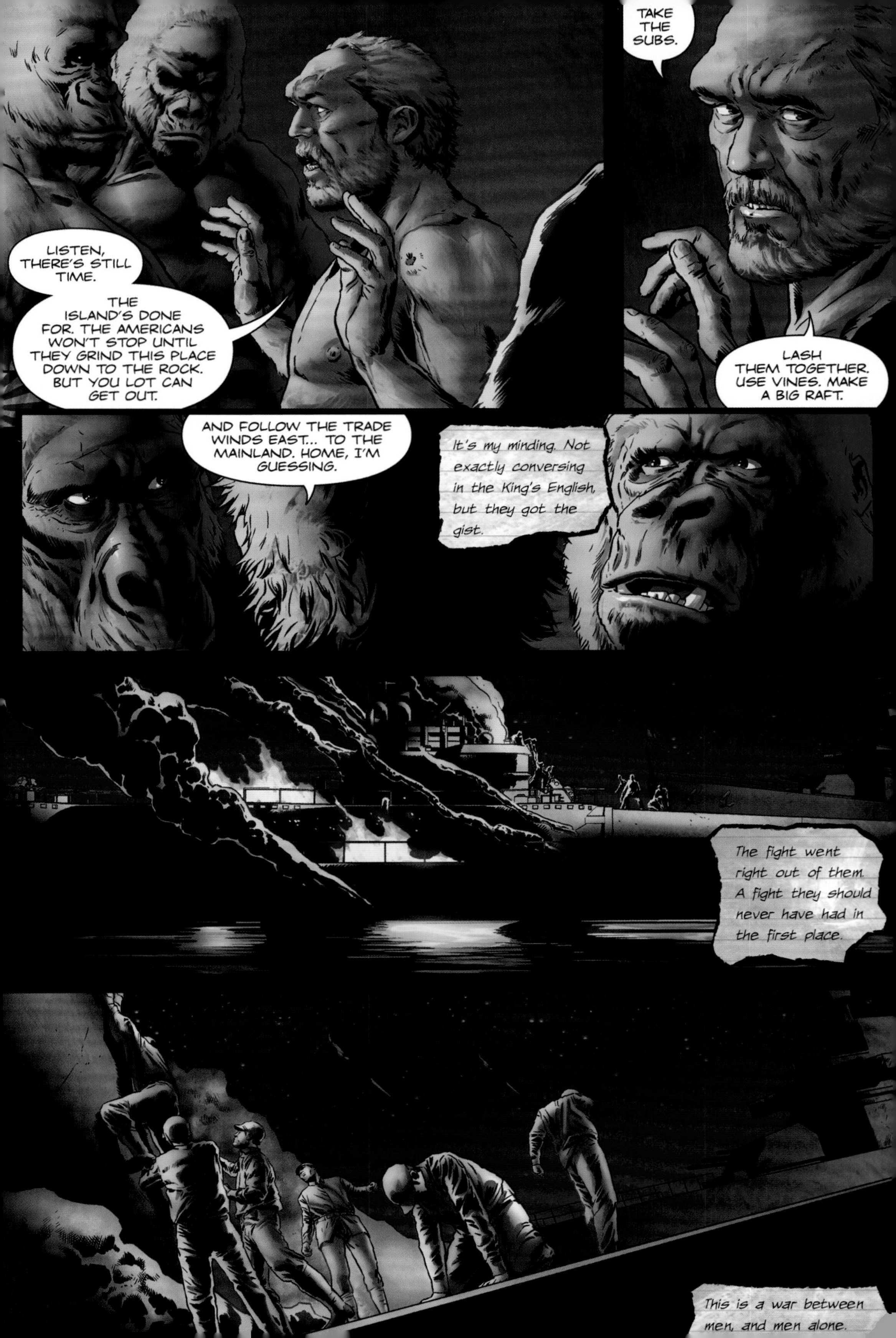
TAKE THE SUBS.
LISTEN, THERE'S STILL TIME.
THE ISLAND'S DONE FOR. THE AMERICANS WON'T STOP UNTIL THEY GRIND THIS PLACE DOWN TO THE ROCK. BUT YOU LOT CAN GET OUT.
LASH THEM TOGETHER. USE VINES. MAKE A BIG RAFT.
AND FOLLOW THE TRADE WINDS EAST... TO THE MAINLAND. HOME, I'M GUESSING.
It's my minding. Not exactly conversing in the King's English, but they got the gist.
The fight went right out of them. A fight they should never have had in the first place.
This is a war between men, and men alone.

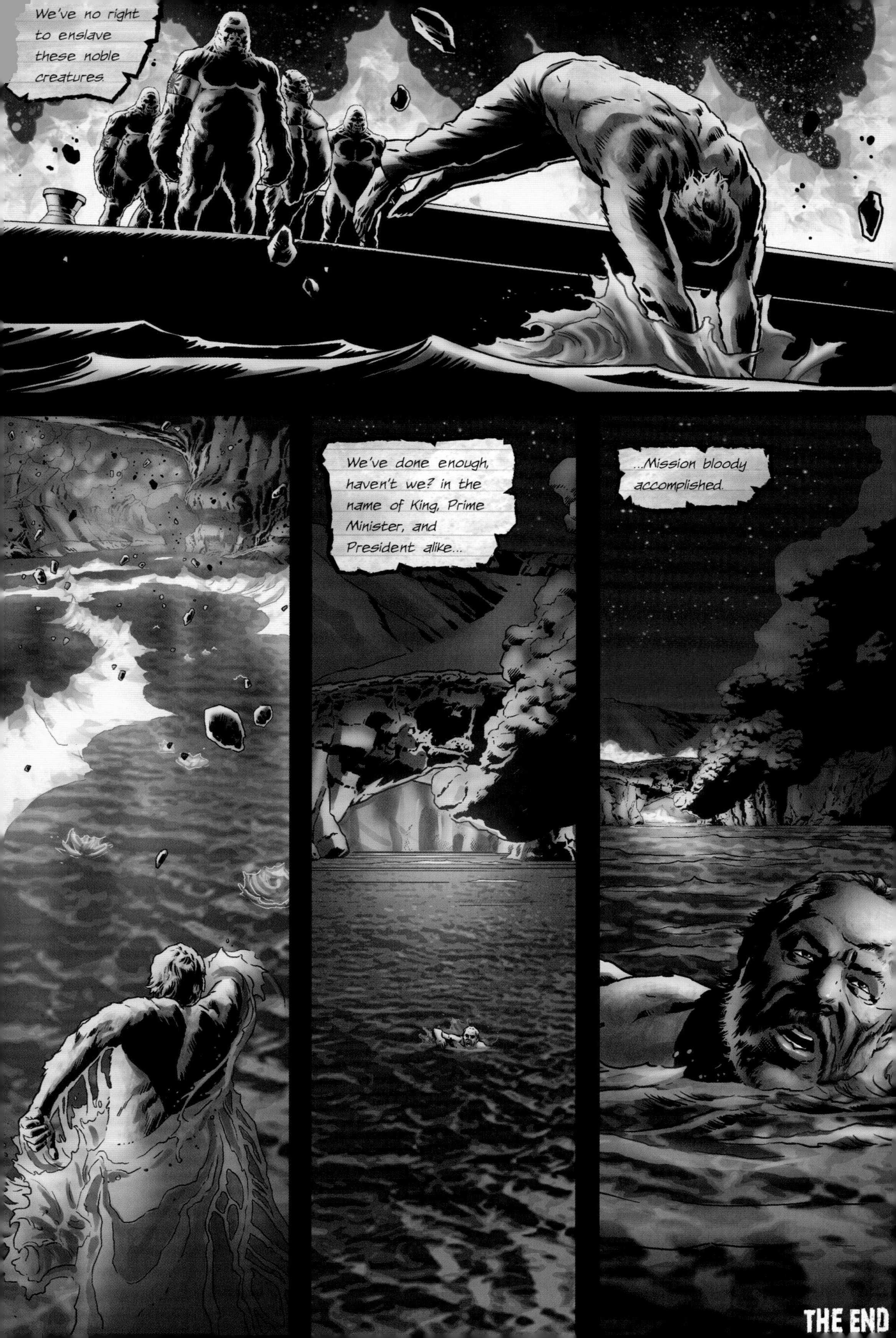
We've no right to enslave these noble creatures.
We've done enough, haven't we? in the name of King, Prime Minister, and President alike...
...Mission bloody accomplished.
THE END

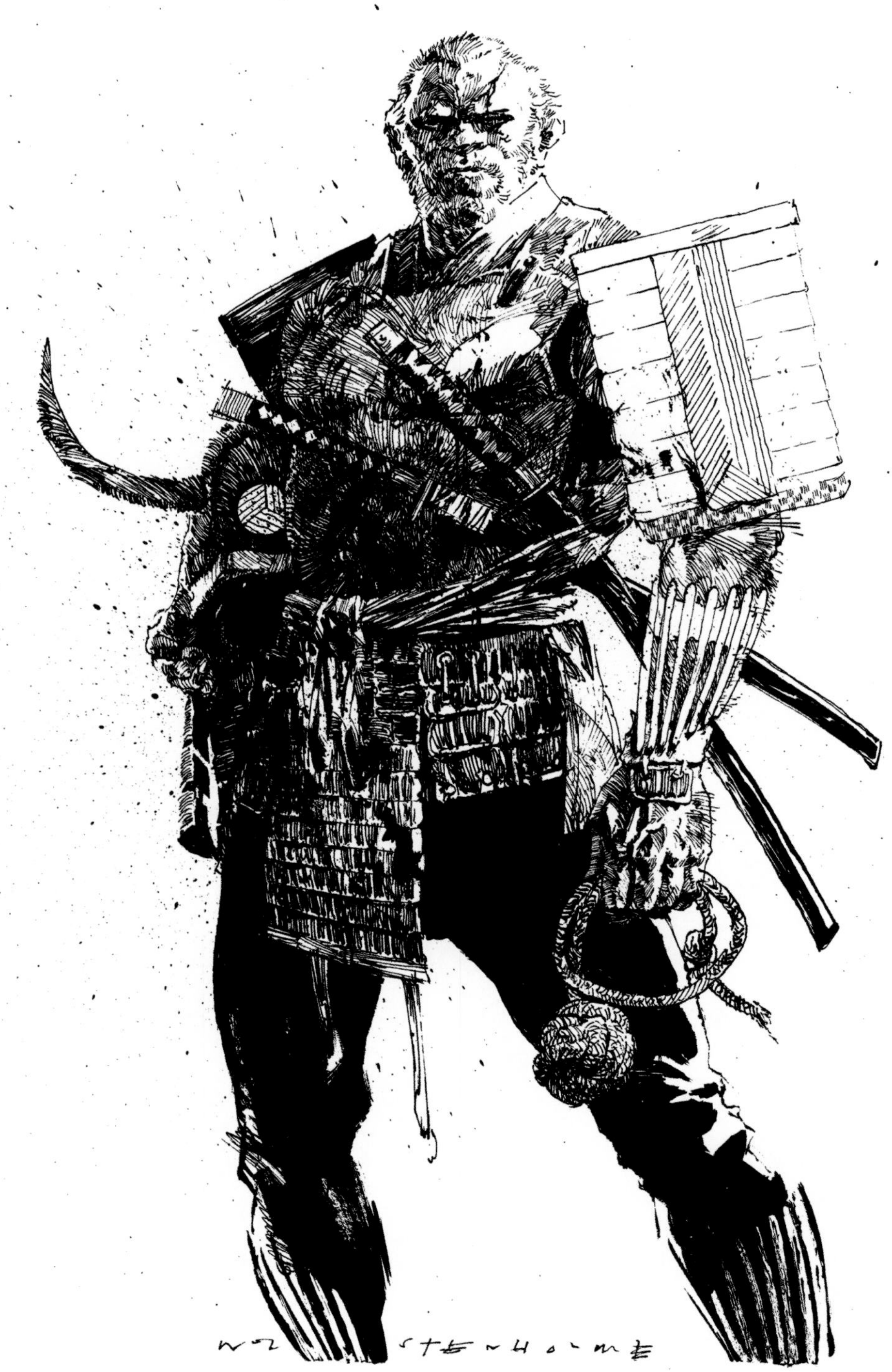

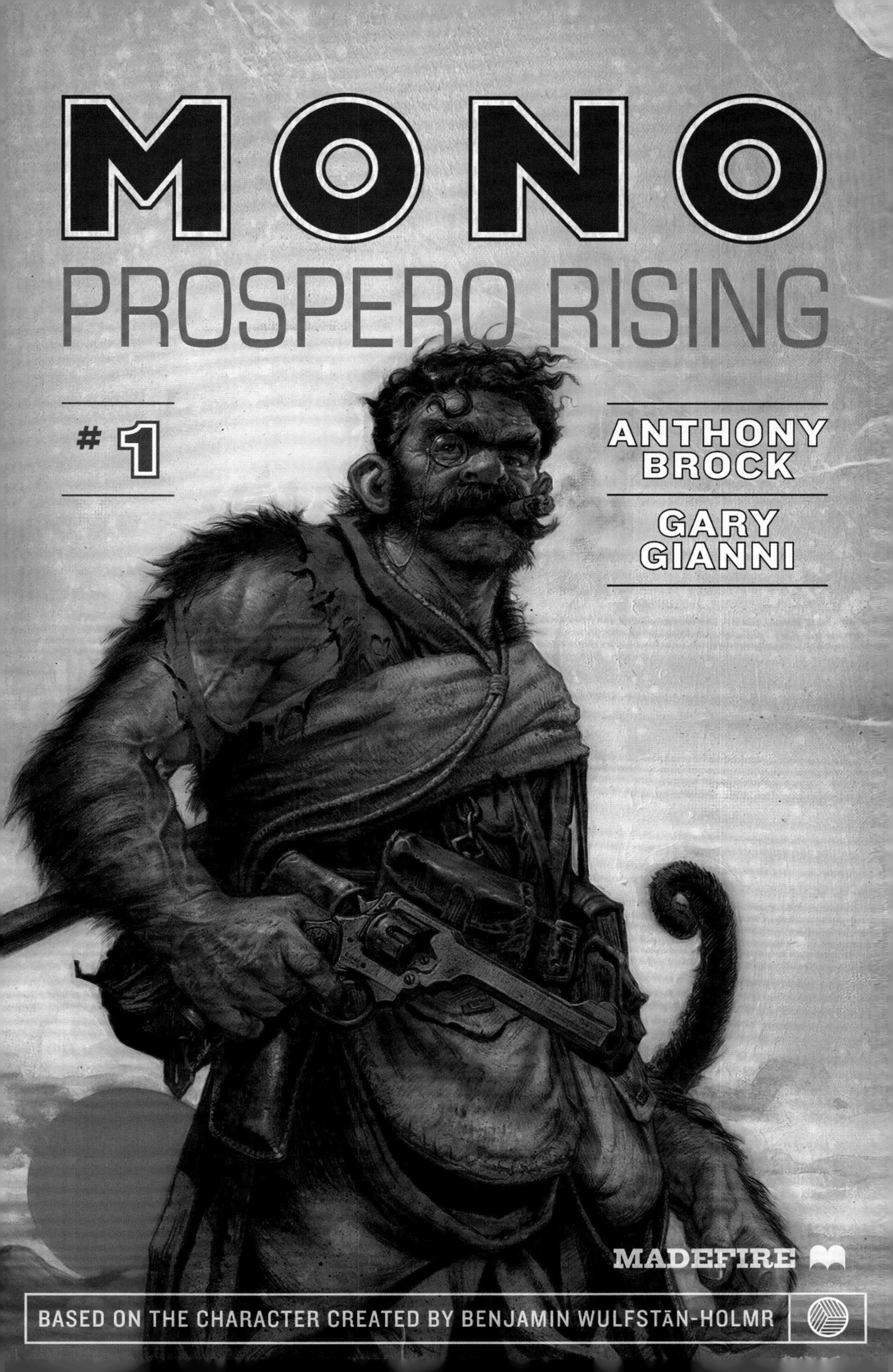
MONO
PROSPERO RISING
#1
ANTHONY BROCK
GARY GIANNI
MADEFIRE
BASED ON THE CHARACTER CREATED BY BENJAMIN WULFSTĀN-HOLMR

MONO

PROSPERO RISING

Written by Anthony Brock

Illustrated by Gary Gianni
Cover art by Greg Staples

Based on the character created by
Benjamin Wulfstān-Holmr

Madefire

INTRODUCTION
by Liam Sharp

Mono, the gentlemanly ape-man, spy and adventurer, first appeared in his own self-titled pulp magazine between January 1939 and March 1941, published by Struth and Shaw Publications, New York. A total of seven short stories were printed in Detective Clues magazine during the same period, and a long running series of novellas followed from 1968 to 1974, published by the Paperbook Library. Created to cash in on the success of Doc Savage, The Shadow and The Avenger, Mono never achieved the same level of popularity, despite the superior prose style and enigmatic protagonist.

The authorship was routinely attributed to Barrington Nash, the house pseudonym of a number of writers working for Struth and Shaw Publications, also credited as the writer/creator of the Frank Scopegate novellas—actually the creation of Malcolm Trout. All but four of the original Mono stories, and all of the later novellas, were in fact written by an elusive and enigmatic Englishman called Anthony Brock, though the creation of the character himself is attributed to one of the owners of Struth and Shaw Publications, Benjamin Wulfstan-Holmr.

Almost nothing is known about Anthony Brock. Mono enthusiasts have speculated that he must—on account of the military details that richly impart a rare sense of reality in his pulp fiction—have fought in either the first or second world war, if not both. How he came to write for a New York publisher is entirely unknown, and for a long while he seems to have lead a peripatetic life-style, moving around Europe before eventually settling in the village of Grazalema in 1950s Spain. This in itself is fascinating, given his clear love of the British establishment, and it has been suggested, rather fancifully, that Brock—much like Ian Fleming—may have served as a British spy. As is the case with the James Bond novels, Mono stories do vividly impart an apparently superior knowledge of how Britain's secret services actually operate. Various 'real' unexplained historic events are rationally explained away in several of the novellas—grist to the mill of imaginative fans in love of a good conspiracy, and even leading, in the most extreme cases, to the preposterous suggestion that the ape-human hybrid Mono was an actual figure in history!

It seems unlikely, but as far as anybody knows Brock is still alive—though he must be into his twelfth decade by now! At some point in the 1970s he stopped writing and disappeared into complete obscurity. Some (un-cited) bios say he was married and had three daughters. He was also said to have primarily worked as an architect, compulsively writing fiction on the side. Others say he returned to the UK and was employed in a senior position at Whitehall. Whatever the truth of the matter, Brock has left a wealth of sprightly, vivid and enthralling tales for us to rediscover. The anthropomorphic beast-man Mono is a wonderful and unique creation quite unlike his fictional peers of the time.

Liam Sharp, March 2014

I

SICILY

Chapter 1
September 1943

Barely discernible in the darkness, a gentle ripple disturbs the oily swell of the Mediterranean as a submarine soundlessly disappears beneath the surface leaving a solitary figure crouched in an inflatable craft. The young man is vigorously paddling with deft quiet strokes, careful not to disturb the phosphorescence in the water below. There is a heavy package wedged into the seat behind him. Everything is black including his face and hands. Ahead of him, a point on a nearby island from where, a few minutes earlier, had come three short flashes.

James 'Jamie' Kerr Robertson knew very little about his mission. He had spent nearly three weeks in Gibraltar acquainting himself with a pack of dogs, two extremely intelligent Airedales and three Alsatians.

He was given to understand that it was important that he master certain control and 'understanding' techniques with the dogs as they were to be an integral part of the primary mission. He was also given some hours of 'dry' instructions in a mini-sub, all of which he had found exciting and intriguing.

He had volunteered, of course, for special services when offered the opportunity. He had enjoyed the induction courses and felt at home in the somewhat rarefied ambience of the language specialists. But, before leaving for his posting, he was fairly sure that the last house he had stayed in was not an official residence of the service. He had not been allowed out, but from what he could perceive from his rooms and the office of his 'instructor', the grounds were extensive and more domestic in character. There were none of the usual signs of either military or security activity. It seemed to him, during this period, that he was undergoing some kind of speciality selection process, as much of his time was spent filling out forms—essays more like!—on a wide variety of subjects. He would

have found this irksome, never having enjoyed his schooling, were it not for the long interviews—that invariably became chats—with the fatherly gentleman who seemed to be in charge. In his usual placid way he assumed that he would be informed if and when necessary of any change in his stated commission. So far this information had not been forthcoming.

Formally all he knew, as he manoeuvred his small craft through the calm autumn night, was that he was on his way to rendezvous with his commander to pass on instructions.

For the period of this operation his code-name was 'Besim', which meant 'smiling one' in Turkish and which he took to be a compliment.

Although he knew that he should be concerned only with the job at hand, he could not stop his thoughts drifting back a few years to his family life on the island of Corfu. This new night-time adventure reminded him of a happy and exciting earlier escapade with his brother when a mutual dare had led to them taking off in the family dinghy well after the hours they were normally permitted. It had been the first time that he had swum in the dark so far from shore, and getting back on the dinghy had proven near disastrous. Of course the blame had fallen squarely on his shoulders in spite of his younger brother's protestations of responsibility.

Another flash from the torch brought him back to the present and the need to avoid some rocks close to his starboard side.

He had lost all sense of what land he was nearing as it had disappeared into an all-engulfing darkness. As if his commander knew what he was thinking there came two more flashes of the torch and he was able to get a sense of distance, about 50 yards, to the small commotion where the sea met the shore. He was making for what appeared, in the reflected light, to be a narrow ledge of rock almost at water level. He became aware of the sound of small waves lapping over rocks and then, suddenly, he felt himself, still in his craft, hoisted onto the ledge.

"No moon tonight," said a deep, rather gruff but well-spoken voice from the dark.

"Then we shall make our own light," Jamie replied, as he had been instructed to. Feeling slightly foolish he clambered from his craft. His boot skidded on the slimy rocks and he had to steady himself to avoid falling against the officer.

"We will carry the boat between us. You at the stern. Mind your footing." As he was saying this the bulky shadow swung the bundle of cans from the back seat to the front, impressing Jamie, again, with the brute strength the action had required.

The young messenger—for that was what he felt himself to be—controlled his nervousness, lifted where instructed and followed the pull of the load along the ledge. It was gently inclined and, before long, they had risen some feet above the water line. Eventually they came to a halt.

"Let the boat lie here," came the order.

Jamie could make out what looked like the mouth of a cave. Crouching he followed the agile form of the Commander. After manoeuvring around more rocks with the help of brief illuminating flashes from the torch ahead, they finally came to a hidden chamber. By the light of a caged electric lamp hanging from a small outcrop he was now able to discern the full measure of the man he had come to fetch.

very strong have for others. Jamie held his imagination in check and told himself that in such bad light one should not rush to conclusions. Not attractive by any standard Jamie would care to apply, his first impression of the Commander was of a stern warrior in his bulky, battered uniform. The one redeeming feature, which gave Jamie some degree of comfort, was a capricious suggestion of warmth that he thought he detected in the piercing eyes: dark and too close together under heavy brows, they should have been frightening. It could have been the simple relief in finding that he was not afraid that left him with the impression of friendliness. Whatever the case, Jamie was certain that this reaction was no accident and that the Commander could have any effect he wished on the person before him.

From inside his jacket he pulled out the two brass document tubes.

"I am to give you these messages immediately, Sir."

A large, long-fingered and very hairy hand took the containers. Cracking open first the tube with the banded wax seal, the Commander unrolled the two sheets of paper and held them up to the lamp. He read their content attentively, looking twice at Jamie before returning them to him. He unscrewed the second tube, glanced at it briefly, then said that he would read that one later.

Jamie was reminded of his first encounter with the boxing instructor at school. Here, though, was a man to fear, not to learn from. What Jamie could see, by the dim light, was a bulky fighter's frame topped by a great, unshaven, heavy-featured face. There seemed no hint of aggression or hostility in the countenance or the massive arms that hung aimlessly as if waiting for instruction. Yet something in his manner and bearing suggested the kind of indifference that the

"Do you know what's on those?" the Commander asked, indicating the papers in Jamie's hand.

"No, Sir."

The Commander nodded his assent for Jamie to look at them. The young man was taken aback to find them completely blank.

With a short laugh the Commander broke the atmosphere of formality between them and said: "Schoolboy stuff but efficient, eh?"

"Those papers were your credentials and

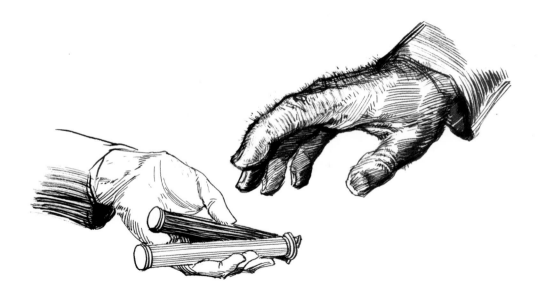

my briefing. Apparently for the duration of this mission you are to refer to me as 'Prospero', if necessary, and I am to call you Besim. Odd names. Somebody we both may know having a little joke, no doubt. I prefer your correct name, in private, if you have no objection."

"None, Sir," he agreed quickly, wondering about the 'somebody'.

"Now we must work before daylight. You can collapse and stow your boat in the cave while I bring in the fuel and the parts, which should be in that package. I have repairs to my craft to undertake and you must get some sleep as I will be requiring your assistance later."

Chapter 2
Action

Jamie had slept fretfully in the hammock slung at the back of the cave. Always more of an open-air person, he could not escape the irony of finding himself on a mission that involved sleeping in a cave and taking to sea in a submarine. When he saw the vessel for the first time by the eerie morning light filtering through the squat cave mouth his sense of anxiety caused him to exclaim audibly and without thinking. The Commander turned to him enquiringly.

"Golly, she's small, Sir," was all he could think to say by way of explanation.

It was unlike any vessel he had ever seen. He guessed it to be about 50ft in length—a third, or less, of the length of the sub that had brought him from Gibraltar, and smaller than the one he had been given instructions in while there. This boat—he couldn`t bring himself to think of her as a ship—seemed to have two sterns. Jamie, with his limited nautical knowledge, assumed that the two flaps pointing together, which he could see breaking the surface at each end, must be stowed

rudders. He hoped that their resemblance to hands in prayer was not an omen. His impression of a Heath Robinson affair was not improved by an odd coil of copper tube mounted before the stubby conning tower and from which surface-mounted copper tubes went fore and aft on both sides of the craft. On the other side of the conning tower was the only item that leant the vessel any semblance of a war machine: a small, wrapped cannon was mounted low between two curved armour shields.

The Commander had been working on the repair until now and was anxious to get under way. He had roused Jamie brusquely with a shake and a grunt about the time.

Having rushed his ablutions, and still chewing the one biscuit he'd had time to grab, Jamie was clambering through the hatch as Prospero cast off.

Down below, the tubes and hull closed around him and he became aware of the dull throb of a diesel engine somewhere deep within. He was relieved to find that the cluster of pipes, handles and dials comforted him and made him feel as if part of the machine. This sensation intrigued him, and he wondered if it would last.

The shape of the Commander filled the hatchway as he descended into the cockpit, stopping to close the hatch.

"Welcome aboard MS3 young man. We must submerge to snorkel depth for the tower to clear the rock so I will take the helm for the moment. Once clear I will be asking you to stay on a course and will try to rest for a period."

The controls looked different to the ones Jamie had experienced in Gibraltar. He hoped that he would be given some rudimentary instruction for the handling of the craft. He was not to be disappointed. Once clear of the island and at periscope depth, the Commander yielded the helm to Jamie and set about guiding him in the basics of controlling the vessel. They set a north-westerly course with the intention of stationing themselves roughly 100 miles north of the island of Alicudi. The Commander told Jamie that this position ought to provide them with the broadest surveillance sweep for enemy submarine activity. Until now his orders had been to deter the enemy and interfere with their navigation systems, and thereby hope to introduce the perception in the enemy of a naturally occurring area of magnetic aberration. He thought that he had achieved this in a wide area to the south of this position by successfully crippling three submarines in the time that he had been there.

His new orders, as of last night, were to encounter and destroy. For this purpose they were equipped with six mines that they could arm and detach from the underbelly of MS3. With that information to digest, and already beginning to feel comfortable with the handling and the registers around him, Jamie was left to follow the set course.

For nearly two hours Jamie was able to leave the Commander to get some necessary rest, wrapped in the rubber-lined swivel-seat next to him, with his head slumped forward on his chest. Essentially at the command of his vessel, Jamie had time to think about and wonder at the remarkable change that had occurred in his life since he had volunteered for duty. He was still not sure what precisely had spurred him to the decision. It certainly was not hatred for the enemy or patriotic fervour. If his education, upbringing and travels had taught him anything, it was that there were no fundamental differences between peoples. He supposed that somewhere in his motivation, beyond mere curiosity and experience seeking, was a hope that his rather ambiguous ideas of principle might be given more definition.

He was brought back to his immediate task when a large domed red light started to flash on the dial panel in front of him.

He nudged the Commander who sat upright as if never asleep. With the turn of a handle and a deft flicking of three switches the engine rumble ceased and Jamie understood that they were now being propelled by the electric motor. Jamie had released his wheel as soon as the Commander had signalled that he would take the helm and was, once again, a passenger, ready and alert.

He watched as Prospero steered with his right hand while grasping, with his left, what looked like a joystick—a sturdy, rubber-clad shaft with a large copper button protruding from the top. When the Commander pressed this button with his thumb the needles on some of the dials in front of him began to flicker and dance.

Without being told Jamie knew that they had picked up the trace of another vessel and by the Commander's reaction it would appear that he was treating it as a potential enemy. Before Jamie could ask how they would be able to identify an enemy submarine from a friendly one, the Commander was murmuring to him that all Allied vessels in the vicinity would be fitted with a small device that emitted an otherwise undetectable magnetic signal, but which would be enough to identify them to him. This was the first time that Jamie thought that he could discern a hint of pride, a slight nod of self-satisfaction in the Commander's demeanour. It was oddly reassuring to discover that this quiet, imposing, uncommunicative mass of a man might have simple recognisable emotions.

Jamie was reflecting on this and the other shocking realisation that they were about to enter into combat—his first blunder into the reality of war, here in this tube, against a monstrous, invisible entity; a great object out there beyond their metal sheath which, given the chance, will try to crush them. Again he was glad of the bulky presence next to him and the steady determination with which the Commander was attending to his tasks.

"Jamie, when I say 'alpha' you will pull down on the large red lever in the centre of the dials between us. The cabin will darken and you will place your feet on the rail below your seat and keep your hands away from anything metallic. Do you understand?"

"Yes Sir."

"When I say 'beta' you will push the handle up again. If you need to hold onto something then do so using only the rubber covered bar that runs to the deck either side of your wheel. Under no circumstances put your hands through the wheel. If I have not given the order 'beta' and you need to manipulate the helm you must first don the gloves that are hanging from your seat."

"Aye, aye, Sir." He found strange comfort, again, in those familiar words.

Jamie looked now more closely at the levers and dials arrayed before him. He had not been especially attentive of them before as they were much like those in the control room of the instruction submarine in Gibraltar. The depth and air pressure gauges, engine monitors, gyro, level gauges, even the ship's clock were similar if not the same. But he did not recognise the lever in question and followed the rod to which it was connected to a multiple housing below the pressure pipes that ran along below the canopy. To his untrained eye it seemed that the rod was connected to five stubby ones, which terminated in casings clamped to a conduit running beneath each one.

"It isolates all that might be sensitive from the general circuitry," murmured the Commander in a rumbling voice, which, in his case, served as a whisper. He must have noticed Jamie's inquisitive scrutiny.

Jamie now thought that he could hear, almost feel, the thrashing propeller of the closing submarine.

The Commander seemed to be transfixed by the large indicator immediately before his face. Two long needles within the same display had been twitching in unison and were gradually turning down toward each other. They steadied and continued getting closer together.

"Alpha," growled the Commander.

Jamie snapped forward, grabbed the lever with both hands and pulled down.

Darkness. All but for a low red glow from the same domed warning light.

The Commander threw a large switch on the lower panel and for a second they were in complete darkness.

Suddenly they were thrown to one side as if prodded by giant fingers and a sharp, prolonged screeching sound told them that they had brushed some part of the German submarine.

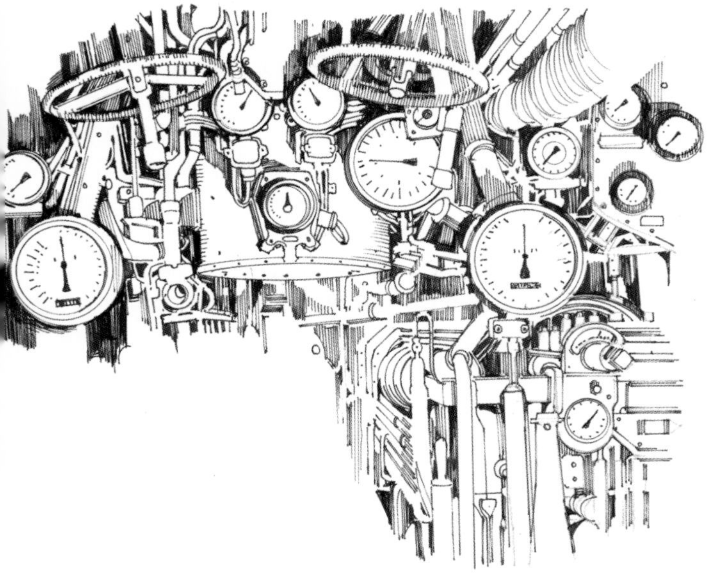

Thrown almost on their side and swinging out of control, the gyro was spinning wildly.

"Probably the radio cable," grunted the Commander.

"Beta, beta!"

Jamie's hands were around the lever again. Up it went and the lights were on again.

The throb and woosh of the U-boat, which had grown so loud, was now retreating to their stern.

"Keep her steady," ordered the Commander. "Hard to port."

Jamie swung the wheel between his hands rapidly to the left, then steadied.

The Commander was concentrating again on the location instrument before him. The needles

were pointing up and the left one slightly outward. Gradually it swung over and they began to converge.

"He's stopped," he said. "Probably heard us."

The needles were steady but getting no closer.

"We must go down after him."

Jamie watched the depth gauge begin to swing and felt, instinctively, the pressure around them increasing. At 120ft the craft began to complain with small metallic groans and Jamie was relieved to see the needles coming together again on the Commander's locator dial.

They levelled and when the needles flicked together the Commander seemed to close his eyes in concentration then tripped the release of the first mine to leave the bay beneath MS3. The sound of a faint clang from somewhere under their feet was enough to swing the Commander into action and turning the motors to full ahead, he ordered his vessel: "Up 20."

Jamie snapped out of his trance-like state, set the plane angle and asked, "Course, Sir?"

"Hard to port. For the moment we have to make distance."

They could hear the enemy sub put on power, her propeller throbbing as she seemed to be heading for the surface, passing them on their right side.

"Stay level," ordered the Commander. "If she's going up we'd better stay deep. Full ahead on current course."

When the explosion came it was with an appalling thunderclap, not fingers this time, but a giant fist grasped their tight little tube, trying to shake it to pieces. The German submarine must have been close to the surface but not more than 100ft from them. There came a second explosion that was more contained. This was followed by more sounds that were unrecognisable but, nevertheless, unnatural.

Jamie's attention was drawn from his anxiety for their own safety to thoughts of the crew of the stricken submarine. He decided that an imagination was not good company in battle conditions. In fact, he was fortunate that his inexperienced imagination could not extend to the brutal reality of the sinking vessel close at hand.

With its conning tower having broken surface, and the main hatch open, the charge had detonated on the bow of the submarine, ripping it open in one searing blast. The explosion had passed through the twisting plates and tripped a torpedo that had been primed for a possible attack at the surface. The whole craft bucked as water rushed into the gaping rupture. The forward rush to the surface was, at once, punched to a stop with the weight of the imploding sea taking her down by the nose. There was no time for her crew to close the first forward bulkhead. They were struggling to close the second against the cataract flooding the entire front section of the vessel. The captain ordered his crew to abandon the stricken submarine and there was a disorderly scramble for the main ladder and for the galley escape hatch as men struggled against the deluge. The few who made it to the surface were not much luckier than their comrades below.

On board MS3 Jamie and his Commander had their own concerns. The little ship had been battered by the concussions. While Jamie struggled to level the craft lengthwise and steady the wildly rotating gyro compass, the Commander hurriedly worked on the ballast pump, closing valves to control a hissing leak that threatened to leave them uselessly heeled over. A seeping thread of water from a crack in the direction finder dial had an ominous look about it. The engines, though, still responded, as did the rudders. The other controls, as if reluctant, gradually allowed themselves to be tamed. At last MS3 began to feel more sturdy again. The two men briefly looked at each other and, with a slight nod, acknowledged their relief.

"We should make some distance before surfacing," said the Commander.

The following night, for several hours they remained at the surface with the diesel motor running softly to recharge the batteries and with the hatch open to replenish the air aboard. They took turns to sit at the hatch exit and keep watch. The Commander busied himself while below, checking the systems and repairing or bracing, where possible, the minor fractures that they had detected.

One hour before they were to return to patrol, the Commander called him up to the conning tower. The sea was calm and the night sky clear and pristine dark. The stars shone as if recently polished and the Milky Way trailed over them as confident as a giant torch beam. This magnificent, peaceful firmament seemed so entirely at odds with the turmoil being waged on earth that the two of them were reduced to a chastened silence. The Commander was standing on the deck just behind the tower, gazing at the sky.

"I have always found the magnificence and breadth of this southern sky so humbling. All our shoddy scrabbling seems so meaningless. Don't you think, Sir?"

He had not meant to say anything, least of all something so emotional and, as if sensing his discomfort, the Commander replied, "Doc reports very highly of you."

"I am surprised that she feels able to make any assessment considering the short time I was at the base," said Jamie, relieved at the lightening of tone, and adding, "She seems quite a remarkable woman in such an uncommon place."

"She is my wife and I would not know how to be objective about her. But I can only agree with you concerning her remarkableness. For me, she has always shone in any assembly no matter how distinguished the company."

Jamie was having difficulty ordering his thoughts. The very idea that the larger-than-life person next to him had just confessed to being married to the enigmatic woman, apparently in charge of an undefined but obviously important and secretive department of the military establishment in Gibraltar, had confused his already disturbed sense of overstepping permitted boundaries. Something to do with the very incongruity of their circumstance was, surely, compelling him heedlessly into these rash observations.

"It must be difficult for you both, as for any family in these times."

"Indeed so. But we have always lived a life of adventure. Not for us, it would seem, the pastoral quiet of a small farm or the domestic regularity of normal employment. As you might have judged I am not complaining. And your own family?"

"My family? Well..." he hesitated and gave a quick sigh. "This sky and this sea make me feel very close to them—to my mother at least. I have no idea where my younger brother might be but my mother, when last I heard from her, was still living at our house on Corfu, near a small village on the west coast. So you can understand my feeling of being near home." He was silent for a while then continued, "I grew up on the island and although I went to school in England, I could never wait to get back there, to the village and the sea, for all my holidays. I am not sure that I have any real idea of what you might call domestic regularity. All that I do know is that, in most respects, I would not have wanted any other life."

"I too had a childhood that was anything but normal," said the older man. He was wondering in what respect the boy would have wished for a different life, and he thought of his own infancy.

"You could say that I practically ran wild. Some very gentle people, of great principle, came to my aid and helped me shape my own path. But all of that is a very long story and we are becoming distracted from our task." He went on to describe what he knew of the invasion of the mainland of Italy that was under way at that very moment. Hence the change in his orders and the need for them to be especially vigilant for the next few hours.

Before they went below he did have one more question for Jamie and it concerned the gentleman who had interviewed the young man during his stay at the house in the south of England. Had this gentleman been a personal friend or acquaintance of Jamie before that period? When the answer came back as "no", all that the Commander had to add was that he was intrigued, then, by what might have triggered Jamie's selection for this particular branch of the service. Jamie explained this in the same terms as it had been explained to him—it was by virtue of his classical education (much of it from his mother) and his particular fluency in the languages of the eastern Mediterranean, specifically Greek and Turkish. His easy relationship and experience with animals had also been a determining factor.

The Commander was left with the feeling that the answer to the real question that was at the root of his curiosity—how someone so relatively young should have been selected for this particular assignment—must have to do with influence from a person close to the boy, who knew him well and had followed his up-bringing. He resolved to advance his knowl-edge of the boy's family, but at a more propitious time.

As the sky began to lighten they were again patrolling at periscope and snorkel depth. The swell was still sufficiently flat for them to be able to run the diesel without excessive risk of water choking the air intake and they wanted to conserve battery power for as long as possible.

The Commander was at the handle of his locator device, about which, in spite of their closer relationship, Jamie had still not had the courage to enquire. He rather assumed, in any event, that he would be told that it was highly secret. Its range of effectiveness seemed, almost, to be governed by the Commander's power of concentration. As if to illustrate this very fact, it was from a state approaching a trance that the Commander suddenly ordered: "Switch to battery. Dive to 50ft."

Pressing hard on the 'locator button', as Jamie was already thinking of it, the Commander scrutinised the indicator dial. The two needles, already shivering slightly toward each other at the top of the dial, began to move more steadily, and the Commander hunched his shoulders in grim determination. The enemy ship was approaching fast.

"Up 30," snapped the Commander.

"Aye, aye, Sir," Jamie responded, pulling back on the hydroplane levers.

"The art will be to place ourselves directly over his path. Slow ahead."

They were both keenly attentive to the increasing volume of the propeller noise from the closing vessel. Jamie could sense, rather than hear, that the German was bearing down on them from somewhere below their bow. He trusted his Commander to be able to judge the correct position and moment for the attack. It was as if the gruff giant next to him, combined with his technical instruments, was possessed of sensitivities so specialised and refined from years of practice that they seemed entirely natural.

"Prepare for Alpha," came the command. Jamie reached for the red lever. At that moment the right hand needle on the Commander's indicator twitched over to the right and back, and the red light began to flicker above them.

"Another sub!" exclaimed the Commander in a low curse, but nonetheless commanding: "Alpha."

Jamie pulled down the lever. The Commander was switching with one hand and releasing the charge with the other. Everything went dark.

"Beta!" he barked. "Surface. All ahead full."

Jamie set her hard up while the motors churned with a will to get them away from what was coming at speed. They broke the surface quicker than Jamie had thought possible and the Commander immediately started up the diesel engine to make more speed.

The locator dial, with the Commander's thumb on the button, left them in no doubt that the other sub had located them. The two needles were swinging to the bottom of the dial and converging rapidly. The Commander ordered to turn and face the on-comer. He switched again to the electric motor and hoped to position himself above the second subma-rine. They had completed their turn, were counting down the seconds till the first mine would explode, when the needles came together and the Commander released the second mine. With a grinding, whining wrench they were thrown out of their seats as their craft was thrown on its side. The explosion seemed to go on for ever and their stricken vessel was tossed like a cork in a cauldron of boiling water.

The two men struggled back to their positions. Dials had cracked open and pipes had burst all around them. The Commander started to close valves above them and indicated, with gestures, which ones Jamie should be caring for. A serious sound of water forcing in was coming from the stern and Jamie was sent to close the engine room bulkhead. As he gave the instruction the Commander told Jamie that the first impact must have been a physical contact with the other sub and that the mine on the first had exploded almost at the same time. Apart from limiting the damage from this double concussion they needed to separate themselves as much as possible from the imminent explosion of the second mine. Jamie scrambled aft, clambering to the engine room through a growing torrent of water. It took all his energy and strength to close the door and swing the lock. Having screwed home the stays he stumbled forward to the control room, slipping on the wet surface as it tilted ever more forward. They were going down.

About to rejoin the Commander in the control room there came the most ear-shattering, mind-crushing roar and Jamie was thrown off his feet, hit the bulkhead frame with the side of his head and blacked out.

Jamie recovered consciousness to find himself strapped in his control. Still dazed, with his head throbbing and to one side, he was aware of the dim red light flickering crazily. The angle of the boat was all wrong and the pressure straining on his every sense.

Out of the corner of his half-open eye he saw the Commander at his station in an attitude of what looked, inexplicably, like prayer, with his great, primitive head, clothed in a fur cap, thrown back and staring at the canopy with his arms thrust forward. Jamie knew that, if not dead already, they soon would be. He was not afraid. Welcome warm blackness enveloped him.

A wash of cold air and spray brought him awake. He was propped in the conning-tower hatch with his head in the cold dusk air. The sea was agitated around him and they were making slow headway against a blustery wind. The right side of his head was pure agony and he could feel some kind of padding inside a bandage that went round below his chin and over his crown. He thought he might be hallucinating and tried to move his hands to touch the metal around him. He felt a tug at his leg and was grabbed from below and eased down into the cockpit control room. The Commander was smiling, almost childishly, as he gave Jamie some water from the flask.

"We were lucky to have found ourselves in such friendly waters," he exclaimed. The statement left no margin for Jamie to question its meaning. It would have seemed petulant or pedantic to have dwelt on the subject of their rescue from that deep and pulverising fate. He was left, merely, to enjoy his salvation and to study the damage that had been wreaked on the instruments and plumbing of their little submarine.

Their air replenished, and unable to repair the damaged diesel motor, they were forced to make way with the electric motor. This meant staying just below the surface. The batteries were low and many instruments were shattered. The gyro compass had become unbalanced and needed to be struck to give a reading. Fortunately the radio still worked and, at dusk, with the antenna above the surface, they were able to make contact with the relief submarine, which was, no doubt, already stationed off the Commander's island waiting to pick them up. A new position was agreed for the rendezvous that would save their power.

The next three hours they passed silently under dimmed light, the Commander regularly checking his vessel detection device and Jamie nursing both himself and the controls of the battered craft.

Their transport submarine surfaced nearby. It was not the same ship that had delivered Jamie three nights ago. This one was equipped with a transport cradle aft of its tower especially constructed to carry MS3 or a similar craft. With the swell that continued to run it was decided to tow the smaller craft to calmer waters or make for the shelter of the western shores of Sicily, whichever came sooner.

For the remainder of that night Jamie had no opportunity to enquire of his Commander about the manner of their salvation from what he was beginning to feel, with ever more conviction, should have been a certain death deep in the troubled waters of the Mediterranean. With a line from the towing submarine made fast to their bow it was essential for one of the men to maintain a watch from the conning tower as they pitched and yawed through the constant spray. With consideration for Jamie's injury the Commander ordered him below and took the duty for himself.

Throughout those long hours of discomfort and semi-consciousness Jamie would relive those moments when he had seen, as if from a distorted angle, the Commander in that strange posture. He could not throw off the image of a man in fervent prayer. In that dim red glow, an El Greco St. Francis, as it were, emerging in the chemical liquid in his schoolboy darkroom. He felt sure that his feverish mind was hallucinating this wild illusion and his practical mind refused any spiritual interpretation. Although he had only known the Commander these few hours he was sure that the man, though serious and intense, was not of a religious persuasion. In spite of his confused state he resolved to remain alert for an explanation for what he had witnessed and for how they had found themselves at the surface after their catastrophic plunge.

An hour before dawn, about two miles east of Trapani, they were able to perform the docking operation, which required the carrier sub Skimmer to submerge to periscope depth and allow the Commander to manoeuvre his craft into the cradle on the stern of the larger vessel. With MS3 securely clamped to the welcoming marsupial bulk of the mother ship, the two weary crew members were finally welcomed aboard Skimmer by the captain and officers. Jamie was quite certain that the deference with which they were received sprang from sincere admiration and not simply out of respect for his commander's rank. Personally, though moved by the warmth of their reception and strengthened by the hot strong tea, liberally laced with rum, he was, quite suddenly, more concerned by how hungry he felt.

The return journey to Gibraltar should have allowed him time to acquaint himself more with his commander. This was not to be. There was no opportunity aboard Skimmer to advance his quest for an explanation of their salvation. Except for the briefing in the captain's cabin they bunked in separate quarters, only meeting to eat in the wardroom, where they were in the company of other officers. Since the night aboard the mini-sub after that first day's action Jamie had not had a conversation, alone, with the Commander. Instructions, orders, damage reports or comments concerning their situation, position or weather conditions had been the limit of their communications. Moved, as he was, by a genuine but complex brew of emotions, including respect, filial admiration and a growing sense of friendship, Jamie knew that he was motivated by much more than mere curiosity. He resolved, therefore, to wait for anything that might help him shape a clearer image of this figure who now loomed so large in his life yet remained so mysterious.

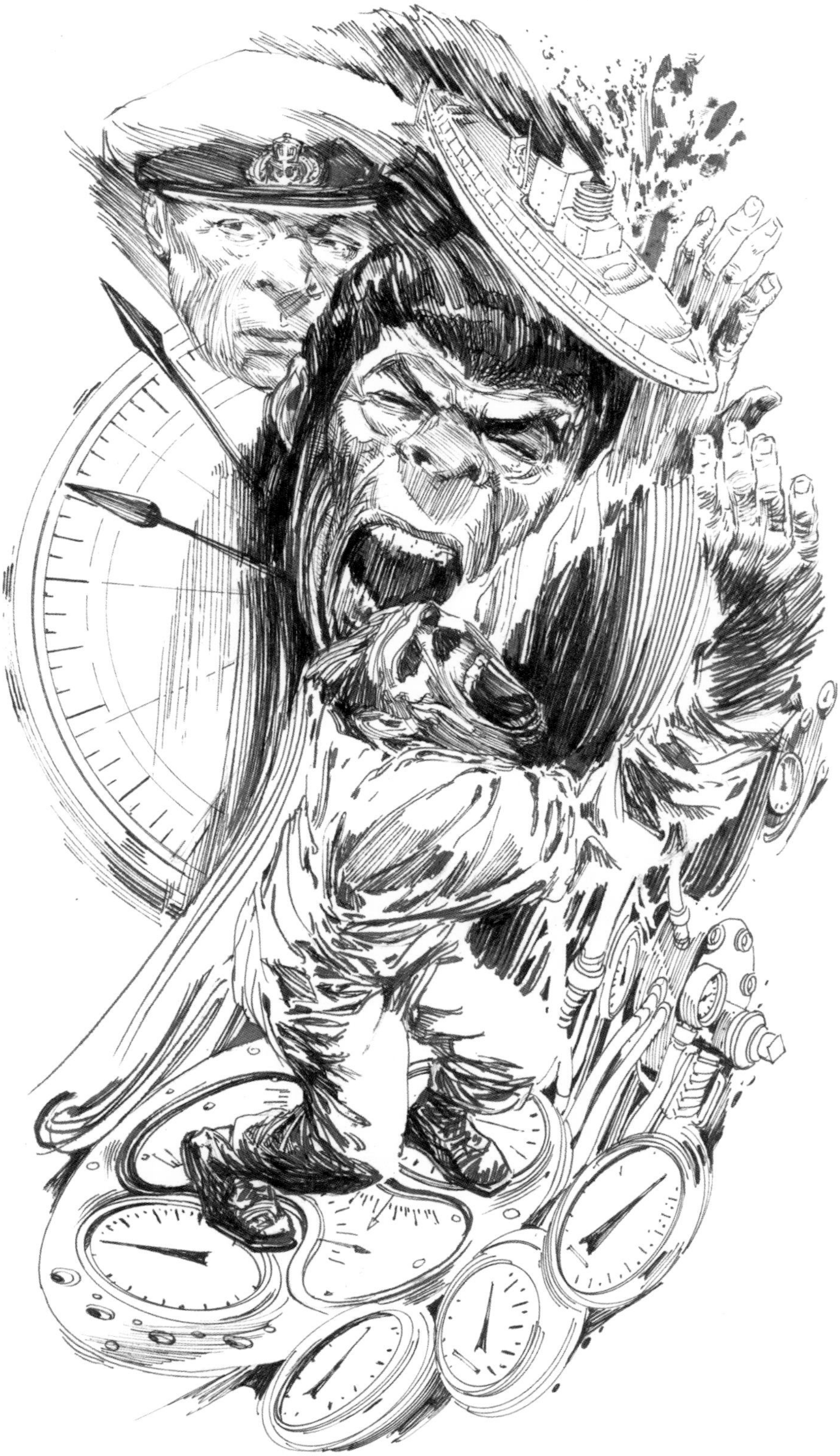

Almost one month later, after what he considered to be an unnecessary extended period of training, he had come to terms with the possibility that his submarine adventure, alongside the Commander, had become a singularly exotic period of his life, the memory of which he might, one day, retell to his grandchildren. In the intervening period the character who had been so close and important for those intense few days had disappeared from view. Jamie was briefly reminded of him when he coincided with 'Doc' at training sessions with the mini-subs, the last occasion being when he singularly failed to master whatever skill it required to manipulate a version of the vessel indicating device.

He had been relieved to return to training with the dogs and was even quite proud of his performance in one exercise for which he had to subsist on the 'Rock', with only a dog for company and for as long as possible without being discovered. The trial of clandestine survival earned him a special badge for staying undetected while performing the required tasks for 12 days, although he had not confessed to the fact that he had willingly been discovered as he was tiring of the game and had not been sure whether he might have exceeded his brief. He was certain that he and 'Mutt', his canine accomplice, could have 'survived' indefinitely, such a team had they become. Indeed it had been the dog who had taken him to a hiding place of such comfort that it seemed unlikely to have been pure chance. Who, he had wondered, had been there before? So it was that he felt small merit in the achievement and when neither the Commander, nor 'Doc' had attended the short prize-giving ceremony he had not been surprised. Unwilling to enquire after them, he was sure that they had slipped out of his life.

Then, without explanation, he had been summoned to appear before the commanding officer. Concerned that he had, in some way, transgressed or been deficient he found himself anxiously installed in a large leather chair, waiting for his appointment in the ante-room to the CO's office, when Prospero passed before him. The great man stopped, turned, saluted then shook his hand and gave him a fleeting smile. He knocked and opened the office door beckoning Jamie to follow. From that moment Jamie had no idea what to expect but felt certain that it was going to be interesting.

Jamie and the Commander's adventure will continue in
MONO: Prospero Rising **in 2015...**

Creating
The Old Curiosity Shop

Mr. Liam Sharp
—Story, Script

There's so much legacy attached to a character like MONO.

There's a debt owed to the creators that came before, a need to honor their work, whilst building on it, and hopefully creating something fresh.

Ben Wolstenholme introduced me to the character some six years ago — I confess to complete ignorance, which is a bit embarrassing given that I've been steeped in pulp material my entire life. How had I missed it? Ben had dreams of drawing MONO in the form of a comic book, and I remember the day he told me about it very clearly.

Let me be honest with you — Ben was, and is, a very talented artist. I've known him since he was 12 years old, and I used to give him tips when I was starting out, a very long time ago it seems. But as I looked at his sketches, his squat, characterful (I'm being kind here) figure work and clumsy, inelegant ink work, I thought it was a bit of a pipe dream. He had a long way to go before his work, in my opinion, was of a professional quality.

And yet it had something. It was lively, and committed. It was engaging. And MONO was definitely asking for the comic treatment. If Ben didn't do it, somebody else was sure to re-discover the man-ape assassin and spy. I wondered if it might help if I wrote it? That way I could at least guide the process, lend the project a bit of experience. It was a long-shot, a bit risky, and frankly I judged the whole endeavor very unlikely to ever amount to anything!

I should have known better, and I need not have worried.

Do this: Look at our narrator Heston on the first pages, and then at Heston on the last page.

Yup.

Staggering.

'The Old Curiosity Shop' is more than just a comic, it is an artistic journey. And the learning curve from unpublished beginner to exceptional draughtsman happens not over a series of issues, but in a matter of pages. By the time Ben hit the spread of war-torn Caen he was, in my opinion, one of the most unique and accomplished artists in the entire industry. It was pretty astonishing to witness, and more than a little bit humbling!

Once Ben hit his stride everything changed again. The plot shifted. The writing took on a life of its own, particularly as it became infused with the primal, charnel

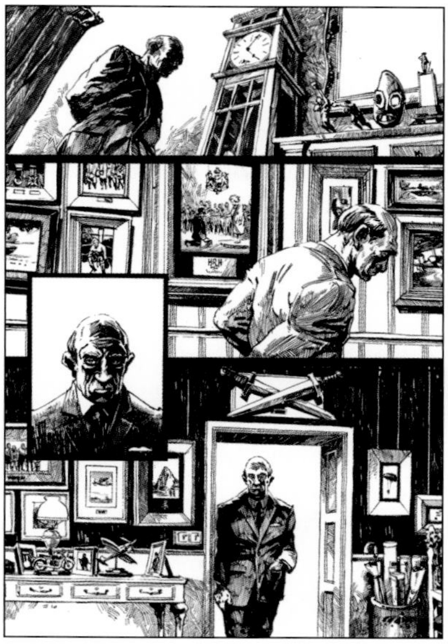

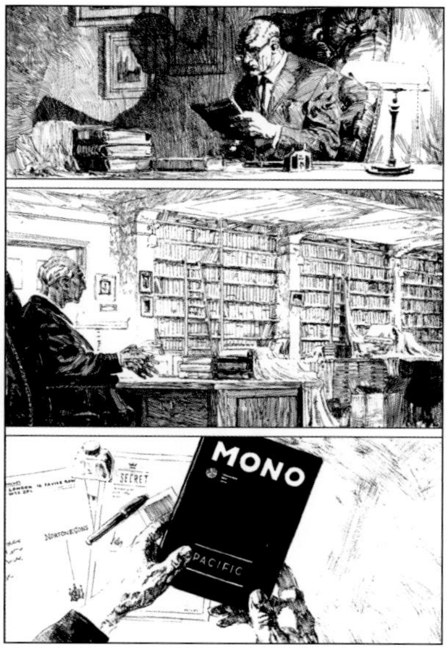
SECRET
MONO
PACIFIC

poems of Wilfred Owen – a perfect voice for this story. We had started with the ambition of a Frank Miller-esque narrative, but Owen ended up being the biggest influence by far, and that profoundly changed the nature of the story. I wrote, and rewrote every episode as Ben's art continued to inspire and evolve. It became a much more organic process, and we started to stretch out scenes, thinking about the long-form read. We juxtaposed misleading information in the words against the brutality of the action.

As an example, Ben introduced the dogs into the story – the Nagazi. And the concept of Nazi Nagazi grew out of that – dogs bred to hunt humans. The fight MONO has with these enormous bear-bating dogs becomes a metaphysical tussle, in which he tries his hardest to put the wrong done to them right. MONO, as suggested by the pulps, has the ability to connect with all animals on a psychic level – something mysteriously referred to as 'minding'. We wanted to touch on that in a way that seemed more believable, less preposterous. So in our story MONO really knows dogs, and how to reset them, return them to their natural states, whilst also rendering them unconscious by exploiting their pressure points.

Ben manages to put this across on paper with amazing clarity, and some drop-dead gorgeous drawing. MONO lying supine on the unconscious dogs might well be my favourite single image of the whole series.

For me, though, it is the final, inevitable punch-up with the General – a scene that lasts almost an entire issue – that is the stand-out. Ben choreographed the fight through a floor plan of the chateaux he created, even going so far as to design a color 'mood' map for the whole issue. It's an obsessively considered, virtuoso piece of storytelling. It leads the eye left to right until a crucial turning point – at which juncture MONO is suddenly rooted, rendered an immovable object. Enough, as they say, is enough! And then... well, you'll just have to go read it. Then read it again. It's remarkable.

You may not know it, but the events in this story really happened. The general, the terrible things done to the city of Caen – mostly by the allied forces – these are historical. And MONO, as is always the way with the pulp incarnation, plays a part. He's there, where the balance of power pivots.

The question then is – why?

And then – what next?

These are things I look forward to exploring with Ben in future stories! —LS

Mr. Ben Wolstenholme
—Story, Pencils, Inks

What was I thinking?

As I pull this first volume of MONO together it makes me realize what a blur this whole experience has been.

When we set out as Madefire in 2011 we had multiple goals; we wanted to explore the edges of digital storytelling as we developed 'Motion Books'; we also wanted to remain authentic to comics and the centuries of words-and-pictures storytelling that has gone before us. On top of that agenda it's farcical, not to say a little troubling, to think I put myself forward for MONO. As Liam has (too eloquently!) mentioned, I have no prior experience in comics, let alone the emergent 'grammar' of Motion Books. I knew that I wanted to improve as a storyteller, and so I made a start. But soon I was wondering what I had gotten myself into, and as such I owe a huge debt to Liam. At Madefire we're surrounded by some extraordinary creators and if it wasn't for Liam's encouragement I would have retired and sat back from the whole creative process. Instead, working on The Old Curiosity Shop story, and seeing it through, has had a profound effect on me. Thank you, Liam.

And so, with that said, here are a few things that I have found particularly useful along the way:

First off, this medium is all about words and pictures, and Liam conveyed a strong belief that you don't need to 'say it' and 'show it' at the same time. I've tried to let the visuals take a different path to the written word – so that they may augment or juxtapose one another.

Where I have had prior experience is in storyboarding, particularly planning for film and animation. This background became the anchor to my approach. I would begin by breaking Liam's script down into individual thumbnails, regardless of eventual layout. The things to consider here are vast: character, action-and-acting, camera, lighting, styling, editing, pace. Then I would start to consider the sequence as a whole on the page or screen – the general hierarchy of visuals, positive and negative space, and, of course, where dialogue and text will appear. I now know that this list is essentially the same for drawing any printed comic, a serious endeavor.

I would ask myself:

"What is the most important moment or panel?"

"Where would the camera be best placed for the action?"

"What is the right number of shots or steps for this sequence?"

"How can the page layout accentuate the pace and drama?"

"How would I shoot this?"

Both The Old Curiosity Shop and MONO Pacific were released 'digital-first' as Motion Books. Motion Books take advantage of the opportunity 'screens' provide by incorporating motion, depth and sound. Working towards an onscreen reading experience there is both 'more' and 'less' to consider at the same time. For example, not everything needs to be shown on the screen at once, so there is more room to expand the art of the panels. Unlike print comics, there is also an added variable of time and user-control. Pauses and interactive 'tap points' are used to introduce new text or additional panels – this creates more flexibility in layout.

Through timing and interactivity, we can now lead the reader through the story, giving us new ways to surprise and delight. Comics no longer have to start from top left and lead the eye across a static page, although, I believe that there is an important rigor and restraint found in print that needs to remain in the digital execution. I'd liken it to a design process: Whether designing for print, or designing for screen, great design needs to have a strong sense of hierarchy – of what is *most* important. Strong design also demands a system approach, be it in the use of grids, typography, or placement of imagery – these practices have been honed in print over many years and should be heeded. Onscreen there is more room for theatre, but there is often a lot less discipline and rigor around layout, typography, hierarchy – and what not-to-do. I am a big believer that 'less is more' – in other words, if you can say it with less then it becomes more impactful. I have found it very useful to create MONO through traditional page layouts – not only so that it can

easily be printed – but also I find the discipline and restraint of the original design accentuates the importance of transitions and movement when they occur onscreen.

In terms of art, MONO straddles the chasm between educated man, and primordial beast, so my goal with the look of MONO was to combine a classical, timeless sentiment with an urgent and visceral violence. I am still early in inking as a craft and as such have been exploring the best approach, you'll see that I started with dip pen and brush, then moved for a little while to digital inking, then back to physical again. The return to ink and paper was mainly to allow for a real range of mark-making, and a sense of consequence in every stroke, but each have their advantages. To me the inks are about creating tension and pace in the blacks and through negative space. These can imply movement or calm in themselves. Once the inks are complete, I send them to the Fin Cramb in Scotland for coloring – now there's a patient, and incredibly gifted man!

So, in summary, I hope you've enjoyed joining MONO on a couple of his early adventures. I know I can't wait to open another of his journals. This process has been the start of an education – I wouldn't go as far as to say ignorance is bliss, but it certainly helped in my case. —BW

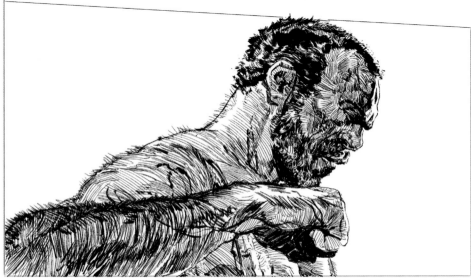

Mono

Nolstenholme

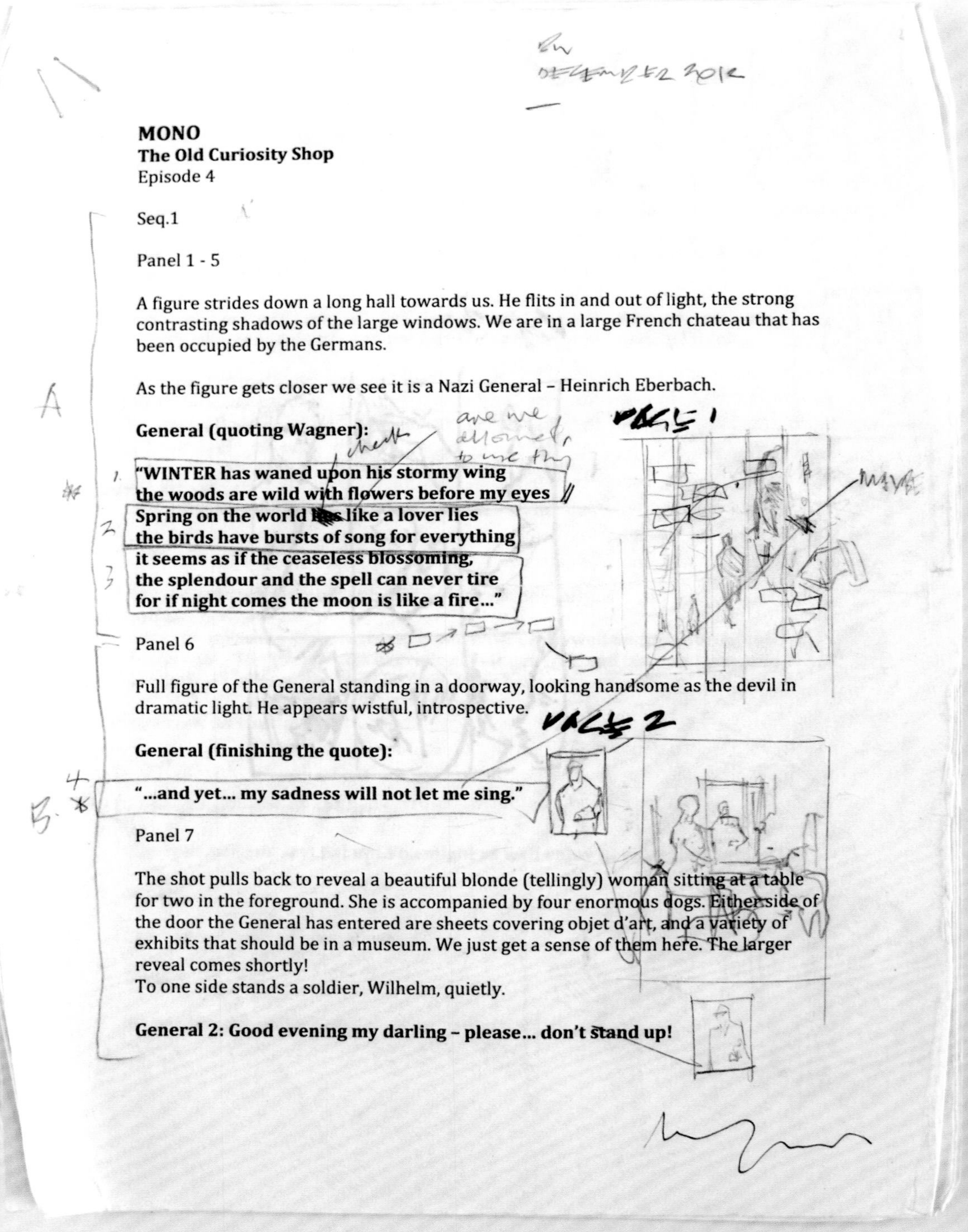

MONO
The Old Curiosity Shop
Episode 4

Seq.1

Panel 1 - 5

A figure strides down a long hall towards us. He flits in and out of light, the strong contrasting shadows of the large windows. We are in a large French chateau that has been occupied by the Germans.

As the figure gets closer we see it is a Nazi General – Heinrich Eberbach.

General (quoting Wagner):

"WINTER has waned upon his stormy wing
the woods are wild with flowers before my eyes
Spring on the world like a lover lies
the birds have bursts of song for everything
it seems as if the ceaseless blossoming,
the splendour and the spell can never tire
for if night comes the moon is like a fire…"

Panel 6

Full figure of the General standing in a doorway, looking handsome as the devil in dramatic light. He appears wistful, introspective.

General (finishing the quote):

"…and yet… my sadness will not let me sing."

Panel 7

The shot pulls back to reveal a beautiful blonde (tellingly) woman sitting at a table for two in the foreground. She is accompanied by four enormous dogs. Either side of the door the General has entered are sheets covering objet d'art, and a variety of exhibits that should be in a museum. We just get a sense of them here. The larger reveal comes shortly!
To one side stands a soldier, Wilhelm, quietly.

General 2: Good evening my darling – please… don't stand up!

Liam is both a writer and an artist; as a result he writes very visual scripts. This visual guidance was a massive help as I learnt the ropes.

The introduction of the General in stark contrast to his poetic recital makes for a striking entry. *—Above & Opposite.*

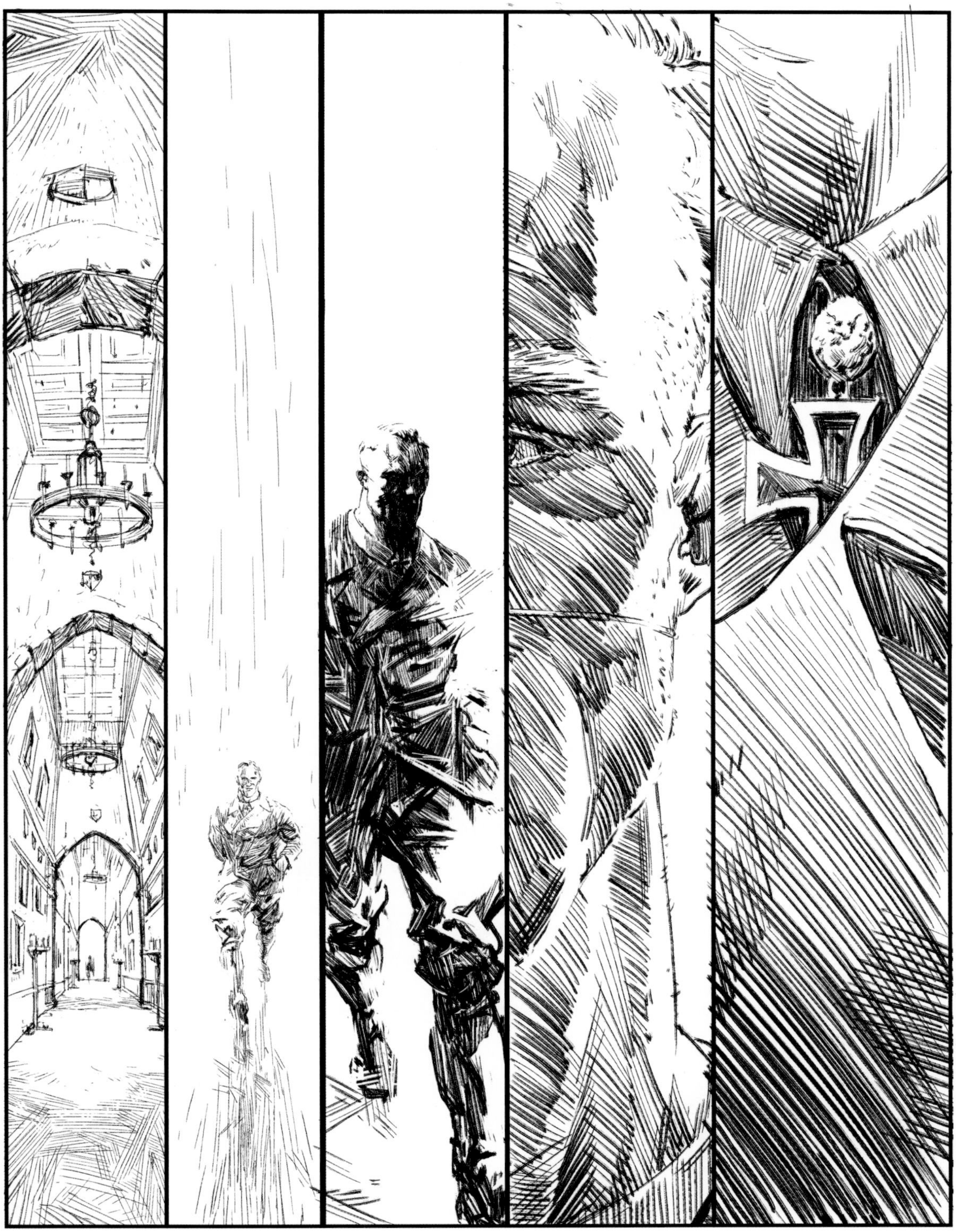

MONO EPISODE 4
MARCH 2013

WOLSTENHOLME

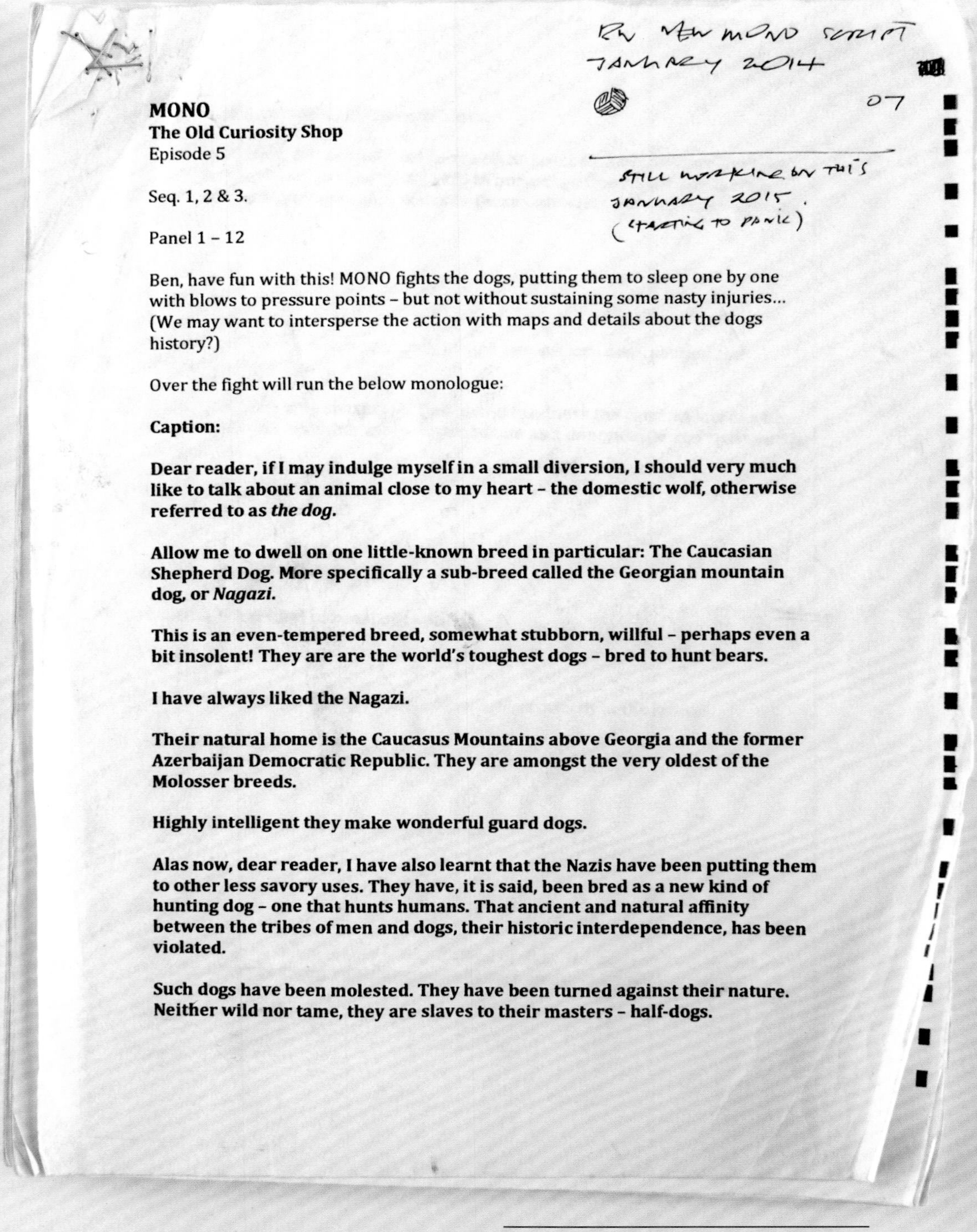

RW NEW MONO SCRIPT
JANUARY 2014
07

STILL WORKING ON THIS
JANUARY 2015.
(STARTING TO PANIC)

MONO
The Old Curiosity Shop
Episode 5

Seq. 1, 2 & 3.

Panel 1 – 12

Ben, have fun with this! MONO fights the dogs, putting them to sleep one by one with blows to pressure points – but not without sustaining some nasty injuries... (We may want to intersperse the action with maps and details about the dogs history?)

Over the fight will run the below monologue:

Caption:

Dear reader, if I may indulge myself in a small diversion, I should very much like to talk about an animal close to my heart – the domestic wolf, otherwise referred to as *the dog*.

Allow me to dwell on one little-known breed in particular: The Caucasian Shepherd Dog. More specifically a sub-breed called the Georgian mountain dog, or *Nagazi*.

This is an even-tempered breed, somewhat stubborn, willful – perhaps even a bit insolent! They are are the world's toughest dogs – bred to hunt bears.

I have always liked the Nagazi.

Their natural home is the Caucasus Mountains above Georgia and the former Azerbaijan Democratic Republic. They are amongst the very oldest of the Molosser breeds.

Highly intelligent they make wonderful guard dogs.

Alas now, dear reader, I have also learnt that the Nazis have been putting them to other less savory uses. They have, it is said, been bred as a new kind of hunting dog – one that hunts humans. That ancient and natural affinity between the tribes of men and dogs, their historic interdependence, has been violated.

Such dogs have been molested. They have been turned against their nature. Neither wild nor tame, they are slaves to their masters – half-dogs.

This script was very intimidating as the action was left so open-ended. It did give me a lot of room to experiment, however.

I think Liam was just messing with me to see what I would do! —*Above & Opposite.*

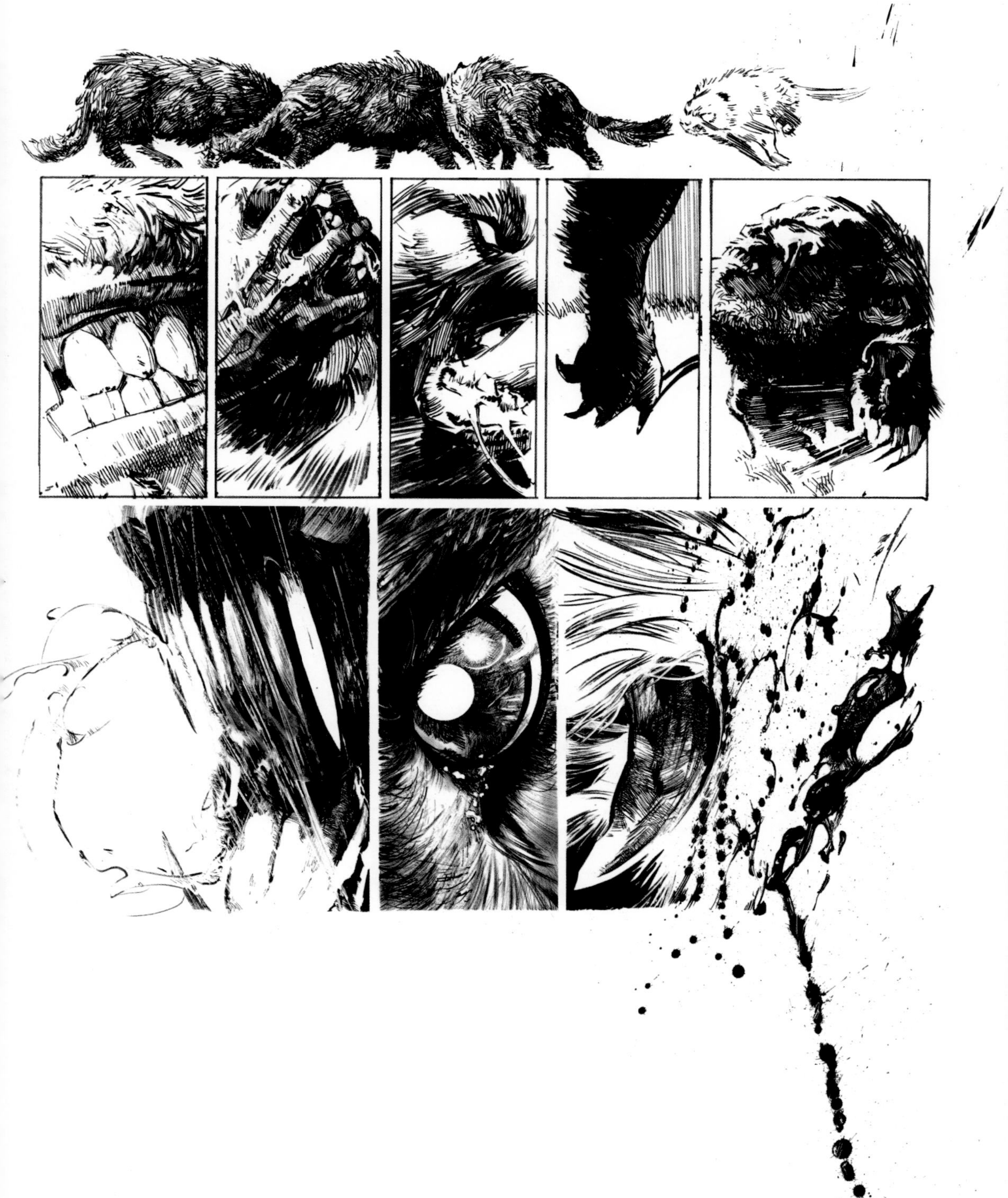

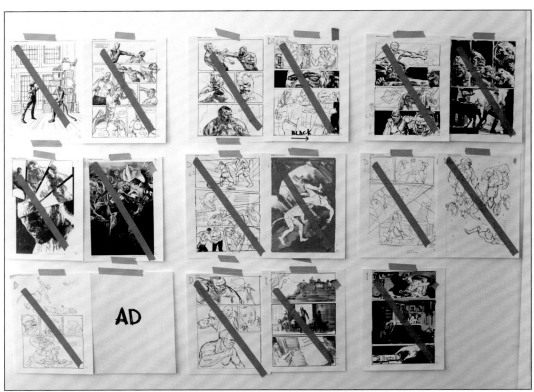

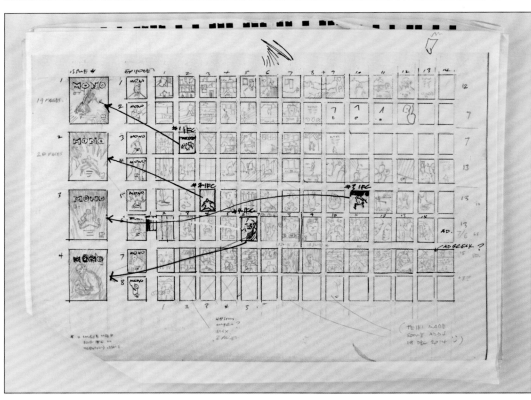

Keeping track of the pages as a whole arc. And tracking my progress on the last pages of the MONO Motion Book series. —*Above.*

Master schematic to show how the seven Motion Book episodes combine into four printed Issues. —***Below.***

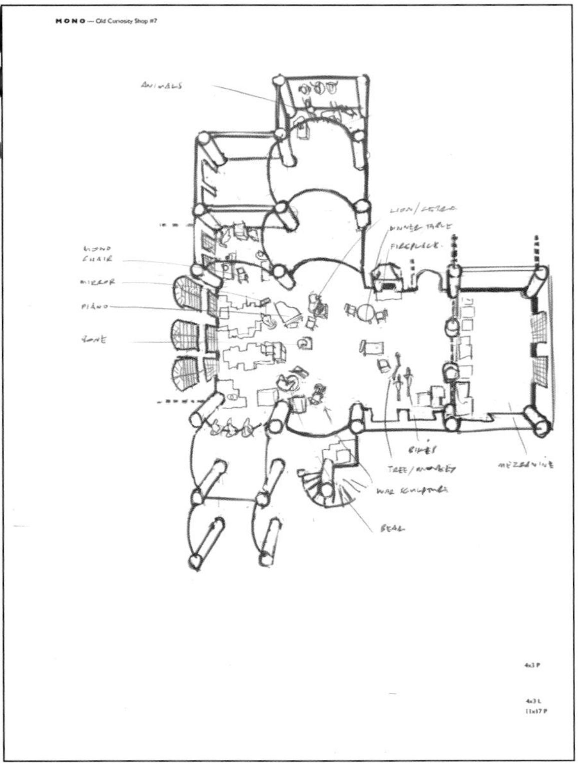
MONO — Old Curiosity Shop #7

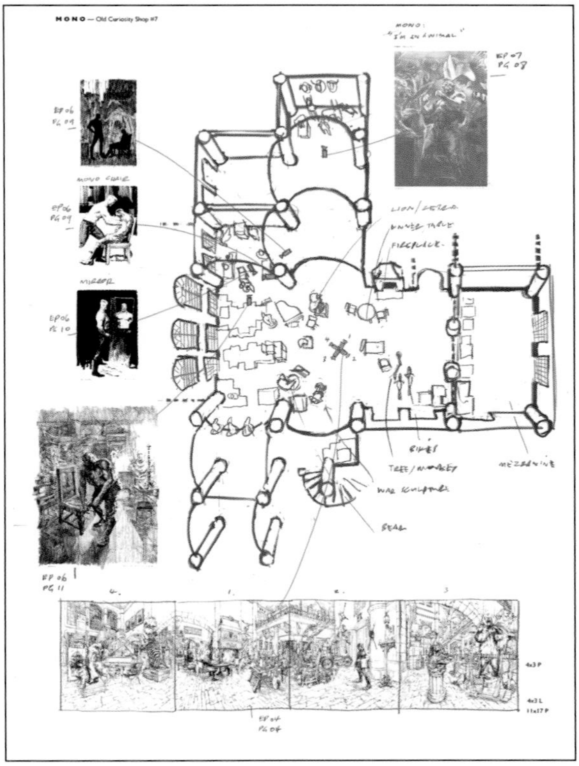
MONO — Old Curiosity Shop #7

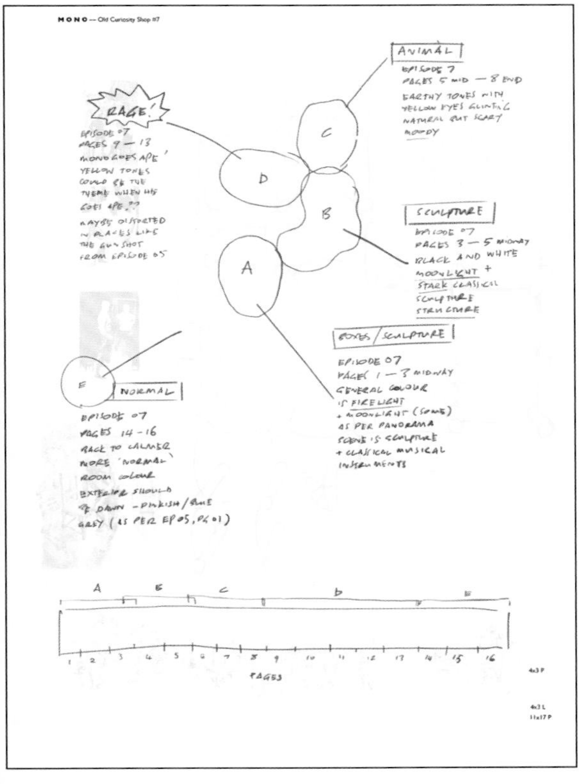
MONO — Old Curiosity Shop #7

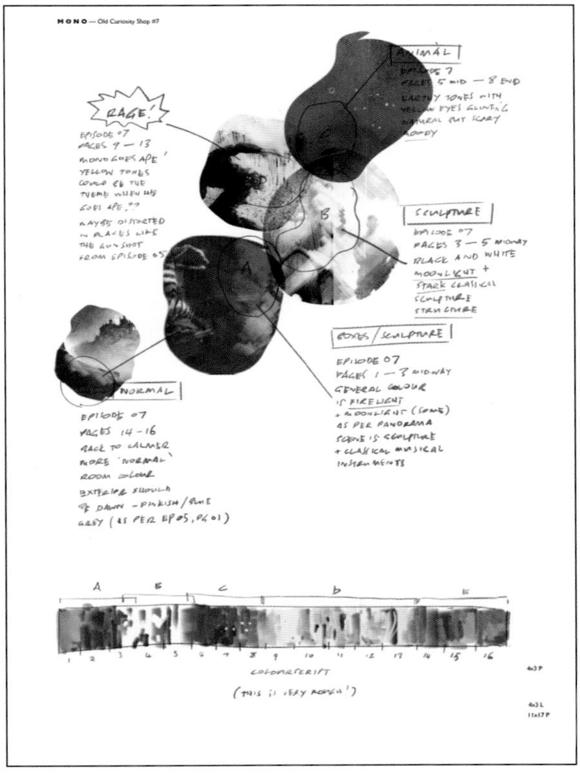
MONO — Old Curiosity Shop #7

Notes to Fin on the overall layout of The Old Curiosity Shop and key objects. ***—Top left.***

Making sure the final scenes tie together with the master panorama as seen in issue #2. ***—Top right.***

Mapping the final sequence into key sections as the fight progresses from a backdrop of 'human' sculptures to 'animal' taxidermy. ***—Bottom left.***

Colorscript to describe the changing emotion of the scene as a build up to MONO going 'Ape' (yellows). ***—Bottom right.***

'I imagine the panels like a Victorian cut paper theatre, with foreground, middle-ground & background.'

Mr. Fin Cramb
—Color

One of the most rewarding things about working on the colors for MONO: The Old Curiosity Shop was the level of collaboration going on. Putting the technicalities of the coloring process aside for a minute, I think that was the real strength of it for me – thoughts and ideas were swapped and encouraged all the time between the creative folk involved – my ideal way to work!

I imagine the panels like a Victorian cut paper theatre, the foreground, middle-ground and background separations being the most important thing in both the clarity of the panel and a feeling of how it might move. I'll often begin by breaking up the page into flat colors or grey tones with each ground, figure or asset separated out – so, before I've even started the real colors, the page is prepped in such a way that I can later pass it to the animator, or 'builder', to work their magic.

The coloring of MONO was like a playground for me; I love to employ a mix of both digital and traditional materials and I really like to try out new techniques. The Madefire tool offers up a huge amount of extra storytelling possibilities and Ben often experiments with his linework – shifting his subtleties and methods – it's cool to be able to react to those kinds of things in the color.

Some of the things I'm most proud of in the book are the odd bit of emotional and expressive coloring. For example, when MONO is being beaten, his world begins to grey out and lose its color. It's a real narrative strength in comics, and something I enjoy as a reader. Also some of the technical tricks – making a wine glass truly clear so that the background can move behind it, or figuring out how the bloom from a light might fill the space between two moving figures – I got really into all that stuff. —FC

'The Motion Book is a new frontier for the visual storyteller, a blend between comic book & motion picture.'

Mr. Evan Limberger —Build

Building, as we call it at Madefire, is unique both in presentation and process.

As a builder I feel like I must have the mind of a sequential artist and a film director. Sequential artists are thinking of how to lead the eye of the reader, and directors are sensitive to the overall mood and pace of a story. In this sense, a builder's process is very unique.

The majority of my time is spent planning out the build. From deciding the pacing of each page and how each panel is revealed, to the extent of motion within each panel. Building the finale of MONO (the Motion Book series) was a particular pleasure, not only because I am a fan of the series, but also because Ben and Liam have already established a specific art direction for the story. That makes my job a lot easier. After talking with the creators, I can set the pace throughout the story, pace is very important in my job.

During the finale, there are distinct pace changes that occur – we go from a very formal boxing match, which is precise and academic, to a savage assault, which is brutal and primeval. I emphasize this distinction by evolving the presentation of each panel throughout the fight. While the General is in control, the panels come on screen in a uniform fashion: left to right, or top to bottom. Furthermore, I kept the motion within each panel contained within the panel borders and stayed true to a formal comic page. Edges are crisp, 90° angles and motions are precise.

It isn't until MONO takes over that my panel transitions become raw and jagged, more dynamic, and enter the page in a sharper way. During those sequences I envisioned jaws snapping, and the motion is more exaggerated. I also start to break those traditional panel borders and the motion begins to enter the negative space around the panels. For instance, on one page blood splatters in the background around the panels to help emphasize the power of each of MONO's punches.

This episode was a heavy hitter, with dozens of punches. Ben did a great job drawing each differently, so when it came to building this episode I also varied how each blow was presented. Some punches are simply a fist swinging into a body part, others I'm moving the entire panel to emphasize the movement. Some use motion blurs. Some I add a flash of light for shock value. It's this constant challenge to keep things fresh and diverse that makes the creative process of building so enjoyable for me. —EL

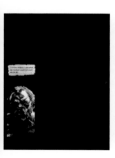

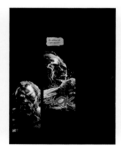

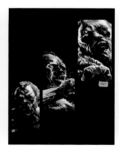

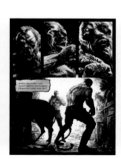

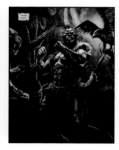

Black & White Gallery

BEN WOLSTENHOLME

A note of thanks to my family – Nanu, Teifi and Neve for being so patient and supportive ever since this ape-man invaded our lives.

And to Madefire; my co-founders Liam & Eugene, and to the whole team for all the encouragement.

—Thank you.

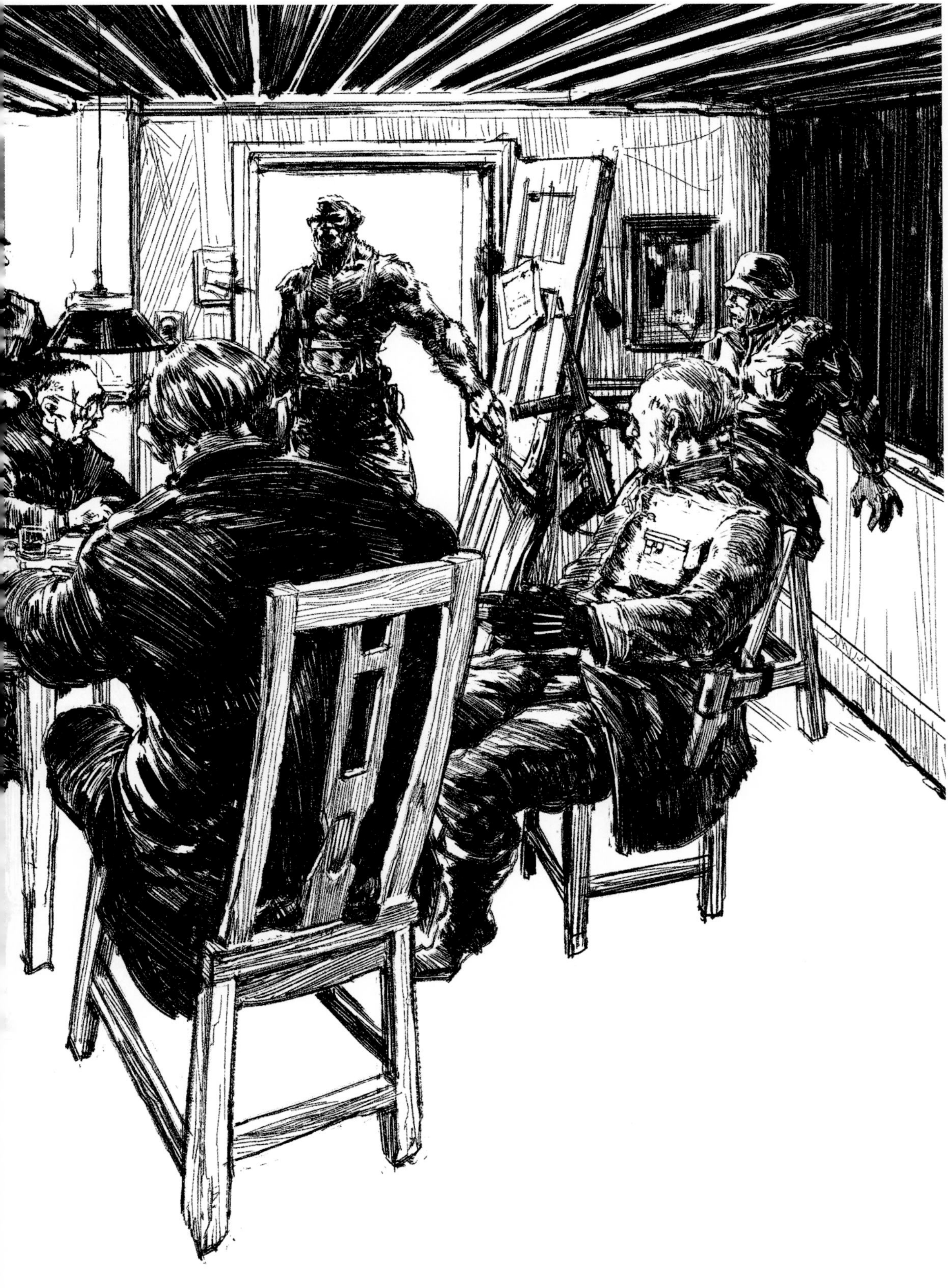

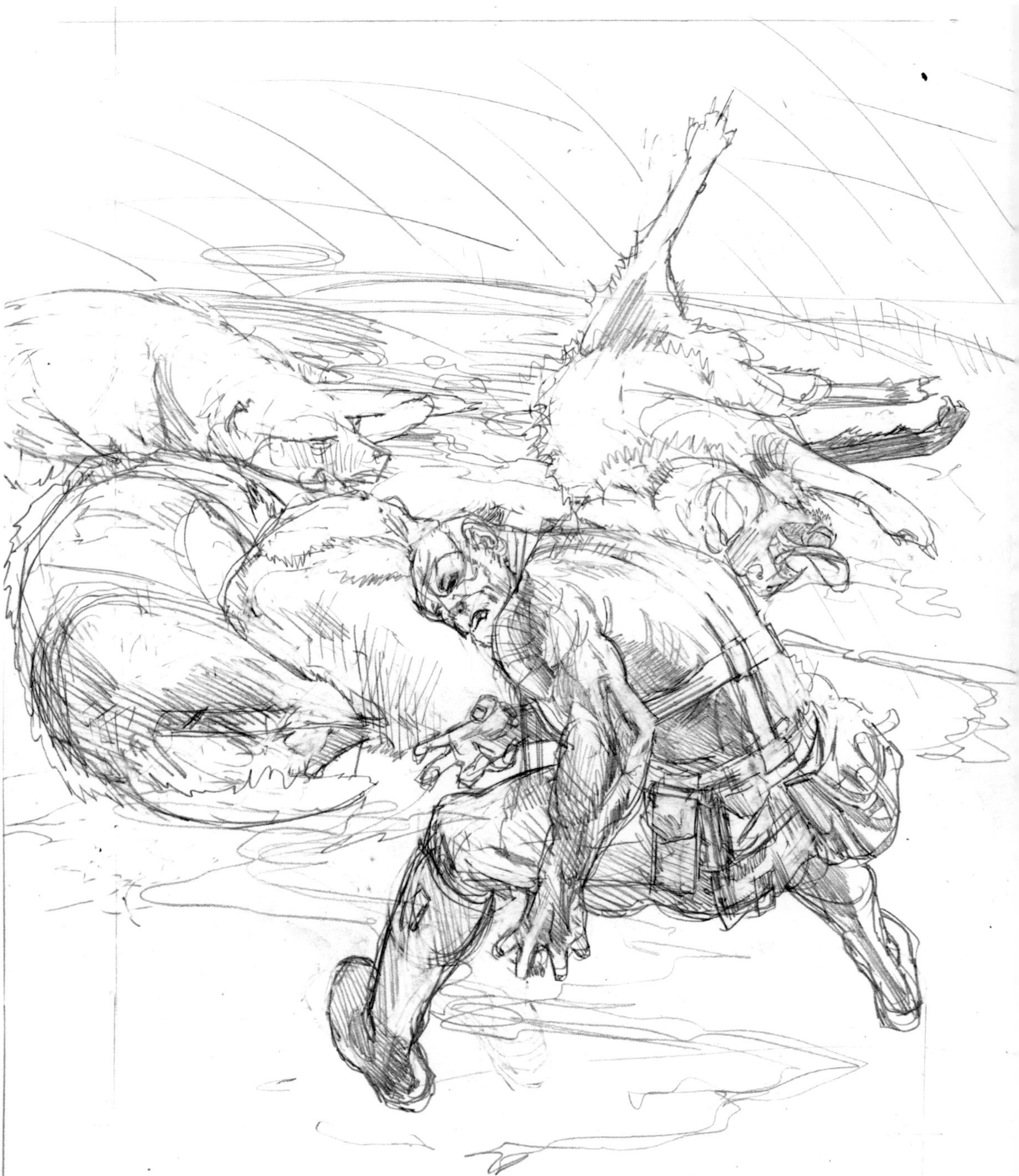

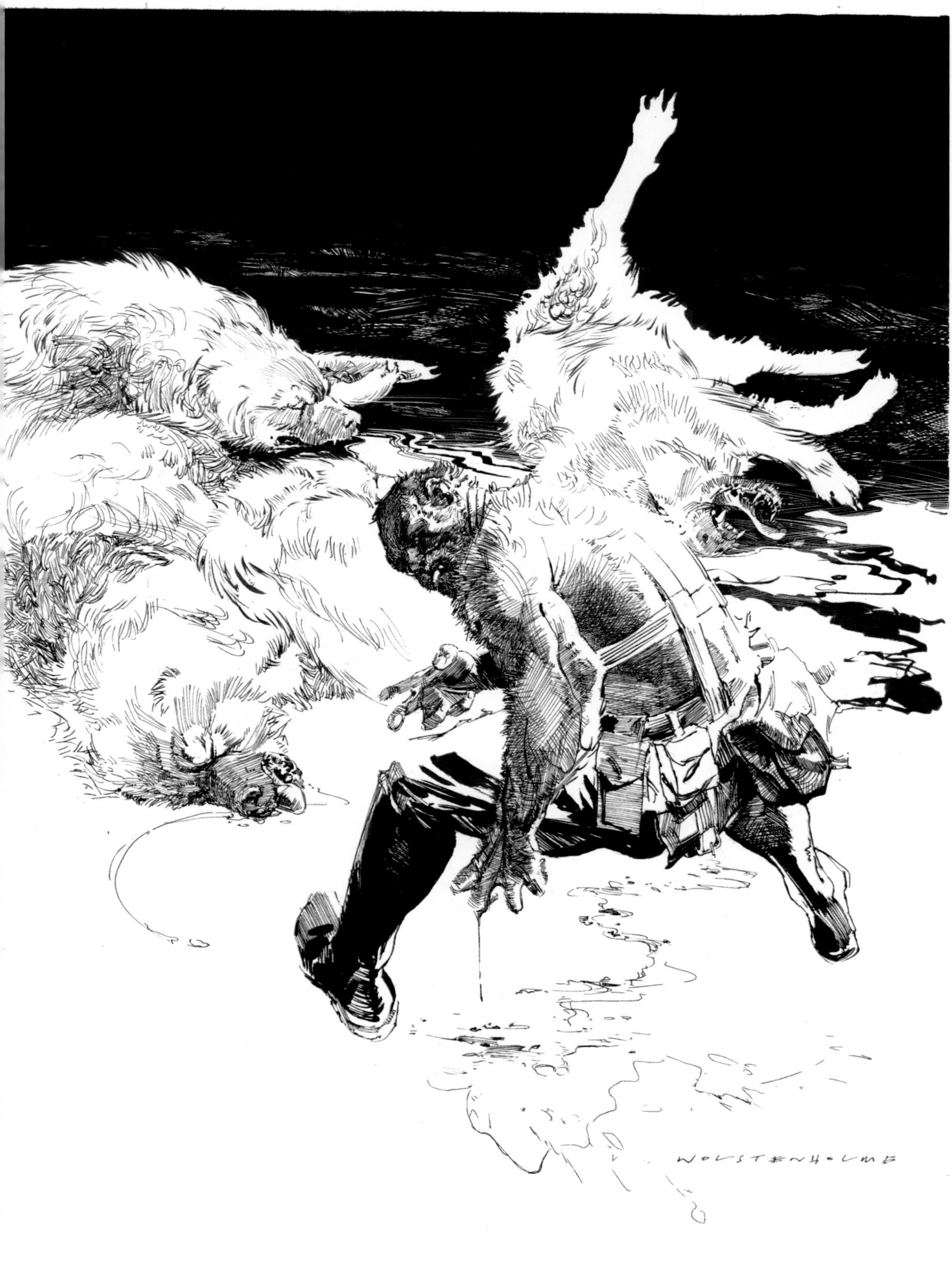
WOLSTENHOLME

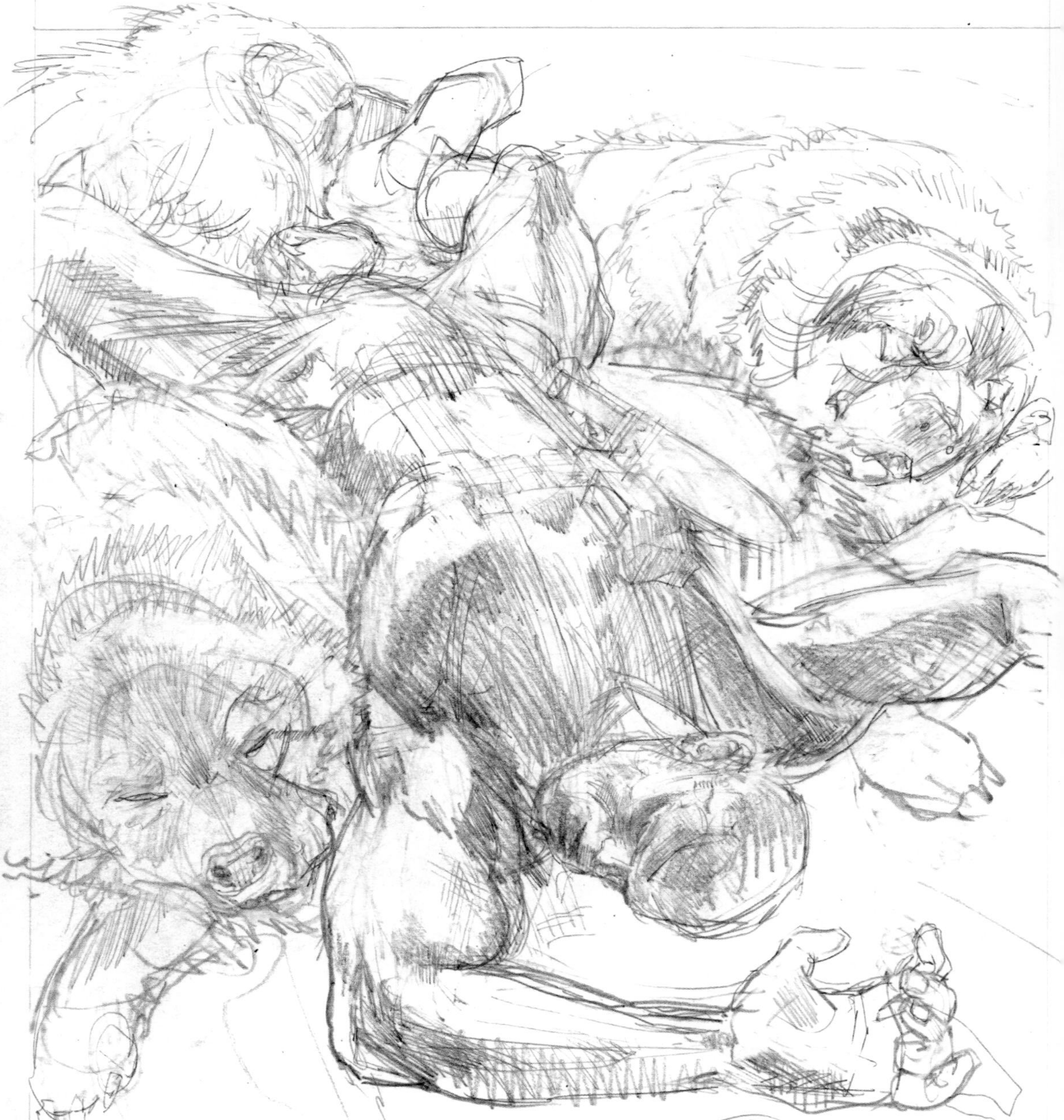

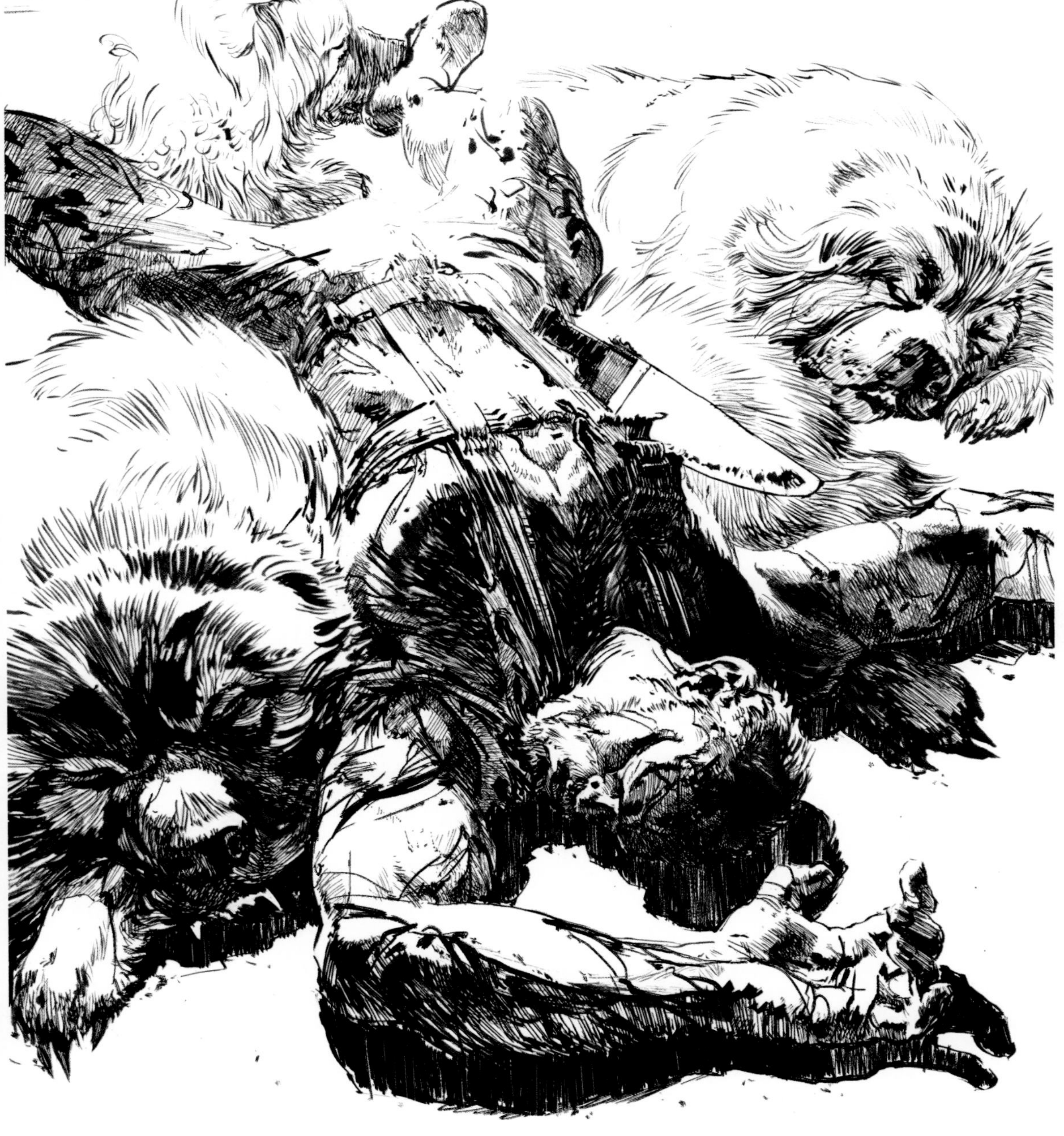

WOLSTENHOLME
MONO

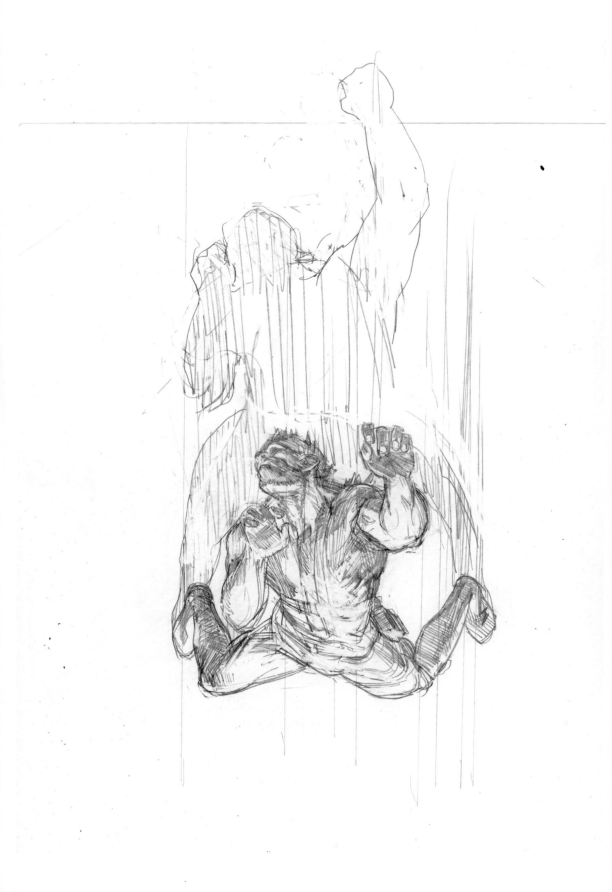

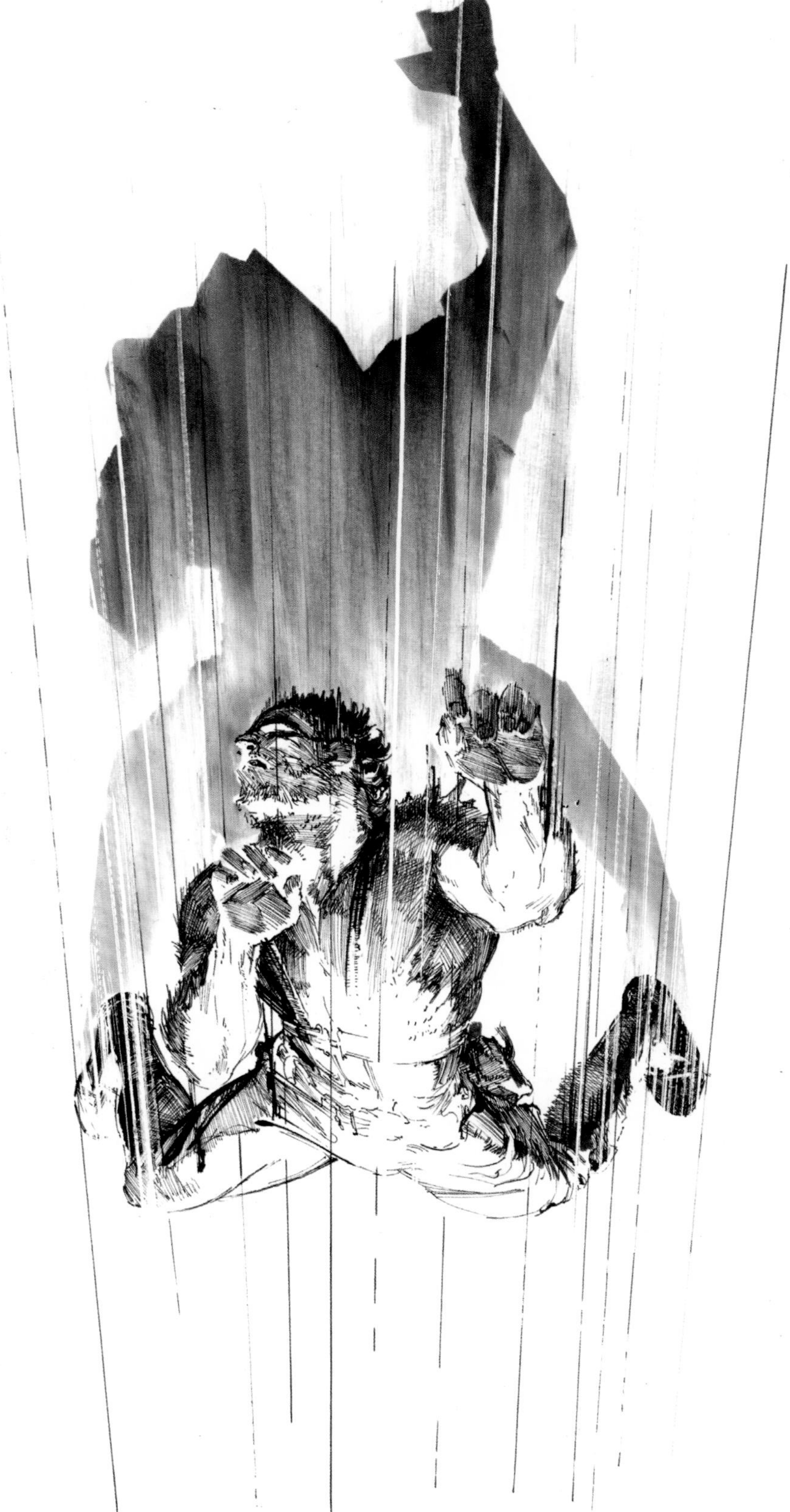

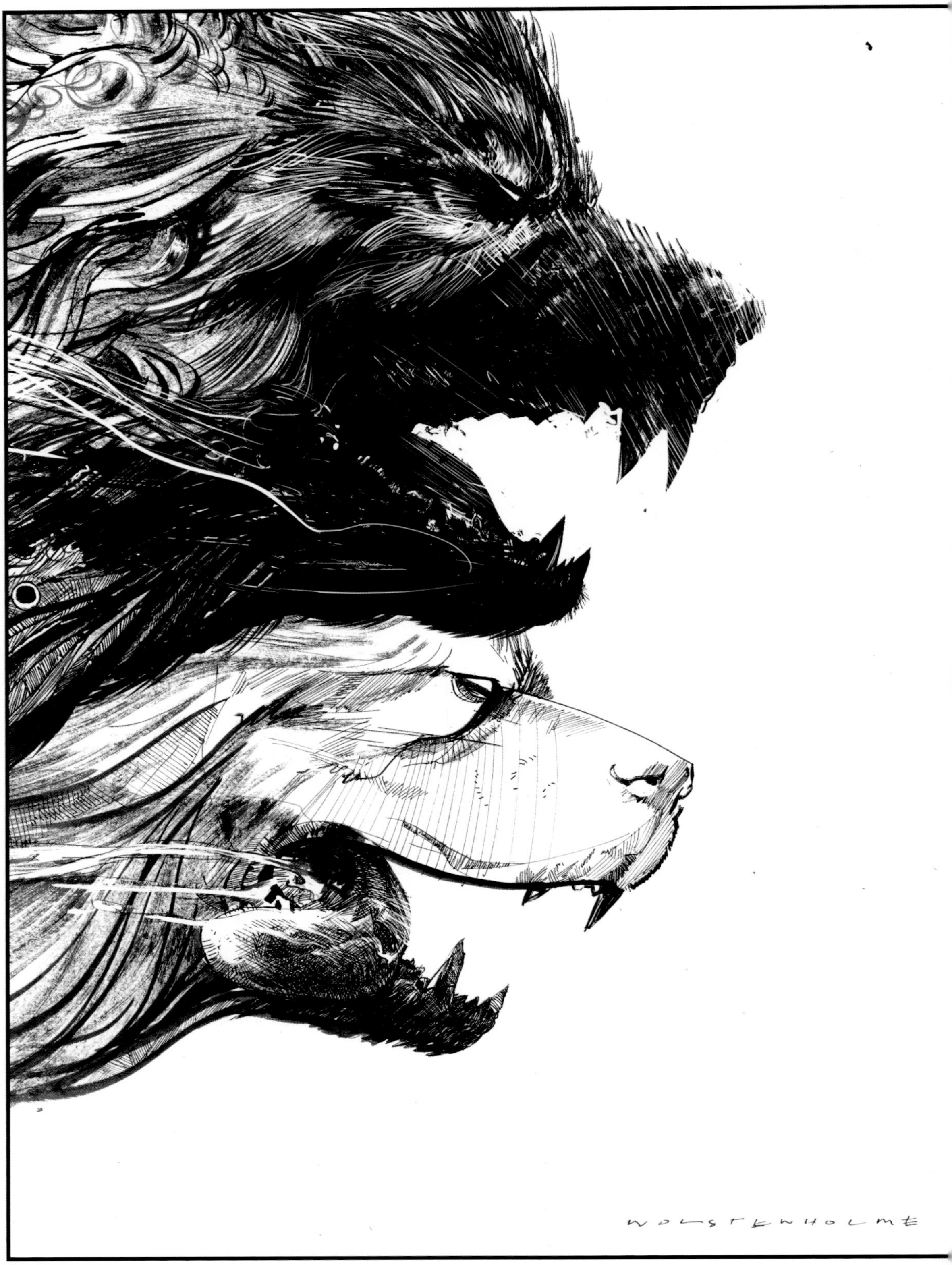
WOLSTENHOLME

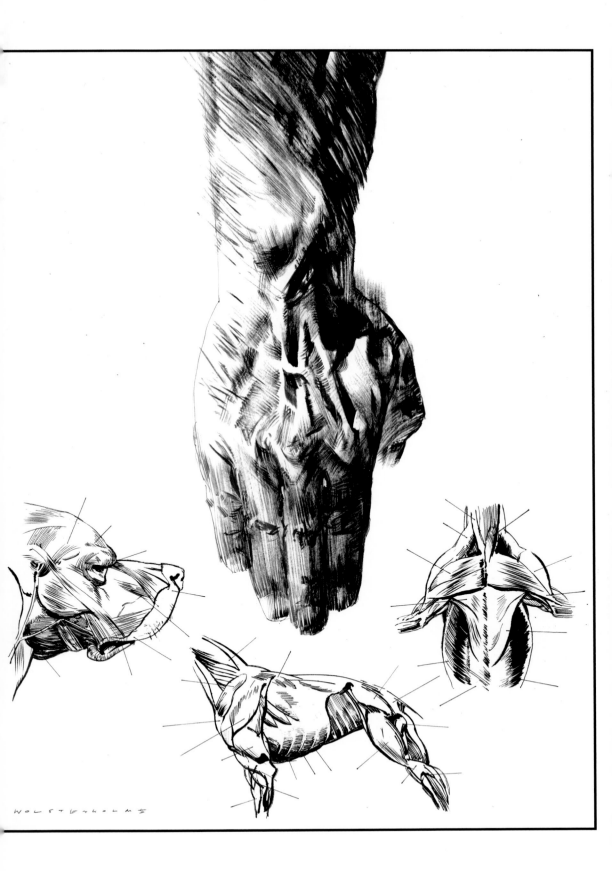

WOLSTENHOLME

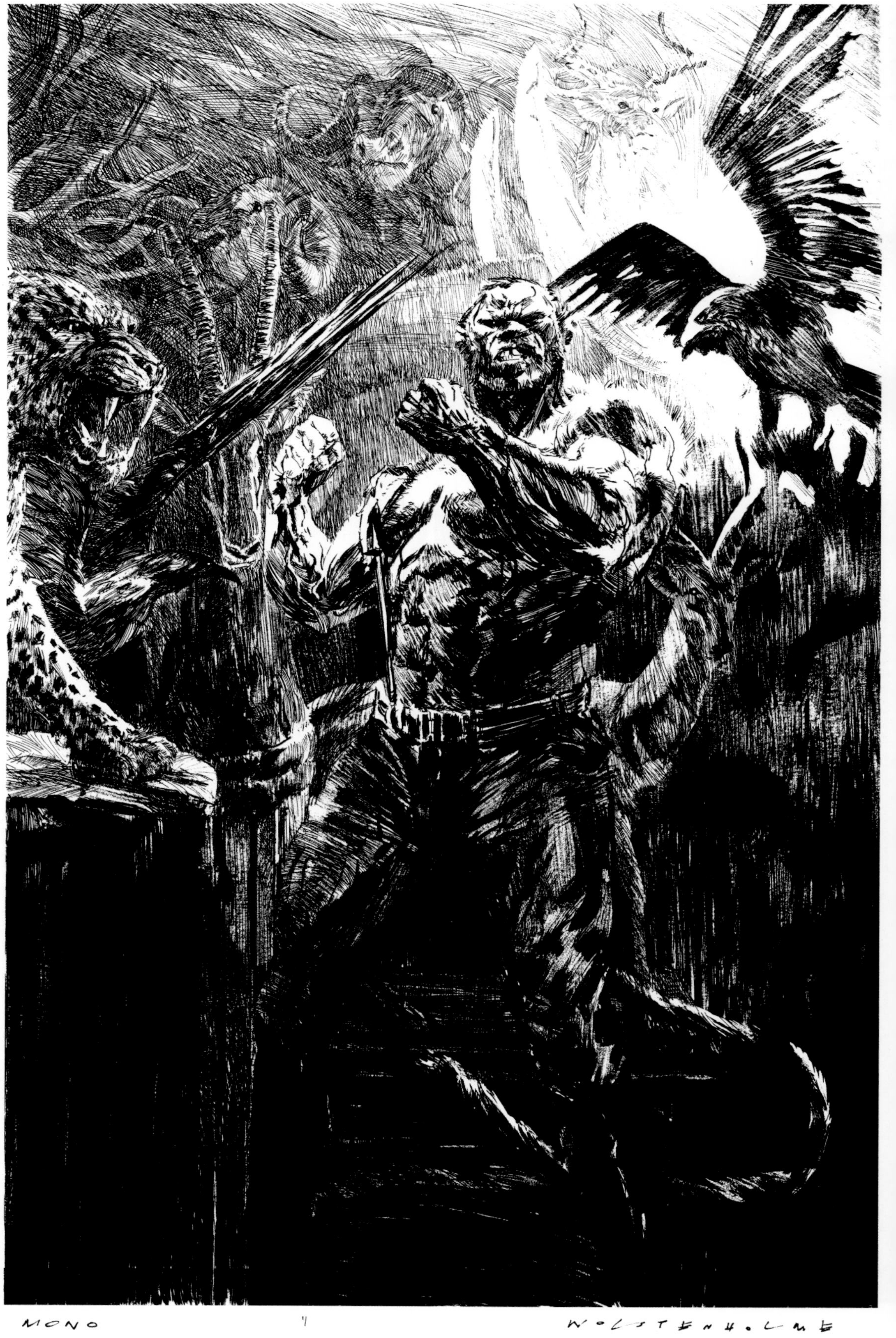

MONO WOLSTENHOLME